FREEDOM OF SPEECH

FREEDOM OF SPEECH

Rights and Liberties under the Law

KEN I. KERSCH

ABC⬥CLIO

Santa Barbara, California • Denver, Colorado • Oxford, England

Library of Congress Cataloging-in-Publication Data
Kersch, Kenneth Ira, 1964–
    Freedom of speech : rights and liberties under the law / Ken I. Kersch.
        p. cm. — (America's freedoms)
Includes bibliographical references and index.
    ISBN 1-57607-600-8 (hardcover : alk. paper) e-book ISBN 1-57607-607-5
    1. Freedom of speech—United States.   I. Title.   II. Series.

    KF4772.K47   2003
    342.73'0853—dc21

                                                    2003002634

ABC-CLIO, Inc.
130 Cremona Drive, P.O. Box 1911
Santa Barbara, California 93116-1911
This book is printed on acid-free paper.
Manufactured in the United States of America

For my students

To me the question whether liberty is a good or a bad thing appears as irrational as the question whether fire is a good or a bad thing? It is both good and bad according to time, place, and circumstance, and a complete answer to the question, In what cases is liberty good and in what cases is it bad? would involve not merely a universal history of mankind, but a complete solution of the problems which such a history would offer.

JAMES FITZJAMES STEPHEN
Liberty, Equality, Fraternity

CONTENTS

SERIES FOREWORD

America's Freedoms promises a series of books that address the origin, development, meaning, and future of the nation's fundamental liberties, as well as the individuals, circumstances, and events that have shaped them. These freedoms are chiefly enshrined explicitly or implicitly in the Bill of Rights and other amendments to the Constitution of the United States and have much to do with the quality of life Americans enjoy. Without them, America would be a far different place in which to live. Oddly enough, however, the Constitution was drafted and signed in Philadelphia in 1787 without a bill of rights. That was an afterthought, emerging only after a debate among the foremost political minds of the day.

At the time, Thomas Jefferson was in France on a diplomatic mission. Upon receiving a copy of the proposed Constitution from his friend James Madison, who had helped write the document, Jefferson let him know as fast as the slow sailing-ship mails of the day allowed that the new plan of government suffered one major defect—it lacked a bill of rights. This, Jefferson argued, "is what the people are entitled to against every government on earth." Madison should not have been surprised at Jefferson's reaction. The Declaration of Independence of 1776 had largely been Jefferson's handiwork, including its core statement of principle:

We hold these truths to be self-evident, that all men are created equal, that they are endowed by their Creator with certain unalienable Rights, that among these are Life, Liberty, and the pursuit of Happiness. That to secure these rights, Governments are instituted among Men, deriving their just powers from the consent of the governed.

Jefferson rejected the conclusion of many of the framers that the Constitution's design—a system of both separation of powers among the legislative, executive, and judicial branches, and a federal division of powers between national and state governments—would safeguard liberty. Even when combined with elections, he believed strongly that such structural checks would fall short.

Jefferson and other critics of the proposed Constitution ultimately had their way. In one of the first items of business in the First Congress in 1789, Madison, as a member of the House of Representatives from Virginia, introduced amendments to protect liberty. Ten were ratified by 1791 and have become known as the Bill of Rights.

America's Bill of Rights reflects the founding generation's understanding of the necessary link between personal freedom and representative government, as well as their experience with threats to liberty. The First Amendment protects expression—in speech, press, assembly, petition, and religion—and guards against a union of church and state. The Second Amendment secures liberty against national tyranny by affirming the self-defense of the states. Members of state-authorized local militia—citizens primarily, soldiers occasionally—retained a right to bear arms. The ban in the Third Amendment on forcibly quartering troops in houses reflects the emphasis the framers placed on the integrity and sanctity of the home.

Other provisions in the Fourth, Fifth, Sixth, Seventh, and Eighth amendments safeguard freedom by setting forth standards that government must follow in administering the law, especially regarding persons accused of crimes. The framers knew firsthand the dangers that government-as-prosecutor could pose to liberty. Even today, authoritarian regimes in other lands routinely use the tools of law enforcement—arrests, searches, detentions, as well as trials—to squelch peaceful political opposition. Limits in the Bill of Rights on crime-fighting powers thus help maintain democracy by demanding a high level of legal scrutiny of the government's practices.

In addition, one clause in the Fifth Amendment forbids the taking of private property for public use without paying the owner just compensation, and thereby limits the power of eminent domain, the authority to seize a person's property. Along with taxation and conscription, eminent domain is one of the most awesome powers any government can possess.

The Ninth Amendment makes sure that the listing of some rights does not imply that others necessarily have been abandoned. If the Ninth offered reassurances to the people, the Tenth Amendment was designed to reassure the states that they or the people retained those powers not delegated to the national government. Today, the Tenth is a reminder of the integral role states play in the federal plan of union that the Constitution ordained.

Despite this legacy of freedom, however, we Americans today sometimes wonder about the origin, development, meaning, and future of our liberties. This concern is entirely understandable, because liberty is central to the idea of what it means *to be American.* In this way, the United States stands apart from virtually every other nation on earth. Other countries typically define their national identities through a common ethnicity, origin, ancestral bond, religion, or history. But none of these accounts for the American identity. In terms of ethnicity, ancestry, and religion, the United States is the most diverse place on earth. From the beginning, America has been a land of immigrants. Neither is there a single historical experience to which all current citizens can directly relate: someone who arrived a decade ago from, say, southeast Asia and was naturalized as a citizen only last year is just as much an American as someone whose forebears served in General George Washington's army at Valley Forge during the American War of Independence (1776–1783). In religious as in political affairs, the United States has been a beacon to those suffering oppression abroad: "the last, best hope of earth," Abraham Lincoln said. So, the American identity is ideological. It consists of faith in the value and importance of liberty for each individual.

Nonetheless, a longstanding consensus among Americans on the *principle* that individual liberty is essential, highly prized, and widely shared hardly assures agreement about liberty *in practice.* This is because the concept of liberty, as it has developed in the United States, has several dimensions.

First, there is an unavoidable tension between liberty and restraint. Liberty means freedom: we say that a person has a "right" to do this or that. But that *right* is meaningless unless there is a corresponding *duty* on the part of others (such as police officers and elected officials) not to interfere. Thus, protection of the liberty of one person necessarily involves restraints imposed on someone else. This is why we speak of a *civil* right or a *civil* liberty: it is a claim on the behavior of another that is enforceable through the legal process. Moreover, some degree of order (restrictions on the behavior of all) is necessary if everyone's liberties are to be protected. Just as too much order crushes freedom, too little invites social chaos that also threatens freedom. Determining the proper balance between freedom and order, however, is more easily sought than found. "To make a government requires no great prudence," declared English statesman and political philosopher Edmund Burke in 1790. "Settle the seat of power; teach obedience; and the work is done. To give freedom is still more easy. It is not necessary to guide; it only requires to let go the rein. But to form a *free government;* that is, to temper together these opposite elements of liberty and restraint in one consistent work, requires much thought; deep reflection; a sagacious, powerful, and combining mind."

Second, the Constitution does not define the freedoms that it protects. Chief Justice John Marshall once acknowledged that the Constitution was a document "of enumeration, and not of definition." There are, for example, lists of the powers of Congress in Article I, or the rights of individuals in the Bill of Rights, but those powers and limitations are not explained. What is the "freedom of speech" that the First Amendment guarantees? What are "unreasonable searches and seizures" that are proscribed by the Fourth Amendment? What is the "due process of law" secured by both the Fifth and Fourteenth amendments? Reasonable people, all of whom favor individual liberty, can arrive at very different answers to these questions.

A third dimension—breadth—is closely related to the second. How widely shared is a particular freedom? Consider voting, for example. One could write a political history of the United States by cataloging the efforts to extend the vote or franchise to groups such as women and nonwhites that had been previously excluded. Or, consider the First Amendment's freedom of speech. Does it include the expression of *all* points of view or merely *some?* Does the same amendment's protection of the "free exercise of religion" include all faiths, even obscure ones that may seem weird or even irritating? At different times questions like these have yielded different answers.

Similarly, the historical record contains notorious lapses. Despite all the safeguards that are supposed to shore up freedom's foundations, constitutional protections have sometimes been worth the least when they have been desperately needed. In our history the most frequent and often the most serious threats to freedom have come not from people intent on throwing the Bill of Rights away outright, but from well-meaning people who find the

Bill of Rights a temporary bother, standing in the way of some objective they want to reach.

There is also a question that dates to the very beginning of American government under the Constitution. Does the Constitution protect rights not spelled out in, or fairly implied by, the words of the document? The answer to that question largely depends on what a person concludes about the source of rights. One tradition, reflected in the Declaration of Independence, asserts that rights predate government and that government's chief duty is to protect the rights that everyone naturally possesses. Thus, if the Constitution is read as a document designed, among other things, to protect liberty, then protected liberties are not limited to those in the text of the Constitution but may also be derived from experience, for example, or from one's assessment of the requirements of a free society. This tradition places a lot of discretion in the hands of judges, because in the American political system, it is largely the judiciary that decides what the Constitution means. Partly due to this dynamic, a competing tradition looks to the text of the Constitution, as well as to statutes passed consistent with the Constitution, as a *complete* code of law containing *all* the liberties that Americans possess. Judges, therefore, are not free to go outside the text to "discover" rights that the people, through the process of lawmaking and constitutional amendment, have not declared. Doing so is undemocratic because it bypasses "rule by the people." The tension between these two ways of thinking explains the ongoing debate about a right to privacy, itself nowhere mentioned in the words of the Constitution. "I like my privacy as well as the next one," once admitted Justice Hugo Black, "but I am nevertheless compelled to admit that government has a right to invade it unless prohibited by some specific constitutional provision." Otherwise, he said, judges are forced "to determine what is or is not constitutional on the basis of their own appraisal of what laws are unwise or unnecessary."

Black thought that was the job of elected legislators who would answer to the people.

Fifth, it is often forgotten that at the outset, and for many years afterward, the Bill of Rights applied only to the national government, not to the states. Except for a very few restrictions, such as those in section 10 of Article I in the main body of the Constitution, which expressly limited state power, states were restrained only by their individual constitutions and state laws, not by the U.S. Bill of Rights. So, Pennsylvania or any other state, for example, could shut down a newspaper or barricade the doors of a church without violating the First Amendment. For many in the founding generation, the new central government loomed as a colossus that might threaten liberty. Few at that time thought that individual freedom needed *national* protection against *state* invasions of the rights of the people.

The first step in removing this double standard came with ratification of the Fourteenth Amendment after the Civil War in 1868. Section 1 contained majestic, but undefined, checks on states: "*No State* shall make or enforce any law which shall abridge the privileges or immunities of citizens of the United States; nor shall any *State* deprive any person of life, liberty, or property, without due process of law; nor deny to any person within its jurisdiction the equal protections of the laws" (emphasis added). Such vague language begged for interpretation. In a series of cases mainly between 1920 and 1968, the Supreme Court construed the Fourteenth Amendment to include within its meaning almost every provision of the Bill of Rights. This process of "incorporation" (applying the Bill of Rights to the states by way of the Fourteenth Amendment) was the second step in eliminating the double standard of 1791. State and local governments became bound by the same restrictions that had applied all along to the national government. The consequences of this development scarcely can be exaggerated because most governmental action in the United States is the work of state and local governments. For instance, ordinary citizens are far more likely to encounter a local police officer than an agent of the Federal Bureau of Investigation or the Secret Service.

A sixth dimension reflects an irony. A society premised on individual freedom assumes not only the worth of each person but citizens capable of rational thought, considered judgment, and measured actions. Otherwise democratic government would be futile. Yet, we lodge the most important freedoms in the Constitution precisely because we want to give those freedoms extra protection. "The very purpose of a Bill of Rights was to . . . place [certain subjects] beyond the reach of majorities and officials and to establish them as legal principles to be applied by the courts," explained Justice Robert H. Jackson. "One's right to life, liberty, and property, to free speech, a free press, freedom of worship and assembly, and other fundamental rights may not be submitted to vote; they depend on the outcome of no elections." Jackson referred to a hard lesson learned from experience: basic rights require extra protection because they are fragile. On occasion, people have been willing to violate the freedoms of others. That reality demanded a written constitution.

This irony reflects the changing nature of a bill of rights in history. Americans did not invent the idea of a bill of rights in 1791. Instead it drew from and was inspired by colonial documents such as the Pennsylvania colony's Charter of Liberties (1701) and the English Bill of Rights (1689), Petition of Right (1628), and Magna Carta (1215). However, these early and often unsuccessful attempts to limit government power were devices to protect the many (the people) from the few (the English Crown). With the emergence of democratic political systems in the eighteenth century, however, political power shifted from the few to the many. The right to rule belonged to the person who received the most votes in an election, not necessarily to the firstborn, the wealthiest, or the most physically powerful. So the focus of a bill of rights had to shift too. No longer was it designed to shelter the majority from the minority, but to shelter the minority from the majority. "Wherever the real power in a Government lies, there is the danger of oppression," commented Madison in his exchange of letters with Jefferson in 1788. "In our Government, the real power lies in the majority of the Community, and the invasion of private rights is *chiefly* to be apprehended, not from acts of government contrary to the sense of its constituents, but from acts in which the Government is the mere instrument of the major number of the Constituents."

Americans, however, do deserve credit for having discovered a way to enforce a bill of rights. Without an enforcement mechanism, a bill of rights is no more than a list of aspirations: standards to aim for, but with no redress other than violent protest or revolution. Indeed this had been the experience in England with which the framers were thoroughly familiar. Thanks to judicial review—the authority courts in the United States possess to invalidate actions taken by the other branches of government which, in the judges' view, conflict with the Constitution—the provisions in the Bill of Rights and other constitutionally protected liberties became judicially enforceable.

Judicial review was a tradition that was beginning to emerge in the states on a small scale in the 1780s and 1790s and that would blossom in the U.S. Supreme Court in the nineteenth century and twentieth centuries. "In the arguments in favor of a declaration of rights," Jefferson presciently told Madison in the late winter of 1789 after the Constitution had been ratified, "you omit one which has great weight with me, the legal check which it puts into the hands of the judiciary." This is the reason why each of the volumes in this series focuses extensively on judicial decisions. Liberties have largely been defined by judges in the context of deciding cases in situations where individuals thought the power of government extended too far.

Designed to help democracy protect itself, the Constitution ultimately needs the support of those—the majority—who endure its restraints. Without sufficient support among the people, its freedoms rest on a weak foundation. The earnest hope of *America's Freedoms* is that this series will offer Americans a renewed appreciation and understanding of their heritage of liberty.

Yet there would be no series on America's freedoms without the interest and support of Alicia Merritt at ABC-CLIO. The series was her idea. She approached me originally about the series and was very adept at overcoming my initial hesitations as series editor. She not only helped me shape the particular topics that the series would include, but guided me toward prospective authors. As a result, the topic of each book has been matched with the most appropriate person as author. The goal in each instance has been to pair topics with authors who are recognized teachers and scholars in their field. The results have been gratifying. A series editor could hardly wish for authors who have been more cooperative, helpful, and accommodating.

Donald Grier Stephenson, Jr.

PREFACE

This is a book about the freedom of speech in the United States, aimed at those who are new, or relatively new, to the subject. The first inclination of such readers will probably be to imagine that the subject is primarily legal and almost exclusively concerned with decisions of the U.S. Supreme Court. To approach the subject in that way, however, would be to distort what the freedom of speech has meant over the long term of U.S. history. Certainly, beginning in twentieth century, the Court, citing the First Amendment, came to loom large in matters of free speech. But before that, the scope of what one could or could not say was rarely determined in the High Court. Often it was a matter for lower-court judges, applying not the U.S. Constitution but rather the judge-made common law, as that law had developed in England and the United States over the course of centuries. But even more often, the scope of permissible speech was set outside of courts by social and private pressures, cultural currents, legislation, and hard-fought political struggles.

This book discusses contemporary Supreme Court–created First Amendment doctrine and the landmark decisions in which that doctrine was announced and shaped. But it sets the emergence of that doctrine in a much broader context. The book is attentive to what free speech meant before what the Court said about it mattered. Even when the Court moves to center stage of our story, the book pays more attention than is typical to the ways cultural and political forces influenced how it ruled and what it said.

In this orientation, the book reflects what I see as a healthy trend among contemporary constitutional scholars: the trend toward situating legal and constitutional doctrine in political and historical contexts and emphasizing the ways constitutional meaning is constructed outside of courts. My aim is to give readers a better idea of how Americans actually think about and live their key commitments. Readers will see, I hope, that the nature and scope of those commitments as they are actually practiced, including the commitment to the freedom of speech, changes significantly over time. Only by seeing the law as intertwined with culture and politics and as perpetually subject to change, can readers gain an accurate understanding of the law— present, past, and future.

This book is also different from traditional accounts of civil liberties in that (until recently, at least) those accounts treated questions of individual rights separately from questions of institutional and constitutional structure and from the long-term trajectory of the development of the U.S. state. The problem with making this separation is that the way we think of the Bill of Rights today—as principles of individual rights enforced by federal courts against repressive acts undertaken by legislative majorities—is not the way the Bill of Rights was understood by most people at the time it was ratified. That enumeration of rights was primarily aimed at limiting the national government, not the state governments. It was not at all clear (or, to many, even desirable) that its promise lay in its enforcement by courts, especially federal courts. To gain an accurate picture of the meaning of the freedom of speech in the United States, we must be sensitive to the way the right as a principle related to the right as it was lived in institutional practice. Our current ways of attributing meaning to the freedom of speech, as well as enforcing it, were not stipulated at the time of the nation's founding. They were created.

In approaching the subject from several angles at once, we leave behind a narrative that says the nation's founders enshrined the freedom of speech in the First Amendment to the U.S. Constitution because they believed it to be the most important of our freedoms, a narrative that then casts the rest of constitutional history as a long march (broken by periods of reactionary backsliding) toward the realization of the promise of the right in the 1960s. The story I tell here is less directional and consequently less reassuring. Every age, even our more liberated time, has forms of speech that it prefers and others of which it is deeply wary. Different eras, including our own, are structured by unique constellations of hopes and fears. In other words, I suggest that far from amounting to a movement "ever upward" toward an ideal, the dynamics of the freedom of speech in our country have shown a much greater mutability than is commonly supposed.

Moreover, even if one does conclude, on balance, that speech has become freer over time, it would not necessarily mean that freedom as a whole has increased. Liberty is not so easily sealed into hermetic packets of separate individual rights, with the progress of each charted separately from the others. To the extent that in recent years the federal courts have become the primary protectors of our free speech rights, the rights of both local communities and legislatures (both state and federal) to set public policy have been constrained. In many ways, in the current environment, the more speech rights are extended, the more democratic rights—and, one might even say mischievously, the right to vote—have been constrained. To look at speech alone, and not as a component of a broader focus on general questions of liberty and self-government, is to miss much of what constitutes the true meaning of the freedom of speech.

The story I tell here reflects my own thinking about the dynamics of constitutional development and the nature of constitutional change concerning civil liberties. In that sense—and I believe it is an important one—the book is an original work. I should say, however, that I have written this book (unlike my others) not primarily for scholars but for general readers, including students. My views, some of which are distinctive, are reflected most clearly in the shape of the narrative. In its substance, much of the book is a work of synthesis. In coming to this project, my expertise was not in First Amendment law but rather in the broader field of constitutional development, constitutional change, civil liberties, and U.S. political thought. I have profited greatly in this work from the primary research of others, published in works that are listed in the references section at the end of each chapter. At the urging of my editors, footnotes and in-text references have been kept to a minimum. I recommend that readers refer to these engaging works for more comprehensive treatments of key aspects of the subject.

Overview

One of the chief purposes of this book is to underline that things were not always as they are today. Although the later chapters will describe the growing role of the Supreme Court in deciding public policy on free speech, the beginning chapters will discuss an earlier era when law and policy were set primarily by state and local courts and even more by social norms, legislation, and the political process.

Chapter 1 begins by providing the reader with a general introduction to the concept of free speech in U.S. society and the place that freedom has assumed within the country's constitutional tradition. The chapter then offers an introductory overview of the philosophy behind this freedom by considering both the justifications offered in its defense and the criticisms calling attention to its dangers. After this overview of free speech theory, the chapter concludes with a short summary of the ways in which free speech principles have been embodied in the constitutional doctrines of the U.S. Supreme Court over the course of the twentieth century.

Chapter 2 will chart the ways American law and thought concerning free speech emerged as part of political and common law legal traditions going back to at least sixteenth-century England. Although our free speech laws were profoundly influenced by our English inheritance, Americans, in response to their peculiar circumstances and experiences, began to develop their own traditions and interpretations as far back as colonial times. After the American Revolution and the constitutional Founding, this process proceeded apace, and U.S. understandings of free speech were shaped by political controversies over such issues as the Sedition Act in 1798, the rise of a vigorous antislavery movement in the 1830s, the Civil War, and the rise of mass politics, mass publishing, and the growing political radicalism of the late nineteenth century.

Chapter 3 will discuss twentieth-century developments in free speech, with an emphasis, albeit not an exclusive one, on the role of the U.S. Supreme Court in framing the contours of constitutional doctrine on free speech. The Court assumed a central role in free speech law as part of its general institutional ascendancy. Given the political and social turmoil of the twentieth century—the radicalism early in the century and the attendant government crackdowns, the creation of a new and powerful central state, the Cold War, the civil rights, antiwar, student, feminist, multicultural, and conservative movements—the Court hardly found it necessary to cast about for disputes. The cases poured in, and the Court assumed a large role in shaping the nation's law, policy, and culture.

The fourth chapter will consider the issues and prospects for free speech in the twenty-first century. The major forces shaping the Court's doctrines in the years to come will probably involve technological change, in particular the rise of the Internet, and the rise of globalization. Globalization, of course, includes the

Internet, but it also includes the internationalization of "human rights" standards and treaties and the rise of global and regional institutions acting to police those standards, of which free speech is a part. Because speech, to many, seems to be getting freer and freer, it will also be useful to think about the ways an ideology positing increasing openness may be obscuring the ways new prejudices and institutions are working in new ways to inhibit the freedom of speech.

Chapter 5, an alphabetically ordered reference chapter, provides the reader with brief definitions or descriptions of key doctrines, terms, people, events, laws, and constitutional provisions alluded to in the book's narrative chapters. Chapter 6 presents in chronological order edited excerpts from important original documents involving the freedom of speech. These include books, pamphlets, speeches, constitutional provisions, statutes, international agreements, and U.S. Supreme Court opinions. These documents are often sharply written and provocative, and may provide an engaging focus for discussion and debate.

Considered as a whole, this book attempts to give readers a broad view of freedom of speech in the United States as a matter of law, as a matter of politics, and as a matter of culture. All vantage points on the freedom of speech are related in profound and complicated ways. It is this complexity that lends a lively interest to the subject.

ACKNOWLEDGMENTS

My first extended foray into free speech was taken at the invitation of Jim Stoner and Dick Morgan at their Liberty Fund Conference on the freedom of speech held in Freeport, Maine, in the summer of 1999. I am grateful to them for inviting me to the conference and to the Liberty Fund for sponsoring it. Matt Berke devoted a considerable amount of time to carefully reading over the manuscript and helping me clarify the argument and the prose.

It is a much better book for his help. Clem Fatovic and Ted Holsten also read large portions of the manuscript, often on short notice, and made highly useful suggestions. The James Madison Program in American Ideals and Institutions at Princeton, under the leadership of Robert P. George, named me the Ann and Herbert W. Vaughan Fellow for 2001–2002, thus providing me with the leave time and the congenial intellectual environment I needed to complete the manuscript. Grier Stephenson, series editor, and Alicia Merritt, acquisitions editor, shepherded me along with consideration and patience. I am thankful for their help and good cheer. Melanie Stafford and Kathy Delfosse provided production and editorial assistance, respectively. My students, as always, provided the inspiration. To them this book is dedicated.

Ken I. Kersch

1

INTRODUCTION

*T*HROUGHOUT ITS HISTORY, foreign visitors to this country have been struck by the widely held U.S. belief that they live in the greatest and freest country in the world. Such pride is expressed today in the praises to "the land of the free" sung before every baseball game, or the sometimes prickly, sometimes resigned commonplace that one can do or say whatever one wants because, after all, "It's a free country." The extent of this pride was apparent to Fanny Trollope, an English visitor to the United States in the 1820s, who noted with surprise how quickly Americans took hot exception to the notion that they might perhaps not be the greatest, freest country in the world. "Other nations have been called thin-skinned, but the citizens of the Union have, apparently, no skins at all; they wince if a breeze blows over them, unless it be tempered with adulation" (Trollope [1832] 1960, 355). In conversing with a milkman during her visit, Trollope, as a subject of another great, free nation, was shocked to hear a simple milkman declare that only in America could the poor eat, could the people protect their property from arbitrary seizure, and could "we says and prints just whatever we likes." When Trollope parried these claims by questioning the singularity of American freedom, the milkman gruffly remarked on "how little you knows of a free country." (Trollope [1832] 1960, 102).

The right to say and print "whatever we likes" holds a special place in the American heart, so special a place that we might call it the quintessentially American freedom. The guarantee of the "freedom of speech," after all, is announced in the First Amendment to the Constitution of the United States. Along with rights to religious liberty, liberty of the press, and the liberty to peaceably assemble and to petition the government for a redress of grievances, the First Amendment declares that "Congress shall make no law . . . abridging the freedom of speech." It was drafted by James Madison, the "Father of the Constitution" and, hence, one of our nation's principal Founding Fathers. If Americans are the freest people in the world, so the understanding goes, it is largely because the founders accorded to free speech what scholars have called "a preferred position," first among our constitutional rights.

This heart warming story is too simple, however. Americans' belief that freedom of speech is part of their national birthright, a birthright that sets the United States above other nations, has been a constant throughout U.S. history, as many foreign visitors have observed. But the scope of that freedom has shifted radically over the course of U.S. history. In understanding these shifts, and hence, the uniqueness of the nature of free speech in the United States today, we must rid ourselves of certain myths and misreadings of America's constitutional history.

One common mistake in understanding freedom of speech in the United States is to confuse the freedom itself with the law concerning free speech. It is true that the clearest case of a restriction on one's speech is being arrested or fined or put in the stocks for it. But Frenchman Alexis de Tocqueville, another early-nineteenth-century commentator on the American democratic experiment, saw that when it came to free speech and free thought, Americans seemed constrained by more than mere law. American culture itself, Tocqueville observed, led citizens to go along to get along, to keep their mouths shut if they held opinions that contradicted the majority view. To do otherwise would expose them not to legal prosecution but to "all kinds of unpleasantness and everyday persecution" from their neighbors (Tocqueville [1833] 1969, 255). As Tocqueville put it in *Democracy in America,* "While the majority is in doubt, one talks; but when it has irrevocably pronounced, everyone is silent, and friends and enemies alike seem to make for its bandwagon" (Tocqueville [1833] 1969, 254).

In their fear of popular sanction, Tocqueville found Americans more timid than the subjects of the supposedly unfree monarchies of Europe—not in spite of the country's democracy but indeed because of it. European monarchs certainly had the power to forbid unwanted speech, but their dictates had no deep moral authority. But in a democracy, Tocqueville said, "the majority is invested with both the physical and moral authority" (Tocqueville [1833] 1969, 254). Ironically, then, Tocqueville concluded, "I know no country in which, speaking generally, there is less independence of mind and true freedom of discussion than in America" (Tocqueville [1833] 1969, 234–235).

A second common mistake concerning freedom of speech is to misread the Constitution itself. A quick study of the First Amendment's deceptively simple language leads many students to suppose that no law may be passed that abridges a person's speech. In fact, however, what the First Amendment actually says is that Congress shall not abridge the people's *"freedom* of speech."* There is an important distinction here. A stricture against abridging speech is absolute: It implies that Congress cannot forbid people from saying what they want. The Constitution's actual language, however, is not absolute at all. Rather, it seems to beg the question. If Congress cannot abridge the freedom of speech, it cannot constitutionally forbid one to say whatever one has a right, or the "freedom," to say. Conversely, Congress *can* forbid one from saying whatever one does not have a right to say. Congress, in other words, is at liberty to abridge one's speech; it just cannot abridge one's freedom of speech.

The distinction between abridging speech and abridging the freedom of speech may seem confusing in the abstract, but it is easy enough to see in action. If, for example, a citizen hates the president's policies on education or health care and makes a verbal threat to assassinate him, he is summarily arrested. He might plead freedom of speech, but he will not have a chance in court because although forbidding threats on the president's life is a restriction on *speech*, it is not a restriction on the *freedom of speech*. One has no freedom to threaten to kill the president.

"The most stringent protection of free speech," Supreme Court Justice Oliver Wendell Holmes, Jr. once declared, "would not protect a man in falsely shouting fire in a theatre and causing panic" (*Schenck v. United States*, 249 U.S. 47 [1919], 52). And there are many other restrictions on speech that are not considered restrictions on the *freedom of* speech. One is not free, for example, to perjure oneself—to lie under oath in a court of law. One is not free to propose a bribe to a political official. Because of antitrust laws, businesses in competition with each other are not free to talk to each other about fixing the price of goods or services. Nor are they free to use false or misleading advertising. Under the labor laws passed in the 1930s, corporate managers cannot say nasty things about labor unions. Under civil service laws, government employees are sharply limited in the expression of their political opinions. Repeated comments by workers or supervisors about a fellow employee's sex, race, or physical attractiveness can result in legal action or dismissal, First Amendment notwithstanding. Obscenity remains legally punishable, as does talking dirty to children. In short, the speech of Americans is and always has been abridged in many ways. It is only their freedom of speech that is protected. And just what constitutes freedom of speech has changed over time.

Historical change also leads us to gloss over other language in the First Amendment. That amendment clearly states that "*Congress shall make no law*," and the word "Congress" was chosen advisedly. The Bill of Rights, including the First Amendment's free speech provision, was added to the Constitution to allay Anti-Federalist fears that the new central government was too distant from the people to protect their fundamental rights. Indeed, many feared that that government would soon have designs on their rights. Those who insisted on a guarantee of the freedom of speech were principally concerned about incursions on that right from what they took to be the distant, out-of-touch, and quasi-aristocratic federal Congress. As for restrictions on free speech by state legislatures and local governments (to say nothing of employers, teachers, or ministers), the Constitution—including the famous First Amendment—was utterly silent. At the time it was written and for a very long time afterward, the free speech provision did not apply to other agencies. The First Amendment guaranteed only that Congress could "make no law . . . abridging the freedom of speech."

Moreover, the First Amendment was not even actually the first at the time it was proposed. Today, we tend to think that it was placed first in the Bill of Rights because its guarantees were foremost in the hearts of the framers. But the fact that the constitutional guarantee against congressional restrictions on freedom of speech is first is really a fortuitous quirk of history. The two amendments that preceded it—amendments dealing with governmental structure rather than constitutional rights—were not ratified. The original (but unratified) "first amendment" was concerned with setting a proper ratio of constituents to members of Congress. Next in line was an amendment setting up procedures for congressional pay raises (this "Rip Van Winkle" amendment, the twenty-seventh, was finally ratified in 1992). Only because these measures failed did the First Amendment as we know it get bumped up to the head of the queue.

INSTITUTIONAL PROTECTIONS FOR
THE FREEDOM OF SPEECH

Ever since the famous school desegregation decision in *Brown v. Board of Education* (347 U.S. 483 [1954]), most Americans instinctively see the Supreme Court as the glorious and final protector of our basic rights and freedoms, particularly the freedom of speech. Whenever a plaintiff seeks "equal justice under law" (as the inscription over the entrance to the High Court in Washington promises), whenever an indigent criminal defendant asserts a right to legal counsel at public expense (as did small-time Florida criminal Clarence Earl Gideon), or whenever a public school student is punished for denouncing an unpopular war (as in the case of Iowa's Tinker children in the 1960s), they fight for their equality and freedom by, as we say, "taking their case all the way to the Supreme Court."

The story of the little guy who fights all the way to the Supreme Court to vindicate the promise of fundamental constitutional freedoms has become for us a kind of American folktale. Hollywood has helped impress this narrative on the public mind through numerous movies. One thinks of Henry Fonda playing Clarence Earl Gideon in *Gideon's Trumpet*, a film adaptation of the Anthony Lewis book, or of *The Norma McCorvey Story*, a made-for-TV movie about the abortion rights decision in *Roe v. Wade* (410 U.S. 113 [1973]). ("Roe" was a pseudonym McCorvey used in bringing the case.) Television news magazines constantly run stories about the wronged vindicating their claims in court, including, at times, the Supreme Court. Inspired in their youth by the heroic *Brown v. Board of Education* decision, many academics and legal scholars have come to venerate the Court as the ultimate protector of our basic rights and liberties. And this view is elaborated in books centered on the story of underdogs defending justice and freedom by taking their cases to the Supreme Court. Most constitutional law textbooks reinforce this view by presenting the story of our constitutional freedoms through instructing by a succession (or "line") of Supreme Court cases.

In many ways, however, this post-*Brown* vision of the Court as the protector of the little guy masks the reality of U.S. constitutional history and distorts the ways rights and liberties were traditionally protected under the Constitution. As far as free speech is concerned, the popular image of the little guy protecting his speech rights by taking his battle all the way to the Supreme Court is almost purely the product of institutional and constitutional developments of the twentieth century. It was not until the 1960s that the federal courts came to define free speech rights in the basic form in which we know them today.

For one thing, the Supreme Court was until fairly recently a relatively weak institution. It attained its current level of power only after a period of intense institutional struggle. Although the homes of the federal government's legislative and executive branches, the U.S. Capitol and the White House, respectively, were built when the country decided to move its peripatetic capital to a permanent home in Washington, D.C., in 1800, no one at the time bothered to build a home for the judicial branch. For much of its history, the U.S. Supreme Court, far from operating in glorious splendor, actually heard its cases in digs in the U.S. Capitol basement. The imposing "Marble Palace" that we know today, with the inscription "Equal Justice Under Law" chiseled into its very stone, was erected only in 1935.

The power of the Court was gradually built up through the skillful husbandry of its two great pre–Civil War chief justices, John Marshall (1801–1835) and Roger Brooke Taney (1836–1864). Marshall, a staunch Federalist appointee of President John Adams, is often considered by scholars to be the greatest justice ever to sit on the Court. Marshall deployed his considerable intellectual talents and personal charm to build up the authority of the Court as a strong governing institution. He then goaded the Court to use its growing authority to interpret the Constitution to grant the national government broad powers to promote commerce and economic development. In *Marbury v. Madison* (5 U.S. 137 [1803]), considered by many to be the most brilliant and important Supreme Court decision in U.S. history, Marshall declared for the first time that the Court possessed the power of judicial review—the power, that is, to measure any ordinary law passed in the United States against the nation's fundamental law, the Constitution, and to render void any law contrary to constitutional requirements. The power of judicial review, of course, provides the basis for the current Court's free speech rulings. Today, when the Supreme Court invalidates either a federal or a state law because it is inconsistent with the First Amendment, it exercises the power that John Marshall established in *Marbury v. Madison.*

In *Marbury* and in other decisions, Marshall claimed broad powers on behalf of both the Court and Congress. But in certain landmark decisions, Marshall argued that although the national government's power to regulate commerce among the several states was broad, states retained significant residual "police powers" to regulate matters of health, safety, and morals. Many claims of unconstitutional restrictions on free speech arose from challenges to state laws. When these laws were challenged in court, many were defended on the grounds that states have a legitimate and constitutional right to enact laws aimed at the advancement of public health, safety, and morals. Moreover, in his decision in *Barron v. Baltimore* (32 U.S. 243 [1833]), Marshall anchored in a constitutional opinion what many had assumed to be true since 1791: namely, that the Bill of Rights, including the First Amendment, provided protection only against infringements by the federal government. The Bill of Rights did not impose any constitutional constraints on the conduct of states.

Although this reading of the scope of the Bill of Rights may today seem like a setback for individual rights, in the early nineteenth century, it was actually the proponents of the Bill of Rights and their political successors who argued most vigorously that the

Bill of Rights applied only to the federal government. They considered it a fundamental democratic right for the people to come together and act via majority rule in the compact political communities of their states without interference from the far-off federal government and the quasi-aristocratic, life-tenured judges of the federal courts.

This understanding of the scope of the Bill of Rights, however, did not mean majority rule went wholly unchecked in the states. States had their own constitutions and courts and, typically, their own bills of rights. So far as state laws were concerned (explicitly after *Barron v. Baltimore*, and implicitly before), freedom of speech issues were matters for states under state law. Since the federal government legislated relatively infrequently for most of the nineteenth century, the Supreme Court thus had almost nothing to say about the Bill of Rights, including freedom of speech, for more than a full century after their addition to the Constitution in 1791.

The importance of the Supreme Court as an institution within the U.S. government continued to grow over the course of the nineteenth century, with various ebbs and flows in different political eras. After losing authority during the Civil War era, in part because of its disastrous decision in the *Dred Scott v. Sandford* (60 U.S. 393 [1857]) slavery case, the Court rebounded to become an aggressive defender and promoter of individual rights. As it turned out, the great charter of the Court's modern rise to power was the Constitution's Fourteenth Amendment (1868), one of its Civil War amendments. The Fourteenth Amendment, in line with the results of the Civil War, gave the national government broad authority to protect rights and to protect those rights against violations by the states. The amendment provides, in part, that

No State shall make or enforce any law which shall abridge the privileges and immunities of citizens of the United States; nor shall any State deprive any person of life, liberty, or property without due process of law; nor deny to any person within its jurisdiction the equal protection of the laws.

The Fourteenth Amendment proved to be crucial to the development of the law of civil rights and civil liberties in the United States. Prior to the Civil War, it was fairly clear to most Americans that their fundamental rights and liberties were to be protected first and foremost not by the national government (of which they were suspicious) but rather by the states. By creating what Madison called a "compound republic" in which power was carefully divided between the national government and the states (which is also called federalism), by stipulating that the national government was to be a government of "enumerated," or listed, powers only, with all the residual powers assumed to be the province of the states, and by providing for the election of the best men to national office, men who would understand not only the possibilities but also the limits of their authority, liberty would be vouchsafed to the broadest extent humanly possible. When Anti-Federalist opponents of the Constitution objected that these structural protections for rights and liberties were insufficient and that a Bill of Rights was necessary, one of the nation's most influential founders, Alexander Hamilton, responded vigorously that the structural protections for rights and liberties were, all things considered, the best protections. "The truth is, after all the declamations we have heard," Hamilton wrote, "that the Constitution is itself, in every rational sense, and to every useful purpose, a Bill of Rights" (*Federalist Paper* no. 84, in Hamilton, Madison, and Jay [1787–1788] 1999, 483). In this dispute, the Anti-Federalists lost the war but won the battle: The 1787 Constitution (which they opposed as a dangerous step toward centralized power) was ratified, but as part of a political deal to secure ratification, the Federalists agreed to add a Bill of Rights. Even then, as we have seen, the Bill of Rights was intended to limit national government, not the states, and in this way to set human liberty on its firmest foundations.

But after the Civil War, could anyone really believe that a national acquiescence to the claims of the states to govern themselves was the best way to preserve human liberty? Hadn't the southern states, when left to freely govern themselves, violated the most fundamental of human freedoms, the right not to be enslaved and thus subject to the arbitrary will of another? Hadn't the southern states, when left to freely govern themselves, permitted some to appropriate the fruits of others' labor and to sell others' parents, spouses, and children? Indeed, hadn't the southern states given some humans the right to exercise over others the Godly power over life and death itself?

And how had fundamental individual freedoms been restored? By the vigorous and bloody assertion of national power over the power of the states. In the Civil War, for the first time in the constitutional history of the United States, national power and the cause of liberty were joined together unambiguously. Thus, with the opening command of the Fourteenth Amendment, "No State shall . . .," the order of 1789 was changed forever. In the Reconstruction years, the national government aggressively and to an unprecedented extent policed the conduct of the states. At the same time that the South was governed by an occupying army in the wake of the Union victory, Congress worked to consolidate the governing authority of the national government over the states in all spheres. Significantly, Congress in the postwar years repeatedly extended the jurisdiction of federal courts, which were, after all, arms of the national government. And it was not long before those courts began hearing cases mounting constitutional challenges to the conduct of the states under the terms of the Fourteenth Amendment.

In a long series of cases involving mostly economic rights, the Supreme Court moved aggressively to protect what it deemed to be fundamental rights under the privileges and immunities and due process clauses of the Fourteenth Amendment. (It was one of the great tragedies of the Civil War amendments that following the end of Reconstruction in 1877, they were rarely used successfully to advance in court the interests and claims of the freed slaves and their descendants.) In the name of "the liberty of contract," the Court invalidated minimum-wage laws, maximumhours laws, and other laws regulating the contractual relations between employers and employees (see *Allgeyer v. Louisiana*, 165 U.S. 578 [1897]; *Lochner v. New York*, 198 U.S. 45 [1905]; *Coppage v. Kansas*, 236 U.S. 1 [1915]; *Adkins v. Children's Hospital*, 261 U.S. 525 [1923]).

One of the chief questions for judges, lawyers, and legal scholars in the late nineteenth and early twentieth centuries was how to define the parameters of the "liberty" newly protected against state action under the Fourteenth Amendment due process clause. Some argued that a judge seeking to define that liberty should look to Anglo-American constitutional history and tradition to define that liberty. Others seemed to look to some inchoate sense of "justice" or "natural law." Still others, however, made the historical argument that those who drafted and ratified the Fourteenth Amendment understood the "liberty" now protected against state action to be coextensive with parts or all of the Bill of Rights. This process came to be called "absorption" and later, "incorporation." This amounted to a constitutional argument that the Fourteenth Amendment effectively overruled the standing constitutional order (as reflected by Chief Justice Marshall's opinion in *Barron v. Baltimore*) that the Bill of Rights did not limit the conduct of the states. In 1897, in *Chicago, Burlington, and Quincy Railroad Co. v. Chicago* (166 U.S. 226 [1897]), the Supreme Court for the first time incorporated a provision of the Bill of Rights against the states, the Fifth Amendment's takings clause, which provides that private property shall not be taken for public use without just compensation. Next in line for incorporation was the First Amendment's protection of freedom of speech, which occurred in the 1925 case of *Gitlow v. New York* (268 U.S. 652 [1925]), involving the criminal anarchy prosecution of a prominent socialist. Others followed over the course of the twentieth century. It is thus plain that our contemporary understanding of the ways free speech is protected by the federal courts owes quite a bit to the constitutional revolution and the "new birth of freedom" set out in Abraham Lincoln's Gettysburg Address at the time of the Civil War (November 19, 1863).

WHY FREE SPEECH?
FIRST AMENDMENT THEORY

Over the long course of Anglo-American political history, many theories have been formulated concerning the justification for and proper scope of the freedom of speech. Contemporary theories are created mainly by law school professors and are published in books and student-edited law journals. Most of these law professors are paid not only to teach but also to devise and publicize novel theories about the law. If their theories seem plausible, the professors are hired by parties to lawsuits, either to argue their cases in court (most law school professors are lawyers) or, alternatively, to submit briefs to the courts arguing on behalf of a particular interpretation of the First Amendment.

Theories of free speech come to the attention of judges in two ways. First, as part of their consideration of how to decide a free speech case, judges read law review articles concerning that freedom (the articles are often brought to their attention by one side or the other, for the purpose of influencing the judges to the advantage of their clients). Second, judges listen to law professors directly through amicus curiae briefs and through oral argument in courts of appeals and in the U.S. Supreme Court. The Latin term *amicus curiae* literally means "friend of the court." The term refers to legal briefs submitted to the court by experts or interested groups and individuals who are not parties to the case but who believe that the information or arguments they bring to the court will be useful to it. Such groups or individuals may also hope to sway the court to a certain result. When they go to court, litigants with enough money often pay law professors large sums to file amicus briefs or to argue their free speech cases in court. When the litigant is poor and cannot pay, some law professors who wish either to help a litigant or to advance their own views on free speech will offer to file an amicus brief or to argue a case for free (known as working pro bono). Either way, in the United States today, the views of academics powerfully influence free speech cases before the U.S. Supreme Court.

The arguments made on behalf of free speech were not always so strongly influenced by academic theorists. Over the course of Anglo-American legal history, most of the arguments were formulated by people whose lives were, at one time or another, openly devoted to political combat. These people were engaged in political fights, and they argued for freer speech as a way of advancing their political goals. The seventeenth-century English poet and political pamphleteer John Milton, for example, wrote *Areopagitica* (1644), one of the earliest arguments on behalf of speech as a means to truth. Milton was a prominent Puritan agitator whose goal was not free speech in the abstract but freedom from the censorship imposed on dissenting Puritan publications by the Crown and by the realm's established Anglican church. One of the most expansive early arguments on behalf of free speech in America was made by Andrew Hamilton, the lawyer for John Peter Zenger, an eighteenth-century newspaper publisher from New York City. Zenger had been prosecuted for harshly criticizing the colony's royal English governor. Hamilton pioneered the argument that the truth of an utterance should be a defense in actions for seditious libel (libel, that is, against the government and government officials).

In the nineteenth century, professional philosophers like John Stuart Mill advanced theories of free speech under the influence less of politics than of that century's scientific revolution. In *On Liberty* (1859), Mill argued that the search for truth as a scientific endeavor is best advanced by an open trade in ideas, even if some of those ideas turned out to be false.

Mill, in his time, was an independent philosopher and intellectual without a university affiliation. In the early-twentieth-century United States, however, university-based academic theorists became the most prominent defenders of free speech. The most broadly influential of these were progressives like Columbia University philosopher John Dewey and Harvard Law School professor Zechariah Chafee. Both linked their theories of speech to broader theories of participatory democratic politics.

The views of Mill, Dewey, and Chafee, in turn, spread well beyond philosophy books and student tests. In the early twentieth century, some of America's most brilliant justices, such as Louis D. Brandeis and Oliver Wendell Holmes Jr., imbued with the age's worship of scientific progress, picked up on Mill's ideas and applied them to the science of social organization. They argued that social progress is possible only through the open expression of ideas. This new free speech theorizing by the judges, in turn, spurred law professors to begin devising their own arguments on behalf of free speech.

A distinction has already been drawn between "academic" and "political" theories of free speech. This distinction relies upon the questionable assumption that academics are not political activists. In the twentieth century, though, beginning with Holmes and Brandeis, progressive judges joined up with progressive academics (both Brandeis and Holmes were graduates of Harvard Law School and had close ties to the faculty of that institution) to formulate a progressive political agenda for free speech law. Law review scholarship, more perhaps than most scholarship, is advocacy scholarship. Much of it is published to advance a distinctly political agenda. Nineteenth-century law concerning speech had for the most part been relatively stable. The twentieth century became the golden age not only of theorizing concerning the ends of freedom of speech but also of pushing for political progress insofar as free speech doctrines were concerned. The twentieth century was the era of free speech theory and "progressive" free speech change. But historically speaking, what were the arguments on behalf of freer speech?

PRO–FREE SPEECH ARGUMENTS

That Man Be Free to Worship God According to the Dictates of His Own Conscience

Contemporary constitutional doctrine often treats free speech rights and the right to freely exercise one's religion as distinct and separate rights. It was not always thus. In fact, historically speaking, the secular right that we know as the freedom of speech arose out of the religious claim on behalf of the freedom of conscience. This was true in both England and America, and in America, it was readily apparent in the debates over the ratification of the Constitution. For example, in writing in 1787 in defense of the Constitution's provision that "no religious Test shall ever be required as a Qualification to any Office or public Trust under the United States" (art. 6, clause 3), founder and Chief Justice (1796–1800) Oliver Ellsworth of Connecticut declared that

> The business of a civil government is to protect the citizen in his rights, to defend the community from hostile powers, and to promote the general welfare. Civil government has no business to meddle with the private opinions of the people. If I demean myself as a good citizen, I am accountable, not to man but to God, for the religious opinions which I embrace, and the manner in which I worship the Supreme being. If such had been the universal sentiments of mankind, and they had acted accordingly, persecution, the bane of truth and nurse of error, with her bloody axe and flaming hand, would never have turned so great a part of the world into a field of blood. (Quoted in Kurland and Lerner 1987, 639–641).

In more modern times, constitutional disputes have arisen in which the connection between free speech and free exercise rights is apparent. The Supreme Court's famous 1943 flag salute decision, *West Virginia State Board of Education v. Barnette* (319 U.S. 624 [1943]), upheld the religious claim of Jehovah's Witness schoolchildren who refused to salute the flag because it violated the biblical injunction against worshipping a graven image. In this case, Justice Robert Jackson defended claims of conscience as a defense of the wider principle of freedom of speech. In melding religious and secular claims in his opinion, Justice Jackson defended the "freedom to be intellectually and spiritually diverse," and declared, "If there is any fixed star in our constitutional constellation, it is that no official, high or petty, can prescribe what shall be orthodox in politics, nationalism, religion, or other matters of opinion or force citizens to confess by word or act their faith therein" (*West Virginia State Board of Education v. Barnette* [1943], *642*).

More recently, in a case involving a decision by the University of Virginia to deny student activities fees to a student-run religious publication, *Rosenberger v. University of Virginia* (515 U.S. 819 [1995]), the students argued that the university's decision violated not only their free exercise rights but also their free speech rights. Their joint free exercise/free speech claim persuaded a narrow majority of the Court, which awarded them a 5–4 victory in the case. In short, the right to speak freely is in many respects a right of conscience, and as such, it is linked historically and conceptually to claims on behalf of religious liberty.

Free Speech as a Means to Truth and a Check against Error

When we think of the virtues of giving people great latitude concerning what they say, our thoughts might naturally turn to the immediate benefits to ourselves of the pleasures of freedom over frustration. But freedom of speech also serves a social purpose. A society that prefers the rational to the irrational will necessarily have a preference for informed judgment and decisionmaking. And the best judgments and decisions, we believe, are usually made after an individual or governing body—a body that may be so wide as to amount to the whole of society itself—has gathered the widest array of facts, points of view, and arguments. Only after hearing the arguments and counterarguments can people make a truly informed decision. To suppress information and to stifle relevant arguments that may make us uncomfortable is a recipe for irrationality, bad judgment, and bad decisionmaking.

This is true in many walks of life. Certainly it is true in science, where many suppressed arguments later proved to be true—such as Copernicus's argument that the earth revolves around the sun and not the reverse. Our knowledge about the world and ourselves, so the argument goes, is best advanced through free and open discussion. It may also be true about public policy arguments, for example, concerning the likelihood that a nation could win a war, such as the war in Vietnam. Not surprisingly, defenses of a latitudinarian conception of free speech are closely linked in history with the intellectual movement known as the Enlightenment, which privileged rational thought and inquiry over religious faith and revelation as the best way to understand life and the world. The founders most devoted to Enlightenment thought, such as Thomas Jefferson—who was a scientist and inventor as well as a statesman and political theorist—were also the ones most likely to deploy this justification in defense of a latitudinarian conception of the freedom of speech.

But the roots of the argument that speech is a means to truth predate the founding of the United States, and the argument's justifications, though adopted by many Americans, were often formulated on foreign (often English) shores. In writing against a system that required all books printed to be preapproved and licensed by the Crown, John Milton demanded, "Let [Truth] and falsehood grapple; whoever knew Truth put to the worst in a free and open encounter?" (Milton 1951, 50). John Stuart Mill made a similar albeit much more extended argument in *On Liberty*. Mill favored the widest possible latitude for the freedom of speech, whether true or false, on the grounds that both types of speech aid in the search for truth. If the truth is banned, then society is directly deprived of its benefit. If falsehoods are suppressed, however, the search for truth cannot benefit from the vigorous dialectical clashes that elevate the quality of a dispute. Moreover, one can better appreciate the nature and quality of one's own beliefs if they are questioned and challenged rather than held largely as a prejudice. As a practical matter, moreover, Mill argued that in the frequently chaotic process of debate, truth and error seem to become inextricably intertwined. (Thus we say colloquially, for example, that an argument we take to be false contains "a grain of truth.") In a world of at times bewildering complexity, freedom of discussion is the best hope that the false can be effectively separated from the true.

In the U.S. constitutional tradition, the Millian conception of the value of free speech to the pursuit of the true was perhaps most famously articulated by Justice Oliver Wendell Holmes, Jr. (a devoted reader of Mill) in his dissent in the 1919 Red Scare case of *Abrams v. United States* (250 U.S. 616 [1919]). In *Abrams*, Holmes explained,

Persecution for the expression of opinions seems to me perfectly logical. If you have no doubt of your premises or your power and want a certain result with all your heart you naturally express your wishes in law and sweep away all opposition. To allow opposition by speech seems to indicate that you think the speech impotent, as when a man says that he has squared the circle, or that you do not care wholeheartedly for the result, or that you doubt either your power or your premises. But when men have realized that time has upset many fighting faiths, they may come to believe even more than they believe the very foundations of their own conduct that the ultimate good desired is better reached by free trade in ideas—that the best test of truth is the power of the thought to get itself accepted in the competition of the market, and that truth is the only ground upon which their wishes can safely be carried out. That at any rate is the theory of our Constitution. It is an experiment, as all life is an experiment. (630)

Free Speech as a Form of Minority Rights

One of the most familiar contemporary arguments on behalf of a latitudinarian conception of the freedom of speech is that free speech is a means of protecting the liberty of minorities and minority arguments and ideas. People in the majority and those advancing views and opinions held by the majority are unlikely to encounter legal restrictions on what they can say. After all, in a democracy such as ours, majorities elect the people who write the laws. And although time lags can take place, representatives who take too much trouble to oppose the will of the majority will before long find themselves out of a job.

But what of people who belong to unpopular social groups, such as ethnic and religious minorities, or people who boldly express highly unpopular ideas such as may be held by communists, anarchists, sexual radicals, campus conservatives, and civil rights advocates? Members of such groups, as well as lone-wolf individualists who, as Henry David Thoreau once put it, step to the sound of a different drummer, cannot look with any assurance to majoritarian institutions to protect their right to speak as they wish on matters of great controversy and of great anxiety. In the contemporary United States, the place such groups and individuals have sought protection for the freedom of speech is in the federal courts. In those courts, they can make First Amendment appeals to judges who are unelected and life tenured, and who are hence relatively free from majoritarian political pressures and the passions of the moment. The federal courts are, in Alexander Bickel's phrase, "counter-majoritarian" institutions, and as such they play an important structural role in our constitutional democracy. In short, according to this argument, pluralism goes hand in hand with vigorous judicial protection of the First Amendment's guarantee of free speech.

Free Speech for Self-Government and Democracy

One persistent argument in favor of free speech is that effective self-government requires a latitudinarian conception of the freedom of speech. In early-seventeenth-century England, members of Parliament famously argued that speech and debate in the legislature should be conducted freely without interference from the Crown. James Madison made similar arguments concerning the importance of free speech in America's founding era, as did John Stuart Mill in the nineteenth century. In the twentieth, progressives such as John Dewey and Alexander Meiklejohn insisted that open debate amounted to "the thinking process of the community" (Meiklejohn 1948, 26). More recently, Robert Bork and other conservatives have claimed that free speech is a requirement of self-government but that there is no blanket constitutional protection for nonpolitical speech (such as certain forms of artistic expression that have little or no political relevance). On the other hand, the free speech position of contemporary "civic republicans," such as Cass Sunstein, defend more latitudinarian protections for speech on the grounds that it serves not just individual needs but broader social interests.

In *New York Times v. Sullivan* (376 U.S. 254 [1964]), Justice William Brennan famously declared that the United States has "a profound national commitment to the principle that debate on public issues should be uninhibited, robust, and wide-open" (270). What significant public purposes are served by such debate? To the extent that open debate makes it more likely that truth will win out over falsehood, public policy will be better formulated and less error prone under a regime that welcomes open discussion and debate. Open discussion and debate are needed, moreover, to prevent powerful interests from imposing intellectual and institutional stagnation on the community. Under a regime that values free speech, dissenters of all sorts are free to challenge the status quo and make the case for social change. Indeed, as John Stuart Mill argued, such changes also force us to better understand why some old ideas and institutions are worth preserving. Free speech also serves as a check on the arbitrary exercise or abuse of power, which would culminate in tyranny—the very opposite of self-government. Free speech creates a space for early warning signs of incipient despotism.

Free Speech on Behalf of Individual Autonomy

Some theories of free speech promote it not because it serves a collective social purpose but rather because it promotes individual autonomy. (John Stuart Mill advocated free speech for both reasons.) And these theories regard individual autonomy as a valuable end in itself. The Supreme Court has frequently recognized this justification for free speech. In the early-twentieth-century case of *Whitney v. California* (274 U.S. 357 [1927]), for example, Justice Louis D. Brandeis, in a famous concurrence, declared that "those who won our independence believed that the final end of the state was to make men free to develop their faculties" (375).

Since Brandeis's day, the autonomy argument has slowly gained adherents on the Court, particularly as the wider culture, at least since the 1960s and 1970s, placed increasing value on the right—indeed, the imperative—of pursuing personal fulfillment or "self-actualization." By the mid-1960s, things had gone so far that Justice William O. Douglas, in a dissenting opinion in *Ginzburg v. United States* (383 U.S. 463 [1966]), opined about the "therapeutical value" of sexual masochism and sexual fetishes on both individual and communal grounds. This value, Douglas argued, lies in the general society's "communication" with a "masochistic community" that loosens conventions that straitjacket human freedom and expression.

It is unlikely today that a justice of the Supreme Court would draft an opinion as Justice Douglas did in his dissent in *Ginzburg v. United States*. Since the 1970s, the culture and the Court have been reassessing the primacy of individual autonomy. One can see this shift in the renewed debates over the consequences and wisdom of no-fault divorce, abortion on demand, and tolerance of racist speech. Such debates have been raging not only in the courts but also in the legislatures and the broader culture.

Preservationist Defenses of Free Speech

Most contemporary free speech theorists advance progressive theories in favor of free speech, defending wide latitude for speech and debate as a means of promoting social change. Only through vigorous and open debate, so progressives argue, is it possible for individuals and society to change and grow and for scientific knowledge to advance. There is, however, a preservationist defense of free speech that has deep roots in Anglo-American history. That defense is most prominently associated with early-eighteenth-century "country party" opposition to the corruption of the "court party," which dominated the king's court in London. John Trenchard and Thomas Gordon's *Cato's Letters* (1720–1723), one of the most famous expressions of country resistance (they were reprinted and widely read by the American colonists during the revolutionary era), referred to freedom of speech as "the Great Bulwark of Liberty" and as essential to the triumph of knowledge over ignorance (*Cato's Letter* no. 15, in Rosenberg 1986, 37–38). For Trenchard and Gordon, knowledge was the great preserver of liberty. They considered England to be the freest country in the world and its constitution the very best. The greatness of English liberty was made possible by free speech, and only recognition of this fact could prevent degeneration in those liberties through corruption and ill-advised innovation.

Echoes of Trenchard and Gordon's preservationist arguments for free speech are sometimes heard today on the college campuses of the contemporary United States, particularly at elite universities. Students and professors who defend patriotism and U.S. traditions are frequently attacked, and sometimes disciplined, for decrying radical social change in the guise of feminism, racial preferences for minorities, and the decline of religious values. These self-identified conservatives contend that the guarantee of free speech principles is essential to their goal of protecting the entire package of U.S. freedoms.

Free Speech as Essential to a Tolerant Society

One of the conditions for the flourishing of a diverse liberal society is a broad toleration for those who practice different religions, hold different political views, and follow different ways of life. Lee Bollinger has argued that the very diversity of our society itself makes intolerance a perpetual threat. Thus, Bollinger argues, only by permitting the broadest possible scope for the freedom of speech can society become a school for tolerance. And the value of tolerance should be at the heart of controversies over the scope of the freedom of speech (Bollinger 1986).

Free Speech as a Form of Prudence

Most arguments we use to defend giving wide latitude to freedom of speech reflect a particular legal understanding of the scope of the issue. But the real-world parameters of free speech have always been shaped by people making political and not simply legal decisions. The criminal law itself, as printed on the page of U.S. statute books, may seem purely legal, but prosecution of a person for violating the law is a matter of political choice. As such, many concerns, and not just the reading of what lawyers call the "black letter" law, or the statutes or rules themselves, as plainly expressed in print, are relevant. Prosecutors look at the time and money it will cost them to see a case to completion, and they weigh these concerns in light of the total caseload they must handle at any given time. And a prosecutor may, for example, consider which sorts of prosecutions will help him attain a judgeship or elected office. Changes in the leadership of prosecutors' offices and in the salience of particular issues will often alter criminal prosecutors' priorities. At various times in U.S. history, blasphemy and obscenity prosecutions were common issues, and in a place like Utah, obscenity still is. The prosecution of drug crimes may be important to prosecutors in one place but not in another. The same is true with violations of labor laws. Prosecutors, in short, make political calculations in deciding which laws to enforce and how often and how rigorously to enforce them.

Regarding free speech, prosecutors must consider the prudence of prosecution in light of popular opinion, which puts great stock in a latitudinarian conception of the freedom of speech. If there is considerable public sympathy for a controversial view (and sometimes even if there is not), prosecution can end up making the defendant into a martyr in the cause of free speech. In the late 1880s, when political radicals exploded bombs in Chicago's Haymarket Square, historian Henry Adams defended the free speech right of anarchists: Laws limiting anarchist speech, Adams contended, would only serve the anarchist cause, which the conservative Adams strongly opposed. In the twentieth century, prosecutions of the American Nazi Party, the Ku Klux Klan, and the American Communist Party (CPUSA) actually gave these illiberal and intolerant groups a political platform and an opportunity to pose as sympathetic defenders of core U.S. values. Communists, in particular, whose political creed scorned the constitutional rights of the "bourgeois" U.S. state, by dint of government persecution became heroes in the cause of free speech.

That said, however, it is not clear that the prosecutions of American Communists in the 1940s and 1950s significantly increased domestic support for the CPUSA. But in some cases, prosecution can go well beyond making free speech martyrs and cause a backlash against the accusers. In George Washington's administration, for example, Alexander Hamilton continually urged the president to prosecute those who were attacking both his character and his leadership. On the advice of a succession of his attorneys general, however, the Federalist Washington, fearing he would thus play into the hands of Democratic-Republican adversaries, refused. His successor, President John Adams, was not so wise, however, and Adams's zealous prosecutions of the Democratic-Republicans under the Sedition Act played a decisive role in delivering the election of 1800 to Thomas Jefferson, the head of the opposing party.

Similarly, repressing speech can turn political allies into political enemies. During World War I, Woodrow Wilson, a Democrat, prosecuted liberals, radicals, and pacifists who opposed the war. Once the war was over, these antiwar activists might have voted for Wilson on account of his progressive domestic agenda. Instead, however, by his conduct during the war years, Wilson imprudently squandered the opportunity for winning their eventual support. Wilson did not censor or prosecute his conservative opponents, a policy that, ironically, put them in a position to work effectively to defeat the president's domestic initiatives after the war ended.

In short, a wide latitude for free speech makes good, practical sense. It is, as William Blackstone put it, sound policy to tolerate free speech, even when it could be prosecuted, because legal action often has social and political ramifications beyond the courthouse doors.

ANTI–FREE SPEECH ARGUMENTS

Claims on Behalf of an Orderly and Effective Self-Government and the Conventions of Decency

As we have seen, one of the main defenses of "uninhibited, robust, and wide-open" speech is that it is indispensable to self-government (*New York Times v. Sullivan*, 376 U.S. 254 [1964], 270). Yet important political thinkers have also asserted the opposite, that in fact, restraint is the sine qua non of self-government. This is apparent in the origins of the phrase "self-government" itself. We usually take the phrase to mean something akin to democracy or republican government, in which the people, acting collectively, make their own laws. But in earlier centuries, "self-government" also referred to the rule that individuals exercised over themselves, checking or "governing" their own passions, impulses, and desires. Jean-Jacques Rousseau argued that democracies in particular can function efficiently only with citizens possessing the virtues of self-control. Tyrannies, he said, do not require any particular type of character among the citizenry, because under tyranny, citizens are told what they must do. On the other hand, where authority is exercised with a lighter touch, as in a democracy, much of the duty of ruling or "governing" falls upon the citizen, whose internal system of self-government makes the less onerous exercise of external authority possible. In the U.S. context, Alexis de Tocqueville similarly argued that restraint is the sine qua non of freedom. Striving to understand and explain the United States of the 1830s, Tocqueville declared that the nation's great freedom derived in large part from the religiosity of its people. In the United States, religiously inspired self-restraint was a precondition of political freedom. The requisite restraints might not be legal restraints, as religious tenets were not legal restraints, but their limits were essential to self-government all the same. Writing in the early twentieth century, Sigmund Freud traced the implications of this argument by arguing that civilized life would be impossible without the suppression and sublimation of elemental passions, urges, and desires.

Today, one sees the relationship between social and cultural restraints and good government in discussions concerning the observance and enforcement of manners and civility. The words "civility," "civic," and "civilization" all stem from the same Latin root. Although it is considered one of the chief accomplishments of the Anglo-American democratic tradition that legislators have the right to speak freely when they are in session, they must still obey rules requiring civility, respect, and collegiality. Clearly, rules of civility in legislative debate do not limit but rather facilitate debate, thereby advancing the cause of effective self-government. At one time, such laws were also enforced in the wider society: Laws against blasphemy, obscenity, "fighting words," slander, and libel helped enforce public standards of civility in the interest of the common good.

The argument for rules of civility and restraint contends that some utterances are socially worthless and therefore either add nothing to political and social discourse or shut it down altogether. What benefit is provided by the protection of the right to call someone a "damn fascist" or to refer to one's opponent using racial, sexual, or religious epithets? Of what social value is hardcore pornography? Can one claim with a straight face that the protection of such language and speech advances the search for truth and the cause of intelligent self-government? Isn't it just as likely that tolerating such speech in a public forum will shut down reasoned discussion rather than stimulate it? And if it has these effects, wouldn't its claim to protection be very thin indeed?

One might think so. But the truth is that such speech has found considerable favor in contemporary jurisprudence. In 1971, for example, the U.S. Supreme Court ruled that Paul Robert Cohen had a constitutional right to walk around a Los Angeles courtroom wearing a denim jacket emblazoned with the phrase "Fuck the draft." Justice John Marshall Harlan argued that this form of expression should be protected because the words should be valued "as much for their emotive as their cognitive force" (*Cohen v. California*, 403 U.S. 15 [1971], 26). In this case, as in others, civility is not valued very highly.

Despite these trends, some thinkers continue to believe otherwise. Walter Berns has pointed out that the Supreme Court would be very unlikely indeed to tolerate such a display in its own courtroom. Nor is vulgar and rude expression permitted on the floor of Congress. Belief in self-restraint and rules of conduct, although still under siege, remains strong (Berns 1976).

Liberation, Egalitarianism, and Concerns of Power

The United States, political philosophers have argued, is the world's most "liberal" society. These philosophers use the word "liberal" as a term of art. It does not mean the politics of the left wing of the contemporary Democratic Party or of Ralph Nader or Jesse Jackson. It is rather a temperament and set of beliefs whose chief value is the formal rights of individuals to make free choices about their lives within a society governed by the rule of law. For a liberal, defenses of free speech come naturally and easily. The individual, after all, should be free to say what he or she chooses. Others, in turn, can listen to him and either accept his arguments or reject them, as they choose. Thus, liberty and equality—the equal right to speak and be heard—go hand in hand. The playing field of debate is open to all, and none are excluded.

Of course, there have always been critics of the notion that a formally open playing field serves the interests of all equally. The nineteenth-century French novelist Anatole France, for example, once famously criticized the notion that neutral laws are equal laws. "The law, in its majestic equality," he scornfully noted, "forbids the rich as well as the poor to sleep under bridges, to beg in the streets, and to steal bread." Law, in other words, may be directed equally at all, but equal laws may greatly favor the rich and powerful. Thus, many have argued, paradoxically, that the way to true equality—a top priority for egalitarians—is to throw out the fiction of neutrality and to simply enact laws that advance the interests of those who are poor and disenfranchised.

One contemporary controversy in the law of free speech involves this very issue. In the *Buckley v. Valeo* (424 U.S. 1 [1976]) decision, the Supreme Court held that financial contributions to political campaigns are a form of political speech and are thus protected by the First Amendment. The decision, in effect, said that the rich and the poor alike have an equal right to make campaign contributions, thereby influencing the outcome of elections. Various limits on campaign contributions were held by the Court to be unconstitutional. Ever since, however, advocates of campaign finance reform—people on the political left as well as some spirited Republicans, such as Senator John McCain—have decried the way the formalities of free speech law have skewed power in politics toward the interests of the rich. They have urged repeatedly that *Buckley* be overturned in the interest of equal citizenship rights.

Analogous arguments have been urged on behalf of other poor and politically disadvantaged groups. Political philosopher Herbert Marcuse, a hero to the New Left and the student movements of the 1960s, made this argument in his widely read essay "Repressive Tolerance." Since then (and building on the work of Marcuse), feminist, black nationalist, "queer," and other left-wing professors, administrators, and students have argued that free speech on campus leaves women, racial minorities, and gays and lesbians more vulnerable to injury and insult than it does male, white, heterosexual students. Under the rubric of equalizing power relations, they have called for and have succeeded in passing campus speech codes that penalize specific forms of expression, stigmatized as "hate speech." The codes at the University of Wisconsin–Madison and the University of Michigan–Ann Arbor were struck down by federal judges as unconstitutional abridgments of the freedom of speech. Campus and workplace sexual harassment regulations forbidding speech that creates a hostile environment for women, however, have been upheld and even encouraged by courts. In the contemporary United States, egalitarianism is one of the most prominent and most effective devices used by activists seeking to limit the freedom of speech.

Pluralist and Anti-Theories of the Freedom of Speech

In recent years, after looking at the long history of the freedom of speech as it is actually practiced in the United States, many scholars, such as Robert Post, have come to the conclusion that it is impossible to attribute any single purpose to the First Amendment because it serves multiple purposes. Some of these scholars argue that free speech promotes certain values as it is practiced within certain institutions. Others, however, such as Stanley Fish, argue that First Amendment doctrine is in truth not principled at all. Nor, they argue, could it ever be. Everything is politics and power, Fish contends. And, what is more, this is not a question of judges' failure of will to abide by principles. Rather, it is inevitable. Since desirable values routinely conflict with one another, choices have to be made. Given the inevitability of conflict, decisions must be determined on political rather than principled grounds. Attempts to formulate unified theories identifying the First Amendment's guiding "purpose" are themselves actually political acts. Indeed, such purportedly "neutral" theories are in fact smoke screens that conceal political agendas.

FREE SPEECH TODAY

Free speech—once a matter of intense debate among the American people and within the nation's institutions—has been largely colonized and domesticated by political, bureaucratic, and legal elites. What is permissible and impermissible speech today is determined less by the ebb and flow of political competition than by rulings from unelected judges in the federal courts. To be sure, the disputes weighed and debated by judges and legal scholars have bubbled up from society itself, whether they are about protests at abortion clinics, university codes prohibiting hate speech, or efforts to prohibit obscenity on the Internet. But the last word on the matters of free speech typically comes from the judiciary.

Accordingly, now more than at any other time in our history, the parameters of permissible speech are defined by the U.S. Supreme Court. As noted earlier, the Court's sustained foray into free speech law began in the early twentieth century. For the first half of that century, the Court worked to impose a conceptual order on the ambiguous free speech clause of the First Amendment. First, it proposed and then sought to apply various "tests" as to whether the speech in question is constitutionally protected or not. (The Court proceeds via "tests" in other areas as well, principally when the plain text, because of vagueness or ambiguity, cannot provide a useful guide to real-world situations.) The point of departure concerning free speech in the early twentieth century was the old common law Bad Tendency test, which let the government regulate speech pursuant to its police powers to protect the public health, safety, and morals. Over time, in a series of cases involving early-twentieth-century political radicalism (mainly anarchists and socialists), the justices of the Court retired the Bad Tendency test and replaced it with a more speech-protective Clear and Present Danger test proposed by Justice Oliver Wendell Holmes, Jr. in 1919. In determining whether speech was constitutionally protected, the Clear and Present Danger test asked not whether the words had a bad tendency but rather "whether the words used are used in such circumstances and are of such a nature as to create a clear and present danger that they will bring about the substantive evils that Congress has a right to prevent" (*Schenck v. United States*, 249 U.S. 47 [1919], 52). In applying this test, the Court at first tended to rule against political radicals. But before long the Court began to apply the Clear and Present Danger test much more vigorously, affording new protections to political radicals (an approach we may call the Heightened Clear and Present Danger test).

In the early 1940s, the Court expanded First Amendment protection even further, according speech a preferred position among the constellation of constitutional rights. But with the rise of the Cold War against the Soviet Union and the general concern about Communist espionage and subversion, the opponents of a latitudinarian conception of free speech gained the upper hand. *Dennis v. United States* (341 U.S. 494 [1951]), the so-called Smith Act case, ended the long-standing hegemony of the Clear and Present Danger test. In *Dennis,* the Court's majority based the decision on the so-called Hand test (named after its author, federal appellate court judge Learned Hand). The majority declared, "In each case [courts] must ask whether the gravity of the 'evil,' discounted by its improbability, justifies such invasion of free speech as is necessary to avoid the danger" (510). Justices Felix Frankfurter and Robert Jackson concurred in the *Dennis* opinion, but they declared that they would not apply the Hand test to reach that result. Frankfurter declared that it was the place of Congress and not the courts to balance free speech against domestic security and to make the constitutional call in this case. Justice Jackson would have hewn to the Clear and Present Danger test in appropriate cases, such as "hot-headed speech on a street corner or circulation of a few incendiary pamphlets, or parading by some zealots behind a red flag" (568). In the case of "a well-organized, nation-wide [Communist] conspiracy," however, the government must be allowed greater latitude in protecting national security (580). Dissenters Hugo Black and William O. Douglas, on the other hand, rejected all the prior tests. Declaring the First Amendment to be "the keystone of our Government," they insisted that in effect, the speech could be banned only if it was such as would bring the country to the brink of imminent revolution. Soon, Black and Douglas would become known as proponents of "First Amendment absolutism," which rejected all tests and declared simply that the amendment stated that "Congress shall make no law . . ." and that that is precisely what it meant. Congress could always prohibit conduct. But it could never prohibit speech. By the late 1960s, this view became mainstream Supreme Court doctrine, wholly displacing the old Clear and Present Danger approach.

In 1969, in an era of massive social upheaval, the Supreme Court announced its final test, the highly speech-protective Imminent and Lawless Harm test, under which speech can be restricted only when it "is directed to inciting or producing imminent law-less action and is likely to incite or produce such action" (*Bran-denburg v. Ohio*, 395 U.S. 444 [1969], 447). This test, however, was in principle so accepting of almost any sort of speech that in most cases it provided little effective guidance to courts. This turned out to be the end of the line of free speech tests, and the Court began turning its attention away from formulating sweep-ing pronouncements and toward an approach to free speech based on careful categorical analysis.

The contemporary constitutional analysis of free speech ques-tions is based not so much on the free speech tests of the past as on a variety of categorical legal distinctions. The most fundamen-tal is the distinction between speech and conduct. The govern-ment has always had the constitutional power to regulate behav-ior. It is only speech, defined as verbal expression, that is clearly protected by the First Amendment. Needless to say, the categories can blur. In a famous case from the late 1960s involving whether children could wear black armbands to school to protest the Viet-nam War, the Court's majority declared the students' actions to be a form of protected expression or speech. The Court has declared that "symbolic speech" such as wearing an armband or burning a flag, which is on the borderline between speech and conduct, is constitutionally protected under the First Amendment. It has also declared that "speech plus," involving such things as picketing, marching, and distributing leaflets, is also a form of constitution-ally protected speech. Hugo Black, in dissent, however, declared the wearing of the armbands to be unprotected conduct rather than protected speech.

To make matters even more complicated, the Court has long distinguished unprotected low-value speech from protected high-value speech. "Obscenity," for example, is speech, but the Court nonetheless has deemed obscenity to be low-value speech, having so little social worth as to fall outside constitutional protections. The Court has similarly declared "fighting words" a form of unprotected speech, although the so-called Fighting Words doctrine has been watered down so much since it was announced in the 1940s that it now seems to live on in name only. Conversely, in the course of its rulings, the Court has designated several categories of speech as clearly valued and hence protected, such as political speech, artistic speech, indecent speech, symbolic speech, personal expression, and (more recently) commercial speech.

Of course, even protected speech may be subject to government regulation. The contemporary Supreme Court's chief concern is that speech not be regulated on the basis of its content. As the Court puts it, the regulation of speech must be "content neutral." One cannot be denied a permit for a march on the grounds that the government does not like the content of what one is going to say, whether one is calling, for example, for civil rights legislation, the end of a war, or even the restoration of white supremacy. The government can, however, impose content-neutral time, place, and manner restrictions on speakers. So, for example, it can forbid someone from articulating pro–civil rights, antiwar, or white-supremacist views by blaring them at high volume out of a sound truck at 3 A.M. in a residential neighborhood. It can require permits for rallies, marches, and parades in order to provide adequate security and to keep the roads open. Moreover, the Court has declared that it will be more skeptical of the constitutionality of speech regulations depending on where the speech takes place. It is least skeptical of speech regulation involving such nonpublic forums as private homes. (Limits on picketing private homes—to protect abortion providers, for instance—have been upheld as permissible restrictions.) The Court has been most skeptical of speech restrictions in such traditional public forums as public parks. Needless to say, there has been much dispute over how to categorize particular spaces. What of airports? Privately owned shopping malls? The streets in front of abortion clinics? Reasonable time, place, and manner restrictions are, of course, permissible when applied to speech taking place even in highly protected public forums.

Contemporary free speech law has grown into a tangled garden of bewildering doctrinal complexity. The current confusion raises the question of whether the Court's midcentury switch from a test-based to a categorical approach has actually simplified the law of the freedom of speech. One thing is certain, however: As in many other areas, such as criminal procedure, for example, free speech jurisprudence now places law and policy decisions once reserved to the other branches of government squarely in the hands of the U.S. Supreme Court.

References and Further Reading

Abel, Richard L. 1998. *Speaking Respect, Respecting Speech.* Chicago: University of Chicago Press.

Alexander, Larry, and Paul Horton. 1983. "The Impossibility of a Free Speech Principle." *Northwestern University Law Review* 78: 1319–1357.

Amar, Akhil Reed. 1998. *The Bill of Rights: Creation and Reconstruction.* New Haven: Yale University Press.

Baker, C. Edwin. 1989. *Human Liberty and the Freedom of Speech.* New York: Oxford University Press.

Berns, Walter. 1976. *The First Amendment and the Future of American Democracy.* New York: Basic Books.

Bickel, Alexander M. 1962. *The Least Dangerous Branch: The Supreme Court at the Bar of Politics.* Indianapolis, IN: Bobbs-Merrill.

Blasi, Vincent. 1977. "The Checking Value of the First Amendment." *American Bar Foundation Research Journal* 521.

Bollinger, Lee. 1986. *The Tolerant Society: Freedom of Speech and Extremist Speech in America.* New York: Oxford University Press.

Bollinger, Lee, and Geoffrey Stone, eds. 2002. *Eternally Vigilant: Free Speech in the Modern Era.* Chicago: University of Chicago Press.

Bork, Robert. 1971. "Neutral Principles and Some First Amendment Problems." *Indiana Law Journal* 47: 1.

Butler, Judith. 1997. *Excitable Speech: A Politics of the Performative.* New York: Routledge.

Chafee, Zechariah Jr. 1941. *Free Speech in the United States.* Cambridge, MA: Harvard University Press.

Cohen, Joshua. 1993. "Freedom of Expression." *Philosophy and Public Affairs* 22: 207–263.

Emerson, Thomas I. 1967. *Toward a General Theory of the First Amendment.* New York: Vintage Books.

Farber, Daniel A. 1991. "Free Speech without Romance: Public Choice and the First Amendment." *Harvard Law Review* 105: 554.

Fish, Stanley. 1994. *There's No Such Thing as Free Speech, and It's a Good Thing, Too.* New York: Oxford University Press.

Fiss, Owen. 1996. *The Irony of Free Speech.* Cambridge, MA: Harvard University Press.

Greenawalt, Kent. 1989. "Free Speech Justifications." *Columbia Law Review* 89: 119.

———. 1995. *Fighting Words: Individuals, Communities, and Liberties of Speech.* Princeton: Princeton University Press.

Hall, Kermit, ed. 1999. *The Oxford Companion to the Supreme Court of the United States.* New York: Oxford University Press.

Hamilton, Alexander, James Madison, and John Jay. [1787–1788] 1999. *The Federalist Papers.* Ed. Clinton Rossiter. Notes and introduction by Charles Kessler. New York: Mentor Books.

Irons, Peter. 1999. *A People's History of the Supreme Court.* New York: Penguin Books.

Karst, Kenneth. 1975. "Equality as a Central Principle in the First Amendment." *University of Chicago Law Review* 43: 20.

Kendall, Willmoore. 1960. "The 'Open Society' and Its Fallacies." *American Political Science Review* 54: 972.

Klarman, Michael J. 1996. "Rethinking the Civil Rights and Civil Liberties Revolutions." *Virginia Law Review* 82: 1–67.

Kurland, Philip, and Ralph Lerner, eds. 1987. *The Founders' Constitution.* Vol. 4. Chicago: University of Chicago Press.

Lowenthal, David. 1997. *No Liberty for License: The Forgotten Logic of the First Amendment.* Dallas, TX: Spence Publishing.

MacKinnon, Catherine A. 1993. *Only Words.* Cambridge, MA: Harvard University Press.

Marcuse, Herbert. 1969. "Repressive Tolerance." In *A Critique of Pure Tolerance,* by Robert Paul Wolff, Barrington Moore Jr., and Herbert Marcuse. Boston: Beacon Press.

Matsuda, Mari J., Charles R. Lawrence III, Richard Delgado, and Kimberle Williams Crenshaw. 1993. *Words That Wound: Critical Race Theory, Assaultive Speech, and the First Amendment.* Boulder, CO: Westview Press.

McCloskey, Robert G. 2000. *The American Supreme Court.* Revised by Sanford Levinson. Chicago: University of Chicago Press.

Meiklejohn, Alexander. 1948. *Free Speech and Its Relation to Self Government.* New York: Harper Brothers.

Mill, John Stuart. 1975. *Three Essays: On Liberty, Representative Government, The Subjection of Women.* Oxford: Oxford University Press.

Milton, John. 1951. *Areopagitica and of Education.* Ed. George H. Sabine. Northbrook, IL: AHM Publishing.

Murphy, Paul L. 1979. *World War I and the Origin of Civil Liberties in the United States.* New York: Norton.

Posner, Richard A. 1986. "Free Speech in an Economic Perspective." *Suffolk Law Review* 20: 1.

Post, Robert. 1995. "Recuperating First Amendment Doctrine." *Stanford Law Review* 47: 1249.

Redish, Martin. 1982. "The Value of Free Speech." *University of Pennsylvania Law Review* 130: 591.

———. 1984. *Freedom of Expression: A Critical Analysis.* Charlottesville, VA: Michie.

Richards, David A. J. 1999. *Free Speech and the Politics of Identity.* New York: Oxford University Press.

Rosenberg, Norman L. 1986. *Protecting the Best Men: An Interpretive History of the Law of Libel.* Chapel Hill: University of North Carolina Press.

Rousseau, Jean-Jacques. 1968. *Politics and the Arts: A Letter to d'Alembert.* Ed. Allan Bloom. Ithaca, NY: Cornell University Press.

Scanlon, Thomas. 1972. "A Theory of Freedom of Expression." *Philosophy and Public Affairs* 1: 204.

Schauer, Frederick. 1982. *Free Speech: A Philosophical Enquiry.* Cambridge: Cambridge University Press.

Schiffrin, Stephen. 1990. *The First Amendment, Democracy, and Romance.* Cambridge, MA: Harvard University Press.

Smolla, Rodney. 1992. *Free Speech in an Open Society.* New York: Knopf.

Sullivan, Kathleen M., and Gerald Gunther. 1999. *First Amendment Law.* New York: Foundation Press.

Sunstein, Cass. 1993. *Democracy and the Problem of Free Speech.* New York: Free Press.

Tocqueville, Alexis de. [1833] 1969. *Democracy in America.* Ed. J. P. Mayer. Trans. George Lawrence. New York: Perennial Library.

Trollope, Frances. [1832] 1960. *Domestic Manners of the Americans.* New York: Vintage Books.

Volokh, Eugene. 1995. "How Harassment Law Restricts Free Speech." *Rutgers Law Review* 47: 561–578.

White, G. Edward. 1996. "The First Amendment Comes of Age." *Michigan Law Review* 95: 299–392.

2

ORIGINS AND
EARLY DEVELOPMENT

*F*OR AMERICANS TODAY, freedom of speech is a constitutionally protected personal liberty, a fundamental and self-evident right of each of us. But the idea of a right to "freedom of speech" did not originally entail a personal right available equally to everyone. How, after all, could society function and sustain itself in a chaotic free-for-all in which authority figures could be criticized and mocked and in which animosities between individuals and factions could be stirred and inflamed? The idea that ordinary individuals had a right to free speech, though perhaps not beyond imagining, was a marginal idea for much of the Anglo-American legal tradition.

Does this mean that in earlier periods of Anglo-American legal history, ordinary people believed they had no general immunity from prosecution for what they said? Not completely. For centuries, people had demanded a right to speak freely, chiefly to pray and to praise God as they saw fit. Other than that, though, they kept a careful lid on their public utterances. Failure to do so, they knew, could lead them into serious trouble. In medieval England, for instance, one could be hauled into the king's courts for getting into a heated argument with a lord or neighbor, since an exchange of harsh words could escalate into physical violence that would disrupt public order and tranquillity—the king's peace, as it was called. In 1275, the English Parliament enacted a statute known as *De scandalis magnatum,* which made it a crime to slander the realm's most prominent men. The theory of *De scandalis magnatum* (which was reenacted several times over the course of the next hundred years) was that although slanders against one's social equals might disturb the king's peace, slander of important personages was especially dangerous because it undermined respect for the honor and dignity of those in authority. In a hierarchical society, social deference is an essential foundation of good governance.

Even in early modern times, when the concept of free speech first became part of English political discourse, it was understood not as a widely available individual right but rather as a specifically parliamentary right: the right of legislators, in the performance of their public duties, to speak freely and openly. Only through open deliberation and dialogue could legislators enact sensible laws and thereby serve the common good.

But this limited concession to free speech did not permit anyone to stir up dangerous trouble. Today, Americans tend to take the stability of government that protects our lives, property, and personal rights for granted as part of our birthright. For most of human history, however, stable government was the exception rather than the rule, and there was a keen sense that peace and prosperity were relatively rare and precarious blessings. Democracy was seen as an inherently unstable form of government. In democracies, Machiavelli warned, people make claims to "think all things, speak all things, write all things." Such liberty, he said, can be tolerated, but only up to a point. Once people feel free to criticize and mock the authorities, public order starts to crumble, and society begins its descent into chaos and destruction (quoted in Levy 1960, 89).

In this regard, the parliamentary right to free speech was often perceived as being as much of a threat as the personal right. In 1523, Thomas More, the speaker of the English House of Commons, tried to persuade England's powerful monarch, Henry VIII, that the Commons could give useful, disinterested "advice and counsel" only if its members were free from fear of punishment. Later, in 1576, the Puritan parliamentarian Peter Wentworth delivered his famous speech "On the Liberty of the Commons," pleading for open discussion as a means of advancing the Crown's interests and criticizing Queen Elizabeth for a number of ill-advised decisions. Despite his good intentions and his sincere appeal to the queen to "discern faithful advice from traitorous, sugared speeches," Wentworth's 1576 speech was denounced as radical and destabilizing, and he was swiftly imprisoned in the Tower of London.

U.S. constitutional tradition was influenced less by the sixteenth-century arguments of More and Wentworth than by the seventeenth-century struggles between the king and Parliament. In 1620, James I of England, the monarch who commissioned the great Bible translation that bears his name, issued a royal proclamation alluding to and even defending the freedom of speech. But at the same time, the king insisted that freedom be limited, that it should help rather than hinder sound, effective government. It could not possibly extend to grave matters of state, which "are no Theames, or subjects fit for vulgar persons, or common meetings" (quoted in Levy 1960, 5 n.9).

The arguments of More and Wentworth were repeated and developed after Charles I, in 1642, tried to enter the House of Commons and arrest five of its members on the floor of the chamber. This royal action came to be seen in England (and later in America) as an effort by the king to assert his personal will at the expense of the common good. Many came to believe that threats against members of Parliament, even if never carried out, harmed the nation by intimidating the people's representatives and chilling the public debate. If such threats were allowed, members of Parliament would incline toward simply flattering the powerful few rather than protecting the interest of the many. Thus, if speech were chilled, every other liberty, including the right of self-government, would eventually be snuffed out. Political freedom, narrowly constrained by the arbitrary will of a king or an aristocracy, was thus no freedom at all. By the seventeenth century, free speech, at least in Parliament, had become for Englishmen the sine qua non of every other freedom.

This turn in political thought proved so powerful that in 1689 the English included a clause in their Bill of Rights conferring upon members of Parliament immunity from prosecution for anything they might say there. The American founders borrowed this provision and made it part of the U.S. Constitution: The speech and debate clause (art. 1, sec. 6) provides that members of Congress "for any Speech or Debate in either House . . . shall not be questioned in any other Place."

Over time, people came to regard freedom of speech as an obvious personal and civil right that applied to all forms of speech and "expression," political and otherwise. Today we tend to credit these changes to a small core of good "progressive" people, such as those who comprised the civil rights movement. In reality, the forces leading to these changes ran much deeper in human thinking and history. In fact, it is these forces themselves that make progressive rights crusading possible.

The idea of free speech as a personal right grew out of the Protestant belief in the right of conscience. In the seventeenth and eighteenth centuries, Protestants held that the individual needs to exercise his or her own judgment and conscience in order to be a good Christian. Thus, it was a religious impulse that inspired the linkage between individual freedom and conscience in the Anglo-American political tradition. This religious idea, interestingly enough, made possible both radically new claims for individual liberty and, at the same time, aggressive campaigns against that liberty. Since Protestants rooted the right of conscience in the free exercise of individual judgment in the service of God, they viewed Catholics, obedient to church hierarchy rather than to the individual conscience, as enemies of truth and freedom. Accordingly, they thought it was fully consistent with freedom of conscience to ban "papist" teachings and utterances and to subject them to various legal restrictions.

Religious antagonisms played an important part in the development of the scope of the freedom of speech in England. England had been a Catholic country for much of its history, and Catholicism was the established church of the realm. In order to procure a divorce, which the church had refused him, Henry VIII broke England's spiritual connection to Rome in 1534 and established the Church of England, or the Anglican church, with himself as its head. By the 1600s, a series of dissenting religious sects, often referred to collectively as the Puritans, began to spring up in England in opposition to the Church of England. At various times, Catholics, Anglicans, and Puritans assumed power in England. Because each believed in the absolute truth of its own creed, each tried to restrict the religious speech of its rivals.

For complicated historical reasons, religious disputes in Europe were political disputes as well. Church and state, after all, were closely linked in Europe. After the Protestant Reformation of the sixteenth century, which denied the authority of the pope and the church of Rome, each reformed nation made its earthly monarch the head of its national church as well. Thus, challenges to a nation's established church became in effect attacks on king and country and acts of insurrection and revolution. In England, for instance, in the Court of Star Chamber (named for the famous paintings on its ceiling), members of dissenting sects were punished for their religious speech on the grounds that it was sedition as well as heresy and blasphemy.

There was a resurgence of censorship in this era because of technological changes that were taking place at the same time: For the first time in history, via the printing press, books were widely available, and they made possible the quick and broad dissemination of heretical, blasphemous, and seditious ideas. Such mass publication, along with an increased literacy rate, made political and religious dissent all the more dangerous. England's Tudor monarchs, Henry VIII and Elizabeth I, sought to control spiritual and temporal threats to their authority by insisting that no book or pamphlet could be published in the realm until it had been submitted to and approved by an official "censor," who would read it and assure that it was productive and healthy rather than destructive and dangerous. Approved documents would be given a license indicated by an official stamp, known as an "imprimatur." Unapproved documents were subject to "prior restraints." Printing anything unlicensed and hence not bearing the royal imprimatur was a criminal offense.

Seditious libel cases arising under the censorship laws were heard in London in the English Court of Star Chamber, founded in 1606. Because of the harsh penalties it meted out, Star Chamber soon became identified with political and religious oppression. After growing political unrest caused the hated Star Chamber to be shut down in 1641, libel cases were transferred to the country's common law courts. Even so, the system of royal censorship continued.

One of the earliest and most eloquent pamphlets protesting against this censorship was penned by John Milton, a seventeenth-century Puritan who, in time, came to be recognized as one of the greatest poets in the history of the English language. In 1625, Milton's father, a convert from Catholicism to Puritanism, sent his son to study at Cambridge, an institution powerfully influenced by Puritan thought. During the English religious civil war, Milton wrote a number of widely read polemics against the Church of England. These pamphlets, along with his advocacy of easier access to divorce, scandalized the religious and civil authorities. In 1644, he published *Areopagitica,* his great attack on press censorship. In later writings, he argued passionately on behalf of individual freedom on the religious grounds that "all men naturally were born free, being the image . . . of God himself" (Milton 1649). On the eve of England's Puritan revolution, Milton defended republican government and attacked monarchy, even going so far as to justify the 1649 beheading of Charles I. The English commonwealth he fought for, however, was short-lived, and with the restoration of the monarchy, both he and his ideas fell into disrepute. Retiring from public life, Milton spent his time supplementing his political writings like *Areopagitica* with monumental poems like *Paradise Lost* (1667).

Despite his withdrawal from public life, Milton's views on press censorship did eventually have some effect: The English system of *royal* censorship was ended with the Glorious Revolution of 1688, which, while leaving the king on the throne, established parliamentary supremacy as a defining feature of the (unwritten) English Constitution. Royal censorship was replaced with a system of parliamentary censorship, which, despite the continuing restrictions, was at least a case of popular governance. Parliamentary censorship continued in England until 1694, when the licensing statute expired. It was not renewed.

THE REGULATION OF SPEECH UNDER ENGLISH COMMON LAW

The licensing scheme for written documents was not the only way the government regulated speech in the realm. English common law also routinely distinguished between "liberty," or speech broadly conducive to the public good, and "license," or speech that was harmful to society.

For most of English history, most of the rules governing the country were created not by a legislature passing statutes or the king issuing commands but rather by judges. The rules set down by these judges in decisions made over the course of centuries in thousands of individual cases became known as common law, so-called because the rules of these cases were uniform or "common" throughout the realm. The English regard their common law as one of their civilization's greatest achievements, an estimation shared by early settlers of North America, who brought it with them to the New World. Much of U.S. law as we know it—such as the law of contracts, of torts (noncriminal injuries), of crimes, and of property—was developed over hundreds of years by English judges as they adjudicated individual disputes in those areas.

The common law, and not just the king and Parliament, had plenty to say about what speech was permissible and what was not. Its chief prohibition was against libel. In the earlier stages of Anglo-American jurisprudence, libel was a much broader category than it is today, when it tends to apply mainly to published statements that exhibit actual malice and a disregard for the truth. In a famous 1606 Star Chamber decision known as *De libellis famosis*, the great English common law judge Sir Edward Coke wrote that it is entirely appropriate to punish criminally scurrilous assertions—libels—made against private individuals and government officials even if they are true. These assertions, he ruled, harm not only the libeled party but also the king's peace, which the king's courts are bound to protect. Some individuals, after all, will be provoked to anger by such statements and take violent action against those who made them. Attacks on government officials may not only provoke violence but may also undermine the government's authority and hence its ability to keep order. Libelous statements that are actually true are all the more dangerous because they impose greater humiliation on the injured party and bring them into greater disrepute.

Common law libels came in several varieties. Blasphemous libel inhibited freedom of religion and undercut the authority of the established church. Obscene libel lowered public morality and debased literary and artistic expression. Private libel damaged an individual's standing in the community ("Good name in man or

woman, dear my lord / Is the immediate jewel of their souls /
Who steals my purse steals trash / But he that filches from me my
good name / Robs me of what not enriches him / And makes me
poor indeed" [*Othello,* Act III, Scene III, l. 180–186]). And seditious libel condemning or mocking the government undermined
its authority.

William Blackstone's *Commentaries on the Laws of England*
(1765–1769), the first book compassing the thousands of case decisions that comprised the common law and summarizing them in
a readily readable form, concisely set out the meaning of libel in
Anglo-American jurisprudence from the eighteenth century well
into the nineteenth. Libels, Blackstone said, are

> malicious defamations of any person, and especially a magistrate,
> made public by either printing, writing, signs, or pictures, in order to
> provoke him to wrath, or expose him to public hatred, contempt, and
> ridicule. . . . The direct tendency of these libels is the breach of the
> public peace, by stirring up the objects of them to revenge, and per-
> haps to bloodshed. . . . [And] it is immaterial with respect to the of-
> fense of a libel, whether the matter of it be true or false, since the
> provocation, and not the falsity, is the thing to be punished criminally.
> (Quoted in Kurland and Lerner 1987, 119)

In civil suits for libel, rather than in criminal actions, however,
the common law in the eighteenth century held that truth could
indeed serve as a defense. Whether a libel was dangerous enough
to be prosecuted criminally, of course, was a matter for the government to decide.

The common law of libel may sound fairly restrictive today.
But in his *Commentaries,* Blackstone took evident pride in what
he considered the great liberality of the English common law. Under that law, after all, no licensing was required and no imprimatur was necessary. English common law was remarkably tolerant, Blackstone argued, because there were no "prior restraints"

on what could be said or published, though after the fact, of course, one could be prosecuted or sued for disseminating harmful statements or ideas. ("If he publishes what is improper, mischievous, or illegal, he must take the consequence of his own temerity" [Blackstone (1765–1769) 1979, 152]). Blackstone acknowledged that "[e]very freeman has an undoubted right to lay what sentiments he pleases before the public." Making one's views public, however, is very different from the right to freedom of one's private thought, for "a man . . . may be allowed to keep poisons in his closet, but not to publicly vend them as cordials." Therefore, he continues, "[t]o punish . . . any dangerous or offensive writings, which, when published, shall on a fair and impartial trial be adjudged of a pernicious tendency, is necessary for the preservation of peace and good order, of government and religion, the only solid foundation of civil liberty." Under English common law, in short, liberty was assured but "license" prohibited. In fact, punishment for license was absolutely necessary to the maintenance of liberty (Blackstone [1765–1769] 1979, 151–152).

CONTINUITY AND CHANGE IN THE COLONIES AND EARLY AMERICAN LAW

In the colonial and early national periods, American laws regulating permissible and impermissible speech were very different from the laws that exist in the United States today. The most striking difference for us, perhaps, would be the abundance of civil defamation suits by ordinary citizens seeking apologies and money damages from other ordinary citizens. Such suits were almost as common as personal injury suits (such as auto accident and "slip and fall" cases) are today. People in colonial America were very serious about their personal reputation for honor and truthfulness—and not simply out of pride or vanity. In small, isolated rural towns, a bad reputation could ruin one's life, personally and financially, so restoring one's good name was essential to one's social survival.

In many cases, a dispute could be resolved informally without a trial through go-betweens, conciliators, and mediators. Even those civil defamation cases that did go to trial seem, by modern standards, to have been resolved rather informally. The trials, for example, typically proceeded without the aid of lawyers (who were expensive and scarce). Juries usually knew the litigants very well and often had some knowledge of the facts in dispute (as in the early jury system of medieval England). Since the real stake in such defamation suits was to restore one's reputation, the damages awarded were usually small. What mattered most was to receive a public apology and to have the defendant retract the defamatory remarks. This result was in fact very common, and it was necessary for healing tears in the social fabric. In small, rural towns, news of apologies spread fast, and following a successful defamation suit, the status quo ante was more or less restored.

Several American colonies, such as Rhode Island, Pennsylvania, and Connecticut, had criminal laws against libel and slander. Concerned as ever with the tenuousness of law and order in the wilderness at the edge of the British Empire, many colonies enacted prohibitions against speech that, though neither slanderous nor libelous, was still inflammatory and therefore dangerous. There were, for example, laws that punished "any persons [who] shall be clamorous, scolding and railing with their tongues" (Rosenberg 1986, 17). The punishment for violating such laws were various, starting with warnings and fines and proceeding upward to whippings, mutilations (such as cutting the ears), and an assortment of public humiliations (like being put in the stockades or in the town square with a sign around one's neck). The requirement that the transgressor apologize and retract the offending statement was as common in criminal cases as it was in civil defamation cases. In what today would be considered an unlawful "prior restraint," colonists were frequently required to post "good behavior bonds," which they forfeited if they engaged in intemperate speech.

By the seventeenth century, common law courts in England, increasingly preoccupied with commercial matters, moved actively to discourage civil slander suits, which they increasingly regarded as a waste of time. The same progression soon began in the American colonies, where growing commerce, with its concomitant rise in litigation, led colonial jurists to seek guidance from the evolving body of defamation law in England. The scope of actionable slander was tightened, the ability of the winner to recover court costs from the loser was cut back, and criminal defamation statutes went unenforced. By the nineteenth century, such suits—except against newspapers—would become relative rarities in the United States.

During the colonial period, America was still part of England, its inhabitants were mainly of English origin, and its jurists looked to English common law for precedents to follow, including with respect to freedom of speech and the press. Some of these jurists had been at Oxford where Blackstone taught; others had been at Cambridge. Some had studied law at the Inns of Court in London, where English barristers trained. Most, however, learned the law on American soil by reading books imported from England, chiefly of Sir Edward Coke's *Institutes of the Laws of England* (1628–1644) and Blackstone's *Commentaries*. Americans readily adopted the English definition of free speech as an absence of prior restraint and the distinction between permissible liberty and impermissible license. The English law of seditious libel also became American law.

Prior to the eighteenth century, there were few newspapers in America and little of the freewheeling, nasty journalistic agitation that would characterize the nation's press in later years. Technological and economic change, however, led to the proliferation of newspapers over the course of the eighteenth century. Print shops, eager to keep their employees occupied during slack time and to earn advertising dollars, began to publish newspapers. These papers were very conscious of the common law of seditious libel, and most, as Benjamin Franklin pointed out in his "Apology for Printers" (1731), were careful not to publish anything that would bring the public authorities into contempt. To do so, after all, would be to court public criticism and legal action. These early newspapermen walked a fine line between protected liberty and unprotected license.

Partly as a result of these libel laws, relatively little political debate took place in the American colonial press in the first half of the eighteenth century. It would be a mistake, however, to assume that because spirited political debate was not evident in the press that it was absent in the American colonies. Indeed, there was plenty of political discussion, but it took place not in popular forums but rather among the elites, and within the confines of their private clubs and letters. The correspondence between these key figures was in fact so important that contemporary scholars turn to them as a principle source for understanding political thought in colonial and revolutionary America. Only in light of this fact can one understand why later on, in 1787, the founders took special care in Article 1, Section 8 of the Constitution to "establish Post Offices" and why some of the founders, such as Benjamin Rush of Pennsylvania, singled out the Post Office as an essential pillar of the new American republic.

Although free speech law in America was anchored firmly in the law of England, the unique circumstances of America eventually put the United States on a different path. As Americans began to have disputes among themselves and with the English, they began to devise arguments for free speech that went beyond those of English common law.

One famous legal innovation arose out of the 1735 trial of John Peter Zenger, a newspaper publisher in New York City. Zenger had rather harshly criticized the governor general of New York, who at the time was an important official of the English government. Zenger was brought up on charges of seditious libel. Such charges, though fairly common in England itself (especially in the late seventeenth century) had been rare in the colonies. Incensed by what seemed a terrible injustice wrought by the enforcement of the English law of seditious libels on this side of the Atlantic, Zenger's lawyer presented the English judge in New York with an innovative and provocative argument: First, he asserted, the truth of the alleged libel should be allowed as a defense (reversing the standard rule in English law), and second, the American jury rather than the English judge should decide whether Zenger was in fact guilty of sedition or malicious intent. Given that English law plainly gave authority to the judge and not the jury on these issues, the judge unsurprisingly dismissed the lawyer's argument and refused to disregard the existing law. The jury, however, defied his instructions on the requirements of English law and held for Zenger. It was an early sign that Americans were determined to shape the inherited English tradition in their own distinctly American way.

As the colonists began to quarrel with the mother country, departures from English legal precedent became more frequent. Sometimes, Americans made heroes of Englishmen who broke the laws of England, especially those who criticized the king or the Parliament. In the context of contemporaneous disputes over taxation and other matters, such tales thrilled disgruntled colonists from Massachusetts to Georgia.

A case in point was that of the English member of Parliament John Wilkes, who, in 1763, wrote an anonymous pamphlet, the *North Briton no. 45*, vehemently attacking King George III and his government. The English authorities were so infuriated by this brazen sedition that it issued a general search warrant empowering government officials to enter any house and seize any evidence that might help identify the pamphlet's author. (In large part because of the Wilkes case, the U.S. Constitution's Fourth Amendment requires a specific warrant regarding "the place to be searched, and the persons or things to be seized."). Wilkes was finally found and arrested. He was later released, though, and he sued the government for its violation of his liberties and won a huge damages award from the English judge, Lord Camden. To Americans who had their own grievances against George III, Wilkes, who was clearly guilty of seditious libel, became a hero and a symbol of freedom. Counties and cities and towns across the Atlantic were named after Camden and Wilkes: We have Camden, New Jersey; Camden, Maine; Camden Yards in Baltimore, Maryland; Wilkes-Barre, Pennsylvania; and Wilkes counties in Georgia and North Carolina, to name but a few. Some people even named their children after this doughty defender of liberty, including the parents of John Wilkes Booth, the later assassin of Abraham Lincoln.

Between 1750 and 1776, when the American colonies declared their independence, there was a dramatic decline in the enforcement of the orthodox law of seditious libel in the American colonies. This decline had less to do with liberal sentiments about free speech than with the fact that colonial officials came to realize that a stringent enforcement of the libel laws would actually backfire. Strict enforcement of seditious libel laws would only make their critics into martyrs and incite public sentiment against their rule.

At the same time, tolerating open criticism of the government did not reduce the growing intensity of colonial grievances against the mother country. Rather, such tolerance actually allowed those grievances to reach a fever pitch in the 1760s, when patriots Samuel Adams and James Otis Jr. published a series of devastating articles denouncing the governor and lieutenant governor of Massachusetts. Adams and Otis were hauled before a grand jury and accused of conspiring to overthrow British rule in America. The grand jury, however, being made up of sympathetic colonists, refused to indict. Such cases explain in part the American reverence for the jury system as an indispensable protector of the people's rights and, ultimately, of self-government and democracy: The Fifth and Sixth Amendments to the Constitution, part of the Bill of Rights, as well as Article 3, provide for broad protections for trial and indictment by juries.

As the Revolution approached, the press grew more outspoken. Elaborate paeans to the virtues of a free press were common, and theories about free speech began to change. In the pre-revolutionary era, Anglo-American theories of free speech fell into several categories. One understanding, with hoary English roots, would have punished any speech, whether true or not, that tended to bring public authority into disrepute. Another, also anchored in English law, held that one could criticize political leaders but only in moderate and respectful terms and only if the speech was patently aimed at advancing the public good.

But another view began to take hold in America by the time of the Samuel Adams and James Otis controversies, namely, that the broadest possible range of speech should be protected. Moreover, its proponents argued, such speech amounts to a safety valve for social tension and resentment, and it is better, they said, to have open speech than suppressed speech that festers until it explodes in a wave of mob violence. Political leaders can anticipate and take preventative measures, the latitudinarian argument continued, only if they understand popular passions and grievances. Such arguments did not by any means emerge fully formed and triumphant on the eve of the American Revolution. The actual laws of the colonies were a motley mix of old and new ideas. Yet on the whole, the revolutionary context, with its freewheeling ideas and opportunistic sloganeering, provided latitudinarian understandings of free speech with tremendous opportunity. The dominance of the old law of seditious libel was being undermined by new social forces.

One need no more evidence of the highly political nature of free speech arguments than to note that during the Revolution, some of the Americans who denounced British censorship were themselves involved in attacking and shutting down pro-British, loyalist printing presses. Libertarian theories notwithstanding, American patriots initiated seditious libel proceedings against loyalists who had made pro-British statements. As the Revolution progressed, after all, the patriots themselves had to worry about instability. As the revolutionaries assumed power, they too became concerned that public criticism would undermine public authority.

Founding Worries

The Constitution designed by the founders envisaged a national government of limited powers. In Article 1, "all legislative powers herein granted" were assigned to Congress as part of a system of enumerated powers. The idea was that Congress could not pass any laws on subjects other than those directly related to the powers "herein granted." Concerning freedom of speech and of the press, the Federalists, in defending the new Constitution, argued that the document changed nothing: The power to regulate speech or the press was not part of Congress's enumerated powers under Article 1. In short, under the new Constitution, speech and press were as free as ever from federal interference.

The Anti-Federalists, however, constantly worried that the aggrandizement of national power would diminish the power of the states and the liberties of the people. They did not accept Federalist assurances. Instead, they followed "Cincinnatus," an anonymous one of their number, who, in a 1787 letter to James Wilson, urged "that the freedom of the press may be *previously* secured as a *constitutional* and *unalienable right*, and not left to the precarious care of popular privileges which may or may not influence our new rulers" (Kurland and Lerner 1987, 122). In short, the Anti-Federalists worried that without a bill of rights, freedom of speech and of the press would be imperiled under the new Constitution.

One worry, expressed by an Anti-Federalist writer known as the "Federal Farmer," was that absent a bill of rights, Congress would use its enumerated power under Article 1, Section 8 to lay and collect taxes, duties, imposts, and excises in order to tax critical newspapers into submission. The power to tax, argued the Federal Farmer (setting out a formulation later used by Chief Justice John Marshall in *McCulloch v. Maryland,* 17 U.S. 316 [1819]), is the power to destroy. Precautions must be taken, he warned, because freedom of the press was "the key stone" of civil liberty (Kurland and Lerner 1987, 123).

As part of their campaign for ratification of the Constitution, the Federalists promised that in the first Congress they would draft a bill of rights to be added to the text via the Article 5 amendment process. James Madison, "Father of the Constitution" and at the time a congressman from Virginia, took on the task of drafting a bill of rights. At first, Madison was not enthusiastic about a bill of rights, and on the floor of the House of Representatives he declared, "I will own that I never considered this provision so essential to the federal constitution, as to make it improper to ratify it, until such an amendment was added; at the same time, I always conceived, that in a certain form, and to a certain extent, such a provision was neither improper nor altogether useless" (quoted in Kurland and Lerner 1987, 128). The first ten Amendments, ratified in 1791, became what we now know as the Bill of Rights. At the time, the First Amendment's guarantee of the "freedom of speech" was barely discussed.

SPEECH IN THE EARLY NATIONAL ERA

In response to new political struggles and social needs, U.S. law began to evolve, in the process generating controversies about its true meaning and purpose. Hamilton and Madison, among the most significant players in writing and ratifying the Constitution, disagreed sharply over the meaning and latitude of free speech.

Hamilton held that Blackstone's definition of the freedom of speech applied in the United States no less than in England. Madison countered with the argument that the United States was different, that given the unique nature of U.S. society and government, its law of free speech should accord speech much greater latitude than allowed under English common law.

Madison had not initially held this view. In time, though, he became one of the earliest and most cogent U.S. defenders of a latitudinarian understanding of free speech. Madison's defense of a departure from the English common law concerning free speech was shaped by his active participation in the great political events of late-eighteenth-century America—particularly the Revolution, the Founding, and the emergence of a two-party system that (with different parties, of course) has continued to the present day.

Free speech controversies often arise out of clashes between destabilizing speech and the imperatives of public order. In the popular mind, what Catherine Drinker Bowen has called "The Miracle at Philadelphia" was a glorious culmination in which the chaos and uncertainty of the preceding era was overcome and a "new order of the ages" was instituted—in large part through a timely intervention by the great and majestic George Washington, whose blessing on the proceedings dissipated the most significant dissent and discord. In this edifying tale, the Federalists, who favored ratification of the 1787 Constitution, also appear as heroic lawgivers. Their triumph over the nay-saying Anti-Federalists, with their inordinate fears of a national government, finally brings peace and stability to a new nation.

In fact, nothing could be further from the truth. Granted, the Federalists did win, through a combination of political savvy (among other things, they took the ratification decision out of the hands of the hostile state legislatures and assigned it to special state conventions and had the national government assume state war debts). But many Americans remained deeply suspicious of a new government that they saw as far removed from ordinary people and beholden to the interests of cities in general and finance capitalists in particular. They worried too about a possible reestablishment of monarchy. Such fears and anxieties were most fully articulated by Thomas Jefferson, whose own antipathy toward centralized power and urban, mercantile interests resonated with those Americans—many of whom would later be collectively identified as "Jeffersonians." Defenders of the new Constitution, still called Federalists, looked to Alexander Hamilton for leadership. Both men served in Washington's cabinet, Jefferson as secretary of state and Hamilton as secretary of treasury, and both sought to persuade Washington to adopt a particular vision of America's future: Jefferson praising a nation populated by study, self-sufficient yeomen farmers and Hamilton holding out the promise of a nation of bustling commercial cities. Over time, it became clear that Hamilton's thinking had the upper hand. Frustrated, worried, and indignant, Jefferson resigned from Washington's cabinet and returned to Virginia, where he and his old friend James Madison began the Democratic-Republican Party as a counter to Federalist policies. Thus, the two-party system was born in the United States.

From our standpoint, the establishment of a two-party system in the late-eighteenth-century United States seems a healthy step toward a balanced political order. To contemporaries, however, it looked like a recipe for chaos. As they saw it, the great men who had come together to win the war against England and build a new nation were now joining hostile and divisive "factions"—a term that at the time referred to quarrelsome and self-interested groups seeking their own advantage at the cost of the common good. For the founding generation, the spirit of faction represented the end of patriotism and unity and the beginning of selfishness and division.

Their sense of peril was aggravated by other political realities. There was great fear, for instance, that one or more European powers would take advantage of disunity in the United States by seizing territories in North America. Moreover, it was plain by the late eighteenth century that revolutions robed in noble purpose did not necessarily end nobly. The French Revolution had devolved into an unprecedented Reign of Terror. The Marquis de Lafayette, Washington's aide and a hero of the American Revolution, barely escaped the guillotine. Hundreds of others were not so lucky, and in Paris's Place de la Concorde, the guillotine unloosed a torrent of blood of the "enemies of the revolution." To make matters worse, radical activists from revolutionary France were arriving in significant numbers on American shores. Americans were split in their opinions about the French. Fear of a French-style revolution grew when U.S. farmers actively defied the authority of the new national government in the Whiskey Rebellion of the early 1790s, when farmers in western Pennsylvania repeatedly attacked federal agents trying to collect a new tax on whiskey. As antitax riots spread, Washington himself led a militia of 13,000 federal troops to put down what had by then become a general rebellion. The mood in the country was contentious, uncertain, tense.

During the early years of the American republic, charges of press bias and de facto censorship proliferated. The claim was not that the government was telling the nation's newspapers what they could publish but rather that the richest, most influential newspapers favored the Federalists and their policies centralizing government and commercializing society. The old Anti-Federalists complained that their views, particularly on economic policy, were not getting adequate coverage. In this tense and uncertain environment, the spirit of faction seemed to many to pervade the printing houses. Concealing their identities behind pseudonyms, political partisans launched vitriolic attacks on government officials, often recalling the English rhetoric of the country party versus the court party. Americans had earlier used such rhetoric to justify the Revolution. In this new battle, the old Anti-Federalists accused the Federalists of imitating the corrupt court of the English king, and presented themselves as defenders of the purer virtues of the country party.

The Federalists, whose instinct for toleration was wearing thin under sustained and sometimes personal attacks, still had recourse to the law of seditious libel. But during the colonial and revolutionary eras, so much fury had been aroused by seditious libel prosecutions of Americans by the English Crown that many Federalists were reluctant to employ it. When some did resort to prosecutions for sedition, grand juries usually refused to indict. Although the constitutions of some states—Pennsylvania and Massachusetts, for example—expressly protected free speech, it was the jury system rather than specific textual guarantees that did the most to ensure a latitudinarian approach to free speech.

Out of these bitter political battles emerged a consensus for the strong free speech provision of the First Amendment. The Anti-Federalists feared that they would be prosecuted for libel in federal courts, often staffed by Federalist judges. And even the Federalists, faithful to their revolutionary past, favored the principle of open political discussion.

Although there was agreement on the broad principle of free speech, there was little agreement as to what institutions would best preserve it. At this stage, "freedom of speech" was not widely understood as the judicially protected right that it later became. The Anti-Federalists, who, as already noted, had been the prime advocates for the Bill of Rights, were also the Americans most distrustful of the federal courts, and for that matter, of the federal Congress. They sought to lodge most of the nation's governing power in state legislatures and state courts. Moreover, it was understood at the time that one of the essential tasks of the Bill of Rights was to educate the people with regard to their rights, with the hope and expectation that they would carry that education with them into public political debate rather than into the office of their lawyer. In its early drafts, the Bill of Rights was couched in monitory rather than mandatory terms, using the word "ought" rather than "shall." Although the "oughts" were ultimately discarded as reflecting a certain weakness of commitment, the expectation remained that citizens should fight for their rights as a matter of civic responsibility and that that responsibility would be best exercised by supporting or opposing legislation, voting, serving on juries, and so forth, not by taking one's case to federal court. Defending one's rights by bringing one's case "all the way to the Supreme Court" does not, for the most part, become a heroic narrative until the middle of the twentieth century, particularly during the 1960s. The institutional implications of the Bill of Rights, as those implications were understood in the early national period, were very different from the way we understand them today.

At this same time, although commitment to the principle of free speech was strong, agreement on the scope of free speech was wanting. For instance, various theories were proposed concerning the latitude that should be given to political dissent. Blackstone, the great eighteenth-century scholar of English common law, was widely quoted for his dictum that the essence of free speech is the absence of prior restraints. Others, however, suggested that Americans would do well to refine the dictums of Blackstone. In Massachusetts, Caleb Cushing insisted that truth should always be a defense in libel prosecutions. John Adams, however, insisted that truth plus good motive should be the test. Founder and constitutional scholar James Wilson, in his famous *Lectures on Law* (1790–1791), argued that truth should be a complete defense in libel prosecutions because the purpose of libel law is to protect a virtuous man's reputation, and no one is entitled to a sound reputation that is false or undeserved.

In the end, there was no need to establish a single comprehensive theory. Both the Federalists and their opponents had an interest in leaving the matter vague and unresolved. The Federalists got their Constitution with a strong central government to guide the development of a commercial republic that later on would wield its power and wealth on the world stage. The Anti-Federalists were able in many ways to limit federal power and thus protect the rights of the people and the sovereignty of the states. Both could agree that free speech was a very good thing. And they left it at that.

But the question of the concrete scope of free speech was soon implicated in the era's uncivil and turbulent politics. The farmers of the Whiskey Rebellion, for example, signed a petition asserting that "we think it our duty to persist in our remonstrances [against the tax] to Congress, and in every other legal measure that may obstruct the operation of the Law, until we are able to obtain its total repeal" (quoted in Rosenberg 1986, 72). In response, Treasury Secretary Alexander Hamilton pressed Attorney General Edmund Randolph for an opinion on prosecuting the farmers for seditious libel. In an advisory opinion that displeased Hamilton, Randolph drew a distinction between the pure speech of the petition and action or conduct that could be regulated by law. Moreover, Randolph said, unless there is an imminent danger, there are no grounds to prosecute.

Toward the end of the Washington administration, a political opposition, which included many of the old Anti-Federalists, joined together to form the new Democratic-Republican Party. This opposition set itself to challenging both Washington and the Federalists. Washington was furious when, in 1794, a Democratic-Republican Society in Pennsylvania complained that he had failed to keep the Spanish from controlling navigation on the Mississippi River. Once again, Hamilton pushed for prosecutions for seditious libel. But the new attorney general, William Bradford, in an advisory opinion, refused to prosecute on the grounds that such action would violate the spirit of the First Amendment, that it amounted to the prosecution of words rather than punishable actions. Law aside, he argued, prosecution would be imprudent because it would elevate the Democratic-Republicans to martyr status. Allowing them to seize that mantle, he said, would be a very bad idea for the Federalists and their program.

As partisan battles continued, Washington blamed the Democratic-Republicans for the kind of rabble-rousing that resulted in the Whiskey Rebellion. The Democratic-Republicans responded with country party rhetoric about court party corruption in the Washington administration. Hamilton and others champed at the bit to prosecute their adversaries for seditious libel. Although the letter of the law at the time provided them with a good legal case, prosecution was politically impractical. It would only marshal support for the Democratic-Republicans, and juries would probably not convict. The Federalists did sponsor a congressional resolution condemning the statements of the opposition party, and Federalist newspapers printed even more ferocious attacks. When John Adams, Washington's successor—and a staunch Federalist— assumed power in 1797, the Federalists' patience with their opponents had all but run out.

To put things right, Adams, with a Federalist majority in Congress, adopted stronger methods. Congress passed the Sedition Act of 1798, reiterating the common law of seditious libel in statutory form, thereby making it a crime to criticize government officials in ways that undercut their authority or subjected them to ridicule. Despite its apparent harshness, the Sedition Act was actually more protective of free speech than was the English law of seditious libel on which it was based. Because of the legacy of the Zenger trial, the Sedition Act permitted truth to be used as a defense. Questions of law and fact were both put before juries of the people. The prosecution, moreover, had to prove criminal intent. Though clearly unconstitutional by contemporary standards, the Sedition Act was perfectly consistent with free speech jurisprudence as it was defined in that era. In its adherence to the precedent of the Zenger decision (1735), the Sedition Act was actually very tolerant in its forms. Indeed, in the Fox Libel Act of 1792, the English had added similar requirements to their common law of seditious libel, an act that in its time was generally considered a major step forward for English civil liberty.

The common law of seditious libel had been slowly developed by common law judges deciding hundreds of concrete disputes over the centuries, and it could thus appear to be a matter of basic law rather than politics. The Sedition Act, by contrast, was passed as part of bitter partisan struggle aimed at silencing particular people, and it inspired fierce anger and resistance. The Democratic-Republicans immediately raised constitutional objections to the act. The powers of Congress, they argued, were limited to those enumerated in Article 1 of the Constitution, and therefore Congress had absolutely no authority to pass legislation regulating speech—a point reinforced by the Tenth Amendment's stipulation that "powers not delegated to the United States by the Constitution, nor prohibited by it to the States, are reserved to the States respectively, or to the people." Only the states, they said, had the authority to regulate speech or pass laws involving seditious libels. In any event, they insisted that the Sedition Act violated the First Amendment's provision that "Congress shall make no law . . . abridging the freedom of speech."

Spurred on by the Sedition Act, Jefferson and Madison drafted the Kentucky and Virginia Resolutions, respectively, in protest against the improper assertion of federal authority in cases involving basic freedoms, including the freedom of speech. At this time in U.S. history, it was not at all clear that, as John Marshall would later claim in *Marbury v. Madison* (5 U.S. 137 [1803]), federal courts had the authority to exercise judicial review, that is, to invalidate laws it held to be unconstitutional. The Virginia and Kentucky Resolutions declared that *the states* had a right to nullify unconstitutional acts of the national government, like the Sedition Act. The Constitution, they argued, amounted to a compact among the states by which specified and limited powers were delegated to the national government. It was up to the states, as contracting parties, to decide whether the federal government had exceeded those powers and if it had, to disregard the law.

The argument of these resolutions was straightforward and forceful, echoing the early Anti-Federalist worries about the absence of a Bill of Rights. (The irony was that the presence of a Bill of Rights had not prevented the passage of the acts.) They argued that federal powers were limited to those specifically enumerated in the Constitution, and this understanding was reinforced by the Tenth Amendment. Moreover, they argued that a law of this type "was expressly and positively forbidden" by the free speech clause of the First Amendment. As such, Madison argued, the transgression "more than any other ought to produce universal alarm, because it is leveled against the right of freely examining public characters and measures, and of free communication among the people thereon, which has ever been justly deemed the guardian of every other right." Thus the Kentucky Resolution declared the Sedition Act "altogether void, and of no force" (Kurland and Lerner 1987, 131–132, 136).

Despite this barrage of constitutional objections, prosecutions under the Sedition Act began apace, with Federalist judges presiding over most of the cases. (Washington and Adams, the only U.S. presidents up to that time, were Federalists and so, not surprisingly, appointed members of their own party as judges). These judges ruled objections to the act out of order. Vermont congressman Matthew Lyon was prosecuted before a Federalist judge for making disparaging remarks about the regal bearing of President Adams. The court had no trouble convicting Lyon of violating the new act and sentenced him to four months in prison and a $1,000 fine, an enormous sum of money at the time. James Thompson Callender, a notoriously low-minded Jeffersonian journalist (he later turned on Jefferson and printed the first published allegations that Jefferson had fathered a child with his slave Sally Hemmings), was also prosecuted in a trial presided over by Supreme Court Justice Samuel Chase. Chase refused to allow Callender's lawyers to argue before the jury that the Sedition Act was unconstitutional. Indeed, he revealed such bias and animus against the

Jeffersonian journalist and his allies that he was later impeached for his behavior and statements, the first such impeachment in U.S. history.

Outrage over the Sedition Act spurred new arguments concerning the meaning of free speech. Americans who had read their Blackstone knew that freedom of speech and the press consisted of the absence of prior restraints, Madison argued. But isn't the same intimidation accomplished, he asked, by punishing someone after they had spoken?

Madison said nothing new or exceptional regarding the practical consequences of prior restraints. But his broader theoretical argument was innovative and deep. In that argument, Madison observed that England and America recognized entirely different loci of sovereignty. In England, the Parliament was sovereign, and most of the fundamental rights that had been carved out over the long course of English history—particularly the English Bill of Rights—were asserted by Parliament against the king. Thus, in England, new rights tended to reduce the Crown's prerogatives and empower Parliament. By contrast, in the United States (as the Constitution's preamble declared) the people were sovereign. Here too the executive could violate the people's rights—but so could the legislature. "Encroachments are regarded as possible from the one as well as from the other," Madison argued; and for this reason, he further argued, the common law "cannot . . . be the standard of . . . freedom in the United States" (Kurland and Lerner 1987, 142).

Moreover, Madison said, a popular government that is elected, limited, and responsible to the people "may well be supposed to require a greater freedom of animadversion than might be tolerated by the genius of such a government as that of Great Britain." If the government is doing things that bring it into disrepute, it is entirely proper that the people should vigorously criticize it. In the United States, for instance, "it is the duty, as well as right, of intelligent and faithful citizens" to observe, assess, and criticize the actions of their government. In a system of representative government, the people must understand "the comparative merits and demerits of the candidates for public trust." The widest latitude for criticism and debate, therefore, must be protected. In a free representative government founded on the principle of popular sovereignty, Madison concluded, free discussion of public issues is the "only effectual guardian of every other right" (Kurland and Lerner 1987, 142, 144, 145, 146).

Not only was political theory on his side, but so too were cultural and political practice. To be sure, he said, Americans have adopted much of the English law of libel as expounded in Blackstone's *Commentaries*. But in the United States, no matter what the law seems to say, individuals and the press habitually speak their minds well beyond the bounds set by a strict reading of the law. And public opinion, he observed, supports this wide latitude to speak and to criticize the government. Of course, in the throes of roiling debate, people often exceed bounds of propriety and decency. But "[s]ome degree of abuse is inseparable from the proper use of everything" (Kurland and Lerner 1987, 143). Given these considerations, why should Americans be bound to hew to the legal definitions extant in England at the time of the nation's separation from the mother country? Moreover, asserting his own authority as the actual drafter of both the Constitution and the Bill of Rights, Madison argued that when each was written it was not intended that the meaning of free speech in the United States be limited by precedents in England.

Did this mean that the federal government was "destitute of every authority for restraining the licentiousness of the press, and from shielding itself against the libelous attacks which may be made on those who administer it?" Yes, said Madison, answering his own question, "the federal Government is destitute of all such authority" (Kurland and Lerner 1987, 144).

Not only did anger over the 1798 Sedition Act prompt Madison and others to redefine the scope of the freedom of speech in the

United States, but it also became a central issue in the presidential
election campaign of 1800. Since the time of the act's passage, the
danger posed by the French had largely subsided. And the zealous, politically biased prosecutions before Federalist judges also
helped turn public opinion against the Federalist Party. The 1800
campaign pitted Federalist incumbent John Adams, who had
pushed for the passage of the act, against Thomas Jefferson, the
Democratic-Republican whose supporters were the act's chief targets. Jefferson was able to position himself as the defender of basic liberties, and he won the contest (his party took over Congress
as well) largely as a reaction to the perceived unfairness of the
Sedition Act and the attendant criminal prosecutions under it. For
the first time in the country's history, power passed from one political party to another. By the time Jefferson was elected, the Sedition Act had expired, but several prominent individuals who had
been convicted under it while it was in force were still in jail. One
of Jefferson's first official acts as president was to pardon all those
prosecuted under the act, and in his inaugural address, he offered
a paean to toleration and a free press. He called for reflection on
the fact that "having banished from our land that religious intolerance under which mankind so long bled and suffered, we have
yet gained little if we countenance a political intolerance as
despotic, as wicked, and capable of as bitter and bloody persecutions." To this he added a plea for unity: "We are all Republicans,
we are all Federalists." One of the greatest battles over free speech
in U.S. history had come to a close, and the constitutional remedy
had not been a Supreme Court decision but a decisive national
election (U.S. Government Printing 1969, 14).

"FIGHTING WORDS": THE DUEL IN THE EARLY UNITED STATES

An important but often overlooked scheme for governing what
could and could not be said in the early United States was the in-

stitution of the duel, prevalent in the colonial period and remaining strong in the South well into the nineteenth century. Duels involved one man challenging another to a ritualized fight, usually with pistols, in response to an affront. They were fought in response to a wide variety of offenses, from trespassing to disagreements during card games. Many, perhaps most, duels were fought following verbal insults. To avoid the possibility of a duel, a man had to take care not to say something publicly to offend another man's honor or dignity. Sometimes, however, men spoiling for a fight would deliberately provoke a duel through the practice of "posting," or placing a notice in a newspaper or a public place such as a tavern calling his opponent a villain or a coward. Typical in the early nineteenth century was the posting by a man spoiling for a duel against a member of Congress: "I denounce to the world John Randolph, a member of Congress, as a prevaricating, base, calumnating, scoundrel, poltroon and coward" (quoted in Baldick 1965, 118).

Alexander Hamilton, one of the nation's most important founders, was actually killed in a duel. In a private letter that was later published, Hamilton had called Aaron Burr a dangerous man who could not be trusted to run the government. Hamilton had denied Burr the presidency by throwing his support to Hamilton's bitter enemy, Thomas Jefferson, whom Hamilton considered the lesser of the two evils. Burr, infuriated, called upon Hamilton to admit or deny that and other similar remarks. Hamilton acknowledged that he probably did say these things, but that he could not recall every statement he had made over the past fifteen years, particularly those made in the heat of political debate. Burr was not satisfied with this response and demanded a duel, which Hamilton, mindful of his honor and reputation, reluctantly accepted. (Hamilton's son had been killed in a duel, and he morally disapproved of the institution.) On July 11, 1804, in Weehawken, New Jersey, Burr shot and killed Hamilton, simultaneously ending both Hamilton's life and his own political career. The seemingly pointless loss inspired a national revulsion against dueling and ultimately led to its being outlawed in the northern United States.

Old institutions were slower to die in the South, however. A mere two years after Hamilton's death in Weehawken, Andrew Jackson, the future president of the United States, challenged Charles Dickinson to a duel for having slandered his beloved wife. (Jackson, though wounded, ended up killing his opponent.) When Jackson's wife died soon after he was elected president in 1828, he had her described on her tombstone as "[a] being so gentle and yet so virtuous, vile slander might wound but could not dishonor" (quoted in Baldick 1965, 123). Duels continued in the South, reaching a peak in the 1830s and 1840s. By the late 1860s, after the defeat of the Confederacy, antidueling legislation was more strictly enforced throughout the country, and the practice finally died out. Recourse to slanders and other insults assumed more modern forms.

THE MAIN CURRENTS OF THE LAW OF SPEECH IN THE NINETEENTH-CENTURY UNITED STATES

One of the main challenges facing nineteenth-century Americans—and in particular, the country's cultural and political elites—was to invent an artistic, literary, and political tradition that was distinctive and original rather than derivative of European ways. Although many U.S. legal scholars still looked back admiringly to the achievements of English common law, others self-consciously endeavored to supersede Blackstone, the common law's great master and codifier (though they gladly stood on the shoulders of the giant). Thus, the nineteenth century became the great age of legal treatise writing in the United States, with an outpouring of multivolume works that would shape U.S. law no less than Blackstone had shaped the law of England. The leaders of this flowering of American legal thought included such figures as Chancellor James Kent of New York, Joseph Story of Massachusetts, and Thomas Cooley of Michigan.

Kent's *Commentaries on American Law* (1826–1830) was one of the most influential expositions of law in the United States in the first half of the nineteenth century. It served both as a standard reference for practicing lawyers and a text for students of U.S. government. Kent wrote his great treatise after having first served with distinction as a New York judge. Not surprisingly, considering that Kent's appointment was made by Governor John Jay, a former chief justice of the United States and coauthor of *The Federalist Papers,* Kent advanced a Hamiltonian understanding of free speech. Kent, an old Federalist, idolized Alexander Hamilton and, in equal measure, detested Hamilton's political and personal nemesis, Thomas Jefferson. In Kent's view, speech and press were protected only to the extent that they advanced some legitimate public purpose and had no malicious motives. Libel, he contended, had at its heart a malicious motive, and the law should presume false defamatory statements to have malicious intent. True statements, on the other hand, were permissible and immune from prosecution if made with "good motives" and for "justifiable ends." Not surprisingly, this rather vague standard gave enormous discretion to judges in determining the outcome of particular libel suits or prosecutions.

Kent's status as an authority on the law was closely rivaled by that of Joseph Story, Dane Professor of Law at Harvard and, simultaneously, an associate justice of the U.S. Supreme Court (1811–1845). Though in many ways a conservative with close ties to Chief Justice John Marshall, a staunch Federalist, Story was actually appointed to the High Court by James Madison, a Democratic-Republican ally of Thomas Jefferson. Story's *Commentaries on the Constitution of the United States* appeared in 1833, three years after the publication of the final volume of Kent's *Commentaries.* Story's treatise is perhaps best known for helping anchor free speech in the U.S. constitutional order and for its traditional Blackstonian distinction between liberty and license. Story insisted that the First Amendment was never "intended to secure to every citizen an absolute right to speak, or write, or print, whatever he might please, without any responsibility, public or private." Such an interpretation, he declared, was "too wild to be indulged by any rational man" (Kurland and Lerner 1987, 182).

> This would be to allow to every citizen a right to destroy at his pleasure the reputation, the peace, the property, and even the personal safety of every other citizen. A man might out of mere malice and revenge accuse another of the most infamous crimes; might excite against him the indignation of all his fellow citizens by the most atrocious calumnies; might disturb, nay overturn all his domestic peace, and embitter his parental affections; might afflict the most distressing punishments upon the weak, the timid, and the innocent; might prejudice all a man's civil, and political, and private rights; and might stir up sedition, rebellion, and treason even against the government itself, in the wantonness of his passions, or the corruption of his heart. Civil society could not go on under such circumstances. Men would then be obliged to resort to private vengeance, to make up for the deficiencies of the law; and assassinations and savage cruelties would be perpetrated with all the frequency belonging to barbarous and brutal communities. (Story [1833], repinted in Kurland and Lerner 1987, 182)

Moreover, Story concluded, echoing Blackstone:

> It is plain that the language of this amendment imports no more than that every man shall have a right to speak, write, and print his opinions upon any subject whatsoever, without any prior restraint, so always, that he does not injure any other person in his rights, person, property, or reputation; and so always, that he does not thereby disturb the public peace, or attempt to subvert the government. . . . [E]very man shall be at liberty to publish what is true, with good motives and for

justifiable ends. (Story [1833], reprinted in Kurland and Lerner 1987, 182)

In sum, Story favored not a regime of censorship, which would subject utterances to the arbitrary authority of a single man, a state censor, but a freedom overseen by public jury trials. People retained the right to express whatever sentiments they wished in private. Once public damage was done, however, the matter then became a public issue.

ROBUST PARTIES, ANTISLAVERY AGITATION, AND SPEECH IN THE UNITED STATES

No sooner had the ink dried on the great treatises of Kent and Story than did social pressures begin to undermine the authority of the legal standards concerning free speech that they had so confidently set out. The Jacksonian era, which began in the late 1820s, ushered in the age of mass democratic politics. This era was marked by the rise of universal male suffrage and by intense, sometimes fierce, partisan rhetoric, purveyed in significant part through the pamphlets and newspapers of the new "penny press." Wild charges and countercharges moved to the center of the country's political life, as politics itself moved to the center of national culture. The targets of politically motivated charges continued to file libel suits under the old standard. But in this new partisan context, prosecutions and suits sought less to protect one's good name than to punish one's political opponents. Parties would align themselves with plaintiffs or defendants, and the losers would become martyrs to free speech and testaments to the other party's wickedness. Juries sometimes refused to convict their political favorites, or they awarded only nominal damages if they did convict. These experiences led those who thought systematically about the freedom of speech to rethink the old approaches. Although the treatise writers of a few years before had argued that a firm line had to be drawn between liberty and license in the interest of social stability, new theorists, such as Frederick Grimke and William Seward, made the case that intense partisan debate could actually serve as a stabilizing force in the polity. Free speech theory, in short, began to adjust its presuppositions to what seemed to be the lessons of Jacksonian political experience.

But at the very moment that the nation was becoming accustomed to the age of mass politics, accepting raucous, partisan politicking as a healthy and stabilizing force, the emerging debate over slavery was undermining that view. Beginning in the 1830s, opposition to the South's "peculiar institution" ceased to be a marginal political force. Antislavery organizations began to achieve a critical mass, blossoming into a full-fledged social movement. Abolitionism began to pose a real threat to the political and cultural institutions of the South. As noted earlier, broad toleration for free speech has always presupposed a faith in the ultimate stability of the government and the sustainability of the public order. Abolitionist speech and political agitation, however, suddenly threatened that very stability and order. Not surprisingly, efforts to stifle abolitionist speech began to take root in the antebellum United States.

Perhaps the chief and most immediate fear in the South was that of a violent mass uprising of slaves against their masters. Such an uprising had happened in Haiti in 1814, and in 1822, a similar plot was hatched by the former South Carolina slave Denmark Vesey. Vesey's plans were discovered, however, and he was tried and hanged. The worldwide trend seemed to be running against slavery. In the 1820s and 1830s, a wave of South American and Central American countries had abolished the institution. In 1833, Great Britain abolished slavery in the West Indies, not far from the southern shores of the United States, and this action emboldened U.S. abolitionists, who became even more fervent in expressing their views. In 1829, David Walker, a free black man living in Boston, composed an antislavery pamphlet urging slaves to rebel against their masters and sent the pamphlet off for distribution in the South. The state of Georgia responded by passing a law imposing the death penalty on anyone who circulated pamphlets that caused trouble with or among the slaves. In 1831, William Lloyd Garrison launched his famous abolitionist newspaper, the *Liberator.* And two years later, the Nat Turner slave revolt took place in the tidewater region of Virginia. Sixty white Virginians died in the revolt before the uprising was ultimately suppressed by force. Politicians in Virginia and throughout the South were convinced that abolitionist writings and speeches were stoking the flames of insurrection and destabilizing the entire political, social, and economic structure of the southern states. The suppression of this inflammatory speech was taken to be a political imperative. Other states followed Georgia's lead and declared it a criminal offense to disseminate antislavery views within their borders.

Far from being intimidated by these actions, antislavery agitation in the North grew stronger and stronger throughout the 1830s. In 1835, for instance, northern abolitionists undertook a mass mailing of abolitionist literature to the southern states. Huge antislavery meetings and rallies were often met with violent resistance, and they were denounced as the work of dangerous radicals who would divide the Democratic Party, and, ultimately, the Union itself. Despite the demands of southern leaders, the northern states never passed laws restricting the speech of abolitionists, though they gave such measures serious consideration. Some limitations on abolitionist speech in the North were imposed by extralegal means: by violence and threat of violence and by a widespread refusal to let public spaces and churches be used for abolitionist meetings.

Both Congress and the executive branch, however, took action to clamp down on abolitionist speech. In an effort to take the divisive issue of slavery off the table, the U.S. House of Representatives in 1836 passed the infamous "gag rule," which ensured that the flood of antislavery petitions flowing into Congress would never be considered. Abolitionist petitioners regarded the gag rule as a clear violation of the First Amendment right to "petition the Government for a redress of grievances." To make matters worse, President Jackson's postmaster general, Amos Kendall, permitted southern post offices to read all mail passing through their region and to seize whatever antislavery literature they might find. Jackson himself was a slaveholder from Tennessee, but his decision to countenance the censoring of the U.S. mails went beyond the chief executive's proslavery preferences. The southern states had declared such material criminal, and thus, by distributing the abolitionist literature, U.S. postmasters in the South were both committing and abetting criminal acts.

In most cases outside the South, restrictions on free speech were the result not of governmental action but of extralegal, often violent disturbances caused by citizen groups. During the 1830s, over one hundred abolitionist meetings in the North were broken up by violent or menacing proslavery mobs. Presses that printed antislavery literature were destroyed, and in 1837, in the infamous case of Illinois abolitionist Elijah Lovejoy, the mob not only destroyed his press but took his life. In Philadelphia, a bastion of Quaker antislavery sentiment, abolitionists had built a headquarters known as Pennsylvania Hall. In 1838, the hall was burned to the ground by a proslavery mob. A portrait of George Washington was the only thing rescued from the flames.

An even more significant instance of antiabolitionist violence occurred not in the midst of a riot but rather on the floor of the U.S. Senate: In May 1856, U.S. Senator Charles Sumner of Massachusetts, a staunch abolitionist, was savagely beaten with a cane by U.S. Representative Preston Brooks of South Carolina.

The attack came shortly after Sumner had delivered an oration on the evils both of slavery and of its defenders. Sumner's speech was a response to violence between proslavery and antislavery settlers in the Kansas Territory. At stake was whether Kansas would enter the Union as a free or a slave state. The final decision, everyone understood, would have consequences far beyond the Kansas Territory itself, for the admission of each new state as slave or free threatened to tip the political balance of power between North and South in the U.S. Senate. Kansas was being settled simultaneously by proslavery southerners and free-soil northerners, many of whom were encouraged, and in some cases, funded, by Amos Lawrence's Massachusetts Emigrant Aid Society. The northerners referred to the southern settlers as "Pukes," and the southerners reviled the northerners as "Invaders." Although most settlers came to Kansas for reasons that had little to do with slavery (they wanted cheap land, open spaces, and farms), animosities snowballed as the proslavery and antislavery camps used Kansas as a staging area for their larger national struggle. As statehood loomed, proslavery Kansans set up their own territorial government and boasted they would bring Kansas into the Union as a slave state. Kansas's proslavery government passed draconian laws to stifle abolitionist speech, making it a felony to express antislavery sentiments and indicting abolitionist newspapers on criminal charges. Violent mobs, unrestrained by the government, attacked these newspapers' printing presses, wrenched them from newspaper buildings, and threw them in the Platte River. Abolitionist legislators were expelled from the territorial government. A rival free-soil government was set up in opposition.

For Senator Charles Sumner, and for many others, "Bleeding Kansas" was a national outrage. Sumner condemned the proslavery Kansans on the floor of the Senate in the harshest terms possible, most famously in a speech entitled "The Crime against Kansas." Sumner was not much of a legislator. But he knew how to deliver shockingly vitriolic speeches that enraged his enemies. "The Crime against Kansas" was not just an attack upon slavery. It was a personal attack upon those members of Congress who defended slavery, including Illinois's Stephen A. Douglas and South Carolina's Andrew Pickens Butler. The attack on the aged Butler was particularly nasty: Sumner characterized Butler as a babbling and drooling old fool and compared Butler's relationship with the institution of slavery to the sort of relationship a man would have with a particularly hideous whore, "who, though ugly to others, is always lovely to him; though polluted in the sight of the world, is chaste in his sight" (quoted in Donald 1960, 285).

The history of free speech shows that the very concept itself developed out of the perceived need to give legislators (rather than private individuals) the liberty to say whatever they wished as part of legislative debates. And Sumner had his say. But the attack on Butler seemed to many to be simply beyond the pale. After the speech, Sumner was ominously warned to watch his back. And the warning proved prescient. On the following day, Sumner, sitting alone at his Senate desk writing, was set upon from behind with a cane by South Carolina's Representative Brooks. (Brooks was a relation of Senator Butler's, and he was outraged by Sumner's attack not only on his kinsman but also upon southern honor. He declared the speech to be a libel on both Butler and on his home state.) Sumner was beaten so brutally that the cane—a thick and sturdy one—was splintered to pieces, and Sumner was reduced to bloody unconsciousness. He was so injured and traumatized by the event that it would be several years before he would recover his health and return to his place in the Senate chamber. The southern code of honor required that the honor of an insulted man be vindicated via retaliation rather than a lawsuit (to which Sumner would probably have been immune under the Constitution's speech and debate clause). Though ultimately fined for assault, Brooks's colleagues refused to expel him from the House. He became a hero in the South. And Sumner became an abolitionist martyr in the North. In political speeches, moreover, the beating of Sumner was cited as an example of how the institution of chattel slavery not only binds the slave but also eats away at the liberties of all Americans, including the freedom of speech. Sumner became a symbol of the relationship between free speech and free government.

It was not at all clear that the enactment of criminal laws against abolitionist speech in the South, the antiabolitionist mob violence in the North, the gag rule and censorship of the mails, and the beating of Charles Sumner on the floor of the Senate ultimately hurt the abolitionist cause. For abolitionists, not surprisingly, free speech became a rallying cry that had an electrifying effect. The suppression of abolitionist speech seemed to vindicate one of the central claims that the abolitionists had made all along about slavery: that as an institution, it was an assault not just on the liberty of the enslaved but rather on that of all Americans. Slavery was a base and corrosive institution, and one could never say where its evil influence would stop. The suppression of abolitionist speech actually played a major part in helping spread abolitionist ideas and led many waiverers and moderates to reconsider their assessment of the abolitionists as hopeless quixotics and fanatics.

Besides strengthening the abolitionist cause, the suppression of abolitionist speech also proved to have strong constitutional implications that have persisted to the present day. The suppression of abolitionist speech on the eve of the Civil War launched the beginning of a wholesale reassessment of the long-standing assumption that the protection of fundamental "privileges and immunities," such as the freedom of speech, were state rather than federal matters. Beginning in the 1830s, such rights increasingly came to be seen as inherently national, as belonging to citizens everywhere in the United States.

The suppression of antislavery sentiments continued right up until the outbreak of war. *The Impending Crisis,* by southerner Hinton Helper, called for abolitionist action by nonslaveholding southerners. The book was published just before the radical abolitionist John Brown staged his 1859 raid on the arsenal at Harpers Ferry, Virginia, where he hoped to seize arms for his war on slavery and in the process (as the profoundly religious Brown described it in a final letter before going to the gallows), to purge this land with blood. Helper's book had been praised by members of the newly launched Republican Party, and following the raid at Harpers Ferry, the Democrats charged both the party and Helper with inciting abolitionist violence and insurrection in the South. Not surprisingly, such condemnations created enormous public interest in *The Impending Crisis*, catapulting it to the status of a national best-seller.

FREEDOM AND CIVIL WAR

One of the great paradoxes of civil liberty, as we have seen, is that it requires a state strong enough to preserve it. Thus, when the power of that state is threatened, civil liberties must often be temporarily abridged to preserve the means of their long-term protection. Of course, when freedom is curtailed in a moment of crisis, it is often denounced as a hypocritical power grab on the part of a government that purports to be a defender of freedom. But the underlying truth—that liberty depends upon a bedrock of limitations—is a real one. The apparent paradox runs deep in the science and theory of free government premised upon the rule of law.

This problem surfaced in U.S. politics during the Civil War. Abolitionists argued that slavery menaced not only the freedom of the slaves but also the freedom of all. Not long after the war began, it evolved from a struggle for national integrity into a crusade for the permanent eradication of chattel slavery in the United States. But to end slavery and to vindicate liberty, it was essential that the Union win the war. And to ensure the North's ultimate victory, political leaders and others insisted that certain freedoms needed to be temporarily abridged. The right to criticize the government, for example, one of the most basic rights, was in some cases regarded as a species of treason. "The safety of the nation," the *New York Times* editorialized during the Civil War, "is the Supreme Law."

This was true on both sides of the Mason-Dixon line. In the Confederate states, unionists were arrested for stating their views, and in extreme cases, they were driven from their homes or executed. While Lincoln was president, thousands of northerners who wrote editorials or criticized the president, the Republican Party, or the war effort were tried (often in military rather than civilian courts) and sent to jail. Others were released only after they agreed to sign an oath of loyalty to the American Union. The right to freedom of speech may have originated in England as a protection for legislators, but in the United States during the Civil War, even these public figures were far from safe. In 1861, a group of Maryland legislators suspected of harboring Confederate sympathies were summarily arrested and thrown in jail out of fear that if they were permitted to speak their minds, they would help corral the state into passing articles of secession. Prior to the Civil War, as we have seen, President Andrew Jackson had ordered his postmaster general to find and destroy antislavery literature in mail headed for the South. Similarly, Lincoln ordered his own postmaster general, Montgomery Blair, to weed out of the mails several northern newspapers whose editorials were sympathetic to the southern cause. One such paper was banned by the government until its owners agreed to sell it to a pro-Union publisher. When another paper tried to evade Post Office censorship by using a private messenger service, the government deployed armed marshals to seize the shipments. Overwhelmingly, U.S. courts tolerated such infringements on free speech, though in fact the courts did not often hear such cases, since protests about the new restrictions were exceedingly rare.

This is not to say that the United States was a proto-totalitarian state during the war. Repression hardly set the tone in most of the country. Although there were prosecutions, there was also a great deal of free speech and spirited debate. Democratic Party newspapers continued to churn out savage criticism of the Republican Party and the Lincoln administration. Even during wartime, the American people were simply too independent, too widely dispersed, and too accustomed to democratic freedoms to refrain from speaking out.

POST–CIVIL WAR DOCTRINE:
THOMAS COOLEY'S TREATISE AND FREE SPEECH

In many ways, the United States after the Civil War was another country. During the war, the national government had assumed an unprecedented degree of centralized power. The Civil War amendments, which charged the national government with protecting the rights of all persons in the United States, had further augmented this power. The economy too was undergoing revolutionary changes, as mass industrialization and railroads strengthened the power of a new capitalist order.

What people thought their freedom of speech entailed also seems to have changed at the same time. Libel suits had long been a defining feature of pre–Civil War jurisprudence. But as historian Norman Rosenberg reports, between 1865 and 1876, fewer than twenty libel suits were filed in the entire country (Rosenberg 1986, 156). In the wake of the war, routine suits by individuals anxious about their reputations had by and large become a thing of the past.

Part of the new thinking in the postwar era involved a vigorous theoretical defense of free speech rights by a group of writers described by a present-day political scientist as "conservative libertarians" (Graber 1991, 17). The conservative libertarians were unlike such twentieth-century defenders of civil liberties as Professor Zechariah Chafee of Harvard and Supreme Court Justice Louis Brandeis: These men could be categorized as "liberals" because, broadly speaking, they favored civil liberties *and* an increasingly interventionist government. Conservative libertarians, on the other hand, believed in limited government across the board. Journalists like E. L. Godkin of the *Nation*, historians like Henry Adams, social scientists like Herbert Spencer and William Graham Sumner, legal scholars like Thomas Cooley and Christopher Tiedeman, and Supreme Court justices like David Brewer and the first John Marshall Harlan believed that government should stay out of most things, whether economic affairs (for example, private property and the contractual relationship between employers and employees) or the regulation of what people could say or write. Nineteenth-century conservative libertarian thinkers did not distinguish, as most constitutional thinkers do today, between "economic rights" and "personal rights." They saw the two types of rights as complementary and inseparable. Harking back to the views of the Jeffersonians and Jacksonians, the conservative libertarians argued that economic independence is a precondition to intellectual independence. Only if a person could accumulate property freely would he acquire the independence to say what he thought without fear. And only if he had acquired a modicum of private wealth would he have the leisure to turn his mind from the pressing tasks of brute survival and cultivate his intellectual and spiritual side with no worries about pecuniary reward.

The conservative libertarian tradition was much in evidence in the constitutional thought of the nineteenth century, particularly its argument for limitations on the regulatory power of government, whether federal or state. In the case of *Ex Parte Jackson* (96 U.S. 727 [1877]), for example, Justice Stephen Field wrote a unanimous opinion for the U.S. Supreme Court, which held that although Article 1 of the Constitution may give Congress the power to regulate the mails, it does not give Congress the power to regulate the distribution of printed materials outside the U.S. mails. Two years earlier, in *United States v. Cruikshank* (92 U.S. 542 [1875]), the Court had declared that the newly passed Fourteenth Amendment imposes limits on the power of states to frustrate gatherings of people to discuss public affairs and, ultimately, to petition the government for redress of grievances. After all, they argued, the Fourteenth Amendment provides that "[n]o State shall . . . deprive any person of life, liberty, or property, without due process of law." The liberty protected under that amendment's due process clause, in the conservative libertarian view, included both basic property rights and the right to the freedom of speech.

The conservative libertarian understanding of the value of free speech was spread through the era's most prominent legal treatises, which were commonly read and referred to by lawyers, judges, and scholars. Thomas Cooley's 1868 work *A Treatise on the Constitutional Limitations Which Rest upon the Legislative Power of the States of the American Union* was perhaps the most influential of all. Cooley was one of the most highly regarded scholars and public officials of his age. Between 1859 and 1884, he taught at the University of Michigan Law School, simultaneously serving part of that time (1864–1885) as a justice on the Michigan Supreme Court. Cooley also served as the first head of the nation's Interstate Commerce Commission.

In his masterwork, *A Treatise on the Constitutional Limitations,* Cooley describes an approach to free speech that mirrored his defense of economic competition in a free market. For Cooley, the clash of ideas in the public arena was a prerequisite to political wisdom and progress. Just as the law of tort or personal injury had evolved to accommodate the rise of modern industries such as railroads, so, Cooley argued, the law of libel had to change to accommodate the ascendancy of discourse and debate in the forum of the new mass media. What Cooley advocated was an approach based on a "conditional privilege," which placed a heavy burden on libel plaintiffs if they were either public officials or candidates for public office or if the topic under discussion was one of public importance. In this regard, *A Treatise on the Constitutional Limitations* gave a libertarian cast to his exposition of the meaning of free speech by rejecting the Blackstonian common law argument that the constitutional guarantee of freedom of speech was, in its essence, limited to a prohibition on prior restraints.

It is worth noting that people who thought of themselves as "progressive" during this era did not line up neatly on the side of "free speech." Nor did "conservatives" line up as its opponents. For many scholars, jurists like Cooley are considered "conservative" because their staunch defense of free speech is combined with their defense of free-market economics (a combination that today would be called "libertarianism"). Some progressives—particularly muckraking journalists—were strong defenders of free speech and a free press because these rights enabled them to reveal unjust social conditions and government corruption. Other progressives, however, had worries about a free press in the late nineteenth century. Take Louis Brandeis, for instance, a jurist regarded as one of the great champions of free speech and press. In a famous 1890 law review article entitled "The Right to Privacy," Brandeis and his law partner, Samuel Warren, advocated a new type of private right. People could invoke this right to sue newspapers that printed stories about them involving matters that were ostensibly private but that were also of interest to the public at large. (Society weddings and the doings of the rich and famous were the classic ventures in the nation's "new" newspapers.) In this, Brandeis was clearly asking that judges confine rather than extend the permissible latitude of free speech.

By contrast, Thomas Cooley was one of the nation's most prominent champions of free speech in the late nineteenth century. Aside from his widely read treatise, Cooley as a judge hearing press libel cases set out his views on a conditional privilege for public figures and on matters of public interest. He even made a case for allowing some measure of press error and exaggeration as a necessary cost of a vigorous and open system of free press and free speech. Cooley's position on private libel actions was highly protective of speech. In it, he held that whereas in libel actions involving private figures, defendants bore the burden of proving the truthfulness of their statements, when public issues and officials were involved, a special privilege should be available because such speech was essential to democratic politics and policymaking (*Atkinson v. Detroit Free Press*, 46 Mich. 341 [1881]).

THE ECLIPSE OF PRIVACY AND
RISE OF OBSCENITY

And yet Brandeis's worries about the coarsening and vulgarizing of public discussion continued to nag. One of the most distinctive new developments in U.S. culture in the second half of the nineteenth century was the pervasive sense that what were once private matters were being discussed in public and given wide and scandalous exposure. The modern media—with all its voyeurism and sensationalism—was really born in the late nineteenth century as the result of the rise of inexpensive, mass-circulation newspapers and of the emergence of a political and journalistic culture in which the revelation of public scandal was seen as a necessary precondition to justice and emancipation. The novelty of the late nineteenth century lay in the new antagonism between what historian Rochelle Gurstein calls "the party of reticence," which was under siege from what she dubs "the party of exposure" (Gurstein 1996, 52, 62). At that time, many still believed that smut and vulgarity could be stopped, and laws were passed to that effect. Far from striking down these laws on free speech grounds, U.S. courts by and large supported the efforts of the party of reticence in their efforts to keep personal matters private. By the middle of the twentieth century, all that would change.

Technological change and the rise of the big cities enabled the cheap "penny press" to exert greater and greater influence on U.S. society. The new sensational press broke down old mores and conventions, all the while appealing to the democratic justification that it was simply "giving the people what they want" (while making hefty profits). The magic formula was to print stories about shocking, lurid murders and other crimes; about adultery, divorce, and prostitution; and about the personalities and scandals of high society and the world of entertainment.

The press's fascination with the scandalous and sensational was paralleled by similar developments in the world of serious literature. Both in the United States and in Europe, the literary movements of realism and naturalism dealt with lowly and common subjects—the life of the poor and the working class, of criminals and prostitutes—and told their stories simply and honestly. The naturalist writers strove for an objectivity devoid of sentimentality. This was the path taken by Gustave Flaubert and Emile Zola in France and by Stephen Crane, George Norris, Jack London, Theodore Dreiser, and Sinclair Lewis in the United States. Responding to protests of the literary party of reticence, novelist and critic William Dean Howells argued for democracy, equality, and scientific truth.

The new realist literary elite, probably unwittingly, ended up allying itself with feminists and other sexual radicals. What they all had in common was a desire to explore the dark and private corners of life—sex, health, and life and death. Only by bringing these matters into the open could society be cleansed of its hidden prejudices and inequalities. Only by speaking about the heretofore unspeakable, openly and without shame, could society be transformed.

Thus, women's rights advocate Elizabeth Cady Stanton preached that "Danger lies in darkness and distance," and feminist doctor Mary Putnam Jacobi enjoined her listeners at a public lecture to "Live in the open air!" Sociologist Lester Ward insisted that sexual matters be discussed freely and publicly (cited in Gurstein 1996, 63).

A raft of obscenity laws were drafted in resistance to these disturbing and invasive trends. A few states already had obscenity laws on the books in the early nineteenth century, but most did not. And where those laws existed, "obscenity" was a broader concept than it later became, extending well beyond matters of sex. Alarm over the "French picture postcard trade" in the 1840s led Congress to include as part of the Tariff Act a section allowing the U.S. Customs Office to confiscate and destroy racy images sent over from Paris. In 1857, the power of customs was expanded to cover not only pictures but also articles with a "blue" content even without images. These were, however, relatively minor matters. By the 1870s, much of the country was appalled and offended by the insistence of the nation's sex radicals that raunchy talk and images were the path to personal and sexual liberation. In 1873, Congress passed the famous Comstock Postal Act, which banned from the mail postcards with "indecent or scurrilous epithets," "obscene, lewd, lascivious" books and papers, "indecent" publications, things "intended or adapted for immoral use or nature," and all matters related to contraception, including birth-control devices and instruction in their use (17 St. at L. 598 [March 3, 1873]).

As might be expected, prosecutors availed themselves aggressively of the new law. As the initial cases came to court, the first skirmishes of modern free speech law were fought. In the late nineteenth century, there was little doctrinal drama in these cases, for the First Amendment arguments used against the Comstock Act and similar legal restrictions on obscenity had almost no legal purchase in U.S. courts. The practice of the time was to allow legislatures considerable latitude to ban materials that had "a bad tendency." And the Bad Tendency test, as it was called, was not at all difficult to meet.

If statutes like the Comstock Act did not get a particular material, the strictures of the common law did. The common law test for obscenity was derived from the famous English precedent of *Regina v. Hicklin* (L. R. 3 Q. B 360 [1868]). The *Hicklin* case involved the censorship of a pamphlet that had attacked the depravity of Roman Catholic priests by alleging that women were frequently being seduced in church confessionals. The court declared that the test of obscenity is "whether the tendency of the matter charged as obscenity is to deprave and corrupt the morals of those whose minds are open to such influences, and into whose hands a publication of the sort may fall" (quoted in Gurstein 1996, 74). Under this test, the standard for obscenity is set by the presumed effect on the reader rather than by the author's or distributor's merit or intention or by some broader social purpose that might have been advanced by permitting the material's publication. This common law standard gave significant power to those seeking to control and to prosecute obscenity.

Perhaps the most famous late-nineteenth-century obscenity case is *United States v. Bennett* (16 Blatchford 355 [1879]). D. M. Bennett, a free-thinking journalist, sent through the mails a copy of Ezra Heywood's pamphlet *Cupid's Yokes, or The Binding Forces of Conjugal Love,* a document intended not to provide sexual stimulation but rather to transform sexuality by bringing it "within the domain of reason and moral obligation" (quoted in Gurstein 1996, 67). Applying the *Hicklin* test, the presiding judge declared the reformist political intentions of the pamphlet to be irrelevant. As a legal matter, all that counted was the probable effect of the publication on those who happened to come across it.

In *United States v. Harmon* (45 F. 414 [1891]), publisher Moses Harmon was charged with circulating journals that included materials such as a letter from a New York City doctor detailing the history of the perversions he had seen in his career, including incest, homosexuality, and bestiality. The prosecution once again argued that the medical purpose of Harmon's case studies was irrelevant. All that mattered was the probable effect on public morals.

Sex and domestic life were hardly the only area in the late nineteenth century in which it seemed that the old proprieties, inhibitions, and rules were under siege. Cooley and other conservative libertarians were sanguine in penning bold defenses of free speech and press in part because they believed firmly that such speech helped advance the liberal capitalist society of which they were supporters. But at the very moment of the liberal capitalist zenith, the very foundations of that system were challenged. The economic depressions of the 1870s and 1890s, as well as the typically harsh conditions of factory workers in the new industrial economy, helped spur labor radicalism by such groups as the Knights of Labor. Many of these radicals, including self-proclaimed anarchists, advocated not reform and gradual improvement but revolution. Discussions of questions concerning the exercise of free speech favoring anarchy, labor rights, and revolution were no seminar-style debates at this time. Rather, these were highly charged issues, and their discussion could result in physical violence. The 1886 bombing by anarchists of Haymarket Square in Chicago led to calls for restrictions on radical speech. Such restrictions were in fact enacted into law after 1901, when President William McKinley was assassinated in Buffalo, New York, by an anarchist, Leon Czolgosz. Here, as is so often the case in the history of free speech, the real fear of chaos and violent revolution led to a shift in thinking about the value of uninhibited speech.

To be sure, many conservative libertarians stuck to their guns. Cooley took a position that was highly protective of even the most provocative political speech. The government, he said, could punish only speakers whose intent and purpose was to bring about rebellion and civil war. St. George Tucker, another conservative libertarian, serving as the attorney for the anarchists charged with the Haymarket bombings, argued that the free speech rights of the anarchists were being infringed (*Spies v. Illinois*, 123 U.S. 131 [1887]). Henry Adams, author and scion of the great Massachusetts political dynasty, warned against the prosecution of anarchist speakers in the wake of the Haymarket bombing on the grounds that a social safety value was necessary and that a crackdown would end up making political martyrs of the anarchists, thus helping to advance their cause—which he abhorred.

In this roiling and chaotic context, however, arguments for greater restrictions on permissible speech gained political strength and influence. Those arguments, in turn, were challenged and opposed by powerful opponents. As these forces clashed, the United States was in the grip of revolutionary social, economic, and political transformations. It was in this context that the old order concerning the freedom of speech came to an end and the modern world of free speech was poised to be born.

REFERENCES AND FURTHER READING

Amar, Akhil Reed. 1997. *The Constitution and Criminal Procedure: First Principles.* New Haven: Yale University Press.

———. 1998. *The Bill of Rights: Creation and Reconstruction.* New Haven: Yale University Press.

Bailyn, Bernard. 1967. *The Ideological Origins of the American Revolution.* Cambridge, MA: Belknap Press.

Baldick, Robert. 1965. *The Duel: A History of Dueling.* London: Chapman and Hall.

Blackstone, William. [1765–1769] 1979. *Commentaries on the Laws of England.* Ed. Stanley Katz. Chicago: University of Chicago Press.

Bowen, Catherine Drinker. 1966. *Miracle at Philadelphia: The Story of the Constitutional Convention, May to September 1787.* Boston: Little, Brown.

Boyer, Paul S. 1968. *Purity in Print: The Vice-Society Movement and Book Censorship in America.* New York: Scribner.

Cooley, Thomas M. 1868. *A Treatise on the Constitutional Limitations Which Rest upon the Legislative Power of the States of the American Union.* Boston: Little, Brown.

Curtis, Michael Kent. 2000. *Free Speech, "The People's Darling Privilege": Struggles for Freedom of Expression in American History.* Durham, NC: Duke University Press.

Donald, David Herbert. 1960. *Charles Sumner and the Coming of the Civil War.* Chicago: University of Chicago Press.

Freeman, Joanne B. 2001. *Affairs of Honor: National Politics in the New Republic.* New Haven: Yale University Press.

Graber, Mark A. 1991. *The Transforming Speech: The Ambiguous Legacy of Civil Libertarianism.* Berkeley and Los Angeles: University of California Press.

Gurstein, Rochelle. 1996. *The Repeal of Reticence: A History of America's Cultural and Legal Struggles over Free Speech, Obscenity, Sexual Liberation, and Modern Art.* New York: Hill and Wang.

Kent, James. 1826–1830. *Commentaries on American Law.* New York: O. Halsted.

Kurland, Philip, and Ralph Lerner, eds. 1987. *The Founders' Constitution.* Vol. 5, *Amendments I–XII.* Chicago: University of Chicago Press.

Levy, Leonard W. 1960. *Legacy of Suppression: Freedom of Speech and Press in Early American History.* Cambridge, MA: Belknap Press of Harvard University Press.

————. 1963. *Jefferson and Civil Liberties: The Darker Side.* Chicago: Ivan R. Dee.

————. 1985. *Emergence of a Free Press.* New York: Oxford University Press.

————. 1993. *Blasphemy: Verbal Offenses against the Sacred, from Moses to Salman Rushdie.* New York: Knopf.

Milton, John. 1649. "The Tenure of Kings and Magistrates." Available at http://www.constitution.org/milton/tenure_kings.htm. Cited December 13, 2002.

————. 1999. *Areopagitica, and of Education.* Reprint, Northbrook, IL: AHM Publishing.

Rabban, David M. 1997. *Free Speech in Its Forgotten Years.* Cambridge: Cambridge University Press.

Rakove, Jack N. 1996. *Original Meanings: Politics and Ideas in the Making of the Constitution.* New York: Knopf.

Rehnquist, William H. 1998. *All the Laws but One: Civil Liberties in Wartime.* New York: Knopf.

Rosenberg, Norman. 1986. *Protecting the Best Men: An Interpretive History of the Law of Libel.* Chapel Hill: University of North Carolina Press.

Shakespeare, William. 1957. *The Tragedy of Othello, The Moor of Venice.* New York: Washington Square Press.

Story, Joseph. [1833] 1987. *Commentaries on the Constitution of the United States.* Ed. Ronald D. Rotunda and John E. Nowak. Durham, NC: Carolina Academic Press.

U.S. Government. 1969. *Inaugural Addresses of the Presidents of the United States from George Washington, 1789, to Richard Milhous Nixon, 1969.* Washington, DC: U.S. Government Printing Office.

VanBurkleo, Sandra F. 2001. *"Belonging to the World": Women's Rights and American Constitutional Culture.* New York: Oxford University Press.

Warren, Samuel, and Louis D. Brandeis. 1890. "The Right to Privacy." *Harvard Law Review* 4: 193–220.

Wentworth, Peter. 1576. "On the Liberty of the Commons." Available at http://www.uark.edu/depts/comminfo/cambridge/wentworth.html. Cited December 13, 2002.

Wood, Gordon S. 1969. *The Creation of the American Republic, 1776–1787.* Chapel Hill: University of North Carolina Press.

3

THE TWENTIETH CENTURY

*I*N THE NINETEENTH-CENTURY United States, free speech disputes were as likely to take place in political campaigns, newspaper broadsides, and public streets as in the courts. Certain disputes were staples, to be sure, in lower-level state courts (libel and slander actions, for instance). But these were common law cases: Most never mentioned the First Amendment.

The First Amendment was not invoked much in the federal courts either at this time. This was because for most of the nineteenth century, it was considered basic textbook law that the Bill of Rights, including the First Amendment, set constitutional limits only on the conduct of the federal government. As far as civil liberties were concerned, states were largely free to govern themselves. Add to this the fact that during that time, state governments in the United States did most of the actual governing and that there were relatively few federal statutes on the books, and the upshot was that as the twentieth century dawned, the federal courts (including the U.S. Supreme Court) had said virtually nothing about the freedom of speech.

By the second decade of the twentieth century, though, a radical change was under way. The new century gave birth to the modern United States, a country in which wide areas of political, social, and economic life became less the business of states and localities and more the affairs of a nation. It was in the late nineteenth and early twentieth centuries that the federal government began to assume sweeping responsibilities and to assert unprecedented powers. The national government got into the business of regulating banks, finance, labor-management relations, and the pricing structure of such major industries as the railroads. Soon it would become heavily involved with the provision of social welfare benefits, such as Social Security. Economic nationalization, in other words, had provoked political, regulatory, and in turn, cultural nationalization. The new mass media took on the new task of informing and entertaining audiences coast-to-coast. Newspapers had reached broad national markets by the late nineteenth century, and by the late 1920s, the new media of movies and commercial radio had joined the swelling tide.

Given these developments, it is not surprising that legal questions went national as well. For the first time, people's speech came to be routinely affected by federal as well as state actions. Moreover, the U.S. Supreme Court was now beginning to see rights violations, whether they occurred at the national or state level, as having implications for national policy and national interests. Accordingly, the Court moved to "incorporate" the Bill of Rights, declaring that key provisions of the Bill of Rights, including the First Amendment, were now restrictions on the conduct of the states as well as of the national government. This, of course, made the Court a major player in the world of free speech. Culture and politics still played a significant role in determining what one could or could not say. But as the twentieth century progressed, the task of defining the scope of the freedom of speech was put increasingly into the hands of lawyers and judges. And the nature of that freedom became more and more a matter of legal doctrine. Freedom of speech became what the U.S. Supreme Court said it was. Over the course of the twentieth century, the

High Court devoted a considerable amount of time and energy to building an elaborate edifice of rules, tests, and categories to lend a more precise meaning to what was, after all, a rather vague—if adamant—constitutional promise.

FREE SPEECH AS BOHEMIAN FASHION

The impulse to latitudinarianism that came to characterize free speech in the twentieth century began not as a vision of politicians or lawyers but rather as a social fashion, an urban craze, and, at least for the smart-set writers, artists, and other New York City bohemians, a way of life. In Greenwich Village in the century's earliest years, "rebellious talking" among intellectuals blossomed into a modernist vogue. Frank and shocking talk about sex, art, and politics, talk that self-consciously sniffed at propriety and trampled on convention, became chic, the quintessence of sophistication and downtown cool.

The modernist impulse toward rebellious talking was a reaction by a set of creative urban artists and intellectuals to dizzying social transformations that had discomfited many who had been accustomed to the familiar, the settled, and the stable. It was no coincidence that these transformations and upheavals were displayed most dramatically in New York City itself. On Manhattan Island, one needed only to step out of one's apartment and stroll the short distance between the mansions on Fifth Avenue and the tenements of the Lower East Side to see before one's eyes the newly yawning gap between destitution and opulence. As one strolled the New York streets, one needed only to listen to the Yiddish, Italian, Russian, and Irish brogue filling the city air to know that the America of the old-stock white Anglo-Saxon Protestant (WASP) dominance was on its way out. Attracted to the United States by its ravenous appetite for new workers and driven from their homelands by ethnic and religious persecution, immigrants landed at Ellis Island and other ports of entry at unprecedented (and, to some, alarming) rates. Ethnic and religious juxtapositions proliferated. For many Americans, what once seemed like eternals were now in frightening flux. (For immigrants, this flux was a concomitant of opportunity.) And change seemed afoot on every front. The categories of "man" and "woman," one would think, were eternal. But in New York City, even the sexes themselves seemed up for grabs. Suddenly, women were taking on men's roles: They were working in unprecedented numbers outside the home and became self-supporting and free. They were single. They went out. They drank. They smoked. And they talked. They expressed themselves. They questioned. Change itself had moved into the national marrow.

The New York City bohemians drank in this change as mother's milk. Some were native to the city, but others were drawn into its bosom from conventional, prosperous, and stable towns in California, Iowa, and Illinois by a thirst, even a yearning, for New York's energy and ferment. They were impelled by a conviction that the collapse of the old boundaries and the wonted ways was making the world anew and presenting them with a banquet of intellectual, cultural, personal, and political opportunities. In a season of vitality, the burgs and crossroads where they had been raised suddenly seemed stagnating and stifling. In Greenwich Village and in New York, the world in its infinite variety was in its spring.

In Greenwich Village, Max Eastman, editor of the radical journal *The Masses* (and a country boy with minister parents), declared that "free-thought talk" defined the culture flourishing all around him. Bohemians would gather in clubs and salons specifically created to crack conversation wide open. Free-thought talk was designed to push hard on the long-standing boundaries and break the norms of respectable public speech. At the Liberal Club, founded in 1912, men and women sat face-to-face drinking together (a sharp departure from Victorian convention) and spoke their minds on every conceivable topic, including, of course, sex,

sex, and sex. Well-off and well-educated Americans—like the members of the Liberal Club—had traditionally recognized a sharp division between high art and culture, which was their bailiwick, and popular art and culture, which was fodder for the lower classes. Liberal Club members delighted in setting this old order topsy-turvy. Ragtime was in, and chamber music, out; dance-hall stomps were in, and ballroom dancing, out. Representational painting was passé, and abstract modernism (on parade at the shocking New York City Armory show of 1913) was the vision of the future. Liberal Club denizens adopted and espoused a radical politics unusual for people of their social position. They loudly announced themselves to be in solidarity with the unwashed masses, with striking workers, with tenement dwellers, and with the "oppressed" (in the process serving as stylish models for later waves of intellectuals and college professors).

The New York bohemians stove to make their glamorous lives into liberationist beacons for a constrained and stuffy country, and soon they succeeded. The Liberal Club's membership list amounted to a who's who of famous American writers, including Edna St. Vincent Millay, Eugene O'Neill, Floyd Dell, Upton Sinclair, Lincoln Steffans, Louise Bryant, and John Reed. And the club's ethos spread. Similar clubs sprouted all over New York, including the Heterodoxy Club, a women-only free speech and discussion group that made small-town sewing circles seem quintessentially tame.

Perhaps the most storied site for freewheeling speech in the early-twentieth-century Greenwich Village (and indeed in the United States) was the weekly salon conducted by Mabel Dodge in her home on Fifth Avenue off Washington Square. Convention held that members of the country's upper crust, like Dodge (a Buffalo heiress), should hold genteel gatherings not downtown, in declassé Greenwich Village, but uptown, the home of high society. Convention also had it that only the "right" sort of people should be on the guest list. Dodge, in the spirit of the Liberal and Heterodoxy Clubs, however, set herself to the task of stirring things up. She insisted that the talk at her downtown salons be serious. But that said, all topics, no matter how racy or radical, were on the table. Moreover, as a spur to the creation of and collision between new and divergent ideas, Dodge summoned her invitees with shocking eclecticism. At her weekly salons, socialist radicals, anarchists, poets, painters, journalists, housewives, sex radicals, lawyers, labor activists, factory workers, and psychoanalysts rubbed shoulders, talked, and argued to a degree that was unprecedented. A modern form of conversation and of free speech was being born.

What do these Greenwich Village cultural trends have to do with free speech law? As it turns out, quite a bit. As part of their credo, the bohemians and intellectuals of the Liberal Club, the Heterodoxy Club, and Mabel Dodge's salons embraced a whole series of radical movements and causes, including modern art, women's emancipation, and the labor movement. The Greenwich Village free talkers, moreover, mixed personally with labor, sex, and literary radicals. When the speech of these new radicals ran up against the strictures of the forces of tradition and stability—often in the form of law—disputatious, well-educated, and well-connected New York bohemians and intellectuals came to their defense in published political essays and in courts of law. In the process, New York's free talkers played a crucial role in formulating modern legal theories of the freedom of speech. These theories, in time, would come to reconstitute the spirit of U.S. society and rearrange the contours of U.S. law.

POLITICAL RADICALISM PRIOR
TO WORLD WAR I

Labor radicalism was one of the great causes of New York's bohemian intellectuals. The early twentieth century was a time of mass industrialization, accompanied by intense and often bloody conflicts between workers and management. There was ominous and at times threatening talk of the struggle of class against class as the prelude to a new and more just economic order. Although this call to class struggle (and indeed to class war) inspired many workers, it simultaneously alarmed the middle or upper classes, and perhaps most workers as well. Given the violence of the world around them and the fiery convictions of the radicals, many of these people considered revolution against the capitalist system to be a real possibility. Many had a genuine fear of the social, political, and economic instability generated by the radicalism of the country's labor movement.

The messenger of early-twentieth-century radicalism was often a street-corner orator, commonly a socialist, a militant laborer from the Industrial Workers of the World (IWW, or "Wobblies"), or an anarchist. This incendiary speaker would mount a soapbox in the public square or step up to the podium in the public hall and with flashing eyes and pointed gesticulations, vehemently denounce the rule of the plutocrats and capitalism itself. In the days before radio and television, politics of this sort, politics in the open air and the public hall, was a means of recruiting allies and supporters and of educating and entertaining the broader public.

It would be wrong to look upon the early-twentieth-century street-corner radicals in the United States as akin to the soapbox orators we might find today in London's Hyde Park or New York's Washington Square. Nor are their speeches strictly analogous to today's televised campaign speeches. The fire-breathing radicals who spoke, the indignant and angry crowds who listened, and the staid and solid citizens who feared them both all cared passionately about the cause. What is more, in this era, radical speech and the possibility of radical acts were closely linked. The atmosphere was often tense. Many of the early-century labor radicals preached and practiced violence and fought for violent revolution—for real. In return, many of those who opposed them felt entirely justified in saving themselves and the country by meeting violence with violence. These were serious times.

The great radical orator and galvanizing figure of radical speech at this time was Emma Goldman. A Russian immigrant who had landed in Rochester, New York, as a teenager, Goldman was pulled toward radical politics while suffering through a stint as a low-paid factory worker and suffocating in an arid, middle-class marriage. In 1889, inspired by Chicago's Haymarket radicals, Goldman fled the life in Rochester she despised and headed for the bohemia of New York City. There, Goldman quickly fell in with a man who became her lifelong companion, the anarchist Alexander Berkman. Goldman herself would soon become the most famous anarchist in U.S. history.

Goldman was legendary for her incendiary style as a radical street-corner orator. She toured the country, stimulating and shocking crowds coast-to-coast with her eloquent advocacy of free love outside the bonds of marriage (including homosexuality), high modernist art and literature, and anarchist politics and with her brutal condemnations of marriage, sexual puritanism, Christianity, and capitalism. She supplemented her orations by launching an anarchist journal, *Mother Earth*, and by appearing as a regular on the Greenwich Village free speech circuit of bohemian salons and intellectual clubs.

Goldman was soon considered by the powers-that-be to be a dangerous woman, and not without reason. In the United States of the early twentieth century, anarchist speech was closely related to anarchist acts. Indeed, Goldman herself hardly stood at any great distance from such acts. Her lover, Berkman, had enthusiastically instructed her in the anarchist strategy of the "attentat"— or politics by assassination—that had been used to eliminate Russia's Czar Alexander II in 1881. Berkman himself (with Goldman's help) made an unsuccessful attempt on the life of Henry Clay Frick, the head of the Carnegie Steel Corporation: Goldman was never charged, but Berkman was sent to jail for fourteen years for attempted murder. In 1901, President William McKinley was assassinated in Buffalo by an immigrant anarchist (and a self-professed admirer of Goldman). To many, the claim that the speech of anarchists, who rejected the claims to authority of all governments, was simply a contribution to healthy political debate simply did not ring true.

In the wake of the McKinley assassination, the authorities in many states moved to outlaw certain forms of radical speech. New York, for example, passed a law that prohibited the expression of anarchist views, and prosecutions under that law and others like it soon began apace. At the same time, prosecutions of sex radicals under prevailing obscenity laws continued. In such a world, a woman like Goldman was doubly marked. Goldman herself, in fact, was driven underground by these laws and forced to assume an alias, which only fed her status as a romantic liberationist outlaw. In the process, she became a hero to (and an inspiration for) the new activist movement seeking to expand the legal protections for the freedom of radical political, artistic, and sexual speech.

The crackdown on radical speech in the wake of the McKinley assassination spurred the creation of one of the country's earliest civil liberties groups, the Free Speech League. The league was the brainchild of a small cadre of New York City intellectuals. Its members pledged themselves to defend not all speech, out of some abstract philosophical conviction, but rather radical speech of particular sorts involving anarchism, socialism, atheism, birth control, and sex. Over time, however, the league became much more broadly committed to the general principles of free speech. In following this path, the league paved the way for a political movement that came to be known as "civil libertarianism."

The driving force behind this pioneering and influential civil liberties group was Theodore Schroeder, the son of German immigrants and a Wisconsin native who had moved to New York City after spending his youth and young adulthood traveling the West, working on railroads, and mixing with workers, immigrants, and drifters. Schroeder ultimately got a legal education and settled down to practice law. He soon became a prolific pamphleteer and a relentless iconoclast. One of Schroeder's favorite topics involved tracing the roots of religious belief to sexual maladaption. (His pamphlets on this subject, needless to say, infuriated the devout and got him brought up on charges for sending obscene materials through the U.S. mail.) Upon moving to New York City from Utah to continue a long-standing crusade against Mormonism, Schroeder fell in with a group of the city's downtown free speech radicals and joined the Free Speech League in its earliest years. With indefatigable devotion (it is said that he never spoke of anything else), he began to turn out a thick stream of pamphlets and books defending the cause of a latitudinarian conception of the freedom of speech. Among these writings was his landmark book, *Obscene Literature and Constitutional Law* (1911).

While Schroeder was in New York penning scholarly defenses of the freedom of speech, Goldman was touring the country, adding the freedom of speech itself to her grab bag of political causes. In the process, she joined what was coalescing into a common free speech front with the labor and the birth control movements (she signed on as an ally of the IWW and of Margaret Sanger, a public health nurse and pioneering advocate of contraception). As people were harassed and even arrested under the new laws for giving—and even for attending—these talks, anarchism, the labor movement, and the birth control movement became joined with the cause of free speech in the U.S. political imagination.

THE IWW FREE SPEECH FIGHTS

The late nineteenth and early twentieth centuries witnessed the most spectacular and sustained period of labor unrest in U.S. history. Working conditions in this era were brutal. Many workers put in nearly endless days at low wages and under unsafe conditions. Workers who sought to change things were at substantial risk of losing their jobs. Nonetheless, a strong union movement was forged, and with the help of political progressives, labor activists succeeded in placing an array of reform proposals on the agendas of legislatures throughout the nation, including child-labor, minimum-wage, and maximum-hours laws; health and safety standards; and laws guaranteeing the rights to organize and belong to unions. This agenda, however, did not advance smoothly. Many, both within the business community and outside it, considered unions to be coercive conspiracies hostile to the interests of private property and individual choice. Strikes and boycotts hit the economy's core industries, such as coal, railroads, agriculture, and steel, raising the specter of economic collapse and ruin. Federal courts stepped in to issue injunctions banning strikes, boycotts, and picketing. Company owners deployed private police forces, often augmented by the National Guard and state militias, to enforce these injunctions and to attack striking workers. Moreover, they often blacklisted workers who associated with unions and used company spies to ferret these people out. Striking workers and their supporters were routinely charged with conspiracy, criminal libel, vagrancy, and disturbing the peace. For their part, the unions used violence and intimidation against both management and "scabs"—replacement workers for those on strike—to maintain these strikes.

Perhaps the most radical of U.S. labor unions was the IWW, which was founded in 1905 and came to play a major role in the development of modern free speech law. Unlike craft unions like the American Federation of Labor, which catered to skilled workers and endeavored to reach workable agreements with employers, the IWW was an "industrial union" open to all. The IWW evinced little interest in workable agreements. Its inspiration was Marxist, and its commitment was to the revolutionary overthrow of capitalism. The Wobblies believed that "the working class and the capitalist class have nothing in common" and that "between these two classes a struggle must go on until the workers of the world organize as a class, take possession of the earth and the machinery of production, and abolish the wage system" (Goldstein 2001, 73). To advance these beliefs, the IWW initiated militant, crippling strikes and openly advocated sabotage (which included everything from work slowdowns to the disabling of machinery). In the context of widespread violence, including a series of attempts (some successful) on the lives of the president, governors, cabinet members, and major industrialists, the Wobblies proved immensely controversial, to say the least.

The IWW rose to national prominence with its "free speech fights" of 1909–1913, fights that prompted the modern era's first broad-ranging national discussion of the fundamental principles of the freedom of speech. During these years, the IWW launched a series of organizing campaigns in many U.S. cities. These campaigns involved fiery revolutionary street-corner orations and the public distribution of incendiary literature. Fearing their destabilizing and pernicious influence and in anticipation of their arrival, localities passed a series of ordinances banning public speaking, rallies, and parades. The Wobblies were arrested for flouting these laws (and were happy to be arrested, since their goal was not to avoid arrest but to fill the jails and stir up publicity). IWW newspapers were seized, and IWW leaders were rounded up and run out of town. The Wobblies, in turn, loudly protested that the authorities were violating their fundamental rights to the freedom of speech.

The Wobblies were not without their supporters. For it was soon claimed that they were being attacked by the powers-that-be not so much for their acts as for the radical content of their ideas. The New York bohemians harbored a strong romantic attachment to ideas concerning revolution, class warfare, the destruction of capitalism, and the creation of a workers' state, and this made them particularly inclined to cast the Wobblies as working-class heroes persecuted simply for saying what they believed. The bohemians joined the barricades in Wobbly strikes in the mills of Lawrence, Massachusetts (1912) and Paterson, New Jersey (1913). The Free Speech League signed on to the Wobbly cause. When World War I erupted a few years later and President Woodrow Wilson, among others, began to attack groups like the Wobblies as anti-American and as threats to the successful prosecution of the war, such groups found additional defenders, not just among anarchists and socialists but also among mainstream unionists and elite progressive intellectuals. Many, of course, including other factions of the labor movement, continued to believe that although free speech was fine, the laws the Wobblies had violated had been perfectly appropriate laws under the circumstances. Liberty was all well and good, but license was simply beyond the pale.

THE BIRTH CONTROL MOVEMENT AND FREE SPEECH

At the same time the labor movement fights were at their highest pitch, struggles over free discussion concerning sex were being fought on an array of fronts. None was more prominent than that involving efforts to suppress the publication and distribution of texts and pamphlets on human sexuality and contraception. The Comstock Act had criminalized the dissemination of birth control information and devices, and discussions of contraception in medical textbooks had been deemed obscene since the 1870s. But beginning in 1912, the Greenwich Village bohemians took up birth control as one of their causes, folding it into their broader campaign for sexual liberation and women's rights. A birth control movement soon attained national prominence by forging shrewd alliances with socialist, labor, and free speech activists.

At the forefront of this movement was Margaret Sanger, a radical socialist public health nurse from Corning, New York. Sanger, a predecessor of such celebrity activist entrepreneurs as Jesse Jackson, Al Sharpton, and Gloria Steinem, was convinced that the open public discussion and widespread use of contraception was the key to health and wealth and the foundation of human happiness. Birth control was indispensable to happiness because it decoupled sex from procreation, freeing men and women to arouse themselves to endless waves of orgasmic pleasure. Birth control liberated women from the poverty caused by their helpless breeding of the grubby broods that infested the urban slums (many called contraception the rich woman's secret). Birth control, moreover, shielded women's health by making dangerous abortions unnecessary (Sanger called abortions "a disgrace to civilization"), by keeping husbands at home and out of the whorehouses (where they picked up venereal diseases that they brought home with them like mud on their shoes), and by staving off the psychological damage that stemmed (so Freud had said) from sexual repression (Gurstein 1996, 96).

Sanger married her political commitments to a thirst for publicity and a relish for shocking the middle classes. She published a birth control journal, *The Woman Rebel*, that defiantly proclaimed to "look the whole world in the face with a go-to-hell look in the eyes, to have an ideal, to speak and act in defiance of convention" (quoted in Gurstein 1996, 107). With the help of an anarchist press and the delivery services of Wobblies and other labor radicals, she broadly distributed *Family Limitations*, a contraceptive instruction manual. Sanger's decision to publish *The Woman Rebel* and *Family Limitations*, as well as her decision to open a birth control clinic in Brownsville in Brooklyn, New York, soon landed her behind bars. Far from being dismayed by this turn, Sanger (like the Wobblies and like Al Sharpton in later years) made the dramatic most of her arrests. Since her antics moved papers, newspapers loved her. Supportive pro-Sanger rallies were held in Carnegie Hall. Like Emma Goldman, Sanger became a regular at Mabel Dodge's salon and the Liberal Club. By joining the cause of sexual liberation with support for socialism, the radical labor movement, and free speech (she was advised by Theodore Schroeder's Free Speech League), Sanger helped forge modern left-wing and civil libertarian politics (Stansell 2000, 238).

The activism of Sanger and Goldman and their Greenwich Village circle was important in bringing free speech arguments into the courts. It would be quite a while, however, before those arguments actually persuaded any judges. Faithful to the law as they knew it, the judges continued to hold, often summarily, that legislators had broad authority aimed at protecting the public health, safety, and morals. Lots had to happen before these judges would even begin to see things differently. It was, for instance, 1930 before latitudinarian approaches to sexual speech first prevailed in court. In *United States v. Dennett*, 39 F.2d 564 (1930), the court held that sex education materials, because they were put forth to advance knowledge rather than to excite lascivious urges, could not be considered legally obscene.

WORLD WAR I, FREE SPEECH, AND THE SUPREME COURT

Struggles between governments and anarchists, socialists, labor activists, and sexual radicals in the early twentieth century provoked broad-ranging public discussions on the proper parameters of the freedom of speech. It was World War I, however, that finally brought this simmering discussion to a boil. During the war, both the national and state governments, in conjunction with an array of private voluntary groups, cracked down hard on what they took to be dangerous and counterproductive speech and expression, a crackdown that provoked intense political resistance. These clashes pulled the U.S. Supreme Court into the free speech fray and marked the beginning of the Supreme Court's ascendancy to its current position as the primary arbiter of the freedom of speech.

Although the old battle lines remained, pitting radicals seeking revolutionary changes against conservative defenders of the status quo, new dynamics came into play during the war, and new fault lines opened that separated radicals and progressives. As the country entered the twentieth century, many progressives had big plans for government power, which they hoped to install as a countervailing force against the runaway power of laissez-faire capitalism. In the pursuit of what they were clearly convinced were noble ends, however, many progressives tended to pooh-pooh the objections of those who warned of the dangers of a radically empowered central state. In part because they took their ends to be noble, these progressives were quick to anger when challenged. As they saw it, the naysayers were becoming obstacles in the path of social progress.

These progressives had little patience for the speech of those who stood in the way of economic justice and social progress. This inclination toward intolerance was doubled when President Wilson, a leading progressive himself, reneged on his campaign pledge and led the United States into World War I, a move that Wilson publicly justified on progressive terms as aimed at making the world "safe for democracy" (Wilson 1917).

Radicals, though, remained staunchly opposed to U.S. entry into the war. Pacifists hated the idea of war itself. Socialists and other anticapitalists saw the war as little more than a sop to munitions makers and other capitalists. And liberals, feminists, and those who preached on behalf of domestic social reform for a variety of reasons, signed on to the campaign against the war as well.

The Wilson administration, which saw itself as a force for progress and social justice, did not take kindly to these criticisms. It cracked down on dissenters, in part by supporting laws restricting the freedom of speech. In 1917, in the wake of the Russian Revolution (which thrilled the New York bohemians), Congress made it a federal crime to threaten the U.S. president with physical harm. More sweeping limitations followed. The Espionage Act

(40. Stat. 219 [1917]) made it a federal crime to "make or convey false reports or false statements with the intent to interfere with the operations or success of the military or naval forces of the United States or to promote the success of its enemies," to "willfully cause or attempt to cause insubordination, disloyalty, mutiny, or refusal of duty, in the military or naval forces of the United States," or to "willfully obstruct the recruiting or enlistment service of the United States, to the injury of the service of the United States." Echoing the legal restrictions of the Civil War era, the act, in addition, authorized the postmaster general of the United States to remove from the mails all materials "advocating or urging treason, insurrection, or forcible resistance to any law of the United States." Anyone sending such materials, moreover, was subject to criminal prosecution. In addition, the Trading with the Enemy Act (P.L. 65–91, October 6, 1917) gave the U.S. postmaster general the authority to censor American foreign-language newspapers. In 1918, these statutes were supplemented with two more statutes, the Sedition Act (40 Stat. 553 [1918]), which made it a crime to say, print, or publish anything intended to cause "contempt, scorn, contumely, or disrepute, as regards the form of government of the United States, or the Constitution, or the flag, or the uniform of the Army or Navy" or to hinder the prosecution of the war, and the Alien Act (40 Stat. 1012 [1918]), which made it a deportable offense for aliens to advocate anarchism, syndicalism (that is, rule by the organized working class), or violent revolution.

These laws were not paper tigers, and along with various state sedition laws, they were vigorously enforced. Private initiatives, moreover, reinforced government policy. As the United States entered the war, waves of vigilante justice swept the nation. Those suspected of disloyalty were tarred and feathered and forced to kneel down and kiss the flag. Some were beaten. Others were killed. German books were burned, and Beethoven was banned in Pittsburgh. With the blessing of state governments and the national government, private groups like the American Protective Association (APA) launched "slacker raids," in which APA members stalked cities, alighting on bars, theaters, and rooming houses they believed harbored folks who were not doing their part. The raiders made citizen's arrests of thousands of "slackers." State councils of defense warned the public of the dire consequences that would befall those who were soft on Germany or opposed the war. Many thought it best to say as little as possible. But others took a different route.

THE BIRTH OF MODERN FREE SPEECH LAW: SCHENCK, ABRAMS, DEBS, AND FROHWERK

The Supreme Court's first modern free speech decisions arose out of the prosecution of socialists and anarchists for opposing the U.S. entry into World War I. In all these decisions, the Court's majority voted overwhelmingly *against* those making First Amendment claims on behalf of their freedom of speech. Nonetheless, these decisions both set out the parameters of the old order and planted the seeds of the new.

In the old order, when free speech cases reached the Court—and they rarely did—the Court used the Bad Tendency test to arrive at a decision. This test had ancient roots. It had long been a staple in Blackstone and English common law, and it gave significant weight to the broader public interest in deciding the proper parameters of free speech. The Bad Tendency test held that it was proper for the government to punish people for speech that had a bad tendency, that is, that harmed the public interest, including speech the government reasonably believed had a tendency either to incite illegal conduct or to obstruct government action. This test set a low standard for court review, and its practical effect was that most assertions of First Amendment free speech rights were sure losers.

The Supreme Court reaffirmed its adherence to the Bad Tendency test in a host of prewar decisions. In *Patterson v. Colorado*

(205 U.S. 454 [1907]), Justice Oliver Wendell Holmes, Jr., who later pushed the Court to adopt a test that was more skeptical of government power, declared that it was entirely constitutional for Colorado to prosecute a newspaper editor who had criticized the judge in a pending case. Such criticism, the Court said, no matter how accurate, "tends to obstruct the administration of justice" (462). Moreover, First Amendment guarantees amounted only to a prohibition on prior restraints. In a similar spirit a few years later, the High Court held (with Holmes writing again) that because there were laws against indecent exposure, it was entirely constitutional to prosecute a man for the publication of an article entitled "The Nude and the Prudes," which advocated a boycott of businesses campaigning against nude bathing (*Fox v. Washington*, 236 U.S. 273 [1915]).

The Wilson administration's prosecutions of antiwar socialists and anarchists under the Espionage Act, however, explicitly set in motion forces of change. A mere month after the act was passed, for example, federal judge Learned Hand, in *Masses Publishing Co. v. Patten* (244 Fed. 535 [S.D.N.Y. 1917]), had boldly cast aside the Bad Tendency test to invalidate a postal service embargo on Max Eastman's revolutionary journal *The Masses*, which had run political cartoons showing the Liberty Bell in shambles and which represented the military as the death of youth, the labor movement, and democracy. Hand's ruling was statutory rather than constitutional. (He argued that as a matter of interpretation, the Espionage Act could not have been directed at "intemperate and inflammatory public discussion" but only at words that "directly ... counsel[ed] or advise[d] insubordination," including "direct advocacy of resistance to the recruiting and enlistment service" [541]). But all the same, Hand's test was clearly edging the law in a new direction.

Hand's protective disposition toward speech critical of the government did not immediately win over adherents (and Hand's decision itself was overturned on appeal). That same year, the

Supreme Court upheld the conviction of Charles Schenck, the general secretary of the Socialist Party (at this time one of the nation's most powerful political parties). As the Socialist leader, Schenck had supervised the printing of 15,000 antidraft pamphlets that were distributed to all the young men in Philadelphia who were being drafted. When some of these draftees complained to the authorities, Schenck was arrested and prosecuted under the Espionage Act. He fought back, arguing that the open and honest discussion of important public issues was protected under the First Amendment (*Schenck v. United States,* 249 U.S. 47 [1919]).

Schenck lost unanimously in the Supreme Court. Nonetheless, the *Schenck* case became a free speech landmark. In it, Justice Holmes began outlining a new doctrinal architecture for free speech cases that would eventually come to supplant the Bad Tendency test. Holmes's opinion implicitly proposed that the Court first distinguish different sorts of speech and then apply different tests for each. For political speech (which was at issue in *Schenck*), he suggested that the justices apply a Clear and Present Danger test, asking "whether the words used are used in such circumstances and are of such a nature as to create a clear and present danger that they will bring about the substantive evils that Congress has a right to prevent" (52). Under this test, the Court needed to assess the intent of the speech and the context in which it was uttered. In peacetime, what Schenck did might not have created a clear and present danger. But in 1917, when the dangers to military recruitment were immediate and real, Schenck's actions clearly evinced an intent to have a real-world effect. After all, Holmes wrote, "The most stringent protection of free speech would not protect a man in falsely shouting fire in a theatre and causing a panic," coining what has become a figure of speech (52). The implication was that, seen in context, this is precisely what Charles Schenck had done.

Holmes's opinion was pregnant with questions. If the Clear and Present Danger test applied to political speech, what tests would apply to other sorts of speech? What *were* the other types of speech? Was sexual speech a separate category? Artistic speech? Commercial speech? Once it was decided what these categories were, did they need to be ranked in order of importance to devise their respective tests? What of the assertion that in some sense, all speech is "political"? Even after this categorization and ranking, presumably some regulation was still impermissible. What should be the test for that regulation for each category of speech? The modern law of free speech is, in its essentials, the story of how the Supreme Court came to answer these questions on a case-by-case basis.

It soon became apparent that the *Schenck* case would not stand alone. That same year, the Court upheld the conviction of Socialist labor leader and presidential candidate Eugene V. Debs for making an antiwar speech that (unlike Schenck's pamphlets) stopped short of counseling direct resistance to the draft (*Debs v. United States*, 249 U.S. 211 [1919]). And it upheld the conviction of the owners of a German immigrant newspaper for criticizing the war (*Frohwerk v. United States*, 249 U.S. 204 [1919]). These famous 1919 Espionage Act decisions were sharply criticized by the new civil liberties activist groups and civil libertarian law professors, who set themselves to change the Court's prevailing free speech doctrine through transforming the thinking of the nation's leading lawyers and judges.

When it came to influencing the future course of that doctrine, no group was to be more effective than the American Civil Liberties Union (ACLU), a spin-off of the American Union against Militarism (AUAM), which itself had been created in 1914 to oppose U.S. entry into the war. When the United States joined the war in 1917, the AUAM began fighting the draft, which its members argued violated fundamental principles of U.S. democracy. After a 1917 rift within the AUAM over how oppositionist they should be toward their fellow progressives in the Wilson administration, a spin-off group, the National Civil Liberties Bureau, was created to take a strong anti-Wilson stand. In 1920, this group, headed by the Harvard-educated, antiwar and anticapitalist radical Roger Baldwin, changed its name to the American Civil Liberties Union.

At the same moment that nationwide activist groups like the ACLU were forming, reform-oriented, full-time law professors were also making their debut as a force for the transformation of constitutional doctrine. For most of U.S. history, lawyers had been trained not at law schools but through an apprenticeship system. By the late nineteenth century, though, law schools made up of full-time faculty began to displace the older, practice-based system of legal education. The faculty in these law schools were largely unburdened by the demands of clients, and they devoted a considerable amount of their time to criticizing the direction of the law in a variety of areas and to steering the law in what they took to be desirable new directions. Two giants of the new legal academy, Ernst Freund and Zechariah Chafee, Jr., became absorbed in free speech reform. Freund, a professor at the University of Chicago, advanced systematic arguments on behalf of the social usefulness of a broad understanding of the freedom of speech. He asserted, moreover, that these arguments should be applied to scientific, artistic, and literary as well as political speech. Chafee, a professor at the Harvard Law School, argued in his landmark book *Freedom of Speech* (1920) that free speech law was out of step with the times and needed to be more accommodating of unsettling speech, even during wartime. Speech was properly checked, Chafee argued, praising Learned Hand and damning *Schenck,* only when there was a serious threat to public safety. Chafee managed to win Harvard Law School graduates Holmes and Louis D. Brandeis over to his views, although he nearly got fired for his radicalism in the process. Persuaded by Chafee, Holmes and Brandeis became the catalysts for the High Court's fundamental reassessment and reorientation of the freedom of speech.

A turning point in this reorientation was Holmes's dissent in
Abrams v. United States (250 U.S. 616 [1919]). *Abrams* involved
the prosecution, under the Sedition Act, of immigrant anarchists
in New York City for printing and distributing leaflets attacking
President Wilson's decision to send U.S. troops to Russia and calling for a general strike in protest. Now wielding the Clear and
Present Danger test, the Court upheld the convictions. But in an
eloquent dissent, Holmes, the inventor of that test, lit out for new
territory, radically ratcheting up the level of First Amendment
skepticism. In *Abrams,* Holmes insisted that Congress "constitutionally may punish [only] speech that produces or is intended to
produce a clear and imminent danger that will bring about forthwith certain substantive evils that the United States constitutionally may seek to prevent." What he called "the surreptitious publishing of a silly leaflet by an unknown man" clearly did not pose
such a threat. Then, tracing an argument first made by John Stuart
Mill and more recently advanced by Chafee, Holmes penned a
stirring paean to free speech that praised the "free trade in ideas"
and declared "that the best test of truth is the power of the
thought to get itself accepted in the competition of the market"
(*Abrams v. United States,* 627, 628, 630).

INCORPORATION, THE RED SCARE, AND THE RISE OF THE SUPREME COURT AS THE PREEMINENT AUTHORITY ON FREE SPEECH RIGHTS

The First Amendment opens with the clear declaration that
"*Congress* shall make no law" (emphasis added). But if Holmes
was right—if free speech is essential to the pursuit of truth and, as
he also argued, it is experiments in life that make progress possible—could the Court really afford to take a hands-off approach to
free speech when it was threatened by state (as opposed to federal)

laws? Before the late nineteenth and early twentieth centuries, the notion that the Bill of Rights applied to federal and not state laws was not understood as a constitutional deficiency but rather as a pillar of an institutional order committed to principles of democracy and self-government. This order kept the distant federal government (including the federal courts) out of the way of the more local, self-governing states. Accordingly, under this order, speech would be protected by state legislators, whose actions would be judged by either the voters or the judges of the states, using the state bills of rights as their guides.

In the late nineteenth century, though, many began to argue that the Civil War amendments (the Thirteenth, Fourteenth, and Fifteenth) had fundamentally altered this long-standing theory (and structure) of U.S. government. The war and the war amendments, they insisted, made the national government the primary guarantor of fundamental rights, including the right to freedom of speech. To be sure, the Fourteenth Amendment said nothing about the freedom of speech per se. But it did state that "[n]o State shall make or enforce any law which shall abridge the privileges or immunities of citizens of the United States; nor shall any State deprive any person of life, liberty, or property without due process of law; nor deny to any person within its jurisdiction the equal protection of the laws." Lawyers and judges with national political agendas seized upon the command that "[n]o State shall," and they began to assert that a whole array of fundamental rights were included within the rather vague terms "privileges or immunities" and "due process of law." If provisions of the Bill of Rights were understood to be implicated by the privileges and immunities and due process clauses, after all, federal courts could enforce the Bill of Rights against the conduct of the states—a process known as the "incorporation" of the Bill of Rights. It is only once the incorporation doctrine took hold in the Court that the conduct of city police forces, local school boards, and municipal public officials—not to mention private businesses and clubs that received benefits from states—could be hauled into the federal courts for allegedly violating people's constitutional rights. By adopting the doctrine of incorporation, the Supreme Court gave itself the power it holds to the present day, the power to broadly determine the meaning of the freedom of speech.

The Supreme Court began incorporating the free speech provision of the Bill of Rights in the 1920s during the Red Scare, a wave of anticommunist and antiradical roundups, arrests, and deportations that followed fast upon the crackdown on socialists, anarchists, and pacifists during World War I. During the Red Scare, aliens like Emma Goldman were deported to Russia on one of the so-called Red Arks. Attorney General A. Mitchell Palmer launched raids against the offices of suspected radicals and used federal criminal laws to put them behind bars. (These were known as the Palmer raids.)

The First Amendment was first incorporated in a case involving just such a radical. Benjamin Gitlow, a Communist activist, was arrested for publishing a "Left Wing Manifesto" that called upon workers to violently overthrow the capitalist system. He was charged under New York's Criminal Anarchy Act (passed in the wake of the assassination in Buffalo of President McKinley). Gitlow, defended by the ACLU, asserted that his First and Fourteenth Amendment rights had been violated by his prosecution and conviction. He lost, but in a move that proved to be a harbinger of future developments, the Court held that the freedom of speech was plainly "among the fundamental personal rights and 'liberties' protected by the due process clause of the Fourteenth Amendment from impairment by the states" (*Gitlow v. New York*, 268 U.S. 652 [1925], 666). Gitlow's prosecution did not violate the First Amendment, but if it had, the Court would have protected him against the actions of the state of New York. (See also *Whitney v. California*, 274 U.S. 357 [1927]; *Fiske v. Kansas*, 274 U.S. 380 [1927]; *Gilbert v. Minnesota*, 254 U.S. 325 [1920].)

The *Gitlow* decision clearly signaled that the Court was moving toward a more activist approach to the First Amendment. It followed *Gitlow* with a series of declarations of the amendment's central importance to the U.S. system of constitutional government. By the 1930s, Justice Benjamin Cardozo had ringingly declared that the constitutional freedom of thought and speech was "the matrix, the indispensable condition, of nearly every other form of freedom" (*Palko v. Connecticut*, 302 U.S. 319 [1937], 327). A few years later, when President Franklin D. Roosevelt addressed Congress and the American people in the wake of the Japanese attack on Pearl Harbor, he placed the freedom of speech and expression at the top of the list of his "four freedoms" (joining the freedom of worship, freedom from want, and freedom from fear). These freedoms were not simply U.S. values, Roosevelt asserted, but international ones. Our national mission was to guarantee the achievement of these freedoms both at home and around the world. In this context, a world in which the regulation of speech was a matter of state politics and law became very much a thing of the past. By the late 1940s, Chafee himself had stepped up on the global stage. Chafee joined the U.N. Subcommission on Freedom of Information and the Press, where he advocated that the freedom of speech be advanced as a global human right.

Still, there was much to be done at home. Although many now saw the freedom of speech as a fundamental, court-protected right, it still was not clear what tests should be applied in determining what speech should be free of restrictions, or what the proper parameters of the freedom were. The Court would work these issues out in the context of a series of disputes arising out a broad array of new social and political disturbances.

SPEECH AND THE U.S. WORKER

One of the most influential of these new disturbances was the antagonism between management and organized labor. To a degree that is hard to imagine today (even in an age of e-mail monitoring and workplace regulations enforcing politically correct speech), in the early twentieth century, large companies worked aggressively to control the speech of their employees. In many cases, they went beyond threatening to fire people and physically assaulted them. Whereas in the past, workers had been forced to live in company towns, different forms of monitoring were developed in the twentieth century. In the 1930s, for example, Harry Bennett, the head of the Service Department in the huge Ford Motor Company plant in Flint, Michigan, routinely kept his men in line by "shaking them up in the aisles" or by roughing up any who either held or expressed pro-union views (Kennedy 1999, 309). General Motors (GM) kept a full complement of company spies and wiretappers on the payroll to keep an eye on those who might undermine the company's profitability. In 1936, a U.S. Senate report on these practices generated considerable public sympathy for the labor movement and helped build support for their political causes (Kennedy 1999, 304, 309–310). For this and many other reasons, including union activism and a keen consciousness by many of the hardships that workers were suffering during the Great Depression, the Wagner Act was passed in 1935. That law, which some have called the Declaration of Independence of American labor, guaranteed workers a federal right to organize and to pursue collective bargaining arrangements with their employers.

The Wagner Act created opportunities, but its promise was realized only after a series of dramatic confrontations. In the legendary Flint, Michigan, sit-down strike of 1937, autoworkers occupied and shut down the GM auto body assembly factory for forty-four days. It was in this context that the Supreme Court took its first step toward creating First Amendment doctrine stipulating the appropriateness of different types of regulation for different free speech settings.

The Public Forum doctrine, for instance, arose out of a series of confrontations between Frank Hague, the antiunion mayor of Jersey City, New Jersey, and the Congress of Industrial Organizations (CIO), the most aggressive and largest of the nation's mass industrial unions. A Jersey City ordinance required that any organization that wanted either to hold a meeting or to hand out literature in parks, streets, or other public places had to first get a permit from the city's director of public safety. Mayor Hague, however, made certain that these permits were routinely denied to labor unions. Arguing that such a restriction amounted to an unconstitutional prior restraint, the CIO, backed by the ACLU, won an injunction against Hague. In its opinion in the case, the Court for the first time declared that public streets, parks, and other public places are "public forums" and that as such, they are entitled to special First Amendment protection (*Hague v. CIO*, 307 U.S. 496 [1939]).

As is often the case in constitutional law, the questions resolved by this doctrinal innovation, in turn, raised new ones. For though the Court in *Hague* had made a stirring declaration that as a matter of principle, public forums were to be considered wide open, many soon realized that it could not literally be true. *Some* regulation was necessary. If some regulation was pernicious and some was legitimate, how was one to distinguish between the two? What was the test?

In a series of subsequent cases, the Court proposed a new Content Neutrality test that stipulated that public officials could not discriminate against speech simply because they did not like its message. In addition, to preserve what was good about the traditional government powers to regulate health, safety, and morals, the Court announced that governments were free to regulate speech through content-neutral time, place, and manner rules. These rules might involve, for example, creating a permit system for rallies held in public parks or on public streets. They might forbid rallies on expressways during rush hour or on residential streets in the middle of the night. At the same time, as additional cases arose, the Court declared that it was not enough for time, place, and manner regulations to *seem* constitutionally neutral while actually being directed at particular messages. The Court would void regulations that were neutral on their face but that in fact were being used as a subterfuge to restrict the content of constitutionally protected speech.

A labor case also prompted an important doctrinal innovation concerning the definition of speech itself. The First Amendment had long been held to apply to speech and not conduct. But was labor-union picketing speech or conduct? In an opinion written by Justice Frank Murphy, who had been the pro-labor governor of Michigan during the Flint sit-down strike, the Court blurred the distinction, declaring picketing, because it involved the dissemination of information and ideas, to be a form of constitutionally protected speech. Such dissemination was declared a central concern of the First Amendment (*Thornhill v. Alabama*, 310 U.S. 88 [1940]).

THE JEHOVAH'S WITNESSES AND THE DEVELOPMENT OF THE PUBLIC FORUM DOCTRINE

At the same time as these labor cases were going on, the Court was rather unexpectedly spurred to further doctrinal innovation by a series of confrontations between public authorities and a radical religious sect known as the Jehovah's Witnesses. The Witnesses believed that people would be saved through zealous proselytizing, and they considered each Witness to be an active clergyman, charged by God with the preaching of the word. The Witnesses undertook their duties at a volume and with a tenacity and ferocity rare even amongst evangelists.

For a long time, the Witnesses attracted little notice, but with the outbreak of World War II, they quickly acquired a higher profile. For the Witnesses were forbidden by their religion from saluting the U.S. flag, from joining the armed forces, and even from pitching in through alternative, nonmilitary service to the nation. Since the very future of the country and freedom in the world was at stake, these refusals to participate were no small matter. The Witnesses were quickly branded as spies and traitors. They preached in public from blaring sound trucks, stridently decrying the "false religions" of others and damning their adherents to hell, all the while defying the local police and refusing to serve their country, and they soon ran into serious trouble. Witnesses were fired from their jobs, their businesses were boycotted, and their children were expelled from public schools. They were dosed with castor oil, tarred and feathered, and set upon by angry mobs. Between 1933 and 1951, nearly 20,000 Witnesses were arrested for various offenses. Under the leadership of their lawyer Hayden Covington, however, many of the Witnesses took their cases to court, standing up for what they saw as their freedom of speech. Between 1938 and 1955, this small sect won twenty-four cases (many of them free speech cases) in the U.S. Supreme Court, exerting a profound influence on twentieth-century free speech doctrine.

In one such case, Alma Lovell, a Witness in a small Georgia town, had been convicted of violating a city ordinance requiring written permission to distribute literature of any kind on city streets. Lovell, however, believed that any requirement that she seek worldly permission to distribute her pamphlet, "Golden Age," was "an act of disobedience to His commandment." She refused to get a permit and argued that any requirement that she do so violated her First Amendment rights. The U.S. Supreme Court agreed (*Lovell v. City of Griffin*, 303 U.S. 444 [1938], 448).

In another case, a Witness named Walter Chaplinsky took his proselytizing to the streets of a small New Hampshire town, in the process antagonizing the locals. When a policeman concerned with preserving the peace asked him to move on, however, Chaplinsky called him a "fascist" and a "racketeer." Chaplinsky was arrested for violating a state law outlawing name-calling and offensive public speech. Chaplinsky asserted that the law violated his freedom of speech. In an innovative opinion dividing speech into separate categories, "protected" speech and "unprotected" speech, the Supreme Court sided with the state. The Court declared that Chaplinsky's utterances were "fighting words," a category of speech that (like obscenity and libel) was not entitled to constitutional protection. Explaining this two-tiered approach to the freedom of speech, the Court expounded upon the theories and purposes of the protection: If the purpose of the freedom of speech is the search for truth, the Court reasoned, then calling someone a "fascist" serves no useful purpose. Chaplinsky's outburst was, accordingly, unprotected (*Chaplinsky v. New Hampshire*, 315 U.S. 568 [1942]).

A parade of Witness cases spurred further refinements that were not always consistent or coherent. In one Witness case, for instance, the Court held that a blanket ban on the public use of sound amplification without a permit was unconstitutional (*Saia v. New York*, 334 U.S. 558 [1948]). The next year, however, the Court upheld the constitutionality of a similar ordinance while at the very same time paying tribute to the "preferred position of freedom of speech in a society that cherishes liberty for all" (*Kovacs v. Cooper*, 336 U.S. 77 [1949], 88).

Ironically, given the characteristic loudness of the Witnesses, the most famous Witness cases of all involved a decision by two Witness schoolchildren to sit still and remain silent. In 1940 and 1943, the Court was confronted with two cases in which Witness children refused to salute the flag or say the Pledge of Allegiance in their public-school classrooms, asserting that to do so would be to sacrilegiously worship graven images. In the first case, which was decided as Europe was being overrun by the Nazis and on the eve of the attack on Pearl Harbor, the Court held that the flag salute requirement did not violate the children's religious freedom. The Court did not reach this conclusion lightly. "A grave re-

sponsibility confronts this Court," Justice Felix Frankfurter declared, "whenever . . . it must reconcile the conflicting claims of
liberty and authority. But when the liberty invoked is liberty of
conscience, and the authority is authority to safeguard the nation's
fellowship, judicial conscience is put to its severest test." All the
same, he concluded,

> The ultimate foundation of a free society is the binding tie of cohesive
> sentiment. Such a sentiment is fostered by all those agencies of the
> mind and spirit which may serve to gather up the traditions of a peo
> ple, transmit them from generation to generation, and thereby create
> that continuity of a treasured common life which constitutes a civi
> lization. . . . The flag is a symbol of our national unity, transcending all
> internal differences, however large, within the framework of the Con
> stitution. (*Minersville v. Gobitis*, 310 U.S. 586 [1940], 591, 596)

As a legislator, he may not himself have voted for a compulsory
flag salute, Frankfurter noted. But the purpose behind the law was
both legitimate and important. As such, as a judge he would vote
to hold it constitutional.

Frankfurter's views did not prevail for long. In one of the most
swift and startling reversals in U.S. constitutionalism, the Court
repudiated its *Gobitis* decision just three years later. The problem
was that even if one agreed that Frankfurter's logic was sensible, as
many did, the actual effect of the *Gobitis* decision proved pernicious. Many who had heard about but not actually read the decision took it as an announcement by the Court that the Jehovah's
Witnesses were traitors. Witnesses were beaten by the hundreds in
the streets. Public authorities threatened to take their children
away and send them to reform schools. After several new justices
were appointed and after sustaining a withering fusillade of press
and academic criticism, the Court quickly agreed to hear a second
flag salute case.

This time around, the Court approached the questions from a
new angle, de-emphasizing religion and focusing instead on the

freedom of speech. Justice Robert Jackson now announced that by requiring the children to salute the flag and say the pledge, the state was forcing them to express views that were contrary to their convictions. To force people to speak in opposition to their conscience (whether that conscience was religiously or secularly informed) was a clear free speech issue. In his opinion in *West Virginia State Board of Education v. Barnette* (319 U.S. 624 [1943]), Jackson defended "the freedom to be intellectually and spiritually diverse." "[F]reedom to differ," he declared, "is not limited to things that do not matter much. That would be a mere shadow of freedom. The test of its substance is the right to differ as to things that touch the heart of the existing order." He concluded, "If there is any fixed star in our constitutional constellation it is that no official, high or petty, can prescribe what shall be orthodox in politics, nationalism, religion, or other matters of opinion or force citizens to confess by word or act their faith therein" (641, 642). Justice Frankfurter registered his dissent.

MONITORING THE MOVIES: THE LEGION OF DECENCY AND THE HAYS COMMISSION

In his opinions in the flag salute cases, Justice Frankfurter argued on behalf of the democratic right of elected governments to promote the public good. Although police powers laws have always been a part of our political system, the technological advances of the early twentieth century raised new questions about the relation of those laws to the new medium of moving pictures.

It was clear to many from the earliest days of the movie industry that it would soon have a profound influence on U.S. life and culture. No sooner had the first films been shot than states and cities set up local boards of censorship to police film content to protect the public morals. These boards garnered support from across the political spectrum. Conservatives worried about the unique power of movies to erode moral standards. Progressives worried that movies would promote social ills. (Women's groups were early and aggressive promoters of film censorship.) Given this consensus, constitutional challenges to these boards went nowhere. (See, for example, *Mutual Film v. Ohio*, 236 U.S. 230 [1915]).

By the 1930s, Hollywood was a major force in the national culture, and discussions of the moral effects of movies shifted from the small stage of town halls and state capitals to the grand arena of national politics. The Catholic church put the problem of immorality in movies at the center of its national political agenda. In 1930, the Legion of Decency, a group formed by prominent Catholics, including members of the clergy, sent a petition signed by 11 million U.S. Catholics to the Association of Motion Picture Producers in Hollywood stridently condemning "indecent and immoral" films. The legion petition called upon the industry to limit the depiction of on-screen sex and violence, to weed out profanity, and to promote marriage, the family, and obedience to government and the rule of law. The legion certainly agreed that films should entertain, the petition stated, but in doing so, it went on, they should not subvert community standards. The legion threatened a massive movie boycott by Catholics if its calls for higher standards went unheeded.

Under the leadership of Will Hays, the Motion Picture Producers and Distributors of America decided to sign on to the Legion's program, creating the Hays Code, which called on filmmakers to uphold moral standards and encourage respect for authority and law. A lay Catholic, Joseph Breen, was put in charge of an office administering the code. From then on, no film that failed to meet the code's standards could be shown at any major theater in the country. The legion itself rated every new film and distributed the ratings to the country's Catholic churches. Catholics were told not to see any film that did not meet Legion standards.

The Hays Code shaped the movie industry until the 1960s. It was then swept away in a tide of personal and sexual liberation, and the core of the current movie ratings system was created, classifying films by content. (The new system was aimed less at protecting public morals than at protecting the sensibilities of children.) (See also *Burstyn v. Wilson*, 343 U.S. 495 [1952].) In the 1960s, this new system was denounced as an oppressive form of censorship, but once it became apparent that the system had little effect on the making and distribution of films, such voices died out. Today, even the age limits are rarely enforced.

Nevertheless, it would be wrong to say that since the 1960s, movies are open to all ideas and all points of view. Current films reflect the culture and the politics of Hollywood actors and directors. That community, for example, rarely casts religion in a positive light. And there is a strong movement afoot in Hollywood to ban all depictions of smoking from the silver screen. The efforts of Hollywood to censor such "corrupting" influences echoes similar efforts by progressives in the earliest years of the twentieth century.

WELCOMING SEXUAL SPEECH

When it comes to preserving public morality, few subjects have proved more enduring than sex. Since at least the late nineteenth century, there have been those who, whether for political, personal, or artistic reasons, have deliberately pushed cultural boundaries of the acceptable in sex-related speech. Only in the mid–twentieth century, however, did the Supreme Court take up in a sustained way the issue of sex-related speech, in the process creating a complicated skein of First Amendment doctrine.

In the 1960s and 1970s, for the first time in its history, the Court decided to hear a large number of cases concerning pornography. This led to some strange scenes within the "marble palace" of the U.S. Supreme Court. To judge the constitutionality of pornographic speech, the justices spent a considerable amount of time screening pornographic films, in the process devising a series of highly-specific—and unmentionable—tests to better distinguish "indecency" from "obscenity" and "hard-core" from "soft-core" pornography. (According to Court-created doctrinal tests, obscenity and hard-core pornography were not constitutionally protected speech, whereas indecency and soft-core pornography were). To make matters worse, Justice John Marshall Harlan, who was nearly blind at the time, was forced to ask his law clerks to narrate for him what exactly was going on up on the screen. The 1960s had arrived at the Supreme Court (Woodward and Armstrong 1979).

Why the proliferation of sex cases? It is impossible to say for sure, but a number of social forces seemed to conspire to create a climate of radical cultural change. As women began to work in increasing numbers outside the home during the war, they achieved a new level of economic independence, which brought with it new sexual freedoms. The invention of the birth control pill in the early 1960s radically enhanced this trend, as did the coming of age of the youth population boom. Although men were the prime consumers of pornography, the willingness of women to have sex outside of marriage played a large part in their liberation. By the 1960s, the whole culture had become broadly sexualized. Moreover, at about this time, a therapeutic ethos emerged in the broader culture. This ethos convinced many that what had once been understood to be private and embarrassing subjects were actually healthy routes to self-expression and personal fulfillment. If we add to these trends the new interest by twentieth-century law professors and judges in all matters involving freedom of speech, and the incentives created by early signals from the Court that it would be broadly protective of sexual speech, we can appreciate how this particular turn in constitutional history came to pass.

Sex-related speech was one area of constitutional law (like "fighting words") where content-based regulation had long been permissible. Because of the pernicious effects of obscene speech on the public morals, it was and is permissible to ban it. What began to change, though, was the scope of the meaning of "obscenity." Beginning in the 1920s and 1930s, in response to legal arguments advanced on behalf of writers and New York bohemians, courts had begun to protect artistic depictions of sexual matters in novels by Theodore Dreiser, James Joyce, and D. H. Lawrence. Only in *Roth v. United States* (354 U.S. 476 [1957]), however, did the Court begin to systematically build on this base and construct the modern constitutional law of obscenity. *Roth*, in fact, launched the free speech career of Justice William J. Brennan, Jr., the modern Court's greatest champion of an expansive conception of the freedom of speech.

The case involved the federal prosecution of the publisher of a quarterly erotic magazine called *American Aphrodite*, which was comprised of nude pictures and dirty stories. The magazine's publisher was prosecuted for sending "obscene, lewd, lascivious, or filthy" materials through the mail. In his opinion in *Roth*, Brennan announced that all ideas with "even the slightest redeeming social importance" are constitutionally protected speech. What distinguishes obscene speech from constitutionally protected speech, however, is that obscene speech is devoid of ideas, and hence is "utterly without redeeming social importance." Sex and obscenity are not synonymous. So the question becomes how one is to tell when speech is obscene. Brennan proposed a test asking "whether to the average person applying contemporary community standards, the dominant theme of the material taken as a whole appeals to the prurient interest" (484, 489). In applying the test to the facts of *Roth*, Brennan determined that the law under which Roth was prosecuted was constitutional. As such, the conviction would stand.

As often happens in constitutional law, the actual decision in a case (in this case upholding the *Roth* conviction) was less important than the signals the decision sent. (We also saw this dynamic in the *Schenck* and *Abrams* decisions.) Here, the Court clearly evinced an inclination to be more protective of sexual speech than it had been at any time in history, and not surprisingly, the Court was soon flooded with sex cases. Before long, Justice William O. Douglas was arguing that even obscenity itself should be considered constitutionally protected speech: "What shocks me," he declared, "may be sustenance for my neighbor" (*Miller v. California*, 413 U.S. 15 [1973], 40–41).

The questions proliferated. Is *this* obscene? What about *that*? Is this picture (or magazine, or book) utterly without redeeming social value, or not? Does this sexual speech express an idea? Or is it "utterly devoid" of ideas? Is nude dancing a form of expression that conveys an idea? Is it broadly regulable conduct, or is it constitutionally protected speech? If it is regulable, is the regulation reasonable, or does it go too far? Is the regulation (such as a zoning law for X-rated theaters) "content-neutral" or "content-based"? If the latter, is it per se constitutionally impermissible, or not? Following its *Roth* decision, the Court set off down the long and bewildering road to devising an elaborate system of tests to try to resolve these issues.

To trace the twists and turns of constitutional doctrine in this area would be an arduous task (though the underlying facts of the cases might prove stimulating). It is notable, though, that as the Court tried, applied, and discarded various tests for sexual speech over the course of the 1960s, many Americans came to blame the Court's willingness to wade into the issue for being partly responsible for the coarsening and sexualization of the broader culture. A strong popular backlash developed against the liberal Warren Court (1953–1969), and Republican presidential candidate Richard Nixon made a crusade against "smut" a pillar of his successful campaign for the White House. At the same time, state and local governments began passing new antipornography laws.

By the time Nixon got to appoint his own justices to the Supreme Court, attitudes toward sexual speech were swinging in a new direction. In *Miller v. California*, Chief Justice Warren Burger, a Nixon appointee, penned an opinion that accorded states and local governments more breathing room for their antismut initiatives. In *Miller,* which involved the mass mailing of a sexually explicit flyer advertising adult films and books, the Court set out the new, more restriction-friendly *Miller* test to assess the constitutionality of regulations on sexual speech. Henceforth, the Court would ask (1) "whether 'the average person, applying contemporary community standards' would find that the work, taken as a whole, appeals to the prurient interest"; (2) "whether the work depicts or describes, in a patently offensive way, sexual conduct specifically defined by the applicable state law"; and (3) "whether the work, taken as a whole, lacks serious literary, artistic, political, or scientific value" (24).

The Nixon-era antismut initiatives also influenced First Amendment doctrine in other areas. Cases involving the zoning of X-rated theaters pushed the Court to refine its doctrine concerning various time, place, and manner regulations. During the same term that he penned the *Miller* opinion, Justice Burger also wrote for the Court in *Paris Adult Theatre* that the Court should recognize "legitimate state interests . . . in stemming the tide of commercialized obscenity," in "the quality of life," and in protecting "the total community environment" (*Paris Adult Theatre I v. Slaton,* 413 U.S. 39 [1973], 57, 58). This ruling was applied to a series of zoning ordinances directed at X-rated theaters throughout the 1970s and 1980s. (See, in addition to *Paris Adult Theatre, Young v. American Mini Theatres,* 327 U.S. 50 [1976]; *City of Renton v. Playtime Theatres, Inc.* 475 U.S. 41 [1986]).

THE THREAT AND FEAR OF COMMUNISM

Throughout the twentieth century, Communist ideology, which derives from the works of the German philosopher Karl Marx and promises a radical equality and an end to exploitation and oppression, has had a strong appeal to artists, writers, intellectuals, and more recently, to college professors. Transfixed by the idealism of the Communist vision, many among this group have overlooked or minimized the brutality that has always accompanied the transformation of Communist ideology into concrete political reality, supporting, over the course of the century, Vladimir Ilich Lenin, Joseph Stalin, Mao Tse-tung, Pol Pot, Ho Chi Minh, and (today) Fidel Castro. But Lenin, Stalin, Mao, and Pol Pot form the greatest group of mass murderers in human history, and the lure of idealism and of the end of oppression seduced many twentieth-century progressives and intellectuals into bed with evil on an almost unimaginable scale.

Because those progressives and intellectuals write most of our histories, teach most of our students, and for many years, dominated the publishing industry, *anticommunism* has often been cast as one of the chief enemies of human freedom (Warshow 1953a). Two episodes, the Red Scare of the 1920s and the McCarthy era of the 1950s, are presented as being among the darkest days of U.S. history. The short career of Wisconsin Republican Senator Joseph McCarthy, a reckless Communist hunter who, between 1950 and 1954, sought to root subversives out of government (and who in many cases reprehensibly failed to distinguish between the guilty and the innocent), has thrown a long shadow over the way many people have thought about the relationship between liberty and security in the twentieth century and has diverted attention from the real dangers to human liberty—proven by the evidence uncovered since the opening of the archives of the Soviet secret police and the declassification of U.S. government documents— posed by the rise of totalitarianism, the postwar Soviet expansionism, and the accompanying complicity of the Communist Party of the United States of America (CPUSA) in plans to aid the nation's enemies and to overthrow the U.S. government (Haynes and Klehr 1999; Klehr, Haynes, and Firsov 1995; Klehr, Haynes, and Anderson 1998).

Even so, government concerns about communism predated the relatively brief McCarthy era, as did progressive resistance to government efforts to address those concerns. As we have seen, early-twentieth-century bohemia romanticized communism and the Russian Revolution, and, just as they had with anarchism and sex talk, the New York bohemians came to identify Communist speech with the cause of human liberation itself.

Recent historical revelations have proved, however, that when it came to communism, self-preservation and public safety were very much at stake. The degree to which the law protects the expression of revolutionary views is far from clear: There had always been a balance struck between the aspiration to liberty and the imperatives of security, for, after all, without stability and order, freedom itself is impossible. New laws have thus always been passed to meet new threats. In 1930, the U.S. House of Representatives created the House Special Committee to Investigate Communist Activities. In the wake of this committee's lapse, the House created the MacCormack Committee (1935), aimed at fighting those who would undermine the effectiveness of the nation's military defenses by encouraging the disaffection of its soldiers. Congress created a permanent House Un-American Activities Committee (HUAC) in 1938, which would last for thirty-eight years. HUAC launched public investigations of Communist influence in government, the movies, and labor organizations. Its efforts were stridently opposed by the ACLU and other civil libertarians, who argued that they represented direct assaults on the freedom of speech.

The U.S. government took other initiatives at this time, one of the most dangerous periods in world history. Shortly after Adolph Hitler took over Austria, the U.S. Congress passed the Smith Act (or the Alien Registration Act [54 Stat. 670 [1940]]), which declared it illegal to "advocate, abet, advise, or teach the duty, necessity, desirability, or propriety of overthrowing or destroying any government in the United States by force or violence." The act also barred individuals from joining any organization or from publishing or distributing any material advocating the overthrow of the government. State laws supplemented federal initiatives. Nearly half passed laws requiring public school and university teachers to take loyalty oaths in which they pledged to obey the laws and uphold the Constitution. Some supplemented the oath with a requirement that teachers swear they were not members of groups that advocated the overthrow of the government.

The ACLU opposed these laws, branding them violations of the freedom of speech, and this position was hardly without foundation. In many cases, staunch anticommunists did not distinguish between groups advocating revolution and groups that were simply critical of the government. Civil libertarians, though, also failed to draw critical distinctions, indignantly defending all groups regardless of whether they were truly revolutionary or not. They stood behind a general principle of "academic freedom," or the right of teachers to think, speak, and write what they please, no matter how radical or revolutionary. When local school boards and state legislators initiated investigations to weed Communist teachers out of the system, civil libertarians cried foul. When Communist college professors—or those who were suspected of harboring subversive views—were scrutinized by university presidents, boards of trustees, and the press, civil libertarians cried witch-hunt.

The situation became especially tense in the immediate aftermath of World War II, when the Soviet Union invaded Eastern Europe and imposed totalitarian police states in countries like Poland, Czechoslovakia, and East Germany. During the war, on instructions from Stalin, the CPUSA hewed to a pro-American, patriotic line, since the two nations were allies in the fight against Hitler (this was the Popular Front period). Once the war was over, however, Stalin told the party to drop this line and to once again work for the overthrow of the U.S. government. They began to do so, and as the Soviets announced their acquisition of nuclear weapons, the tensions between the U.S. government and the CPUSA escalated radically. Communist spies with access to high-level government secrets, such as Julius and Ethel Rosenberg and Alger Hiss, were unmasked and prosecuted. Most liberals denied their guilt (which has since been proved by historians) and charged that virtually all forms of anticommunism amounted to a witch-hunt against people who had dared to fight for progressive causes and to voice dissenting views.

It was in this context in the 1950s that HUAC hearings heated up. Some of what took place was wrong. People brought before the committee and accused of being Communists often were not given the opportunity to present evidence in their own defense or to cross-examine their accusers. Moreover, many were caught in HUAC's net because they were affiliated with Communist front organizations directed at worthy causes, such as the legal defense of wrongly accused southern blacks. Many of these people did not know that for propaganda purposes Moscow was bankrolling social justice efforts in the United States. Looking for hard evidence of suspected Communist ties, HUAC launched raids on left-wing groups. In the process, they put many progressives in the mind of the hated Palmer Raids of the 1920s.

There is no denying that the 1950s crackdown was serious. In the McCarran Act of 1950 (the Internal Security Act), the government required that all Communist organizations register with the Subversive Activities Control Board and provide that board with full information on their leadership, finances, and membership. Authorities stamped the mail of registered groups with the label "Communist Organization," and members were ineligible for passports. (This part of the law was later overturned by the Supreme Court, which announced a fundamental right to travel; *Kent v. Dulles,* 357 U.S. 116 [1958].) The McCarran-Walter Immigration Act of 1948 had given the government broad authority to exclude visitors to the United States who held dangerous political views. And the Communist Control Act of 1954 outlawed the CPUSA. These laws were enforced in some high-profile instances. But in many cases they were resisted, most prominently by the

CPUSA itself, which refused either to register or hand over its membership lists.

Needless to say, these struggles over domestic communism brought many First Amendment cases to the Supreme Court. Perhaps the most famous of all was Dennis v. United States (341 U.S. 494 [1951]), which involved the Smith Act indictment at the height of the Korean War of Eugene Dennis and other CPUSA leaders. In the federal appeals court opinion in Dennis, Judge Learned Hand (who had earlier written the opinion in Masses Publishing Co. v. Patten) proposed a refinement of the Clear and Present Danger test that would give legal weight to the political context in which the challenged speech was uttered. Hand declared that in First Amendment cases involving incendiary political speech, the question for the Court should be "whether the gravity of the 'evil,' discounted by its improbability, justifies such invasion of free speech as is necessary to avoid the danger" (United States v. Dennis, 183 F.2d 201 [1950], 212). Hand's court held that Dennis and the CPUSA leaders had violated the Smith Act by advocating the overthrow of the U.S. government and that given Communist expansionism around the world, understood in the context of a hot and a Cold War, one could not imagine "a more probable danger, unless one must wait till the actual eve of hostilities" (213).

Hand's decision was upheld by the Supreme Court in a fractured opinion in which the justices set out an array of First Amendment arguments. Adopting Hand's test as the constitutional standard, Chief Justice Fred Vinson declared that the evidence clearly demonstrated that the CPUSA leaders "were unwilling to work within our framework of democracy, but intended to initiate a violent revolution whenever the propitious occasion appeared. . . . We reject any principle of governmental helplessness," Vinson declared, "in the face of preparation for revolution." Here, he concluded, the threat of the overthrow of the U.S. government was real, and as such, it was completely constitutional for the government act vigorously to avert that danger. "Speech," the Court concluded authoritatively, "is not an absolute" (497, 501, 508).

Other justices, however, approached the question differently. Justice Felix Frankfurter, a Roosevelt appointee, voted with Vinson but emphasized his trust in the people's elected representatives in Congress. "The demands of free speech in a democratic society as well as the interest in national security," Frankfurter wrote, "are better served by candid and informed weighing of the competing interests [than by] dogmas" (524). Frankfurter asserted that Congress, and not unelected judges, were the officials best suited to bring about this balance. Justice Robert Jackson, another Roosevelt appointee, joined Frankfurter and Vinson to uphold Dennis's conviction, but Jackson emphasized the depth and menace of the Communist conspiracy. "The Constitution," Jackson wrote, "does not make conspiracy a civil right" (572).

Justices Hugo Black and William O. Douglas, also Roosevelt appointees, dissented, advancing a highly latitudinarian understanding of free speech. (Their approach would later ripen into what became known as "free speech absolutism.") For his part, Black claimed that the distinction between speech and action was relevant here: The CPUSA leaders, Black noted, "were not charged with an attempt to overthrow the government. They were not charged with overt acts of any kind designed to overthrow the government. . . . The indictment is that they conspired to organize the Communist Party and to use speech or newspapers and other publications in the future to teach and advocate the forcible overthrow of the Government" (579). The Clear and Present Danger test, they argued, should be the benchmark, and, they further argued, there was no such danger in the *Dennis* case. Black added, moreover, that the First Amendment had a special constitutional status. It occupied a "preferred position" among the provisions of our Constitution. "I have always believed," he wrote, "that the First Amendment is the keystone of our Government" (580).

Following Stalin's death in 1953 and Soviet Premier Nikita Khrushchev's 1956 speech acknowledging and stridently denouncing Stalin's crimes, the liberal Warren Court began evincing greater skepticism toward domestic security initiatives targeting Communists. The most celebrated sign of the Court's change of heart took place on Red Monday (June 17, 1957), when the Court simultaneously overturned the contempt of Congress conviction of a man who had refused to answer HUAC's questions, reversed the Smith Act convictions of prominent CPUSA leaders, limited the ability of states to investigate the political allegiances of state university professors, and vitiated the dismissal of an official the government deemed to be a security risk. These decisions angered many in Congress, who threatened to curb the Court by reigning in its power to hear domestic security cases. In response, the Court issued a series of rulings that seemed to retreat somewhat from the Red Monday decisions. By the mid-1960s, though, the Court's broader free speech initiatives concerning sex and civil rights flowed into the continued stream of Communist speech cases, and the Court finally came to settle on a consistently protective attitude toward all types of radical political speech. (See *Watkins v. United States*, 354 U.S. 178 [1957]; *Sweezy v. New Hampshire* 354 U.S. 234 [1957]; *Service v. Dulles* 354 U.S. 363 [1957]; *Yates v. United States* 354 U.S. 298 [1957].)

THE SOCIAL MOVEMENTS OF THE 1950S AND 1960S

One of the chief engines behind the Court's increasing acceptance of destabilizing and dangerous speech was the cresting moral authority of the civil rights movement. As we have seen, free speech had been a major issue for white abolitionists in the nineteenth century. But no sooner had the slaves been freed than black voices were once again silenced by the end of Reconstruction and the rise of the Jim Crow South. In the early twentieth century, though, conditions altered, and change suddenly seemed possible. The labor shortage in northern factories stimulated by World War I was crucial: It launched the Great Migration of southern blacks to northern cities, where they formed vibrant urban cultures, earned good wages, and voted. As an explicitly antiracist war, World War II, in turn, led to a revolution in public morals. Racism could no longer nestle easily for so many white Americans as an accepted part of "our traditions." Racism had suddenly become un-American. What is more, the outbreak of the Cold War made the country's mistreatment of blacks a liability in the global propaganda war for the hearts and minds of the (nonwhite) Third World.

Blacks themselves, of course, sensed this altered environment and heroically seized its opportunities. By the 1940s, black labor leader A. Philip Randolph was building a March on Washington Movement, which Randolph claimed would bring 10,000 Negroes to the nation's capital to march down Pennsylvania Avenue and protest race discrimination in the United States. Randolph demanded that blacks be able to serve as the equal of whites in the country's defense industries and in its military during wartime. (Randolph's march was canceled when President Roosevelt agreed to issue an executive order banning discrimination in the defense industry and creating the Fair Employment Practices Commission.) At the same time, Charles Hamilton Houston, Thurgood Marshall, and the other lawyers at the National Association for the Advancement of Colored People (NAACP) Legal Defense and Education Fund launched a legal campaign against racial discrimination. And soon, in one of the most momentous movements in U.S. history, a young preacher from Atlanta, the Reverend Martin Luther King Jr., took a campaign of civil disobedience to the streets of the Deep South.

In 1955, King initiated the Montgomery (Alabama) bus boycott to protest the city's segregated public transportation system. He followed the boycott with a series of nonviolent protest marches,

which met with violent, sometimes murderous, resistance. Inter-
racial groups of Freedom Riders protested segregation on interstate bus lines by attempting to board those buses and ride them
side by side. In response, they were attacked and beaten. Vicious
dogs and fire hoses were used against peaceful protest marchers.
As the nation watched on live television, civil rights activists attempting to march from Selma, Alabama, to the state capital in
Montgomery to demand the right to vote were beaten on Selma's
Edmund Pettus bridge.

In the bloody decade between 1955 and 1965, blacks protested
their subordination in a variety of ways, many of which involved
what came to be known as "speech plus," or the conveying of a
message through either conduct or the display of symbols (which
were contrasted to "pure speech," or solely verbal expression).
Movement activists staged sit-ins, for example, in the early 1960s
in which they entered "whites only" lunchrooms en masse, sat
down at the counter, and refused to leave until they were served.
Local officials prosecuted them for these sit-ins on charges of disturbing the peace, trespassing, loitering, and failing to obey a police officer's orders. By the early 1960s, though, the Supreme
Court was overturning these convictions in large numbers. Although the Court did not base its decisions in sit-in cases on free
speech, those decisions nonetheless represented clear victories for
the principle that the Constitution protected acts and actions intended to convey an idea or message. (See *Garner v. Louisiana*,
368 U.S. 157 [1961]; *Peterson v. City of Greenville*, 373 U.S. 244
[1963]; *Lombard v. Louisiana*, 373 U.S. 267 [1963].)

When it came to marching itself (a tactic the civil rights movement borrowed from the labor movement before it), the prosecutions raised free speech issues directly. In one case involving the
convictions of nearly two hundred civil rights picketers for disturbing the peace by marching with signs on the grounds of the
South Carolina statehouse, the U.S. Supreme Court, citing the
march's peaceful nature, rejected the state's assertion that the

protesters were uttering "fighting words" likely to provoke violence by segregation proponents. The Court overturned the convictions (*Edwards v. South Carolina*, 372 U.S. 229 [1963]). Similarly, when black students in Baton Rouge, Louisiana, staged pickets outside the city's segregated lunch counters and were arrested and jailed in a local courthouse, a peaceful protest group of about 2,000 people gathered outside, holding signs with civil rights messages and singing "God Bless America" and "We Shall Overcome." A counterprotest of several hundred whites massed on the other side of the street, with the Baton Rouge police between them. The minister leading the march then delivered a rousing speech calling the arrests illegal and advocating the boycott of the city's racially discriminatory businesses. The police called these remarks inflammatory and told the marchers to leave. When they refused to do so, they were arrested. The Supreme Court overturned the marchers' convictions, declaring that they had a First Amendment right to engage in a peaceful political protest in a public place (*Cox v. Louisiana*, 379 U.S. 536 [1965]).

In these decisions, the Court both expanded the constitutional protections afforded political protesters and refined its doctrine concerning "vagueness" and "overbreadth." These doctrines hold that it is unconstitutional to have a law on the books that is either so vague and unclear that one cannot determine whether one is violating it or so broad as to ban both unprotected and protected speech. The Court found that both the South Carolina and Louisiana protest cases involved clear instances of unconstitutional vagueness and overbreadth. (See also *Shuttlesworth v. Birmingham*, 394 U.S. 147 [1969]). At the same time, however, the Court never retreated from its position that reasonable time, place, and manner restrictions on speech—including morally compelling protest marches—were constitutionally legitimate. If a court issued a temporary injunction against a mass protest, even in a civil rights case and even if the ban seemed likely to eventually be overturned, that injunction still had to be obeyed. The doctrinal framework of free speech law as it had been worked out earlier in the century would stand (*Walker v. City of Birmingham*, 388 U.S. 307 [1967]).

One genuine revolution in free speech doctrine, however, was at hand, and that concerned the law of libel. In *New York Times v. Sullivan* (376 U.S. 254 [1964]), the Court announced for the first time that the press had a broad right to publish material critical of public officials, even if that criticism turned out to have been mistaken. The *Sullivan* case centered on an ad placed in the *New York Times* by four black Alabama ministers and headlined "Heed Their Rising Voices." The ad chronicled the civil rights struggles in the South and appealed to readers for donations. It contained factual errors: It stated that student civil rights protesters in Montgomery had sung "My Country 'Tis of Thee" on the statehouse steps when in fact they had sung the "Star Spangled Banner." It stated that the students had been expelled from school for leading the protest when in fact they had been expelled for leading a lunch-counter sit-in at the Montgomery County Court House on a different day. And it stated that the entire student body of the black Alabama State College had protested the students' expulsion when in fact only a majority of the college's students had protested. L. B. Sullivan, a Montgomery city official, sued both the paper and the ministers for libel.

Libel, of course, had long been considered a category of unprotected speech. Truth was a defense in libel actions. But the ad that triggered *Sullivan* contained plain (and admitted) falsehoods. These falsehoods, which led to a legal presumption of malice against the plaintiff, drove the lower court to award Sullivan $500,000 in damages from the paper and from each of the clergymen. This huge award was wildly out of proportion to any actual damage done to the city official (if indeed there had been any), and it spurred the Court, which supported the civil rights movement, to strike back. In one of the broadest declarations on behalf of free speech in U.S. history, the author of the *Sullivan* decision, Justice

William J. Brennan, declared that the law of libel "must be measured by standards that satisfy the First Amendment," which arose out of "a profound national commitment to the principle that debate on public issues should be uninhibited, robust, and wide-open." He further argued that debate properly "include[s] vehement, caustic, and sometimes unpleasantly sharp attacks on government and public officials." But what of the precedents, such as the Sedition Act of 1798, suggesting that it was indeed constitutional to prosecute people for such attacks? Brennan announced that the constitutionality of the Sedition Act prosecutions had been overturned "in the court of history" (270). So far as public debate was concerned, even false statements must be protected "if the freedoms of expression are to have the 'breathing space' that they 'need . . . to survive'" (271). To hold otherwise, he concluded, would lead to "self-censorship" and a chilling of the broad-ranging freedoms essential to a vibrant democratic polity (276). Did this mean one could now say whatever one wanted about public officials, no matter how false? No, Brennan wrote. Public officials could sue for defamation if they could prove what he called "actual malice," namely, "that the statement was made with . . . knowledge that it was false or with reckless disregard of whether it was false or not" (280).

The *Sullivan* decision did more than change the law of libel: It fundamentally transformed the entire orientation of the courts toward free speech. Formerly, speech had been separated into fairly sharp categories of protected and unprotected speech (such as "fighting words," libel, and obscenity). After *Sullivan,* the Court began compromising its categorical approach with "policy" analysis. Courts began to look at each unique situation and ask what concrete effects a pro-speech ruling would have on openness, both in that area and in the wider culture. This "policy of openness" approach was applied not just to political but also to artistic and commercial speech. Thus, after *Sullivan* it became much harder to defend restrictions on speech against constitutional challenges in all sorts of areas. Indeed, free speech as we know it today is really not much older than the 1964 *Sullivan* opinion itself.

As these developments suggest, it is hard to overestimate the influence of the civil rights movement on the course of U.S. law. Some of these effects were less direct than the *Sullivan* ruling. The student and antiwar movements of the 1960s, which changed the law of free speech, were themselves direct outgrowths of the struggle for civil rights. Many of the participants in these movements were young veterans of civil rights movement initiatives like Freedom Summer (1964), which brought northern college students to the South over their summer vacation to register black voters and to agitate for civil rights. Before being sent to the front lines in Mississippi and Alabama, these students were trained in the principles and tactics of nonviolent protest. As they moved from training to action, the gravity of the commitment they had made became clear. Many were spit on and severely beaten by southerners fighting to save the old order. Some of those students were killed.

In the fall, the survivors returned to their classes in the North. And they did so as very different people. They were now seasoned activists—and moral heroes. Moreover, whatever reflexive respect they may have had for their seniors and for people in power had been shattered forever. Young though they were, they knew what was right, and they were willing to fight for it.

The free speech movement at the University of California–Berkeley began immediately following Freedom Summer. At the start of the fall semester, a group of students set up tables on the sidewalk in front of the campus's main gate and distributed political literature to passers-by. University officials (for reasons that remain unclear) ordered them to clear the sidewalks. Whatever the real reasons behind this order, many on campus thought it had been instigated by right-wingers complaining that the tables were distributing literature agitating for civil rights.

A number of students decided to defy the university. On October 1, 1964, a civil rights activist, graduate student Jack Weinberg (who would later utter one of the most famous pronouncements of the 1960s: "You can't trust anyone over thirty") was arrested by the campus police. As he was being hauled away, the squad car in which he was seated was surrounded by thousands of angry students and stopped in its tracks. Chanting and yelling students held the police car hostage throughout the night. Another graduate student, Mario Savio, a Freedom Summer veteran, mounted the roof of the car and made a fiery speech denouncing university officials. The Berkeley free speech movement had begun.

Savio negotiated for Weinberg's release and drew up a list of demands. When these were not met, he initiated a series of mass rallies and a takeover of Sproul Hall, the Berkeley administration building. The campus had been effectively shut down. Savio's attack on Berkeley's powers-that-be was wide-ranging. (He famously attacked university president Clark Kerr's vision of the university as a machine and the students as its raw materials.) But Savio took free speech to be at the heart of his claims. As he explained,

Last summer I went to Mississippi to join the struggle there for civil rights. This fall I am engaged in another phase of the same struggle, this time in Berkeley. The two battlefields may seem quite different to some observers, but this is not the case. The same rights are at stake in both places—the right to participate as citizens in democratic society and the right to due process of law. Further, it is a struggle against the same enemy. In Mississippi an autocratic and powerful minority rules, through organized violence, to suppress the vast, virtually powerless majority. In California, the privileged minority manipulates the University bureaucracy to suppress the student's political expression. That "respectable" bureaucracy masks the financial plutocrats; that impersonal bureaucracy is the efficient enemy in a "Brave New World." (Quoted in McAdam 1988, 169)

By the late 1960s, with the Vietnam War at its height and the draft in full force, student protests proliferated. Among students, most of the major forces spurring innovation in free speech coincided: sexual liberation, the civil rights movement, and (now) the antiwar movement. The cultural and legal effects of this confluence were profound. By the late 1960s, the authority of the argument that one should be able to say whatever one liked had reached its highest point in U.S. history. Pointed, critical, and often raucous speech laying siege to those in authority—whether in the government, in churches, in secondary schools, in the home, or in colleges and universities—became a signature of the era. Many people now interpreted stirring up trouble, making unpopular arguments, shocking the complacent, and fomenting disorder as acts of courage and as engines of progress against racism, militarism, imperialism, repression, oppression, and injustice.

It was in this context that many people came to prefer the phrase "freedom of expression" to the phrase "freedom of speech." "Speech," they thought, was too limiting. "Expression," after all, encompassed not just the spoken word but also conduct that conveyed both ideas and emotions. In 1969, the Court held that an Iowa junior high school interested in preserving discipline could not forbid its students from wearing black armbands to protest the Vietnam War. The Court held that this action by the students was a "symbolic act . . . closely akin to 'pure speech.'" It thus was entitled to full constitutional protection (*Tinker v. Des Moines,* 393 U.S. 503 [1969], 505).

The new mood was transformed by the Court into a matter of principle and was applied by the Court in a wide variety of areas, including those outside the range of the justices' political sympathies. In the same year as the school armband case, for instance, the Court unanimously upheld the rights of Klansmen to burn a cross and to give a speech declaring that white people may need to take revenge if the U.S. government continues "to suppress the white, Caucasian race" (*Brandenburg v. Ohio,* 395 U.S. 444 [1969], 446). In the process, the Court buried the old Clear and

Present Danger test for political speech advocating illegal action and announced that such speech must be adjudged according to the Incitement test: It could be punished only if "such advocacy is directed to inciting or producing imminent lawless action and is likely to incite or produce such action" (447). At about this same time, rights to express profanity, blasphemy, and dirty talk were also extended. In *Cohen v. California* (403 U.S. 15 [1971]), the Court declared that dirty words were not obscene and constituted a form of constitutionally protected speech. Antiwar protester Paul Robert Cohen, the Court decided, had a First Amendment right to appear in the Los Angeles County Municipal Court building wearing a jacket emblazoned with the words "Fuck the draft."

LATE-CENTURY PROGRESSIVE ATTACKS ON FREE SPEECH

By the end of the 1960s, it seemed to many as if, in one extended paroxysm, the constitutional promise of the freedom of speech had at last been realized and that saying anything one felt like saying (which many took to be the essence of this promise) would be the new order for the ages. A closer look, however, reveals that the laws of history had not been repealed by the social movements of the 1960s and supplementary feminist and gay rights movements of the 1970s. For no sooner did 1960s progressives achieve political power (particularly in colleges and universities) than they began to wield power to silence speech they considered hazardous to the public health, safety, and morals.

Progressive arguments against free speech were not invented in the campus political correctness fights of the 1990s, when university professors and administrators moved aggressively, through codes against sexual harassment and hate speech, to ban and punish sexist and racist speech (with those categories broadly defined). Progressive attacks on free speech were an important part of the spirit of the 1960s. In his essay "Repressive Tolerance" (1965), Marxist professor Herbert Marcuse, an intellectual hero of the student movement, launched a vigorous attack on the freedom of speech. He asserted that free speech doctrine's supposed tolerance of diverse viewpoints was a sham. This tolerance, Marcuse argued, had always been selective. If one looks at history, one will see that the powers-that-be only tolerate speech that advances their own interests. Under these conditions, the widespread belief that the United States is a tolerant nation that values free speech serves as an instrument not of liberation but of oppression: It is an ideological opiate that blinds people to the ways their freedom is being crushed by power. Through their belief in toleration, people are repressed, "manipulated and indoctrinated," and they learn to love their intellectual slavery. The only way out of this, Marcuse continued, is to jettison belief in toleration and attack and neutralize the powers-that-be. He advocated "the withdrawal of toleration of speech and assembly from groups and movements which promote aggressive policies, armament, chauvinism, discrimination on the grounds of race and religion, or which oppose the extension of public services, social security, medical care, etc." In short, he advocated silencing people who stood in the way of the progress of the political left (Marcuse 1965, 100).

As the children of the 1960s rose to power as professors themselves, they moved to enact Marcuse's vision on campuses. The intellectual heirs of the New Left, now professors of the humanities, social sciences, and law, pushed their universities to enact speech and sexual harassment codes that attempted to stamp out speech and expression that they declared oppressed the powerless: women, blacks, gays and lesbians, and other minority groups. In other words, they moved to ban "words that wound" (Matsuda, Lawrence, Delgado, and Crenshaw 1993). To permit students to say things like "It's better for society for women to be homemakers rather than out in the working world" (an example of sexual harassment language listed in many university codes), they argue, is to reinforce society's prevailing power relations. To ban such speech, on the other hand, is to help liberate women from that oppression. The heirs of the New Left want to look at such speech the same way earlier eras looked at "fighting words": as unprotected speech that ought to be restricted.

In these arguments, progressives married Marxist political theory to a push for the revival of the free speech doctrine concerning "fighting words" and "group libel" (a doctrine prohibiting the defamation of a race or class of people), which had held sway on the Supreme Court in the 1940s and 1950s (*Chaplinsky v. New Hampshire; Beauharnais v. Illinois,* 343 U.S. 250 [1952]). The courts and a handful of dissident civil libertarian progressives have fought this effort on certain fronts, though they have encouraged it on others (particularly that involving allegedly sexist speech). The First Amendment, however, constrains public institutions but not private ones. By the end of the 1990s, elaborate systems of speech regulation were in place in many, perhaps most, of the nation's private colleges and universities.

DOCTRINE AND ISSUES AT CENTURY'S END

Political correctness has been one of the most prominent free speech issues of the late twentieth century. But as we enter the twenty-first, other issues now join it on the political agenda, including a new, post–September 11 sense of menace concerning radical political speech, the link between free speech and government largesse, the invention and ascendancy of such new technologies as the Internet, and the globalization of human rights. These issues will be discussed in chapter 4.

Given that modern speech law was developed almost entirely in the twentieth century, this chapter had to pass quickly over events. A summary of Court doctrine is perhaps in order. How does the current Supreme Court analyze free speech questions coming before it? The Court hews mainly (though not consistently) to a categorical approach. First, it looks at the speech involved and asks if it is really "speech" at all. Over the course of the twentieth century, the parameters of what the Court has considered speech have expanded significantly, so much, in fact, that the phrase "freedom of expression" is now often preferred to "freedom of speech." "Pure speech," or utterances, have always been considered "speech." But now, "symbolic speech" (hoisting or burning a flag or wearing a black armband in protest, for example) and "speech plus," or nonsymbolic conduct (such as picketing, marching, and distributing leaflets) are also considered protected speech, since both convey ideas.

Once the Court decides that it is dealing with speech, it then asks if that speech is "high-value speech," which is entitled to broad constitutional protection, or "low-value speech," which is not. Certain categories of speech, such as political, scientific, or artistic speech, have been singled out over the years as classic cases of high-value speech. But the Court now commonly moves beyond these categories and presumes that in our open society, almost all speech should be accorded a high value. Nonetheless, the Court has traced out several small islands of low-value speech—such as libel, "fighting words," perjury, price-fixing, criminal solicitation, and obscenity—that it considers exceptions to the rule and accords little or no constitutional protection. Judges commonly identify high-value speech as speech that is in accord with one of the desirable purposes of the First Amendment, as set out in chapter 1, such as being conducive to personal autonomy, democratic deliberation, or the discovery of truth.

Is it the rule, then, that high-value speech is exempt from government regulation? Well, no, but such speech is broadly (if not limitlessly) protected. Since free speech is a fundamental right, regulations affecting (high-value) speech are subjected to strict scrutiny. In rare cases—such as those involving an imminent threat to the safety of the nation—the Court, after the strictest scrutiny, will permit content-based regulation of speech. Outside this context, the Court has said that the government may regulate high-value speech so long as that regulation is "content neutral," or not aimed at the speech simply because it conveys one message as opposed to another. The Court presumes that content-based regulations are unconstitutional. Content-neutral regulations, on the other hand, such as a time, place, or manner regulations, are presumed to be constitutional. In assessing the constitutionality of content-neutral regulations, the Court will also look at the reasonableness of the regulation in light of the public purposes it serves. If the regulation is merely couched in neutral terms but is actually aimed at silencing a particular message, the Court will strike it down. Similarly, the Court will invalidate the regulations if they limit the scope of the speech more than is reasonably necessary to advance the regulation's ostensible purpose.

Constitutional doctrine concerning time, place, and manner regulations is complicated by the fact that the Court applies fluctuating degrees of skepticism toward those regulations depending on where the speech is taking place, that is, depending on the type of forum for the speech. Speech taking place in "traditional public forums" (such as public parks) and "government-designated public forums" (such as state university campuses) will face the sharpest skepticism. The Court will apply a more lenient standard, however, to "public properties" such as airports, where it will hold a broader array of reasonable regulations constitutional.

The Court, moreover, now has designated a whole array of additional speech sites to be unique environments where different (and often imprecisely articulated) standards apply. So, for example, the Court has held that public schools are unique environments. Although students are not without rights, in the interest of good discipline and order, they are properly subject to a range of limitations on their speech. Federal employees are also subject to limitations on their political speech on behalf of partisan political causes. In the interest of promoting the labor movement, businesses face regulations concerning their ability to criticize labor unions. In the interest of equality, employers and employees face regulations concerning the comments they can make about women, racial minorities, and others. The Court has long accepted that the military is a unique environment in which free speech is appropriately restricted much more than would be allowed in the civilian world.

The Court has also set out an elaborate (and often changing) set of standards to evaluate the constitutionality of speech in different media. Newspapers receive the broadest constitutional protection (owing in part to the specific and separate protection accorded to the press in the First Amendment). Nonetheless, the Court has consistently upheld elaborate systems of regulations involving television and radio broadcasts. For example, it is completely constitutional for the government to ban indecency and profanity during daytime hours (when children may be watching). The Court, however, has afforded more constitutional protection to cable television, given the large number of channels available and the fact that they are offered only to subscribers. (As such, from the Court's perspective, cable systems are more like newspapers.) In a series of recent decisions, the Court has accorded the Internet sweeping constitutional protection on the grounds that it is a wide-open forum with no scarcity problem and the content of a website is seen only by those who consent to do so. (In this regard, the Court has concluded that the Internet is more like newspapers and less like radio and television.)

Contemporary free speech law, then, is structured around considerations of both the type of speech and the type of regulation at issue in a particular case. If the structure of the Court's analysis is clear (even if, admittedly, complicated), one may wonder why there continue to be so many free speech disputes. The answer lies in the problem of defining the categories and fitting real-world facts into them. Does a particular utterance incite action that poses an imminent threat to the country? And what is "speech"? Is giving any amount of money one wants to a political candidate constitutionally protected "speech," or is it broadly regulable "conduct"? Is a certain sexual depiction in a magazine or on the Internet "indecent" (and thus high-value speech), or is it "obscene" (and thus unprotected low-value speech)? Are New York City regulations limiting the hours of a radical black protest march led by the Nation of Islam "content neutral," or were they imposed because of the mayor's hostility to the Nation of Islam's message? Or are similar time, place, and manner regulations, even though neutral, overly restrictive and hence unreasonable? Moreover, does some new case show that a certain category has outlived its usefulness or that it should not be applied in that case? Would creating a new category (or eliminating one) clarify—and simplify—the law?

These questions, and others like them, make contemporary First Amendment law a lively and perpetually developing field. So long as new cases are brought before the Court and so long as the social and political contexts in which they are brought change, constitutional questions concerning free speech will be sharply contested.

REFERENCES AND FURTHER READING

Aaron, Daniel. 1961. *Writers on the Left: Episodes in American Literary Communism*. New York: Harcourt, Brace, and World.

Barth, Alan. 1951. *The Loyalty of Free Men*. New York: Viking Press.

Black, Gregory D. 1994. *Hollywood Censored: Morality Codes, Catholics, and the Movies*. New York: Cambridge University Press.

Blanchard, Margaret. 1992. *Revolutionary Sparks: Freedom of Expression in Modern America*. New York: Oxford University Press.

Bloomfield, Maxwell. 2000. *Peaceful Revolution: Constitutional Change and American Culture from Progressivism to the New Deal*. Cambridge, MA: Harvard University Press.

Bollinger, Lee, and Geoffrey Stone, eds. 2002. *Eternally Vigilant: Free Speech in the Modern Era*. Chicago: University of Chicago Press.

Branch, Taylor. 1988. *Parting the Waters: America in the King Years 1954–1963*. New York: Simon and Schuster.

————. 1998. *Pillar of Fire: America in the King Years 1953–1965.* New York: Simon and Schuster.

Chafee, Zechariah, Jr. 1919. "Free Speech during War Time." *Harvard Law Review* 32: 932–973.

————. 1941. *Free Speech in the United States.* Cambridge, MA: Harvard University Press.

Clor, Harry. 1969. *Obscenity and Public Morality.* Chicago: University of Chicago Press.

De Grazia, Edward, and Roger K. Newman. 1982. *Banned Films: Movies, Censors, and the First Amendment.* New York: R. R. Bowker.

Downs, Donald Alexander. 1989. *The New Politics of Pornography.* Chicago: University of Chicago Press.

Draper, Theodore. 1957. *The Roots of American Communism: The Untold Story of the Formative Years of the Communist Party in America.* New York: Viking Press.

Dudziak, Mary. 2000. *Cold War Civil Rights: Race and the Image of American Democracy.* Princeton: Princeton University Press.

Goldstein, Robert Justin. 2001. *Political Repression in Modern America: From 1870 to 1976.* Urbana: University of Illinois Press.

Graber, Mark. 1991. *Transforming Free Speech: The Ambiguous Legacy of Civil Libertarianism.* Berkeley and Los Angeles: University of California Press.

Gurstein, Rochelle. 1996. *The Repeal of Reticence: A History of America's Cultural and Legal Struggles over Free Speech, Obscenity, Sexual Liberation, and Modern Art.* New York: Hill and Wang.

Haynes, John Earl, and Harvey Klehr. 1999. *Venona: Decoding Soviet Espionage in America.* New Haven: Yale University Press.

Hentoff, Nat. 1992. *Free Speech for Me—but Not for Thee: How the American Left and Right Relentlessly Censor Each Other.* New York: Harper-Perennial.

Horowitz, David. 2002. *Uncivil Wars: The Controversy over Reparations for Slavery.* San Francisco: Encounter Books.

Kennedy, David M. 1999. *Freedom from Fear: The American People in Depression and War, 1929–1945.* New York: Oxford University Press.

Klarman, Michael J. 1996. "Rethinking the Civil Rights and Civil Liberties Revolutions." *Virginia Law Review* 82: 1–67.

Klehr, Harvey, John Earl Haynes, and Kyrill M. Anderson. 1998. *The Soviet World of American Communism.* New Haven: Yale University Press.

Klehr, Harvey, John Earl Haynes, and Fridrikh Igorevich Firsov. 1995. *The Secret World of American Communism.* New Haven: Yale University Press.

Kors, Alan Charles, and Harvey Silverglate. 1998. *The Shadow University: The Betrayal of Liberty on America's Campuses.* New York: Harper-Perennial.

Kryder, Daniel. 2000. *Divided Arsenal: Race and the American State during World War II.* Cambridge: Cambridge University Press.

Lewis, Anthony. 1991. *Make No Law: The* Sullivan *Case and the First Amendment.* New York: Random House.

MacKinnon, Catherine A. 1993. *Only Words.* Cambridge, MA: Harvard University Press.

Manwaring, David. 1962. *Render unto Caesar: The Flag Salute Controversy.* Chicago: University of Chicago Press.

Marcuse, Herbert. 1965. "Repressive Tolerance." In *A Critique of Pure Tolerance,* by Robert Paul Wolff, Barrington Moore Jr., and Herbert Marcuse, pp. 81–123. Boston: Beacon Press, 1969.

Matsuda, Mari J., Charles R. Lawrence III, Richard Delgado, and Kimberlé Williams Crenshaw. 1993. *Words That Wound: Critical Race Theory, Assaultive Speech, and the First Amendment.* Boulder, CO: Westview Press.

McAdam, Doug. 1988. *Freedom Summer.* New York. Oxford University Press.

Murphy, Paul L. 1979. *World War I and the Origin of Civil Liberties in the United States.* New York: Norton.

Navasky, Victor S. 1980. *Naming Names.* New York: Penguin Books.

Newton, Merlin Owen. 1995. *Armed with the Constitution: Jehovah's Witnesses in Alabama and the U.S. Supreme Court.* Tuscaloosa: University of Alabama Press.

O'Neill, William L. 1971. *Coming Apart: An Informal History of America in the 1960s.* New York: Times Books.

Peters, Shawn Francis. 2000. *Judging Jehovah's Witnesses: Religious Persecution and the Dawn of the Rights Revolution.* Lawrence: University Press of Kansas.

Polenberg, Richard. 1987. *Fighting Faiths: The* Abrams *Case, The Supreme Court, and Free Speech.* New York: Penguin Books.

Powe, Lucas. 2000. *The Warren Court and American Politics.* Cambridge, MA: Harvard University Press.

Rabban, David. 1997. *Free Speech in Its Forgotten Years.* Cambridge: Cambridge University Press.

Sabin, Arthur J. 1999. *In Calmer Times: The Supreme Court and Red Monday.* Philadelphia: University of Pennsylvania Press.

Schrecker, Ellen. 1986. *No Ivory Tower: McCarthyism and the Universities.* New York: Oxford University Press.

———. 1998. *Many Are the Crimes: McCarthyism in America.* Boston: Little, Brown.

Stansell, Christine. 2000. *American Moderns: Bohemian New York and the Creation of a New Century.* New York: Owl Books.

Walker, Samuel. 1990. *In Defense of American Liberties: A History of the ACLU.* New York: Oxford University Press.

———. 1994. *Hate Speech: The History of an American Controversy.* Lincoln: University of Nebraska Press.

Warshow, Robert. 1947. "The Legacy of the 1930s." In *The Immediate Experience: Movies, Comics, Theatre, and Other Aspects of Popular Culture,* by Robert Warshow, pp. 3–18. Cambridge, MA: Harvard University Press.

———. 1953a. "The Liberal Conscience in *The Crucible.*" In *The Immediate Experience: Movies, Comics, Theatre, and Other Aspects of Popular Culture,* by Robert Warshow, 159–173. Cambridge, MA: Harvard University Press.

———. 1953b. "The 'Idealism' of Julius and Ethel Rosenberg." In *The Immediate Experience: Movies, Comics, Theatre, and Other Aspects of Popular Culture,* by Robert Warshow, pp. 39–51. Cambridge, MA: Harvard University Press.

White, G. Edward. 1996. "The First Amendment Comes of Age." *Michigan Law Review* 95: 299–392.

Wilson, Woodrow. 1917. War Messages, 65th Congress, 1st Session. Senate Doc. No. 5, Serial No. 7264. Washington, DC: U.S. Government Printing Office.

Woodward, Bob, and Scott Armstrong. 1979. *The Brethren: Inside the Supreme Court.* New York: Simon and Schuster.

4

THE FUTURE OF
THE FREEDOM OF SPEECH

*T*HE LAST WAVE OF INNOVATION in the Supreme
Court's free speech doctrine took place in response
to the cultural shifts and social movements of the
1960s. The Warren Court expanded the constitutional protections
accorded to disruptive political speech to libelous publications
and sex-related speech, to name just two prominent areas. In some
areas, the Burger Court (1969–1986) reacted against the extreme
liberalizing initiatives of the Warren era (for example, allowing for
tighter regulation of sex-related speech), but in others it simply
followed the precedent of its predecessors. For example, symbolic
speech of the sort supported by the Court's *Tinker v. Des Moines*
(393 U.S. 503 [1969]) decision continued to be accorded high constitutional protection, even when it was plain that the justices of
the conservative Rehnquist Court (1986–present) did not like the
substance of the expression at issue, be it flag burnings or cross
burnings. (See *Texas v. Johnson*, 491 U.S. 397 [1989]; *R.A.V. v. St.
Paul*, 505 U.S. 377 [1992]).

Nonetheless, as cases continue to come to the Court, it continues to refine its free speech doctrine by looking critically at the

principles and approaches it has previously committed itself to in light of new circumstances and altered contexts. Several legal areas that first rose to prominence in the Court in the late twentieth century will continue to prove important as we enter the twenty-first. One of the gravest changes in context, of course, was the September 11, 2001, attacks on New York City and Washington, D.C., the deadliest act of war by a foreign enemy ever perpetrated on U.S. soil.

THE RETURN OF THE DANGERS OF RADICAL POLITICAL SPEECH

In the 1980s and early 1990s, in Jersey City, New Jersey, a diverse and multicultural city sitting directly across the Hudson River from lower Manhattan, where the twin towers of the World Trade Center once stood, blind Egyptian cleric Omar Abdul Rahman preached a fiery anti-U.S. gospel against "the Great Satan" to groups of young, intensely anti-U.S. Arab men. Rahman was on record as having been delighted by the assassination of the Egyptian president Anwar Sadat, a man who had broken with the rest of the Arab world to launch a bold peace initiative with Israel (many believed Rahman had been a leader in the assassination plot). Among the members of his Jersey City congregation were men convicted of conspiring to assassinate right-wing American Zionist leader Rabbi Meir Kahane, as well as the man who planted the bomb in the first attack on the World Trade Center in 1993. That same year, Rahman himself was convicted of conspiring to blow up major New York City landmarks, including the Holland Tunnel and the headquarters of the United Nations.

Rahman is one of the many on U.S. soil who enjoyed and apparently took advantage of U.S. guarantees of the freedom of speech. His views were protected in a culture that placed a high value on the marketplace of ideas. And when the world of the fundamentalist Muslims of Jersey City came under sharp government and media focus in 1993, some Americans were quick to come to their defense. They argued that the religious bigotry and the Mc-Carthyism that defines U.S. society was moving to suppress minority cultures and unpopular political views. One such enemy of U.S. "McCarthyism," writing eight years before the September 11 attacks, condemned "the media lynching of Sheikh Omar Abdul Rahman," declaring that "the media carnival . . . is doing its greatest service to those who want Islam to replace Communism as the strategic threat of the 1990s" (Williams 1993, 24). At about the same time, the Jordanian man who planted the bomb in the first attack on the World Trade Center in 1993 was defended by the assertion that his prosecution was "a thinly veiled disguise on the part of the FBI to make a scapegoat of people who are simply practicing religious individuals" (quoted in Gladwell 1993, 2).

After September 11, however, simplistic screeds against U.S. oppression lost their purchase. It became clear that the questions involved were now plainly serious. Should people like Rahman who express radical anti-U.S. political views be silenced or put in jail? Should they be deported from the country for expressing those views? Should we distinguish between the expression of such views by foreigners and by U.S. citizens? And what of those who do not publicly express these views themselves but who belong to organizations that are committed as a matter of principle to overthrowing the U.S. government? Should these people be allowed to teach in public schools? Should they be allowed to hold government office? Is to say "no" to any of these questions to take the country back to the dark days of the Red Scare of the 1920s and the McCarthyism of the 1950s? Or in light of the threats that the country now faces, can we now say that the lessons of those times are not quite so simple as they seemed?

In the face of new threats, Congress, as in the past, has acted. In late October 2001—operating in closed session in the face of an anthrax attack—Congress passed the U.S.A. Patriot Act, aimed at "domestic terrorism." The act targeted criminal activities dangerous to human life, aimed at intimidating civilians or the government, or affecting the operations of the government through mass destruction, assassination, or kidnapping. It authorized the Central Intelligence Agency to undertake domestic spying and allowed expanded surveillance of phones and Internet use if that surveillance was directed at gathering information relevant to an investigation of domestic terrorism. A number of groups immediately charged that the U.S.A. Patriot Act's definition of domestic terrorism was unconstitutionally vague and overbroad and, moreover, that it promised to chill legitimate political activism by groups working in opposition to the U.S. government. They added that the act's surveillance provisions chilled freedom of speech and ran roughshod over free assembly rights (115 Stat. 272 [2001]).

Post-September 11, it was also apparent that many schools were taking the flag salute seriously once again. So far, most flag salutes are voluntary (unlike in the earlier cases, *Minersville v. Gobitis*, 310 U.S. 586, 591 [1940] and *West Virginia State Board of Education v. Barnette*, 319 U.S. 624 [1943]). But what if certain states and towns make the flag salute mandatory in their public schools? Under current doctrine, as announced in Justice Jackson's *Barnette* opinion, such a requirement would clearly be unconstitutional. But might a different Court, in a new context, find Justice Frankfurter's dissenting opinion in that case to be newly persuasive?

As these events and initiatives show, the fundamentals of civil liberties remain serious issues, and simplistic civil libertarian stories that pit the good people who care about civil liberties against the bad people who oppose them are moralistic and intellectually shallow (see, e.g., Sigal 2002). We may be back to the dawn of the twentieth century at the dawn of the twenty-first. But if so, this is not because we are stupid or forgetful of our past but because political circumstances have put the fundamental political questions underlying civil liberties back in play. What test do we use to determine which speech is protected and which is not? We may know that current Supreme Court doctrine is highly protective of radical political speech and the claims of conscience against the claims of community. But times like these, we should also know, work to change doctrine. Does a return to the older tests, such as the Bad Tendency test, make more sense? How about the Clear and Present Danger test? In the Communist conspiracy case of *Dennis v. United States* (341 U.S. 494 [1951])—which was handed down after China had fallen to totalitarian Communist rule and while thousands of Americans were dying in the fight against communism during the Korean War—Judge Learned Hand proposed a First Amendment test that took into account the nature of the threat and the surrounding political circumstances. Is the Hand test more sensible now than the Incitement test of the psychedelic 1960s? As we enter the new century, these are precisely the sorts of questions we will once again consider.

GOVERNMENT LARGESSE AND THE FREEDOM OF SPEECH

In the twentieth century, the national government grew to unprecedented size and power. Concomitant with this growth were new laws regulating speech. In wartime, Congress moved to police dangerous political speech. As the economic and technological environment changed, new regulatory agencies instituted rules prohibiting false advertising, price-fixing, and profanity and indecency on radio and television.

Sometimes this regulation was tied to government largesse. As government got bigger and began to spend taxpayers' money on ever more special interest programs, people increasingly realized that their money was subsidizing interests to which they were hostile. Soon taxpayers were objecting to having to pay for speech with which they strongly disagreed. After all, was that not like being forced to speak against one's will?

The first legal assaults on these arrangements came in the cases involving the allocation of public moneys to parochial schools. Beginning right after World War II, the Supreme Court—often spurred on by anti-Catholic and civil libertarian groups like the Americans United for the Separation of Church and State and the ACLU, respectively, and others who saw religion as anti-scientific and, in some cases, as a form of quasi-totalitarian brainwashing— invented the "strict separationist" approach to the establishment clause. That approach sharply limited the flow of public moneys to religious schools, banned both voluntary (teacher-led) prayers and Bible readings in public schools, and banished religious groups from receiving equal funding and holding formal meetings on school grounds. (See *Everson v. Board of Education,* 330 U.S. 1 [1947]; *Engel v. Vitale,* 370 U.S. 421 [1962]; *Lemon v. Kurtzman,* 403 U.S. 602 [1971].)

The religious groups argued that these restrictions were direct, content-based assaults on their freedom of speech. Despite the staunch resistance of the liberal justices, at the beginning of the twenty-first century, the Supreme Court has begun to agree with them (*Lamb's Chapel v. Center Moriches Union Free School District,* 508 U.S. 384 [1993]; *Rosenberger v. University of Virginia,* 515 U.S. 819 [1995]; *Good News Club v. Milford Central School,* 533 U.S. 98 [2001]). The use by religious groups of public spaces like schools remains one of the most hotly disputed areas of constitutional law, and in the years to come, it will undoubtedly be influenced by shifting cultural perceptions of religion in light of Muslim extremism, the sex scandals within the Catholic church, and the reawakening of U.S. patriotism.

In the late twentieth century, questions involving the sorts of restrictions that government could place on the speech that it paid for were raised repeatedly in a wide variety of contexts. In 1976, for example, the Supreme Court held that if a candidate accepted government money for a political campaign, it was perfectly constitutional for the government to force the candidate to abide by government-dictated campaign spending limits (*Buckley v. Valeo*, 424 U.S. 1 [1976]). These regulations affected the quantity of speech. Other regulations, however, were directed at its content, raising the question of whether the principle that government regulation on speech must remain content neutral was in conflict with the notion long recognized in the law that the government, like any other speaker, should be free to say one thing and to not say another. After all, does a commitment to content neutrality really mean that as part of its effort to advance the public interest, the government cannot choose to favor some views and to disfavor others? Can refusing to give someone money that they are not entitled to in the first place really be unconstitutional?

Controversies over these questions arose most prominently in the context of the culture wars involving abortion and the arts. Beginning in the 1970s, the Health and Human Services Administration issued grants to family planning organizations. In the late 1980s, however, in an effort to discourage abortions, the Reagan administration announced that no one receiving these grants could do or say anything that would "encourage, promote or advocate abortion as a method of family planning." When a group of doctors challenged the regulations as a violation of their freedom of speech, the Supreme Court turned them away by a 5–4 vote. Chief Justice William Rehnquist wrote that "[t]o hold that the Government unconstitutionally discriminates on the basis of viewpoint when it chooses to fund a program dedicated to advance certain permissible goals, because the program in advancing those goals necessarily discourages alternative goals would render numerous government programs constitutionally suspect." When Congress, for instance, spends money to promote democracy abroad, he asked, was it really constitutionally required to encourage communism or fascism, to be "neutral"? Since there is no right to receive government aid and since governments by their very nature in their spending decisions favor some views over others, the new regulations were fully constitutional. Justice Harry

Blackmun, writing in dissent, declared that this "gag rule" was viewpoint discrimination, pure and simple, and that the law violated the principle of "unconstitutional conditions," which forbids the government from conditioning its aid on the relinquishment of constitutional rights (here, both free speech and abortion) (*Rust v. Sullivan* 500 U.S. 173 [1991], 180, 194, 207).

Similar issues were raised in the art world. In the 1980s and 1990s, many artists and academic critics considered blasphemy and obscenity to be on the cutting edge of artistic expression, largely *because* they provoked political controversies over the freedom of speech. When, in the 1980s, the public became widely aware that the National Endowment for the Arts (NEA) had funded a display of a Robert Mapplethorpe photograph that included a "transgressive" picture of a bullwhip inserted into a man's anus and Andres Serrano's *Piss Christ*, a photograph of a crucifix submerged in the artist's urine, a political donnybrook erupted. Congress stepped in and mandated that the NEA had to "[take] into consideration general standards of decency and respect for the diverse beliefs and values of the American public" in handing out its grants (*National Endowment for the Arts v. Finley*, 524 U.S. 569 [1998], 512). Outraged by what she claimed to be an assault on her artistic freedom and her First Amendment rights, performance artist Karen Finley (known for smearing her naked body with simulated feces) sued. The Supreme Court upheld the regulations, asserting that the NEA necessarily made content-based judgments concerning speech in deciding which projects it would fund in the first place. Here, Justice Sandra Day O'Connor said, the regulations were not hard and fast requirements. Rather, they simply required the NEA to take "decency and respect" into account as one of several factors in deciding upon its awards. "Government may allocate competitive funding," she concluded, "according to criteria that would be impermissible were direct regulation of speech or a criminal penalty at stake" (587–588). Justice Antonin Scalia agreed with O'Connor that the regulations were constitutional. But he considered her reasoning deeply flawed. Scalia declared that the distinction between "abridging" speech and funding it was "a fundamental divide" and that favoring and disfavoring points of view is what governments do by their nature (599). Justice David H. Souter dissented, declaring the situation to be a textbook case of unconstitutional viewpoint discrimination.

However significant Court cases involving the relation between free speech and public funding are likely to be in the future (and as the size of government grows, they are likely to remain significant), it is also important to recognize that, as a practical matter, Supreme Court rulings are not likely to have the last word. Ultimately, after all, federal funding for the arts is set not by the Court but by Congress. In the 1990s, when it looked as if constitutional doctrine would constrain what the government saw as its right—and its responsibility—to spend its money in an appropriate way, Congress decided that it would save itself the trouble by simply halting the flow of federal money to the arts. In the face of Karen Finley's constitutional challenge, Congress seriously considered eliminating the NEA altogether, and in fact, its budget has been slashed radically. In some contexts, First Amendment claims made in courts of law can amount to very bad politics.

THE CAMPAIGN FINANCE CONTROVERSY: BRIBERY OR CONSTITUTIONALLY PROTECTED POLITICAL SPEECH?

The growth of government in the twentieth century also gave rise to controversies over efforts to regulate money in politics. It is hardly surprising that as the amount of money flowing into Washington, D.C., grew, efforts to influence how it was spent grew as well. Some people consider both lobbying and campaign contributions core political speech. Others, however, see aspects of the latter as little better than bribery.

Efforts to limit the corrupting influence of money in politics date back to at least the late nineteenth century. In 1907, amid widespread popular concern about the pernicious influence of the trusts and the capitalist plutocrats, Congress banned corporate contributions to political candidates. In 1947, it banned similar contributions by labor unions. In the early 1970s, in reaction to the Watergate scandal, Congress set up a complex system of rules regulating campaign contributions and expenditures.

In assessing these rules in *Buckley v. Valeo,* the Supreme Court held for the first time that political contributions were a form of constitutionally protected speech. But at the same time, the Court said that Congress has the power to impose reasonable regulations on speech in the interest of protecting the political process from both corruption and the appearance of corruption. The *Buckley* Court then went on to assess the constitutionality of a host of specific regulations: It upheld limits on individual contributions to political candidates but held that imposing expenditure limits on those candidates violated their First Amendment rights, as did limiting the amount that individuals and groups could give to issue advocacy groups and political parties.

The *Buckley* ruling set out the doctrinal architecture around which subsequent campaign finance regulations have been constructed. In a move that stimulated the rise of political action committees (PACs), the Federal Elections Commission ruled in 1978 that both corporations and unions can make "soft money" contributions, that is, contributions to grassroots political organizations that are not directly tied to the advancement of a particular candidate. Since that time, many have argued that it is now the PACs and the soft money system that corrupt U.S. politics. They argue that the real root of the problem is the Supreme Court's ruling in *Buckley* that "money is speech," and they have pushed for the Court to overrule that decision (262). And some of the justices of the current Supreme Court seem willing to do so. The status of *Buckley* and the constitutionality of new efforts to regulate campaign finance, such as the recently passed McCain-Finegold Campaign Finance Reform Bill banning soft money contributions to political parties, will be important issues in the years to come.

PRIVATE POWER, TECHNOLOGY, AND THE FREEDOM OF SPEECH

In the Sidney Lumet film *Network* (1976), washed-up network news anchor Howard Beale, an old-school journalist at the dawn of the age of the blow-dried newsroom, decides that he is not going to bow out quietly. Convinced that the future of democracy itself depends on the quality and the integrity of the news—which is being thoroughly eroded through the relentless push for corporate profits—Beale announces that at the moment he retires, in two weeks time, he will blow his brains out on live TV. At first, Beale's network yanks him off the air. But an ambitious corporate vice president, seeing pure ratings gold, quickly reverses course. For the next two weeks, Beale speaks freely on the air, railing biblically at the stranglehold that the corporate media has on American minds. "Television is not the truth," Beale tells them. "Television is a goddamn amusement park. Television is a circus, a carnival, a traveling troupe of acrobats, story-tellers, dancers, singers, jugglers, sideshow freaks, lion tamers and football players. We're in the boredom-killing business." To save themselves and the country, Beale raves, Americans have got to stop watching television. But "first you've got to get mad. You've got to say, 'I'm a human being, goddammit! My life has value!'" So, Beale declares, "I want you to get up now." "I want all of you to get up out of your chairs. I want you to get up right now and go to the window, open it, and stick your head out, and yell, 'I'm mad as hell, and I'm not going to take this anymore!'" And tens of thousands do, across New York City and across the United States.

This is too much for the foreign-controlled corporation that owns Beale's network. They call him in and chastise him for his quaintness and his ignorance of political life. "There is no America, there is no democracy," he is instructed by the executives. They continue:

> There is only I.B.M. and I.T.T. and A.T.&T and DuPont, Dow, Union Carbide and Exxon. Those are the nations of the world today. What do you think the Russians talk about in their Council of States? Karl Marx? They sit down with their statistical decision theories, lineal programming charts, and their Mini-Mac solutions and compute the cost-price probabilities of their stocks and transactions, just like we do. We no longer live in a world of nations and ideologies, Mr. Beale. The world is a collage of corporations, all inexorably determined by the immutable by-laws of business. The world is a business, Mr. Beale. . . . Our children, Mr. Beale, will live to see that perfect world in which there is no war or famine, oppression or brutality. One vast and ecumenical holding company for whom all men will work to serve a common profit; in which all will hold a share of stock, all necessities provided for, all anxieties tranquilized, all boredom amused.

He concludes, "At the bottom of all our terrified souls, we know that democracy is a dying giant; a sick, dying, decaying political concept writhing in its final pain." "The whole world's people," the life-blood of a democracy, "are becoming mass-produced, programmed, numbered, insensate things" (*Network*, 1976).

Long before the era of the megacorporation, Tocqueville reminded us that any proper account of the freedom of speech in the United States must take into account the workings of private power. Although this power may take the form of social ostracism, it may also take the form of the exercise of power by businesses, corporations, and colleges and university administrators. Strictly speaking, privately imposed restrictions on speech are not constitutional violations. But they determine what is said all the same.

Corporate power is nothing new. In the era of mass industrialization, companies commonly controlled the lives of workers in shockingly intrusive ways. Factory workers, in many cases, were forced to live in company housing, to shop in company-owned stores, and to watch only company-approved movies and read company-approved books. Criticizing the company or one's boss or holding pro-union views were all tickets to the unemployment line.

The problem extended well beyond the factory gate. Private universities like Columbia and the University of Pennsylvania thought nothing of firing professors for their radical beliefs. Indeed, Harvard's alumni nearly succeeded in getting one of the twentieth century's most prominent theorists of freedom of speech, Zechariah Chafee, fired for his views. (He was saved only by the steadfast support of the university's president.)

Private surveillance and corporate influence over the public sphere remain problems today. With the aid of new technologies, private companies monitor employee e-mail, looking for signs of disloyalty, sexual harassment, and shirking. And profit-chasing corporate giants have a powerful influence over what many Americans see and hear. As these entities suffuse U.S. life and consolidate control over the supply of information to the public, Howard Beale's apocalyptic warnings seem increasingly prophetic.

Or do they? Perhaps the sources of information were being gobbled up by a few megacorporations in the 1970s, when *Network* was made. But given the rise of cable television and the Internet, many contend that we are now living in a golden age of free speech. Indeed, according to some, never in human history have so many platforms for speech been so accessible to so many. The head of California's Electronic Freedom Forum, Mike Godwin, for example, has declared the Internet to be "the first mass medium ever with the potential to give each of us a voice with the reach of a newspaper or TV station, but with the intimacy or responsiveness of the telephone." He adds, "I believe virtual communities promise to restore to Americans at the end of the twentieth century what many of us feel was lost in the decades at the beginning of the century—a stable sense of community, of place" (Godwin 1998, 10, 15). Similarly, the Supreme Court has called the Internet a "vast democratic for[um]" (*Reno v. ACLU*, 521 U.S. 844 [1997], 868).

Some people see things differently. Stanford law professor Lawrence Lessig has argued that as the Internet has matured, corporate censorship is becoming as prominent there as it was in the world Howard Beale saw emerging in the 1970s (Lessig 2001). University of Chicago law professor Cass Sunstein, on the other hand, is troubled not by the concentration of power on the Web but rather by its fragmentation. Sunstein argues that "filtering" and "personalization" allows Internet users to carefully select the sort of information they receive and to effortlessly screen out the rest. The problem, according to Sunstein, is that this filtering drains the reservoir of common experience that makes civic deliberation in a democracy possible. Instead of getting a picture of the world in its manifold variety, what individuals get is "The Daily Me." The result is a polarized public made up of those who never listen to opposing views and who only interact with people with whom they already agree. If the primary purpose of the freedom of speech is to enhance the quality of our political democracy—and Sunstein believes it is—this narrowness is a serious failing. As a solution, the professor has called for new regulations requiring Internet websites to provide links to other sites that advance positions on public issues that run contrary to their own (Sunstein 2001).

The rise of the Internet has raised all sorts of free speech issues, many of which are now coming before courts for the first time. In searching for guideposts in an unfamiliar landscape, judges in cases involving the Internet have made analogies to newspapers, radio, and television, which were once themselves the outgrowth of revolutionary technological change. In *Reno v. ACLU* (521

U.S. 844 [1997]), which voided the Communications Decency Act of 1996, the Court acknowledged that it was perfectly acceptable, from a constitutional standpoint, to regulate indecency on radio and television, since people, including children, could come upon that material accidentally while turning the dial. (See *FCC v. Pacifica Foundation,* 438 U.S. 726 [1978]). But on the Internet, in contrast, one had to seek out such material to receive it. The Court was skeptical of the act's exception for sites with age verification systems because, it argued, by implicitly requiring such systems, Congress was in effect taking a free medium and transforming it into a pay one, a transformation that would sharply limit the flow of information. Other questions soon followed. A federal court in Philadelphia recently struck down the Children's Internet Protection Act of 2000, which denied federal financing to any public library that did not install filtering software on its computers, calling it an unconstitutional prior restraint (*American Library Association v. United States,* 2002 U.S. Dist. LEXIS 9537 [E.D. Pa., May 31, 2002]; see also *Ashcroft v. Free Speech Coalition,* 535 U.S. 234 [2002]).

The easy accessibility of the Internet has created not just opportunities but also serious problems. It is now easier than ever to distribute offensive, hateful, and even dangerous material. Neo-Nazi sites and sites instructing people how to build deadly explosives have proliferated on the Internet. (Sometimes, when informed of the existence of these sites, service providers censor them.) Some Internet cases have raised problems involving possible incitement to imminent and lawless action. One man opposed to abortion, for example, posted pictures of bloody aborted fetuses on his "Nuremberg Files" website and followed those pictures with the names of abortion doctors and their family members, their home and work addresses, and the route they drive to work. He then divided the names of the doctors into the categories "working," "wounded," and "fatality." When a doctor was murdered, the site's owner drew a line through that doctor's name.

When abortion providers and their professional associations sued, a federal court, citing *Brandenburg v. Ohio* (395 U.S. 444 [1969]), held that the site was protected by the First Amendment. Unless the "Nuremberg Files" site "authorized, ratified, or directly threatened" violence, which the court concluded it did not, then its impassioned opposition to "the baby butcher business" is fully protected (*Planned Parenthood v. American Coalition of Life Activists*, 244 F.3d 1007 [9th Cir., 2000]).

THE NEW PUBLIC HEALTH CENSORSHIP AND
THE CONTINUING PROGRESSIVE POLITICAL
CORRECTNESS CAMPAIGN

In the late twentieth century, the status accorded to health and safety and risk-reduction arguments in public policy debates reached all-time highs. There are, of course, few defenders of harm and illness. But in the past, many people were jealous enough of their privacy and freedom that they set sharp limits on the lengths they were willing to go for risk reduction. Those limits have now been sharply reduced, and the trend has been reinforced—and perhaps created—by the proliferation of harm-based interest groups, each fueled by an intense commitment to the eradication of a single danger, like drunk driving or smoking or fatty foods. Although the topic is rarely discussed (since the media currently tends to support the political agenda of risk-reduction interest groups), these groups, and the public health professionals aligned with them, stand today as some of the nation's leading proponents of censorship.

The more righteous the cause, the more invisible the censorship is likely to become. Anyone who has roamed the Internet knows that it is brimming with all manner of material—strange, serious, and extreme—and one might think that the most aggressive efforts to remove offensive sites from the World Wide Web involve the sites of racist hate groups. The truth, however, is that efforts by public health groups have given these efforts a run for their money. In August 2001, for example, at the instigation of the National Eating Disorder Association in Seattle and with the support of public health groups around the country, Yahoo removed and banned all Websites taking a positive position on such eating disorders as anorexia and bulimia. (The sites typically characterize them as "lifestyle choices.") Holly Hoff, the head of the National Eating Disorder Association, boasted that "it was a real challenge to get them removed, because we're up against free speech," and she savored the victory in the name of health (quoted in Holahan 2001).

Public health crusades against speech promoting alcohol, tobacco, and now fatty foods are well under way. For many years, the American Medical Association has been pushing for a total ban on all alcohol-related advertising. Public health groups greeted the recent announcement by NBC that it would once again begin running ads for distilled liquors with such outrage that the network was forced to retreat. Much of Hollywood is now engaged in a campaign to eliminate all positive depictions of smoking from the silver screen. Moreover, the strict limits on tobacco advertising already in place are only likely to grow stronger. In response to these crackdowns, the Supreme Court has begun to articulate a strong defense of free speech rights in advertising (what it calls "commercial speech"). (See *44 Liquormart v. Rhode Island*, 517 U.S. 484 [1996].) But the moral fervor behind the public health crusade seems well on the way to becoming one of the most significant speech-constricting movements in U.S. history.

The political correctness movement, with which the public health crusade is politically aligned, has already become such a speech-constricting movement. This movement, which has strong followings among progressive college students, professors, and administrators, works to ban speech involving offensive epithets, stereotypes, and criticisms of views they attribute to particular oppressed groups. So when conservative activist David Horowitz sought to run advertisements in college newspapers opposing financial reparations for slavery, many newspapers flatly refused to run it. When Horowitz came to campus to make his argument in person, he was repeatedly shouted down and threatened by "progressives" (Horowitz 2002).

With the recent terrorist attacks within the United States and with the stepping up of similar acts of violence around the world, we are probably entering an era of unusual political intensity. This does not bode well for broad toleration for free speech on campus. On September 11, university administrators removed U.S. flags from campus buses, claiming they were "offensive" to foreign students. Professors who defended the United States and criticized Muslim extremism were brought up on harassment charges for making Muslim students feel uncomfortable. On the other side, some anti-American and anti-Israeli speakers were harshly criticized, and a few were themselves brought up on charges. Multiculturalist ideology has proved unable to manage real political conflict, and the prevalence of this ideology on U.S. campuses is only likely to stimulate more clashes over the free speech there in the future.

GLOBALIZATION: POLITICAL CORRECTNESS BY OTHER MEANS?

Trends toward globalization will almost certainly spur developments in the freedom of speech. Telephones, satellite communications, air travel, and the Internet have clearly brought the far corners of the world closer together. The broader forces of market capitalism, buttressed by an array of international agreements, have both stimulated this interconnection and been strengthened by its growth.

In this context, it has been argued to great effect that political and economic integration should go hand in hand. European bureaucratic elites, for example, have succeeded in transforming what was once a common market into an emergent, Europe-wide government. U.N. bureaucrats are similarly striving toward a system of global governance. Many U.S. professors and political activists have now concluded that the future of freedom and justice depend upon fighting U.S. sovereignty and submitting those who happen to live within the current borders of the United States to the presumably more enlightened rule of "the world community."

Both the European Union and the United Nations have made strong commitments on paper to the protection of human rights, including the freedom of expression. Article 19 of the International Covenant on Civil and Political Rights, for example, which came into force in the mid-1970s, declares that "[e]veryone shall have the right to freedom of expression; this right shall include freedom to seek, receive and impart information of all kinds, regardless of frontiers, either orally, in writing or in print, in the form of art, or through any other media of his choice." Unfortunately, however, the very next article of the covenant provides that "[a]ny propaganda for war shall be prohibited by law" and that "[a]ny advocacy of national, racial or religious hatred that constitutes incitement to discrimination, hostility or violence shall be prohibited by law" (21 UN GAOR Supp [No. 16], 53).

The United States has a deeply rooted historical tradition of taking seriously its constitutional obligations (even if occasionally failing to uphold the freedom of speech). The United Nations, on the other hand, has no such history. The International Covenant on Civil and Political Rights, for example, was signed by nations that are among the world's worst abusers of human rights. In fact, China, the Sudan, and Cuba—who repress freedom of speech by imprisonment, torture, and murder—are all current members of the U.N. Human Rights Commission created by the same International Covenant.

Because of a growing tendency among U.S. elites to see themselves as "global citizens," it is probable that in years to come more appeals to European and international standards will be made in domestic disputes concerning the freedom of speech. However, the moral authority of "the world community" might diminish if human rights continue to be as egregiously violated as has recently been the case; if, for example, Europe's rekindled anti-Semitism continues to rage, and the continent's instinct for censoring anti–European Union and antimulticulturalist speech, not to mention gunning down leaders perceived to be antienvironmentalist and opposed to animal rights—is inflamed. For these reasons, the growing concern for global human rights may actually portend increasing restrictions on speech within the United States in the name of peace, feminism, antiracism, risk-reduction, and public health.

Although "human rights" sounds like something that everyone should be in favor of, students of politics should look not just at abstract principles but at how those principles are likely to play out in practice. The global human rights campaign could easily lead to a constriction of civil liberties in the United States.

CONCLUSION

As we enter the twenty-first century, the scope of the freedom of speech is stable in some ways and in flux in others. On the one hand, at this point in history, what "freedom of speech" means, for good and for ill, remains very much the province of the Supreme Court. Over the course of the twentieth century, that Court has spent much of its time crafting and modifying a series of tests, categories, and distinctions that constitute the corpus of free speech law. Free speech controversies of all sorts, whether over pornography on the Internet, antiabortion protests, speech codes at public universities, or crackdowns on revolutionary radicalism, will for the foreseeable future continue to be resolved through the mediation of this doctrinal architecture. At the same time, though, all sorts of events and pressures are operating that call into question the accustomed tests and categories. After all, through the continual interaction of principles and imperatives, categories change. And they change most in periods of novelty, reform, instability, and fear. Politics, culture, and law, at base, are forever linked. In law, as in politics, the questions of what we must do and what we should do are perennial.

REFERENCES AND FURTHER READING

Cole, David. 2002. "Enemy Aliens." *Stanford Law Review* 54: 953–1005.

Cole, David, James X. Dempsey, and Carole E. Goldberg. 2002. *Terrorism and the Constitution: Sacrificing Civil Liberties in the Name of National Security.* 2d ed. New York: The New Press.

Cottle, Michelle. 2002. "The War on Tobacco Becomes the War on Fat." *The New Republic,* May 13, 16–18.

Doyle, Charles. "The USA Patriot Act: A Legal Analysis." April 15, 2002. Washington, DC: Congressional Research Service.

Gladwell, Malcolm. 1993. "Man Charged in Bombing of New York Skyscraper." *The Tech* (March 5): 2.

Godwin, Mike. 1998. *Cyber Rights: Defending Free Speech in the Digital Age.* New York: Times Books.

Hamburger, Philip. 2002. *Separation of Church and State.* Cambridge, MA: Harvard University Press.

Holahan, Catherine. 2001. "Yahoo Removes Pro–Eating Disorder Internet Sites." *Boston Globe,* August 5.

Horowitz, David. 2002. *Uncivil Wars: The Controversy over Reparations for Slavery.* San Francisco: Encounter Books.

International Covenant on Civil and Political Rights. 1976. G.A. res. 2200A (XXI), 21 U.N. GAOR Supp. (No. 16) at 53, U.N. Doc. A/6316 (1966), 999 U.N.T.S. 171, entered into force March 23.

Kors, Alan, and Harvey Silverglate. 1998. *The Shadow University: The Betrayal of Liberty on America's Campuses.* New York: Free Press.

Lessig, Lawrence. 2001. *The Future of Ideas: The Fate of the Commons in a Connected World.* New York: Random House.

Lipschultz, Jeremy Harris. 1999. *Free Expression in the Age of the Internet: Social and Legal Boundaries.* Boulder, CO: Westview Press.

Network. 1976. Directed by Sidney Lumet. Screenplay by Paddy Chayevsky. Metro-Goldwyn-Mayer.

Nolan, James, Jr. 1998. *The Therapeutic State: Justifying Government at Century's End.* New York: New York University Press.

Olson, Elizabeth. 2002. "W.H.O. Treaty Would Ban Cigarette Ads Worldwide." *New York Times,* July 22.

Rabkin, Jeremy. 1998. *Why Sovereignty Matters.* Washington, DC: AEI Press.

————. 2001. "Censorship." In *Oxford Companion to World Politics,* Joel Krieger, Margaret E. Crahan, and Lawrence Jacobs, eds., pp. 117–118. New York: Oxford University Press.

Redish, Martin. 2001. *Money Talks: Speech, Economic Power, and the Values of Democracy.* New York: New York University Press.

Sarouf, Frank. 1992. *Inside Campaign Finance: Myths and Realities.* New Haven: Yale University Press.

Schemo, Diana Jean. 2001. "New Battles in Old War over Freedom of Speech." *New York Times,* November 25, 1B, 6.

Sigal, Clancy. 2002. "John Ashcroft's Palmer Raids." *New York Times,* March 13.

Smith, Bradley. 2001. *Unfree Speech: The Folly of Campaign Finance Reform.* Princeton: Princeton University Press.

Sunstein, Cass. 2001. *Republic.com.* Princeton: Princeton University Press.

Volokh, Eugene. 1995. "How Harassment Law Restricts Free Speech." *Rutgers Law Review* 47: 561–578.

————. 1997. "What Speech Does 'Hostile Work Environment' Harassment Restrict?" *Georgetown Law Journal* 85: 627–648.

Weinstein, James. 1999. *Hate Speech, Pornography, and the Radical Attack on Free Speech Doctrine.* Boulder, CO: Westview Press.

Williams, Ian. 1993. "In the Eye of the Media Storm: Sheikh Omar Abdul Rahman." *Washington Report on Mideast Affairs,* April/May, 24.

5

KEY PEOPLE, CASES, AND EVENTS

American Civil Liberties Union

Founded in 1920 by Roger Baldwin, the American Civil Liberties Union (ACLU) is the most influential civil liberties advocacy group in U.S. history. The group was initially a splinter group of the American Union against Militarism, a group that opposed U.S. entry into World War I. Far from taking a position on a wide range of issues, at its outset the ACLU was concerned chiefly with the Wilson administration's crackdowns on antiwar speech. In its early years, the ACLU devoted its energy to resisting efforts to suppress political speech (refusing to get involved with issues of obscenity, for example). Gradually, however, it came to consider its mission to be defending the principle of free speech, no matter what the subject. The ACLU regularly litigates free speech cases and files influential amicus briefs in the U.S. Supreme Court.

Amicus Curiae

The Latin term *amicus curiae* means "friend of the court." Amicus curiae briefs are legal briefs submitted to a court, with its permission, by interested groups or nonparty experts. In filing amicus briefs, groups and individuals provide the court both with information and with perspectives on specific issues that may not otherwise reach it. These groups and individuals also use amicus briefs to lobby the court, urging it either to use their preferred lines of reasoning or to reach their preferred result (or both). Groups like the American Civil Liberties Union routinely file amicus curiae briefs in free speech cases. In doing so, they exert considerable influence over the development of constitutional law.

Anarchism

Anarchism is a political creed committed to the proposition that government is the enemy of freedom and should be abolished. Anarchism reached its heyday in the United States as a political doctrine in the late nineteenth and early twentieth centuries, when its purchase was especially strong amongst urban, immigrant intellectuals. For many, anarchism was more than a philosophy: It was a call to action. At this time, anarchists participated in a series of bombings and assassinations—including the assassination of President William McKinley (1901)—with the goal of overthrowing the U.S. government. In the wake of the McKinley assassination, both the national and the state governments passed laws punishing anarchist speech. The constitutionality of these laws was challenged in a number of prominent free speech cases, such as *Abrams v. United States* (250 U.S. 616 [1919]). Although some of these early decisions helped lay the groundwork for more latitudinarian free speech doctrine, all of them upheld the constitutionality of the subversive advocacy laws.

Anti-Federalists

The Anti-Federalists were Americans opposed to the adoption of the U.S. Constitution on the grounds that, as written, it gave too much power to the national government and failed to accord sufficient protections for fundamental rights. The Bill of Rights, which included a guarantee of the freedom of speech, was added to the Constitution in 1791 to secure the political support of the Anti-Federalists for the new U.S. government. At the time the Bill of Rights was adopted, it was broadly understood that its provisions limited the national government only, and not the states. In this way, as it was originally understood by most, the Constitution was consistent with the twin Anti-Federalist goals of protecting fundamental rights while, at the same time, according the states broad authority to govern themselves without interference from a distant national government. See *Barron v. Baltimore*, 32 U.S. 243 (1833).

Bad Tendency Test

Until it came under increasing challenge in the early twentieth century, the Bad Tendency test was the prevailing judicial test in the United States for free speech. Under this test, which derived from the English law of libel as set out by William Blackstone, governments had the authority to restrict speech that they had reasonably determined had a tendency to create an evil that they had a right to prevent. This test was highly deferential to government efforts to regulate speech under a claim to serving the public interest. As such, while this test predominated, very few state or federal constitutional free speech claims came before the nation's courts. Over time, the Bad Tendency test was challenged by the more speech-protective Clear and Present Danger test. The Bad Tendency test is largely defunct, though courts do seem to use it (without admitting that they are doing so) in many contexts, such as those involving sexual harassment codes that prohibit speech involving sexual stereotypes.

Bill of Rights (English)

The English Bill of Rights (1689), the result of intense political struggles between the Crown and Parliament in the seventeenth century, provided the basis for many of the provisions of the U.S. Constitution's Bill of Rights. One provision of the English Bill provides "[t]hat the freedom of speech, and debates or proceedings in parliament, ought not to be impeached or questioned in any court or place out of parliament." The speech and debate clause of the U.S. Constitution (art. 1, sec. 6) tracks this English provision.

Bill of Rights (U.S.)

The first ten amendments to the U.S. Constitution, which were approved by the First Congress and ratified in 1791, constitute the U.S. Bill of Rights. It has its roots in the English Bill of Rights (1689) and, more immediately, in George Mason's "Declaration of Rights" from the Virginia State Constitution (1776). The Federalists, the chief proponents of the Constitution, saw no need for a bill of rights. Indeed, in *Federalist Paper* no. 84, Alexander Hamilton argued that the structural features of the Constitution, including representative government, federalism, and the separation of powers, afforded Americans the best hope that their rights would be protected. The Anti-Federalists, however, argued passionately that the adoption of a Bill of Rights was essential to protect the rights of Americans from infringements by the dangerously distant national government. It was only in the late nineteenth century that courts began to hold that the Bill of Rights restricted the conduct of the states. To win Anti-Federalist support for the new Constitution, however, the Federalists promised to add a Bill of Rights to the document soon after it was ratified. The First Amendment's free speech provision is a prominent part of the Bill of Rights. In the twentieth century, some justices of the Supreme Court declared the freedom of speech to be the most important of our constitutional rights. See *Barron v. Baltimore*, 32 U.S. 243 (1833); *Gitlow v. New York*, 268 U.S. 652 (1925); *Palko v. Connecticut*, 302 U.S. 319 (1937); *Dennis v. United States*, 341 U.S. 494 (1951).

Black, Hugo

Hugo Black (1886–1971), a U.S. senator from Alabama and a New Deal Democrat, was appointed to the Supreme Court by President Franklin D. Roosevelt. During his long tenure on the Court (1937–1971), Black rose to become—along with Justices Oliver Wendell Holmes, Jr., Louis D. Brandeis, and William J. Brennan, Jr.—one of the chief architects of the Court's twentieth-century free speech jurisprudence. Black is perhaps best known for his "free speech absolutism," which holds that the First Amendment's declaration that "Congress shall make no law . . . abridging the freedom of speech" means precisely that—without exception. As a self-described absolutist, Black regularly voted to strike down laws limiting obscenity, libel, and subversive speech. As a literalist, he opposed the efforts of others on the Court to balance individual and governmental interests in its determination of the constitutionality of government efforts to regulate speech. At the same time, though, and despite his professed absolutism, Justice Black consistently distinguished "speech" (verbal utterances or writing) from expressive or symbolic "conduct" (such as picketing or wearing a black protest armband). The former, he held, was protected absolutely; the latter was subject to reasonable regulation. Black is also known for being the Court's leading proponent of the full incorporation of the Bill of Rights. See *Kovacs v. Cooper*, 336 U.S. 77 (1949); *Dennis v. United States*, 341 U.S. 494 (1951); *Beauharnais v. Illinois*, 343 U.S. 250 (1952); *Yates v. United States*, 354 U.S. 298 (1957); *Tinker v. Des Moines*, 393 U.S. 503 (1969); *Brandenburg v. Ohio*, 395 U.S. 444 (1969).

Blackstone, William

William Blackstone (1723–1780), a lawyer, judge, member of Parliament, and scholar, was the first professor of English law at Oxford University and that nation's greatest compiler, systematizer, and summarizer of the common law. Blackstone's *Commentaries on the Laws of England* (1765–1769), a four-volume treatise, demonstrated the ways in which judge-made law had evolved gradually over the course of centuries to provide unique protections for liberty under the rule of law. Blackstone's *Commentaries* placed English law at the fingertips of readers on both sides of the Atlantic. It became a major reference work for Americans (including the founders), who were influenced by many of its understandings, including Blackstone's understanding of the freedom of speech. That understanding declared that free speech, in its essence, amounted to the absence of prior restraints on speech. Starting from Blackstone, Americans gradually developed their own approaches to free speech in light of their unique experiences and commitments.

Blasphemy

Blasphemy is speech that defames either God or religion. For much of Anglo-American legal history, blasphemy was considered a common law crime. Despite the U.S. commitment to the freedom of speech, including the ratification of the First Amendment and similar protections in state constitutions, through most of the eighteenth and nineteenth centuries few people believed there were constitutional obstacles to blasphemy prosecutions. Such prosecutions, however, gradually became much less common. Although the Supreme Court has never held a blasphemy prosecution to be unconstitutional, such a prosecution would clearly run counter to contemporary understandings of the freedom of speech.

Brandeis, Louis D.

Louis D. Brandeis (1856–1941) was one of twentieth century's most influential progressive thinkers and one of the Supreme Court's most important justices (1916–1939). Along with his friend and colleague Justice Oliver Wendell Holmes, Jr., with whom he joined in fashioning the Clear and Present Danger test (*Schenck v. United*

States, 249 U.S. 47 [1919]; *Abrams v. United States*, 250 U.S. 616 [1919]), Brandeis is one of the chief architects of contemporary civil libertarian understandings of the freedom of speech. Although Brandeis advocated the constriction of press freedoms to preserve personal privacy, he nonetheless held a latitudinarian conception of free speech in many areas. Brandeis was also a strong proponent of incorporation, which interpreted the Bill of Rights as restrictions on the states as well as on the national government. In his eloquent concurrence in *Whitney v. California* (274 U.S. 357 [1927]), Brandeis famously defended free speech as essential to the discovery of truth and the practice of popular government.

Brennan Jr., William J.

William J. Brennan, Jr. (1906–1997), an associate justice of the Supreme Court (1956–1990), was the intellectual leader of the Warren Court of the 1950s and 1960s and one of the primary architects of modern constitutional doctrine concerning the freedom of speech. Although appointed by Republican President Dwight D. Eisenhower, Brennan is considered by many to be the embodiment of twentieth-century judicial liberalism. While on the Court, Brennan championed the role of the Court in providing aggressive judicial protection for free speech, broadly considered, including sex-related speech and speech critical of public officials. A devout strict separationist, Brennan was also a major force behind removing prayer from the public schools. See *Roth v. United States*, 354 U.S. 476 (1957); *New York Times v. Sullivan*, 376 U.S. 254 (1964); *FCC v. Pacifica Foundation*, 438 U.S. 726 (1978); *Texas v. Johnson*, 491 U.S. 397 (1989).

Bribery

Bribery, which had long been considered a common law crime and is now banned by statute, is the crime of corrupting a public official by offering (or, in the case of the official, by seeking or receiving) anything of value in return for influence in the public decisionmaking process. Speech proposing or soliciting a bribe is considered unprotected, or low-value, speech. At the same time, however, many argue that a form of high-value, constitutionally protected political expression—contributions to the campaigns of politicians who either are or are seeking to become public officials—inevitably influences their behavior in office and hence is tantamount to bribery. Public debate over whether such contributions and expenditures are more akin to bribery or to high-value political speech shape much of the contemporary debate over campaign finance reform. See *Buckley v. Valeo,* 424 U.S. 1 (1976).

Categorical Approach

Over the course of the twentieth century, the Supreme Court began for the first time to hear a large number of free speech cases. In trying to decide this large and diverse array of cases, the Court soon found that, standing alone, the First Amendment's free speech clause was too broad to provide adequate guidance. Accordingly, the Court gradually developed a "categorical" approach to assessing the constitutionality of laws affecting free speech, an approach to which it usually (though not always) adheres. The Court distinguishes high-value speech, such as speech involving political, scientific, and artistic matters, from low-value speech (sometimes called "unprotected speech"), such as falsely shouting "fire" in a crowded theater, "fighting words," bribery, obscenity, and libel. Speech in the former category is highly protected, and restrictions on it are subject to strict scrutiny. Speech in the latter category is unprotected, and the Court has concluded that it has either minimal or no value or is a definite harm to society. See *Schenck v. United States,* 249 U.S. 47 (1919); *Chaplinsky v. New Hampshire,* 315 U.S. 568 (1942); *New York Times v. Sullivan,* 376 U.S. 254 (1964).

Censorship

Although the charge of "censorship" is hurled rather loosely today at any rules or actions that someone believes inappropriately constricts his or her speech, the term originally applied to a requirement that arose in early modern Europe after the invention of the printing press. All printed matter, prior to being published, had to be submitted for a stamp of approval from the "censor," a public official who oversaw an official governmental licensing scheme. England outlawed censorship in 1694, and the procedure never took root in the English colonies. Today, strictly speaking, the rule against "censorship" is enshrined primarily in common law and constitutional doctrine that prohibits most forms of "prior restraint." In a broad, colloquial (and political) sense, allegations of censorship arise in many contemporary free speech cases. See *Rust v. Sullivan*, 500 U.S. 173 (1991); *National Endowment for the Arts v. Finley*, 118 S.Ct. 2168 (1998).

Chafee Jr., Zechariah

Zechariah Chafee, Jr. (1885–1957), a professor at the Harvard Law School (1916–1956), played a major role in the formation of twentieth-century civil libertarian understandings of the freedom of speech. Chafee became interested in free speech issues during the government crackdowns against suspected radicals during World War I. In his many writings, which attracted considerable attention both on the Supreme Court and off, Chafee traced his own civil libertarian views back to the nation's Founding Fathers. Chafee defended broad protections for free speech in time of war and was a major influence on the Court's move away from the Bad Tendency test and toward the Clear and Present Danger test. He also is one of the chief sources of the Court's decision to take a two-tiered approach to free speech, which separated high-value from low-value speech. In recent years, historians have agreed that Chafee's understandings of free speech, although perhaps desirable from a public policy standpoint, could not be traced back in history (as Chafee had claimed and as the lawyers and judges who drew from him believed they could). Rather, his views marked a substantial departure from traditional understandings of the constitutional meaning of the freedom of speech. Despite their historical inaccuracies, Chafee's writings had a profound influence on the course of U.S. law in the twentieth century.

Clear and Present Danger Test

Justice Oliver Wendell Holmes, Jr. first articulated the Clear and Present Danger test in the Red Scare Espionage Act case of *Schenck v. United States* (249 U.S. 47 [1919]), where he declared that "[t]he question in every case is whether the words are used in such circumstances and are of such a nature as to create a clear and present danger that they will bring about the substantive evils that Congress has a right to prevent" (52). Holmes's *Schenck* opinion marks the starting point for the Supreme Court's contemporary civil liberties jurisprudence. Despite the fact that the *Schenck* Court actually upheld Schenck's conviction, over the years both Holmes and others on the Court came to interpret the test in increasingly speech-protective ways, although those interpretations did not always hold in times of national peril. Nonetheless, the Clear and Present Danger test came to set a high standard for government suppression of dangerous political speech. See *Schenck v. United States*, 249 U.S. 47 (1919); *Abrams v. United States*, 250 U.S. 616 (1919); *Gitlow v. New York*, 268 U.S. 652 (1925); *Dennis v. United States*, 341 U.S. 494 (1951); *Brandenburg v. Ohio*, 395 U.S. 444 (1969).

Common Law

One of the defining features of the Anglo-American system of law (as opposed to the "civil law" system of Continental Europe) is that much of its law originates not from statutes passed by legislatures but rather from rules, both explicit and implicit, set out incrementally by judges as a byproduct of their decisions in thousands of individual legal disputes. Prior to the rise of the modern state in the late nineteenth and early twentieth centuries, the lion's share of the law of Anglo-American countries was judge-made common law. Since then, however, the law in England and the United States has consisted of a mixture of statutory and common law. Today, many areas of law, such as contracts and property, are still shaped primarily by common law rules, though many of those rules have since been codified. Before the U.S. Supreme Court became consistently involved in free speech cases in the mid-twentieth century, common law rules concerning the freedom of speech often implicitly set the prevailing constitutional standards for the regulation of speech. These rules set the terms of debate even when they were challenged—as they often were—as unsuited to the changing conditions and circumstances of the United States.

Communism

Communism is a political ideology, advanced in its most sophisticated and influential form by nineteenth-century German philosophers Karl Marx and Friedrich Engels. In its essence, communism involves a sustained critique of the oppressiveness of the capitalist economic system and a sustained argument on behalf of a communist political-economic system, which Marx and Engels took to be a historical inevitability. Under communism, private property would be abolished and the oppressed working class would seize control of the means of production. Only then could human beings achieve true and humanly meaningful freedom and equality. With its commitment to equality and its promise of total liberation, communism proved immensely attractive to many people, particularly to intellectuals. Its glittering ideals, however, clashed fundamentally with the unavoidable limits of human nature. When put into practice in the Soviet Union, the realization of Communist ideals soon required levels of coercion unprecedented in their scope and violence. The pursuit of Communist ideals in the Soviet Union and elsewhere soon led to the greatest sustained project of mass murder in human history. For much of the twentieth century, many U.S. intellectuals and progressives (though certainly not all of them), transfixed by its high ideals of human equality and freedom, either ignored or minimized the evil at the core of Communist ideology and practice. These intellectuals and progressives felt themselves to be out of step with the mainstream of the U.S. public, who took themselves to be at war with Communist ideology for much of the twentieth century. At various times, the mass of the U.S. people supported the passage and enforcement of a series of laws aimed at restricting Communist organizations and associations and the expression of Communist revolutionary views. During the Red Scare of the 1920s and the Cold War, to either publicly advocate communism, to be a member of the American Communist Party (an organization controlled by Soviet dictator Joseph Stalin), or to refuse to swear allegiance—via a loyalty oath—to the U.S. Constitution was often grounds for dismissal from private and public employment and occasionally for criminal prosecution. Those who ran afoul of these laws and policies, some of whom were not Communists, fought back in courts, defending themselves with appeals to the freedom of association and the freedom of speech. See *Dennis v. United States,* 341 U.S. 494(1951); *Yates v. United States,* 354 U.S. 298 (1957).

Comstock Act

The Comstock Act (1873), the brainchild of Anthony Comstock, the highly religious head of the New York Society for the Suppression of Vice, was a federal law that barred "obscene" material from the U.S. mails. At the time the Comstock Act was passed, obscenity was defined broadly and included not only sex-related but also blasphemous and other vulgar materials. Acting pursuant to its authority under the act, the U.S. postal service, which had put Comstock himself in charge of enforcement, seized a wide variety of materials from the mails and prosecuted a large number of individuals for sending it. Most prosecutions under the act involved sex-related works, including literature written by sex radicals extolling free love, birth control, and pornography. Applying the prevailing Bad Tendency test, the courts routinely upheld the constitutionality of Comstock Act prosecutions. Nonetheless, many of the targets of those prosecutions, like birth control activist Margaret Sanger, used those prosecutions to generate publicity for their causes. In the process, these figures and the other activists and legal scholars who came to their defense argued for a transformation in traditional understandings of free speech law. In the long run, they were successful in pioneering modern civil libertarian understandings of the freedom of speech.

Content Neutrality

In assessing the constitutionality of a law under the First Amendment's free speech clause, the modern Supreme Court asks whether the law is impartial as to the message being conveyed, that is, "content neutral," or whether it is aimed at regulating the content of a particular form of speech, that is, "content based." The Court is highly skeptical of the constitutionality of content-based restrictions of high-value speech (such as political speech) because such regulations distort the proper functioning of the marketplace of ideas. Recognizing that reasonable regulations governing the time, place, and manner of speech (such as regulations concerning littering, crowd control, and noise limits) are essential for public order, however, the Court has broadly accepted the constitutionality of content-neutral regulations concerning high-value speech. The Court does allow content-based regulation of (and even bans on) low-value speech, such as obscenity, li-

bel, and criminal advocacy. See *Texas v. Johnson*, 491 U.S. 397
(1989); *R.A.V. v. St. Paul*, 505 U.S. 377 (1992); *National Endowment for the Arts v. Finley*, 118 S.Ct. 2168 (1998).

Cooley, Thomas McIntyre

Thomas Cooley (1824–1898), a University of Michigan law professor, state supreme court justice, and chair of the Interstate
Commerce Commission, was one of the nineteenth century's
most influential treatise writers. Cooley's *Treatise on the Constitutional Limitations Which Rest upon the Legislative Power of the
United States of the American Union* (1868) evinced a broad-ranging suspicion toward concentrated and arbitrary power and was
solicitous of a wide array of individual freedoms, including both
property rights and the freedom of speech. A notable critic of the
Bad Tendency test, Cooley argued that free discussion was of
unique importance in the United States, where free government
was premised upon popular sovereignty.

Defamation

Defamation is the legal wrong done to a person when one publicly
holds him or her up to scorn or ridicule, in the process damaging
his or her reputation. Oral defamation is known as "slander," and
written defamation is known as "libel." The scope of defamation,
and the penalties attached to it, have varied greatly over the course
of Anglo-American legal history. Although in the past, one could
be charged criminally with defamation (as often happened in seditious libel cases), today nearly all defamation actions are civil actions seeking money damages. Under English law, truth was not a
defense in defamation suits (it was said that "the greater the truth,
the greater the libel"). Under contemporary U.S. law, however,
truth is a defense. The U.S. Supreme Court set the parameters of
modern defamation law—which is highly speech protective, at
least insofar as public figures are concerned—in the civil rights

case of *New York Times v. Sullivan* (376 U.S. 254 [1964]). There, concerned about the "chilling effect" on high-value speech that a broad-ranging definition of defamation would create, the Court, in an opinion by Justice Brennan, held that public officials cannot recover damages even for false statements against them unless those statements were made with "actual malice," or, put otherwise, with either knowledge of the statement's falsity or reckless disregard for its truth.

Doctrinal Tests

Many of the provisions of the U.S. Constitution, including the free speech clause, are too broad and abstract to provide courts with adequate guidance to make constitutional rulings in concrete cases. Thus, in actually implementing the Constitution, courts have devised a series of doctrinal tests that put flesh on the bones of those abstract provisions. Over the years, the Court has devised (and altered and abandoned) a number of important doctrinal tests for assessing the constitutionality of laws affecting the freedom of speech. These tests include the Bad Tendency test, the Clear and Present Danger test, the Hand test, and a reasonableness test concerning time, place, and manner regulations. The Court also applies different standards of judgment to regulations of speech depending on where (or in what forum) it takes place, and it applies different standards to laws affecting high-value and low-value speech. To understand the meaning of the First Amendment today, as a practical matter, one must go beyond the document's text and make sense of the way the facts of a particular case fit into the web of prevailing court-created doctrinal categories and tests.

Dodge, Mabel

Mabel Dodge (1879–1962) was a Buffalo heiress whose lower-Fifth-Avenue salon in New York City became one of the centers of "free-thought talk" in the early years of the twentieth century. At Dodge's salons, guests from all walks of life, including anarchists, socialists, union leaders, sex radicals, housewives, artists, and lawyers, were invited to mix and talk openly about serious topics, no matter how controversial. Dodge's salon played an important role in promoting highly latitudinarian understandings of free speech. When sexual and political radicals (many of whom attended Dodge's salons) were prosecuted for expressing their views, these conceptions of free speech were introduced in court. Over time, they came to constitute the core of contemporary free speech law.

Espionage Act

In 1917, Congress passed the Espionage Act, a criminal statute aimed at prosecuting those whom the Wilson administration believed were hindering the U.S. war effort in World War I. The act provoked a storm of controversy, both in Congress and more broadly, in reaction to the restrictions it placed on the freedom of speech. Prosecutions under the act inspired many to become civil libertarians and led to a series of landmark Supreme Court rulings (which nevertheless upheld the act's constitutionality) launching the Court's modern free speech and civil liberties jurisprudence. See *Masses Publishing Co. v. Patten,* 244 Fed. 535 (S.D.N.Y. 1917); *Schenck v. United States,* 249 U.S. 47 (1919); *Abrams v. United States,* 250 U.S. 616 (1919).

Establishment Clause

In addition to guaranteeing the freedom of speech, the First Amendment also provides in its establishment clause that "Congress shall make no law respecting an establishment of religion." Although this clause was originally understood as prohibiting the creation of a national church, in the middle years of the twentieth century, the Supreme Court began to interpret it as requiring that a "wall of separation" exist between church and state. In a series of cases involving voluntary school prayer and incidental moneys going to parochial schools, the Court created a "strict separation" doctrine, which in effect cut off most public moneys from religious schools and banned almost all forms of religious expression from public schools. In a series of cases involving student religious groups requesting meeting space and funding on the same basis as secular groups, however, the late-twentieth- and early-twenty-first-century Supreme Court began to consider its earlier strict separationist establishment clause rulings as unconstitutional viewpoint discrimination that violated the freedom of speech. See *Everson v. Board of Education*, 330 U.S. 1 (1947); *Engel v. Vitale*, 370 U.S. 421 (1962); *Lemon v. Kurtzman*, 403 U.S. 602 (1971); *Lamb's Chapel v. Center Moriches Union Free School District*, 508 U.S. 384 (1993); *Rosenberger v. University of Virginia*, 515 U.S. 819 (1995); *Good News Club v. Milford Central School*, 533 U.S. 98 (2001).

Fairness Doctrine

In 1949, the Federal Communications Commission (FCC), which is charged with the allocation and regulation of the broadcast airwaves in the "public interest, convenience, and necessity," promulgated the fairness doctrine, requiring broadcasters to both devote airtime to and provide balanced coverage of public issues. The Supreme Court, citing the limited available space on the broadcast airwaves (which it contrasted with newspapers), has unanimously upheld the constitutionality of the fairness doctrine. *Red Lion Broadcasting Co. v. FCC*, 395 U.S. 367 (1969).

Federalists

The Federalists were Americans who, believing in the importance of a strong and stable national government, favored the replacement of the Articles of Confederation with the Constitution of the United States (1787). The Anti-Federalists, the chief antagonists of the Federalists, opposed ratification of the Constitution on the grounds that it would consolidate national power to the extent that the country would devolve into a centralized despotism that would sharply curtail their fundamental rights. After successfully persuading the American people to ratify the Constitution, the Federalists grew into a political party that counted George Washington, John Adams, and Alexander Hamilton among its members. Following ratification, many of the rights-based, anticentralizing arguments of the Anti-Federalists were taken up by the partisans of Jeffersonianism, which found a home in the Democratic-Republican Party.

"Fighting Words" Doctrine

In *Chaplinsky v. New Hampshire* (315 U.S. 568 [1942]), the Court upheld the constitutionality of a state law barring public speech that is derisive and offensive, on the grounds that the law was a legitimate means of preserving the public peace. According to the "fighting words" doctrine articulated by the Court in *Chaplinsky*, derisive and offensive statements, like low-value, unprotected obscenity and libel, play "no essential part of any exposition of ideas, and are of such slight social value as a step to truth that any benefit that may be derived from them is clearly outweighed by the social interest in order and morality" (572). Despite this ruling, the Court's subsequent decisions raise serious doubts about whether the "fighting words" doctrine is still good law. See *Terminiello v. Chicago*, 337 U.S. 1 (1949); *Brandenburg v. Ohio*, 395 U.S. 444 (1969); *R.A.V. v. St. Paul*, 505 U.S. 377 (1992).

Forums

Over the course of the twentieth century, the Supreme Court has developed constitutional doctrine that accords different levels of scrutiny to speech depending upon the forum in which it takes place. Strict scrutiny (which holds that the law must be "narrowly tailored in the service of a compelling government interest") is applied to such traditional public forums as public parks and to such government-designated public forums as the campuses of state universities. A lower level of scrutiny (which holds that a regulation is constitutional if it is reasonable), however, is applied to other government properties, such as airport terminals. The First Amendment does not limit restrictions on speech imposed on private property, including the campuses of private colleges and universities. See *Hague v. CIO*, 307 U.S. 496 (1939); *Shuttlesworth v. Birmingham*, 394 U.S. 147 (1969).

Free Speech Absolutism

Free speech absolutism was an approach to free speech championed by Justice Hugo Black (and agreed to by Justice William O. Douglas). It takes a literalist approach to the First Amendment's free speech clause, holding that the amendment says "Congress shall make no law . . ." and that that is precisely what it means. Because Justice Black took the constitutional text at its word and because he was skeptical of judicial power, he opposed efforts by others on the Court to balance the freedom of speech against competing government interests. Although Justice Black's absolutism was highly protective of speech, its effect was mitigated somewhat in practice by his simultaneous commitment to drawing a sharp distinction between speech and conduct. Black held, for example, that wearing a black armband to school to protest the Vietnam War was conduct rather than speech. As such, it was not entitled to First Amendment protection. See *Tinker v. Des Moines*, 393 U.S. 503 (1969).

Free Speech League

The Free Speech League was the first association in the United States specifically devoted to the protection and promotion of the freedom of speech. It was organized in New York City in 1902 by Theodore Schroeder, Emma Goldman, and others in response to the crackdown on anarchists and other radicals in the wake of the assassination of President William McKinley. The league proved highly influential, serving as a predecessor of the American Civil Liberties Union, and its creation marked the beginning of the political and intellectual movement toward contemporary civil libertarian understandings of the freedom of speech.

Gag Rule

In the 1830s, antislavery petitions began to flood into the U.S. Congress, and in 1836, at the behest of Representative Henry Pinckney of South Carolina, the House passed a rule that provided that "all petitions, memorials, resolutions, propositions, or papers relating in any way, or to any extent whatsoever, to the subject of slavery, or the abolition of slavery, shall, without being either printed or referred, be laid upon the table, and no further action whatever shall be had thereon" (quoted in Curtis 2000, 177–178). Abolitionists and their supporters in Congress, including Massachusetts Representative John Quincy Adams, considered this "gag rule" to be a clear violation of their First Amendment right to "petition the Government for a redress of grievances" and campaigned unceasingly against it. With the growth of antislavery sentiment in the North, Adams's efforts finally paid off, and the gag rule was repealed in 1844.

Goldman, Emma

Emma Goldman (1869–1940) was an immigrant anarchist, sex radical, and denizen of the bohemian set in early-twentieth-century Greenwich Village. Although she spent much of her time in New York, Goldman also gave lecture tours around the country, shocking and thrilling her audiences with her outspoken advocacy of the abolition of government and of the bonds of marriage, her excoriation of Christianity and capitalism, and her promotion of free love (including homosexuality), free speech, and other civil liberties. Goldman was prosecuted several times for her dangerous views. The government stripped her of her citizenship in 1908, and she was jailed for opposing the draft during World War I. During the Red Scare, Goldman, who had repeatedly expressed admiration for the Russian Revolution, was deported to the Soviet Union, along with her lover and comrade Alexander Berkman.

Guarantee Clause

Article IV, Section 4 of the Constitution provides that "[t]he United States shall guarantee to every State in this Union a Republican Form of Government." Although the U.S. Supreme Court has only rarely invoked this clause in deciding a case, it has played an important part in constitutional debates arising outside the courts, including those involving the freedom of speech. Liberty of speech, it has been argued, is one of the pillars of the free, republican government vouchsafed by this provision.

Hand Test

The Hand test—named for its creator, the highly respected federal appeals court judge Learned Hand (1872–1961), (often considered the greatest U.S. judge never to sit on the Supreme Court)—is a free speech test that accorded legal weight to the context of that speech. In cases involving provocative political speech, Hand asserted in his appellate opinion in *Dennis v. United States* (183 F.2d 201 [1950]) that the question for a court should be "whether the gravity of the 'evil,' discounted by its improbability, justifies such invasion of free speech as is necessary to avoid the danger" (212). The Supreme Court adopted the *Hand* test in its own decision in *Dennis.* The Hand test was subsequently abandoned for the more speech-protective incitement test. But in environments of high public risk—such as the war against terrorism of 2002—the test, with its appreciation for political necessity and the preservation of the public safety, might well be revived.

Harassment Codes

In the late twentieth century, under the influence of the feminist and multicultural political movements, many U.S. colleges and universities enacted harassment codes that banned not only harassing conduct but also speech involving race, sex, religion, sexual orientation, or national origin that is "intimidating, hostile, or offensive" and is thus held to create a "hostile environment" in alleged violation of the nondiscrimination provisions of the Civil Rights Act of 1964 (29 C.F.R., sec. 1604.11(a) [2001]). (The prohibition on "hostile environments" is not part of the law itself but was imported into it by judicial interpretation at the behest of law professors.) These codes are typically enforced in an arbitrary and politicized manner that reflects the political commitments of those who draft and enforce them (prohibiting, for example, stereotypes of blacks, women, and some foreigners but not of males, whites, or Americans). Many are insulated from constitutional scrutiny because of their adoption by private universities. Even when they are instituted in public settings, most courts have ignored the free speech implications of these codes, though criticism of them on constitutional grounds has become increasingly common.

Hate Speech

During the late 1980s and the 1990s, a number of prominent academics and currents of thought within academia, such as feminism and critical race theory, influenced by the leftist imperatives of the 1960s, began to argue for the regulation of hate speech, or speech that stereotypes, stigmatizes, or offends an individual on the basis of race, ethnicity, religion, sex, sexual orientation, national origin, age, veteran status, or other such factors. Although in theory the hate speech codes that college faculties imposed on many campuses swept broadly, they were designed with specific stereotypes in mind and enforced accordingly. (Transgressions against white men, military veterans, and those whose national origin was American were ignored). As authority for their constitutional legitimacy, those who drafted hate speech regulations both on and off campus cited supportive Supreme Court precedent from the 1940s and 1950s concerning "fighting words" and group libel. Contemporary courts have tended to strike them down, at least in their more explicit guises, however, as blatantly unconstitutional forms of content and viewpoint discrimination. Many survive, however, in private institutions not bound by the First Amendment (such as private universities) and in harassment codes, which the courts have almost uniformly upheld. See *Chaplinsky v. New Hampshire*, 315 U.S. 568 (1942); *Beauharnais v. Illinois*, 343 U.S. 250 (1952); *R.A.V. v. St. Paul*, 505 U.S. 377 (1992).

Hicklin Test

The *Hicklin* test, which was rooted in the English court decision of *Regina v. Hicklin* (L.R.3 Q.B. 360 [1868]), was the common law test for obscenity in the late-nineteenth and early-twentieth-century United States. In following this test, courts were charged with inquiring "whether the tendency of the matter charged as obscenity is to deprave and corrupt the morals of those whose minds are open to such influences, and into whose hands a publication of that sort may fall" (quoted in Gurstein 1996, 74). The *Hicklin* test focused on individual (rather than societal) corruption and trained its attention on the weakest person who might come across the material. As such, it swept a wide array of materials into the category of impermissible obscenity. The *Hicklin* test, like the Comstock Act, was anathema to sex radicals and early civil libertarians, who made sustained and ultimately successful efforts to replace it with more speech-protective constitutional doctrine.

High-Value Speech

The Supreme Court takes a two-tiered approach to free speech issues, distinguishing high-value speech (including political, scientific, and artistic speech), which stands at the core of the First Amendment, from low-value speech, such as libel, obscenity, blackmail, criminal advocacy, and false advertising, which do not. Although the Court is highly protective of high-value speech, it permits extensive regulation of low-value speech and even permits it to be banned altogether. What types of speech fall into which category has altered significantly over the course of U.S. history in response to the alteration of political, economic, and social contexts. Subversive advocacy was once considered low-value speech, as were offensive, indecent, and blasphemous speech. All are currently accorded constitutional protection as high-value speech. In recent years, the Court has become more protective of commercial speech. See *Chaplinsky v. New Hampshire*, 315 U.S. 568 (1942); *Gitlow v. New York*, 268 U.S. 652 (1925); *44 Liquormart v. Rhode Island*, 517 U.S. 484 (1996).

Holmes, Jr., Oliver Wendell

Oliver Wendell Holmes, Jr. (1841–1935), one of the most influential jurists and legal scholars in U.S. history, was a professor of law at Harvard, a justice of the Supreme Judicial Court of Massachusetts, and an associate justice of the U.S. Supreme Court (1902–1932). He was also the author of a number of landmark legal studies. Holmes was skeptical of judicial power and of formalistic and natural rights–based understandings of law. He was a proponent of science and of the power of governments to experiment to advance what they took to be the public interest (though, as a Darwinian and a pessimist, Holmes's arguments were based more on a vision of the inevitable triumph of the powerful than on a belief in progress). Notwithstanding his skepticism concerning judicial power, Holmes was a pioneer in prodding the Supreme Court to become an aggressive protector of the freedom of speech. Holmes was the first justice—typically joined by his friend and colleague Louis D. Brandeis—to challenge the use of the Bad Tendency test in free speech cases and favored replacing it with the more speech-protective Clear and Present Danger test. In his famously eloquent opinions in the Red Scare cases, Holmes, echoing John Stuart Mill, anchored his case for new protections for the freedom of speech in the role free speech plays in the sciencelike search for truth. These cases in many ways mark the beginning not only of the modern law of free speech but also, more broadly, of the modern law of civil liberties. See *Schenck v. United States*, 249 U.S. 47 (1919); *Abrams v. United States*, 250 U.S. 616 (1919); *Gitlow v. New York*, 268 U.S. 652 (1925).

Incitement Test

The Incitement test is a twentieth-century doctrinal test that was advanced by the Court in *Brandenburg v. Ohio* (395 U.S. 444 [1969]), a case involving a cross-burning by the Ku Klux Klan. Under this test, which represents a high-water mark of latitudinarian conceptions of free speech, speech can be restricted only when it "is directed to inciting or producing imminent lawless action and is likely to incite or produce such action" (447). Although the test is broadly worded, in practice it is applied mainly to cases involving radical political speech. It is not considered relevant in cases involving price-fixing, or obscenity, perjury, or a wide variety of other matters. See also *Whitney v. California*, 274 U.S. 357 (1927).

Incorporation

Incorporation is the legal doctrine holding that the Bill of Rights constitutionally limits the conduct of both the national and the state governments. From the Founding through the end of the nineteenth century, the amendments making up the Bill of Rights (including the First Amendment) were understood to limit only the national government. Late in that century, however, the Supreme Court began to assert that the privileges and immunities and the due process clauses of the Fourteenth Amendment (1868) had nationalized the protection of certain fundamental rights. Which rights had become nationalized was a matter of dispute, but over time, the justices came to agree that certain express provisions of the Bill of Rights were so fundamental as to be "incorporated" as protections against the states via the Fourteenth Amendment. In *Gitlow v. New York* (268 U.S. 652 [1925]), the Court held that the freedom of speech was an incorporated right. Today, most free speech cases involve state laws, and hence, technically speaking, they arise under the provisions of both the First and the Fourteenth Amendments. See *Barron v. Baltimore,* 32 U.S. 243 (1833); *Palko v. Connecticut,* 302 U.S. 319 (1937).

Indecent Speech

In the late nineteenth and early twentieth centuries, the category of "indecent speech" was applied broadly in public discourse to refer to various types of speech, including obscenity, profanity, and blasphemy, that were not protected by the law. Today, however, the category of indecent speech applies more narrowly to sex-related speech that is held to be constitutionally protected, in contradistinction to "obscene" speech, which is not. See *Cohen v. California,* 403 U.S. 15 (1971); *FCC v. Pacifica Foundation,* 438 U.S. 726 (1978); *Reno v. ACLU,* 521 U.S. 844 (1997).

Judicial Review

Judicial Review is the power of the courts, including, most prominently, the U.S. Supreme Court, to review a law and to declare it unconstitutional. Although this power was not explicitly granted in the text of the Constitution, many (such as Alexander Hamilton, who justified the practice in *Federalist Paper* no. 78) assumed its existence. John Marshall explicitly announced the Supreme Court's judicial review powers in *Marbury v. Madison* (5 U.S. 137 [1803]), arguing that the Constitution is the fundamental law of the sovereign U.S. people and that thus any statute that violates that law must be void. He added, further, that "it is emphatically the province and duty of the judicial department to say what the law is" (177). However, the Court began routinely exercising the power of judicial review in free speech cases only in the twentieth century. In doing so, it assesses the constitutionality of both state and federal laws.

Kent, James

James Kent (1763–1847) was one of the most influential jurist-scholars and treatise writers in early-nineteenth-century America. Kent practiced law privately, taught law at Columbia University, and served both as chief justice of New York's highest court and as chancellor of the State of New York. (He is often referred to as "Chancellor Kent.") After retiring from the bench, Kent published his *Commentaries on American Law* (1826–1830), which were welcomed as the U.S. counterpart to Blackstone's *Commentaries*. A staunch Federalist and admirer of Alexander Hamilton, Kent revered the common law. In his *Commentaries*, which were widely used as a reference work by scholars and practicing lawyers alike, Kent passed on this reverence. His understanding of free speech was Hamiltonian in its assertion that speech and press were legally protected if the statements at issue were made for a legitimate purpose, without malicious motives, to advance the public good. Kent's *Commentaries* held false statements to be malicious per se. This standard was less libertarian than others advanced later, and it accorded significant power to judges in private lawsuits and criminal libel prosecutions.

Ku Klux Klan

The Ku Klux Klan is a racist, white-supremacist group, known for its distinctive garb of white sheets and hoods, with roots in the post–Civil War U.S. South. The antiblack, anti-Catholic, anti-Jewish, anti-immigrant, and antiforeigner Klan has a history of engaging in murder and lynchings as well as of articulating racist and nativist views. The Klan has put to the test modern First Amendment doctrine's commitment to be "content neutral" in its regulation of free speech, and the contemporary Supreme Court has upheld Klan-initiated cross-burnings, for example, as constitutionally protected forms of symbolic speech. See *Brandenburg v. Ohio*, 395 U.S. 444 (1969).

Law Reviews

Law reviews are student-run scholarly journals published by U.S. law schools. They contain articles authored by law professors on a wide variety of legal topics, including those on the freedom of speech. Law review articles are frequently read and cited by judges in issuing rulings involving the freedom of speech. They are thus one of the primary conduits of influence for professors seeking to advance particular understandings of the purpose and scope of that freedom.

Libel

Libel is defamation by writing. It is distinguished from "slander," which is defamation by oral utterance. Libel law was, in its origins, a product of the common law, and its scope was very broad for much of Anglo-American legal history. Libel law traditionally provided for either civil lawsuits or criminal prosecutions of anyone who printed something that publicly injured, embarrassed, or ridiculed someone else and thus damaged their reputation. Over the years, various defenses to libel developed, the most important being the truth of the assertion. Libel suits were common for much of U.S. history, but such suits, particularly when they involved political issues and newspapers, seemed in many ways to run counter to arguments on behalf of broad protections for free speech and a free press. In the 1960s, in the landmark case of *New York Times v. Sullivan* (376 U.S. 254 [1964]), the scope of the law of libel was sharply limited by constitutional considerations. Today, matters of public interest are largely immune from libel suits, and libel prosecutions are much rarer than they were in earlier times.

Liberal Club

The Liberal Club, founded in 1912, was a private social club that met on MacDougal Street in New York City's Greenwich Village. Its purpose was to create a place where (against the conventions of the time) men and women could meet, drink, and talk freely on topics that had long been considered taboo in polite company. Liberal Club members deliberately sought to shatter social and cultural boundaries by listening to popular music, taking up lowbrow dance steps, championing modern art, and broaching radical ideas about sex, art, and politics. The club hosted visits from Margaret Sanger, Emma Goldman, and other radicals, and it played an important role in germinating wide-ranging, latitudinarian conceptions of free speech.

License

Traditional common law understandings of free speech, as summarized by William Blackstone and adopted by the American colonists, distinguished between legally permissible "liberty" and impermissible "license." For the English and for most Americans before the twentieth century, "liberty" consisted of the freedom of a self-governing individual to say whatever he wanted—provided he had a good motive and promoted (or at least, did not harm) the public good. "License," on the other hand, was ill-governed speech, whether true or not, that was offered out of bad motives or that brought with it harmful social consequences. For Blackstone, for nineteenth-century U.S. treatise writers like Joseph Story, and for lawyers, judges, and others, it was a long-standing article of faith that whereas liberty in speech was either constitutionally protected or immune from common law prosecution or judgment, license was not. In the contemporary United States, this distinction has collapsed, and utterances that would once have been considered licentious may now be theoretically defined as socially useful.

Lovejoy, Elijah

Elijah Lovejoy (1802–1837) was a Presbyterian minister and the outspoken abolitionist editor of the *Alton (Illinois) Observer.* Mobs and vandals repeatedly destroyed Lovejoy's printing presses for stirring up antislavery sentiment. In November 1837, while fighting to defend his fourth press against an angry mob, Lovejoy was shot dead. His death attracted national attention, and Lovejoy became a symbol to abolitionists and others of the ways the denial of liberty inherent in chattel slavery necessarily degraded other constitutional liberties such as the freedom of the press and the freedom of speech.

Low-Value Speech

The Supreme Court takes a two-tiered approach to free speech issues, distinguishing high-value speech (including political, scientific, and artistic speech), which stands at the core of the First Amendment, from low-value speech, such as libel, obscenity, blackmail, criminal advocacy, and false advertising, which do not. Although the Court is highly protective of high-value speech, it permits extensive regulation of low-value speech and even permits it to be banned altogether. What types of speech fall into which category has altered significantly over the course of U.S. history in response to the alteration of political, economic, and social contexts. Subversive advocacy was once considered low-value speech, as were offensive, indecent, and blasphemous speech. All are currently accorded constitutional protection as high-value speech. In recent years, the Court has become more protective of commercial speech. See *Chaplinsky v. New Hampshire*, 315 U.S. 568 (1942); *Gitlow v. New York*, 268 U.S. 652 (1925); *44 Liquormart v. Rhode Island*, 517 U.S. 484 (1996).

Madison, James

James Madison (1751–1836), the draftsman of the Constitution and the Bill of Rights, was a coauthor (with Alexander Hamilton and John Jay) of *The Federalist Papers* and the fourth president of the United States (1809–1817). He was also one of the most influential spokesmen for the adoption of a uniquely American understanding of the freedom of speech. Although Madison did not believe a national Bill of Rights was necessary to preserve American freedoms, he drafted the Bill of Rights, including the First Amendment, after the proponents of the Constitution agreed to add it to the document to win over the opposition. Madison later became a leading proponent of nonestablishment and religious liberty. Madison was a staunch opponent of the Federalist-backed Sedition Act (1798). In opposing that act, Madison influentially argued that U.S. law departed from English common law on matters of speech. Given the theories of popular sovereignty and the commitment to self-government underlying the U.S. Constitution, he contended that in the United States, speech critical of the government was constitutionally protected.

McCain-Feingold Campaign Finance Law

After an extended period of debate about the allegedly corrupting influence of money in political life, President George W. Bush signed the McCain-Feingold Campaign Finance Reform Bill into law in 2002. The law places strict limits on soft money contributions to political parties, which many argued were being used to circumvent the laws limiting contributions to individual candidates. The law also places sharp restrictions on contributions financing broadcast advertisements running within sixty days of an election or thirty days of a party primary. No sooner was this law passed than it was immediately challenged in court as an unconstitutional restriction on the freedom of speech, specifically, on political speech, which stands at the core of the Court's understanding of high-value speech. Others contend, however, that the McCain-Feingold law regulates the contribution of money, not speech. Moreover, it does so in a reasonable effort to advance a legitimate public interest in protecting the political system against corruption and perception of corruption (a purpose approved by the Court in *Buckley v. Valeo,* 424 U.S. 1 [1976]). The constitutionality of the McCain-Feingold law will likely be determined by the U.S. Supreme Court.

McCarthyism

In the twentieth century, fear of communism and of Communist revolution had a considerable influence on thinking concerning the freedom of speech. From the time of the Bolshevik Revolution through World War II, suspicions that Communists were plotting to overthrow the U.S. government led to a significant amount of antisubversive legislation and to congressional and executive-branch investigations. With the fall of China to the Communists, the outbreak of the Korean War, and the Soviet advance into Eastern Europe, U.S. anxieties became particularly intense. It was at this time, in February 1950, that Wisconsin Senator Joseph McCarthy, in a speech in Wheeling, West Virginia, launched an aggressive crusade to root suspected Communists out of the U.S. government, a crusade that McCarthy continued in hearings of the House Un-American Activities Committee. Suspected Communists lost their jobs if they either refused to testify or if, though admitting past or present membership in the American Communist Party, they refused to publicly name other Party members. Though Communist infiltration of the government was a real problem and though seen in the proper historical context, the fears of communism were justified, McCarthy, a reckless alcoholic, cast his accusatory net much too broadly, drawing in noncommunist political opponents and other innocents. Though he received broad support in the country early on, before long he was discredited, and by 1954, even President Dwight D. Eisenhower and Vice President Richard Nixon were criticizing him. What many referred to as the era of McCarthyite witch-hunts (if not the struggle against communism) was over.

McKinley, William

William McKinley (1843–1901), president of the United States from 1897–1901, was assassinated in Buffalo, New York, by Leon Czolgosz, an immigrant anarchist and admirer of Emma Goldman. The McKinley assassination prompted both state and national governments to pass laws either sharply restricting or banning anarchist speech. In reaction to the undesirable effects of these laws, many began to fashion sustained legal and philosophical arguments on behalf of more latitudinarian conceptions of the freedom of speech.

Mill, John Stuart

John Stuart Mill (1806–1873) was an English philosopher, economist, and member of Parliament whose views on the freedom of speech and thought were articulated in his masterpiece, the philosophical work on human freedom *On Liberty* (1859). Mill methodically defended giving broad scope to the freedom of speech on the grounds that it was most conducive to the elimination of error and the discovery of truth. Mill also believed strongly in individual autonomy, which he declared essential to the cultivation of individual genius and realization of human happiness. Mill's defense of free speech and thought were immensely influential amongst philosophers and men of affairs alike. Oliver Wendell Holmes, Jr., who launched the Supreme Court's modern free speech jurisprudence, was an admirer of Mill's, and Mill's arguments proved to have considerable sway in many of the free speech arguments made on the High Court.

Miller Test

The *Miller* test, which was formulated in the Supreme Court's *Miller v. California* (413 U.S. 15 [1973]) decision, is the test the Court currently uses to determine the constitutionality of laws involving sex-related speech. The test adopts the long-standing rule that obscene (as opposed to indecent) materials are not entitled to First Amendment protection. According to the *Miller* test, material is obscene if "the average person, applying contemporary community standards, would find that the work, taken as a whole, appeals to the prurient interest; [and] the work depicts or describes, in a patently offensive way, sexual conduct specifically defined by the applicable state law; and the work, taken as a whole, lacks serious literary, artistic, political, or scientific value" (24).

Milton, John

John Milton (1608–1674), one of the great poets of the English language and the author of *Paradise Lost* (1667), was also a politically active Puritan. As a member of a dissenting sect, Milton publicly opposed the established church and aggressively championed the rights of conscience and the freedom of speech. His *Areopagitica* (1644) is considered one of the most influential defenses of free speech ever penned.

Naturalism

Naturalism is a late-nineteenth-century U.S. literary movement that arose out of the influence of scientific rationalism and Darwinian understandings of social problems. Naturalism emphasized the artistic imperative of frank, objective, and even brutal truth-telling in literature. It was in this spirit that such naturalist writers as Theodore Dreiser, Frank Norris, Stephen Crane, and Jack London took workers, prostitutes, and the poor as their subjects, commonly representing these people as pawns of an inhumane and unjust social order. Many naturalist writers took the further step of arguing that humanity could be redeemed only through the triumph of socialism. During the naturalist heyday, many influential literary critics judged their writings, with its incessant focus on life's low side and on helplessness, depravity, and sexual and personal abjection, to be unartistic and obscene.

Obscenity

Although the epithet "obscene" was long applied broadly to any sort of speech, from blasphemy to sexually explicit speech, that was held to be unprotected by law, the category of "obscenity" was narrowed considerably over the course of the twentieth century. Currently, obscenity is understood to be one of the two categories of sex-related speech—"indecency" being the other—used by courts for purposes of First Amendment analysis. Whereas indecent material is constitutionally protected, obscenity, which is considered low, disgusting, and without redeeming social value, is not. For most of U.S. history, neither definitions of the parameters of obscenity nor the banning of obscene materials aroused much controversy, since a broad consensus existed that such a ban was conducive to the public health, safety, and morals. Controversy was aroused on the fringes, however, in the late nineteenth and early twentieth centuries by sex radicals, and, subsequently, by birth control advocates and bohemians. By the late 1950s, however, assaults on the old norms became pervasive, and commercial pornography was increasingly available. The Court began hearing a larger volume of obscenity cases in the 1950s, and as it did so, it began to refine and alter its doctrine in the area. In *Roth v. United States* (354 U.S. 476 [1957]), Justice William Brennan set out a test for obscenity that asked "whether to the average person, applying contemporary community standards, the dominant theme of the material taken as a whole appeals to the prurient interest." This test was imprecise, and it was refined in a series of subsequent cases, at last reaching some measure of settlement in the case of *Miller v. California* (413 U.S. 15 [1973]), which held that material is obscene if, in the sensibilities of an average member of the community, its predominant theme is prurient, if it depicts sexual conduct in a patently offensive way, and if taken as a whole, it "lacks serious literary, artistic, political, or scientific value." Under contemporary Court doctrine, hard-core pornography may be banned outright. As a practical matter, however, the Internet has made obscene materials more readily available to a broader range of people than at any prior time in human history.

Overbreadth Doctrine

In its "overbreadth doctrine," the Supreme Court has declared that it is a violation of the First Amendment's free speech clause for the government to enforce a law in such a way that the scope of its prohibitions encompass both protected and unprotected expression (at least if that law is "substantially" overbroad). As such, the Court has said that overbroad laws have a "chilling effect" on constitutionally protected speech. For example, a law permitting the police to arrest people who annoy them has been struck down as unconstitutionally overbroad.

Police Powers

The term "police powers" refers to the residual powers of government to pass legislation aimed at advancing the public health, safety, and morals. Under traditional understandings of the U.S. Constitution, police powers were exercised exclusively by state and local governments, with the more limited category of specifically enumerated powers being exercised at the federal level. Today, however, both the national and state governments pass laws pursuant to the police power.

Preferred Freedoms Doctrine

The contemporary vision of the U.S. Supreme Court as the institution of government vitally and uniquely positioned to be the guarantor of fundamental personal rights against majoritarian tyranny was not a part of the original constitutional design. Rather, it was an outgrowth of the "preferred freedoms doctrine," which the Court created in the mid-twentieth century. The original constitutional design understood the Constitution as creating a national government of limited, enumerated powers. Rights and liberties were residual freedoms, or what was left over in the space where the limited national government could not act or intrude. However, when the Court placed its imprimatur on the creation of a national government of general, or unenumerated, powers in the 1930s (which has become the huge national government we know today), it began searching for some way to articulate constitutional limits on government in the new context. It alighted on the view that the constitution protected fundamental personal freedoms—such as the freedom of speech—and it held that these freedoms held a specially prized place in our constitutional system. The Supreme Court then announced itself to be primary institutional guarantor of those "preferred freedoms." Law professors who were politically supportive of this new constitutional vision (as most law professors were) in turn devoted themselves to crafting constitutional theories that effectively institutionalized it, rendering the vision synonymous in the public mind with the essence of U.S. constitutionalism itself.

Prior Restraint

Under the English common law, although one was liable for the harms caused by one's words, one could only be punished after one exercised the right to say what one wanted; that is, there were no prior restraints, such as those imposed by an official censor, on what one could say. For most of Anglo-American legal history, the prohibition on prior restraints constituted the core of the common law protection for the freedom of speech and press. Although the prohibition on prior restraints does not seem especially speech protective by today's standards, William Blackstone and others considered it one of the great achievements of English law. A regime of prior restraints—censorship—had been instituted in England in response to the rise of the printing press and public literacy and the subsequent proliferation of writings that England's Tudor monarchs found blasphemous and politically destabilizing. The Tudors set up a licensing scheme that required that any documents published in the realm be preapproved by a Crown censor. After intense political resistance to this regime, England ended it in the late seventeenth century. The Blackstonian understanding of the freedom of speech, holding that its core was the absence of prior restraints, was imported into American law and predominated in the colonial era and in the nation's early years. Gradually, however, this understanding was challenged by calls for a uniquely American approach to free speech that went beyond the prohibition on prior restraints to guarantee the broad-ranging protection of free speech even after publication.

Public Forum

Traditionally, public places such as streets and parks have been considered the property of the government. As the owner of the streets and parks, the government was presumed to have the right to control the speech there in any way it pleased. Beginning in the 1930s, however, on the theory that the people and not the government were the true owners of the streets and parks, the Supreme Court began to accord "public forums" special constitutional status, in the process sharply restricting the government's traditional ownership rights. Public forums, the Court argued, were unique spaces for assembly and public discussion. It held that reasonable regulation of speech in public forums (time, place, and manner regulations) is permissible. But content-based restrictions are unconstitutional. The question of what constitutes a "public forum" has been disputed in cases involving airports, shopping centers, and other venues. See *Hague v. CIO*, 307 U.S. 496 (1939); *Cox v. Louisiana*, 379 U.S. 536 (1965); *International Society for Krishna Consciousness v. Lee*, 505 U.S. 672 (1992).

Puritans

The Puritans, a dissenting Protestant sect in England, were persecuted for denying the religious authority of the realm's established church, the Church of England. Puritan arguments concerning the liberty of conscience and the related obligation to exercise one's free will on matters of religion and religious practice had a profound influence on the development of a commitment to individual liberty in Anglo-American law. And it was thus not coincidental that devout Puritans such as Peter Wentworth and John Milton were among the earliest and most vehement advocates of the freedom of speech. Because what was to become the United States was initially settled by Puritans and other religious dissenters fleeing religious persecution in England, these commitments to individual liberty became one of the foundations of U.S. law and U.S. political culture.

Realism

Realism is a literary movement that placed supreme value on seeing and depicting life as it really was, directly and honestly, without the distortions of artistic interpretation. Although the realist movement had eighteenth-century roots, it reached its apogee in the late nineteenth and early twentieth centuries, when it dovetailed with a cresting commitment to scientific rationalism that valued objective observation over the stylizations and emotionalisms of romanticism. European writers such as Honoré de Balzac, Gustave Flaubert, Emile Zola, Leo Tolstoy, and Fyodor Dostoyevsky were among the most influential pioneers of literary realism, which in turn influenced the naturalism of such U.S. writers as Theodore Dreiser, Jack London, and Frank Norris. These writers, who in their novels and stories frankly depicted the more brutal and coarser side of U.S. life (often as a form of social criticism), were frequently criticized as dirty, low, and ignoble. As such, many considered their work to be lacking in artistic merit, and the appropriateness of its public dissemination was called into question.

Red Scare

In the aftermath of the Bolshevik Revolution (1917) and the end of the First World War (1918), the United States experienced a wave of anticommunist sentiment and an attendant crackdown on political radicals known as "The Red Scare" (1919–1920). The staunch opposition of socialists and radicals to American entry into the war and the enthusiasm expressed by homegrown and immigrant radicals for bringing anarchism and Bolshevism home to the U.S. laid the groundwork for the Red Scare. But the crackdown itself was sparked by a series of radically destabilizing events, including massive strikes, and attempts on the lives of thirty-eight leading U.S. politicians, including U.S. Attorney General, A. Mitchell Palmer. These events convinced many that the U.S. government was on the verge of being overthrown. The crackdown, which was led by Palmer himself, involved a series of prosecutions under the Espionage Act (1917) and the Sedition Act (1918), as well as the round-up of 10,000 suspected anarchists and Communists in the so-called Palmer Raids (1919). A slightly smaller round of arrests took place in 1920, and many of the suspected radicals were held without access to a lawyer, without being informed of the charges against them, and without trial. Some, including Emma Goldman and Alexander Berkman, were deported to the Soviet Union. Over time, the U.S. people became less fearful that the overthrow of the government was imminent, and Palmer was broadly criticized for his assault on civil liberties.

Sanger, Margaret

Margaret Sanger (1879–1966) was a radical socialist nurse who, in the interest of liberating women (and men) and promoting public health, championed the broad dissemination of birth control information and devices. Her books and other writings made her famous, and her prosecution under the obscenity laws for running a contraception clinic in Brooklyn made her a cause célèbre. Not surprisingly, Sanger became one of the nation's most relentless critics of the federal Comstock Act (1873). She ran with New York's bohemian radicals, frequented the Liberal Club, and supported strikes by the members of the Industrial Workers of the World. That radical labor union, along with Theodore Schroeder's Free Speech League and a raft of Greenwich Village rebels, supported Sanger's cause on free speech grounds. Through her activism, Sanger became a champion and symbol of modern, latitudinarian conceptions of the freedom of speech.

Schroeder, Theodore

Theodore Schroeder (1864–1953), a lawyer and legal activist and theorist, was a pioneer of twentieth-century civil libertarian understandings of the freedom of speech. In his many pamphlets and in his work for New York City's Free Speech League (which commonly defended labor and sexual radicals), Schroeder played a major role in convincing influential people to draw a sharp distinction between the substantive content of obscene and radical speech, which they might find distasteful, and the broader and desirable principle of the freedom of speech. In doing so, Schroeder laid the intellectual groundwork for many of the century's later civil libertarian free speech theorists, who routinely argued that speech was to be protected even if one disagreed with or even abhorred its content. In later years, this view would be adopted by the U.S. Supreme Court, which held that it was unconstitutional to restrict speech on the basis of its content or viewpoint, no matter how distasteful or abhorrent.

Sedition Act

The Sedition Act (1798) was passed by Congress at the urging of Federalist President John Adams. Its aim was to tamp down criticism of the government and public officials in a highly unstable period in the nation's early history. The act subjected an individual to either a fine or imprisonment for defaming or bringing into contempt or disrepute either the government or government officials. The act spawned a number of high-profile and highly politicized prosecutions by Federalists against their Jeffersonian enemies. The Sedition Act prosecutions were adjudicated according to the speech-protective standards set by the Zenger trial (1735). According to these standards, truth was a defense, and the jury, rather than the judge, was charged with assessing the libelousness of the words. Nonetheless, many, both at this time and afterward, believed that the Sedition Act ran counter to fundamental U.S. commitments to free speech principles, if not to the Constitution itself. In 1964, the Supreme Court retrospectively announced that the Sedition Act had been unconstitutional. See *New York Times v. Sullivan,* 376 U.S. 254 (1964).

Seditious Libel

Dating from seventeenth-century England, seditious libel was a crime involving oral or written attacks on the government or public officials. Initially, judges rather than juries were charged with determining whether a libel had occurred. And truth was no defense to the charge. Indeed, the more truth to the attack, the greater the offense was considered because it was held that a truthful attack would probably cause more severe damage to the libeled individual. In the Zenger decision (1735), a colonial American jury famously spurned the English rules concerning seditious libels by declaring truth a defense and transferring the question of the libelousness nature of the statement from the judge to the jury. The Sedition Act of 1798 made seditious libel a crime within the United States (within the limits set out by the Zenger decision), though that statute lapsed in 1801. For much of U.S. history, it was not clear whether seditious libel, a common law crime, ran counter to the strictures of the First Amendment. Many, however, staunchly contended that it did. Accordingly, prosecutions for sedition were relatively rare. (They were most likely to take place in wartime and pursuant to special acts passed with war in mind, such as the Espionage Act during World War I.) Starting at the time of World War I, the Supreme Court began to slowly dismantle most of the old law of seditious libel. Today, it is understood that under most conditions, the First Amendment affords considerable protection to those who criticize the government and public officials. See *Schenck v. United States*, 249 U.S. 47 (1919); *Abrams v. United States*, 250 U.S. 616 (1919); *Gitlow v. New York*, 268 U.S. 652 (1925); *New York Times v. Sullivan*, 376 U.S. 254 (1964).

Slander

Slander is defamation by oral utterance and is distinguished from "libel," or defamation by writing.

Speech and Debate Clause

Article 1, Section 6 of the U.S. Constitution, the "speech and debate clause," provides that members of Congress "for any Speech or Debate in either House . . . shall not be questioned in any other Place." The concerns addressed by this provision arose out of contention between the Crown and Parliament in sixteenth- and seventeenth-century England, when the Crown sought to stifle criticisms leveled against it by prosecuting and imprisoning troublesome members of Parliament. In the aftermath of these struggles, legislators' right to speak their minds freely during legislative deliberations has come to be considered one of the foundational rights of Anglo-American democratic constitutionalism.

Speech Plus

Constitutional guarantees of the freedom of speech had traditionally been understood to apply only to "speech," that is to verbal articulations, and a sharp distinction was drawn between protected speech and unprotected "conduct." Over the course of the twentieth century, however, the Supreme Court came to assert that expressive conduct—conduct that conveys a message—may come in many guises and is a form of constitutionally protected speech. For this reason, picketing, flag and cross-burning, and wearing a protest armband are now protected via the Constitution's guarantee of the freedom of speech. The scope of the protection accorded to expressive speech-plus-conduct, however, is far from clear. Though assassination may be politically expressive conduct, it is not constitutionally protected, nor is defacing a government building with a political or sexual message. See *Thornhill v. Alabama*, 310 U.S. 88 (1940); *Brandenburg v. Ohio*, 395 U.S. 444 (1969); *Tinker v. Des Moines*, 393 U.S. 503 (1969); *Texas v. Johnson*, 491 U.S. 397 (1989).

Story, Joseph

Joseph Story (1779–1845), the author of the three-volume work *Commentaries on the Constitution of the United States* (1833), was one of the most influential scholar-judges of the first half of the nineteenth century. A man of legendary and evident erudition, Story simultaneously served on the Supreme Court (1811–1845) and as Dane Professor of Law at Harvard. Although a Democratic-Republican (he was appointed to the High Court by James Madison), Story quickly fell into the orbit of the staunchly Federalist Chief Justice John Marshall. In the process, he earned a reputation for revering natural law, property rights, and national power and for heatedly opposing Jacksonian democracy. In his *Commentaries*, Story hewed to the traditional Blackstonian distinction between permissible liberty and impermissible license, and he asserted that the First Amendment's free speech guarantee must be understood in light of that distinction. As such, he held that under the U.S. Constitution, men have the right to publish without prior restraint "what is true, with good motives and for justifiable ends" (Story 1833, reprinted in Kurland and Lerner 1987, 182).

Sumner, Charles

Charles Sumner (1811–1874) was a vehemently abolitionist U.S. senator from Massachusetts who in May 1856 was severely beaten on the floor of the Senate by South Carolina Senator Preston Brooks. Brooks went after Sumner for a scathing speech Sumner had delivered on the Senate floor. The speech, entitled "The Crime against Kansas," attacked both slavery and, in highly personal and insulting terms, the members of Congress who defended it. Like the murder of abolitionist newspaper editor Elijah Lovejoy, the caning of Charles Sumner became a political symbol for the ways the continuing toleration of chattel slavery worked to degrade other fundamental freedoms, such as the freedom of speech.

Symbolic Speech

For much of U.S. history, "speech" for constitutional purposes was limited to "pure speech," that is, verbal communication, whether oral or written. During the twentieth century, however, the Supreme Court held that conduct that communicated a message symbolically—such as displaying a red flag, burning a draft card or the American flag, wearing a black armband to protest a war, or burning a cross—is not simply a case of conduct (which would make it subject to broad regulation) but rather a form of high-value, constitutionally protected speech. Today, such "symbolic speech" is a fully protected form of free expression. See *Stromberg v. California*, 283 U.S. 359 (1931); *United States v. O'Brien*, 391 U.S. 367 (1968); *Tinker v. Des Moines*, 393 U.S. 503 (1969); *Texas v. Johnson*, 491 U.S. 397 (1989); *R.A.V. v. St. Paul*, 505 U.S. 377 (1992).

Time, Place, and Manner Regulations

The Supreme Court has held that speech taking place in a public forum such as public streets and parks should be accorded special constitutional protection. But that protection is not absolute. Although it is almost always impermissible to regulate such speech on the basis of its content, the Court has held that the government may impose reasonable "time, place, and manner regulations" upon it. So, for example, the Court has upheld permit requirements for public marches, noise restrictions on public concerts, and time restrictions on sound trucks. The Court has also said that since the freedom of speech is a fundamental right, such regulations must be narrowly tailored to serve a legitimate and content-neutral government interest. See *Kovacs v. Cooper,* 336 U.S. 77 (1949); *Clark v. Community for Creative Non-Violence,* 468 U.S. 288 (1984); *Ward v. Rock against Racism,* 491 U.S. 781 (1989); *Madsen v. Women's Health Center,* 512 U.S. 753 (1994).

Vagueness Doctrine

Under contemporary free speech doctrine, the Supreme Court will hold a law regulating speech "void for vagueness" if a person of average intelligence would be uncertain whether the law would or would not apply to a particular form of expression. From a constitutional perspective, laws that are vague are deficient in two respects: First, they violate a fundamental requirement of the rule of law that people are able to know what the law is and thus able to alter their conduct accordingly. Second, vague laws have what the Court has called a "chilling effect," by which individuals who are uncertain about the law's scope (and hence its penalties) hesitate to exercise the full scope of their right to the freedom of speech. In *Coates v. City of Cincinnati, 402 U.S. 611* (1971), the Supreme Court struck down, on the grounds that it was unconstitutionally vague, a Cincinnati city ordinance that made it illegal for three or more people to meet on sidewalks and behave in a way that was "annoying" to passers-by.

Viewpoint Discrimination

The Supreme Court has held that the banning of discussion not of a topic but of one point of view on that topic amounts to unconstitutional "viewpoint discrimination." Such a ban, in its lack of even-handedness, is a distortion of the marketplace of ideas, which the Court is committed to defending. To ban all discussion of war, for example, would be a form of content discrimination (which is also unconstitutional, at least as it affects high-value speech). But to specifically ban speech advocating war (as does, for example, the International Covenant on Civil and Political Rights [1966]) would be unconstitutional viewpoint discrimination. See *Rust v. Sullivan*, 500 U.S. 173 (1991); *R.A.V. v. St. Paul*, 505 U.S. 377 (1992); *Rosenberger v. University of Virginia*, 515 U.S. 819 (1995); *National Endowment for the Arts v. Finley*, 524 U.S. 569 (1998).

Virginia and Kentucky Resolutions

Thomas Jefferson and James Madison drafted the Kentucky and Virginia Resolutions, respectively, in angry reaction to the Sedition Act (1798), which they considered an unconstitutional federal assault on free speech and other civil liberties. In those resolutions, they (and the Kentucky and Virginia legislatures that passed them) declared that states have the right to declare federal statutes—such as the Sedition Act—unconstitutional and hence null and void. The Constitution, they argued, is properly understood as compact among the states. By the terms of that compact, the national government was delegated specific and limited powers. It was up to the states, as compacting parties, to decide whether or not the national government had exceeded those powers, and if a state concluded that it had, that state had the right to declare the law void within its borders. The Virginia and Kentucky Resolutions are an illustration from the era before the ascendancy of the institutional power of the Supreme Court of the way people acted in legislatures and via other nonjudicial forms to protect constitutional freedoms, including the freedom of speech.

Wentworth, Peter

Peter Wentworth (1533–1593) was an outspoken sixteenth-century English Puritan and parliamentarian. In a speech entitled "On the Liberties of the Commons" (1576), he made one of the earliest and most eloquent pleas for the importance of respecting legislators' freedom of speech. He did so in defense of a speech he had made at Westminster sharply criticizing the powerful Queen Elizabeth I. Wentworth argued that allowing members of Parliament to speak frankly on the floor of the legislature was essential in helping the queen govern effectively, for it helped her more clearly discern both her and the realm's long-term interest. For his troubles, the queen imprisoned Wentworth in the Tower of London. Nonetheless, Wentworth's speech proved influential in shaping the future course of the freedom of speech in the Anglo-American constitutional tradition.

Wilkes, John

John Wilkes (1725–1797) was a member of Parliament who, in an anonymous 1763 pamphlet, the *North Briton* no. 45, vehemently attacked the English government and king. Infuriated by the seditious nature of the pamphlet, the Crown issued general search warrants authorizing officials to enter any house and seize any papers with the aim of uncovering the culprit. Wilkes was found out and arrested but later released. He successfully sued the government for the infringement of his liberties and won a large damages award from the presiding judge, Lord Camden. In the process, Wilkes transformed both himself and Lord Camden into folk heroes in the American colonies. At that same time, the colonists were deeply vexed by the high-handed tactics, including the issuance of general warrants, used on them by the Crown. The Wilkes case inspired the addition of the Fourth Amendment search and seizure protections to the Constitution. It also helped crystallize many Americans' commitment to the principle of the freedom of speech.

Wobblies

Founded in 1905, the Industrial Workers of the World (IWW) was one the nation's most radical labor unions. Its members, known as "Wobblies," prided themselves on working across the lines of race, sex, and ethnicity long before other unions did, and they saw the world as sharply divided into an employer class and a laborer class. They took politics to be a struggle for dominance between these two classes and fought for the revolutionary overthrow of capitalism and the elimination of the wage-labor system. The Wobblies had no interest in working within the system and preferred such aggressive tactics as strikes and sometimes even violence. Between 1909 and 1913, the Wobblies launched a series of organizing campaigns—the IWW Free Speech Campaigns—that involved fiery street-corner orations and the public distribution of revolutionary literature. In an unstable era torn by labor and anarchist violence, cities and towns passed ordinances intended to put a lid on this disruptive speech. The Wobblies defended themselves by declaring that their free speech rights were being violated. They were supported in their claims by New York bohemian artists and writers and by such newly emerging civil liberties groups as the Free Speech League. The Wobbly free speech fights mark one of the earliest political and intellectual mobilizations on behalf of modern, civil libertarian understandings of the freedom of speech.

Zenger, John Peter

The 1735 trial in New York City of John Peter Zenger (1697–1746), the publisher of a weekly newspaper, transformed the law of libel in America and marked an important departure, in favor of a broader conception of free speech, from the libel law of England. Zenger was charged with seditious libel for his sharp criticism of the governor general of New York. In his case, Zenger prevailed with his arguments: First, he argued that the truth of the libel should be allowed as a defense to the charges. (Under English law, the truth was not a defense.) Second, he argued that the jury (composed of Americans) rather than the judge should decide the legal issues of whether Zenger's published criticisms were of a seditious tendency and whether Zenger's intent in publishing it was lawful. (English law plainly provided that both of these issues were to be determined by the judge, not the jury.) The judge in the Zenger case dismissed these innovative arguments out of hand. But the jury in the case held for Zenger. The Zenger case was an early signal that the Americans, although cognizant of English law, would chart their own path when it came to the freedom of speech.

6

DOCUMENTS

PETER WENTWORTH, SPEECH ON THE LIBERTIES OF THE COMMONS (1576)

English Parliamentarian Peter Wentworth, who had harshly criticized the powerful Queen Elizabeth I, defended himself at Westminster, offering one of the earliest and most eloquent arguments on behalf of the freedom of speech of legislators.

Mr. Speaker, I find written in a little volume these words in effect: Sweet is the name of liberty, but the thing itself a value beyond all inestimable treasure. So much the more it behoveth us to take care lest we, contenting ourselves with the sweetness of the name, lose and forego the thing, being of the greatest value that can come unto this noble realm. The inestimable treasure is the use of it in this House. . . .

I conclude that in this House, which is termed a place of free speech, there is nothing so necessary for the preservation of the prince and state as free speech, and without, it is a scorn and mockery to call it a Parliament House, for in truth it is none, but a very school of flattery and dissimulation, and so a fit place to serve the devil and his angels, and not to glorify God and benefit the commonwealth. . . .

[T]wo things do great hurt in this place, of which I do mean to speak. The one is a rumour which runneth about the House, and this it is, "Take heed that you do; the Queen's Majesty liketh not such a matter;

whosoever speaketh against it, she will be much offended with him."
The other: sometimes a message is brought into the House, either of
commanding or inhibiting, very injurious to the freedom of speech and
consultation. I would to God, Mr Speaker, that these two were buried in
hell, I mean rumours and messages, for wicked undoubtedly they are;
the reason is, the devil was the first author of them, from whom pro-
ceedeth nothing but wickedness, . . .

Now the other was a message . . . brought the last sessions into the
House that we should not deal in any matters of religion but first to receive
from the bishops. Surely this was a doleful message, for it was as much as
to say, Sirs, ye shall not deal in God's causes, no, ye shall in no wise seek to
advance his glory. . . . God . . . was the last session shut out of doores. But
what fell out of it, forsooth? His great indignation was therefore poured
upon this House, for he did put into the Queen Majesty's heart to refuse
good and wholesome laws for her own preservation, the which caused
many faithful hearts for grief to burst out with sorrowful tears, and moved
all papists, traitors to God and her Majesty in their sleeves to laugh all the
whole Parliament House to scorn. . . . So certain it is, Mr Speaker, that
none is without fault, no, not our noble Queen, since then her Majesty
hath committed great fault, yea, dangerous faults to herself. . . .

[I]t is a dangerous thing in a prince to oppose or bend herself against
her nobility and people. . . . And how could any prince more unkindly
intreat, abuse, oppose herself against her nobility and people than her
Majesty did the last Parliament? And will not this her Majesty's han-
dling . . . make cold dealing in any of her Majesty's subjects toward her
again? I fear it will. . . . And I beseech . . . God to endue her Majesty
with his wisdom, whereby she may discern faithful advice from
traitorous, sugared speeches, and to send her Majesty a melting, yielding
heart unto sound counsel, that will may not stand for a reason; and then
her Majesty will stand when her enemies are fallen, for no estate can
stand where the prince will not be governed by advice.

JOHN MILTON, *AREOPAGITICA* (1644)

*Here, John Milton, English Puritan and poet, argues that Parliament
should reject a proposal that would outlaw the printing of any document
without prior approval by a government censor.*

I deny not but that it is of greatest concernment in the church and commonwealth to have a vigilant eye how books demean themselves, as well as men, and thereafter to confine, imprison, and do sharpest justice on them as malefactors. For books are not absolutely dead things, but do contain a potency of life in them to be as active as that soul was whose progeny they are; nay, they do preserve as in a vial the purest efficacy and extraction of that living intellect that bred them. I know they are as lively, and as vigorously productive, as those fabulous dragon's teeth; and being up and down, may chance to spring up armed men. And yet, on the other hand, unless wariness be used, as good almost kill a man as kill a good book: who kills a man kills a reasonable creature, God's image; but he who destroys a good book, kills reason itself, kills the image of God, as it were, in the eye. Many a man lives a burden to the earth; but a good book is the precious life-blood of a master spirit, embalmed and treasured up on purpose to a life beyond life. 'Tis true, no age can restore a life, whereof, perhaps, there is no great loss; and revolutions of ages do not oft recover the loss of a rejected truth, for the want of which whole nations fare the worse. . . .

When a man writes to the world, he summons up all his reason and deliberation to assist him; he searches, meditates, is industrious, and likely consults and confers with his judicious friends; after all which done, he takes himself to be informed in what he writes, as well as any that writ before him. If in this, the most consummate act of his fidelity and ripeness, no years, no industry, no former proof of his abilities can bring him to that state of maturity as not to be still mistrusted and suspected (unless he carry all his considerate diligence, all his midnight watchings and expense of Palladian oil, to the hasty view of an unleisured licenser, perhaps much his younger, perhaps far his inferior in judgment, perhaps one who never knew the labor of book-writing), and if he be not repulsed or slighted, must appear in print like a puny with his guardian, and his censor's hand on the back of his title to be his bail and surety that he is no idiot or seducer; it cannot be but a dishonor and derogation to the author, to the book, to the privilege and dignity of learning.

What should ye do then, should ye suppress all this flowery crop of knowledge and new light sprung up and yet springing daily in this city? Should ye set an oligarchy of twenty engrossers over it, to bring a famine upon our minds again, when we shall know nothing but what is measured to us by their bushel? Believe it, Lords and Commons, they who counsel ye to such a suppressing do as good as bid ye suppress yourselves and I will show how. If it be desired to know the immediate cause of all this free writing and free speaking, there cannot be assigned a truer than your own mild and free and humane government; it is the liberty, Lords and Commons, which your own valorous and happy counsels have purchased us, liberty which is the nurse of all great wits. This is that which hath rarefied and enlightened our spirits like the influence of heaven; this is that which hath enfranchised, enlarged, and lifted up our apprehensions degrees above themselves. Ye cannot make us now less capable, less knowing, less eagerly pursuing of the truth, unless ye first make yourselves, that made us so, less the lovers, less the founders of true liberty. We can grow ignorant again, brutish, formal, and slavish, as ye found us; but you then must first become that which ye cannot be, oppressive, arbitrary, and tyrannous, as they were from whom ye have freed us. . . .

JOHN TRENCHARD AND THOMAS GORDON, "OF FREEDOM OF SPEECH"

English Whigs John Trenchard (1662–1723) and Thomas Gordon (d. 1750) were harsh critics of the policies of King William III, of High-Church religious views, and of corruption. Writing under a pseudonym between 1720 and 1723, they published Cato's Letters *in the* London Journal *and the* British Journal. *These eloquent defenses of liberty were popular in both England and America and helped form the understandings of the founding generation concerning the freedom of speech.*

"That the Same Is Inseparable from Publick Liberty," Cato's Letter no. 15 (February 4, 1720)

Without Freedom of Thought, there can be no such Thing as Wisdom; and no such Thing as publick Liberty, without Freedom of Speech: Which is the Right of every Man, as far as by it he does not hurt and controul the Right of another; and this is the only Check which it ought to suffer, the only Bounds which it ought to know.

This sacred Privilege is so essential to free Government, that the Security of Property; and the Freedom of Speech, always go together; and in those wretched Countries where a Man cannot call his Tongue his own, he can scarce call any Thing else his own. Whoever would overthrow the Liberty of the Nation, must begin by subduing the Freedom of Speech; a Thing terrible to publick Traitors.

This Secret was so well known to the Court of King Charles I that his wicked Ministry procured a Proclamation to forbid the People to talk of Parliaments, which those Traitors had laid aside. To assert the undoubted Right of the Subject, and defend his Majesty's Legal Prerogative, was called Disaffection, and punished as Sedition. Nay, People were forbid to talk of Religion in their Families: For the Priests had combined with the Ministers to cook up Tyranny and suppress Truth and the Law. While the late King James, when Duke of York, went avowedly to Mass; Men were fined, imprisoned, and undone, for saying that he was a Papist: And, that King Charles II might live more securely a Papist, there was an Act of Parliament made, declaring it Treason to say that he was one.

That Men ought to speak well of their Governors, is true, while their Governors deserve to be well spoken of; but to do publick Mischief, without hearing of it, is only the Prerogative and Felicity of Tyranny: A free People will be shewing that they are so, by their Freedom of Speech.

The Administration of Government is nothing else, but the Attendance of the Trustees of the People upon the Interest and Affairs of the People. And as it is the Part and Business of the People, for whose Sake alone all publick Matters are, or ought to be, transacted, to see whether they be well or ill transacted; so it is the Interest, and ought to be the Ambition, of all honest Magistrates, to have their Deeds openly examined, and publickly scanned: Only the wicked Governors of Men dread what is said of them. . . .

Freedom of Speech is ever the Symptom, as well as the Effect, of good Government. In old Rome, all was left to the Judgment and Pleasure of the People; who examined the publick Proceedings with such Discretion, and censured those who administered them with such Equity and Mildness, that in the Space of Three Hundred Years, not Five publick

Ministers suffered unjustly. Indeed, whenever the Commons proceeded to Violence, the Great Ones had been the Aggressors. . . .

The best Princes have ever encouraged and promoted Freedom of Speech; they knew that upright Measures would defend themselves, and that all upright Men would defend them. . . .

Misrepresentation of publick Measures is easily overthrown, by representing publick Measures truly: When they are honest, they ought to be publickly known, that they may be publickly commended; but if they be knavish or pernicious, they ought to be publickly exposed, in order to be publickly detested. . . .

Freedom of Speech is the great Bulwark of Liberty; they prosper and die together: And it is the Terror of Traytors and Oppressors, and a Barrier against them. It produces excellent Writers, and encourages men of fine Genius. Tacitus tells us, that the Roman Commonwealth bred great and numerous Authors, who writ with equal Boldness and Eloquence: But when it was enslaved, those great Wits were no more. . . . Tyranny had usurped the Place of Equality, which is the Soul of Liberty, and destroyed publick Courage. The Minds of Men, terrified by unjust Power, degenerated into all the Vilenes[s] and methods of Servitude: Abject Sycophancy and blind Submission grew the only means of Preferment, and indeed of Safety; men durst not open their Mouths, but to flatter. . . .

All Ministers, therefore, who were Oppressors, or intended to be Oppressors, have been loud in their Complaints against Freedom of Speech, and the Licence of the Press; and always restrained, or endeavoured to restrain, both. In consequence of this, they have brow-beaten Writers, punished them violently, and against Law, and burnt their Works. By all which they shewed how much Truth alarmed them, and how much they were at Enmity with Truth. . . .

Freedom of Speech, therefore, being of such infinite Importance to the Preservation of Liberty, every one who loves Liberty ought to encourage Freedom of Speech. Hence it is that I, living in a Country of Liberty, and under the best Prince upon Earth, shall take this very favourable Opportunity of serving Mankind, by warning them of the hideous Mischiefs that they will suffer, if ever corrupt and wicked Men shall hereafter get Possession of any State, and the Power of betraying their Master. . . .

God be thanked, we Englishmen have neither lost our Liberties, nor are in Danger of losing them. Let us always cherish this matchless Blessing, almost peculiar to ourselves; that our Posterity may, many Ages hence, ascribe their Freedom to our Zeal. The Defense of Liberty is a noble, a heavenly Office; which can only be performed where Liberty is. . . .

BENJAMIN FRANKLIN, "AN APOLOGY FOR PRINTERS," *PHILADELPHIA GAZETTE* (JUNE 10, 1731)

Benjamin Franklin (1706–1790), scientist, inventor, patriot, statesman, and founder, was one of the most prominent writers and printers in colonial America. At the time when seditious libel laws were being vigorously enforced in England, Franklin, an admirer of Cato's Letter *no. 15, penned his own widely disseminated statement of the advantages of a free press.*

Being frequently censur'd and condemn'd by different Persons for printing Things which they say ought not to be printed, I have sometimes thought it might be necessary to make a standing Apology for my self, and publish it once a Year, to be read upon all Occasions of that Nature. Much Business has hitherto hindered the execution of this Design; but having very lately given extraordinary Offence . . . I find an Apology more particularly requisite at this Juncture. . . .

I request all who are angry with me on the Account of printing things they don't like, calmly to consider these following Particulars: That the Opinions of Men are almost as various as their Faces; an Observation general enough to become a common Proverb, So many Men so many Minds. . . . That the Business of Printing has chiefly to do with Men's Opinions; most things that are printed tending to promote some, or oppose others. . . . That it is as unreasonable in any one Man or Set of Men to expect to be pleas'd with every thing that is printed, as to think that nobody ought to be pleas'd but themselves.

Printers are educated in the Belief, that when Men differ in Opinion, both Sides ought equally to have the Advantage of being heard by the Publick; and that when Truth and Error have fair Play, the former is al-

ways an overmatch for the latter: Hence they chearfully serve all con-
tending Writers that pay them well, without regarding on which side
they are of the Question in Dispute.

Being thus continually employ'd in serving all Parties, Printers naturally acquire a vast Unconcernedness as to the right or wrong Opinions
contain'd in what they print; regarding it only as the Matter of their
daily labour: They print things full of Spleen and Animosity, with the
utmost Calmness and Indifference, and without the least Ill-will to the
Persons reflected on; who nevertheless unjustly think the Printer as
much their Enemy as the Author, and join both together in their resentment. . . .

That it is unreasonable to imagine Printers approve of every thing
they print, and to censure them on any particular thing accordingly;
since in the way of their Business they print such great variety of things
opposite and contradictory.

That if all Printers were determin'd not to print any thing till they
were sure it would offend no body, there would be very little printed.

That notwithstanding what might be urg'd in behalf of a Man's being
allow'd to do in the Way of his Business whatever he is paid for, yet
Printers do continually discourage the Printing of great Numbers of bad
things, and stifle them in the Birth. I my self have constantly refused to
print any thing that might countenance Vice, or promote Immorality;
tho' by complying in such Cases with the corrupt Taste of the Majority,
I might have got much Money. I have also always refus'd to print such
things as might do real Injury to any Person, how much soever I have
been solicited, and tempted with Offers of great Pay. . . . I have heretofore fallen under the Resentment of large Bodies of Men, for refusing absolutely to print any of their Party or Personal Reflections. In this Manner I have made my self many Enemies, and the constant Fatigue of
denying is almost insupportable.

I take leave to conclude with an old Fable, which some of my Readers have heard before, and some have not.

A certain well-meaning Man and his Son, were traveling towards a
Market Town, with an Ass which they had to sell. The Road was bad;
and the old Man therefore rid, but the Son went a-foot. The first Pas-
senger they met, asked the Father if he was not ashamed to ride by

himself, and suffer the poor Lad to wade along thro' the Mire; this induced him to take up his Son behind him: He had not travelled far when he met others, who said, they were two unmerciful Lubbers to get both on the Back of that poor Ass, in such a deep Road. Upon this the old Man gets off, and let his Son ride alone. The next they met called the Lad a graceless, rascally young Jackanapes, to ride in that Manner thro' the Dirt, while his aged Father trudged along on Foot; and they said the old Man was a Fool, for suffering it. He then bid his Son come down, and walk with him, and they travell'd on leading the Ass by the Halter; 'till they met another Company, who called them a Couple of sensless Blockheads, for going both on Foot in such a dirty Way, when they had an empty Ass with them, which they might ride upon. The old Man could bear no longer; My Son, said he, it grieves me much that we cannot please all these People: Let us throw the Ass over the next Bridge, and be no farther troubled with him.

Had the old Man been seen acting this last Resolution, he would probably have been call'd a Fool for troubling himself about the different Opinions of all that were pleas'd to find Fault with him: Therefore, tho' I have a Temper almost as complying as his, I intend not to imitate him in this last Particular. I consider the Variety of Humours among Men, and despair of pleasing every Body; yet I shall not therefore leave off Printing. I shall continue my Business. I shall not burn my Press and melt my Letters.

Montesquieu, *The Spirit of the Laws*, Book 12, Chapters 12–13 (1748)

French political thinker Montesquieu (1689–1755), who was read scrupulously by the American founders, was one of the most influential advocates of constitutionalism and a major proponent of the separation of powers. Here, in a selection from his most influential book, Montesquieu discusses free speech and draws an important distinction between conduct and speech.

Nothing renders the crime of high treason more arbitrary than declaring people guilty of it for indiscreet speeches. Speech is so subject to interpretation; there is so great a difference between indiscretion and malice; and frequently so little is there of the latter in the freedom of expression, that the law can hardly subject people to a capital punishment for words unless it expressly declares what words they are.

Words do not constitute an overt act; they remain only in idea. When considered by themselves, they have generally no determinate signification; for this depends on the tone in which they are uttered. It often happens that in repeating the same words they have not the same meaning; this depends on their connection with other things, and sometimes more is signified by silence than by any expression whatsoever. Since there can be nothing so equivocal and ambiguous as all this, how is it possible to convert it into a crime of high treason? Where this law is established, there is an end not only of liberty, but even of its very shadow. . . .

Not that I pretend to diminish the just indignation of the public against those who presume to stain the glory of their sovereign; what I mean is, that if despotic princes are willing to moderate their power, a milder chastisement would be more proper on those occasions than the charge of high treason. . . .

Overt acts do not happen every day; they are exposed to the eye of the public; and a false charge with regard to matters of fact may be easily detected. Words carried into action assume the nature of that action. Thus a man who goes into a public market-place to incite the subject to revolt incurs the guilt of high treason, because the words are joined to the action, and partake of its nature. It is not the words that are punished, but an action in which words are employed. They do not become criminal, but when they are annexed to criminal action; everything is confounded if words are construed into a capital crime, instead of considering them only as a mark of that crime.

In writings there is something more permanent than in words, but when they are in no way preparative to high treason they cannot amount to that charge. . . .

JOHN WILKES, *THE NORTH BRITON* NO. 45 (APRIL 25, 1763)

Angered by King George III's appointment of the Earl of Bute to be his prime minister, John Wilkes, a member of Parliament, lashed out at the king, anonymously attacking him in The North Briton *no. 45. The king's successful use of a general search warrant in ransacking houses to discover the pamphlet's author and Wilkes's subsequent prosecution became for the American colonists a symbol of English tyranny. And Wilkes's subsequent victory in winning damages for the trespass on his liberties made him an American hero.*

The government have sent the spirit of discord through the land, and I will prophesy, that it will never be extinguished, but by the extinction of their power. A nation as sensible as the English, will see that a spirit of concord, when they are oppressed, means a tame submission to injury, and that a spirit of liberty ought then to arise, and I am sure ever will, in proportion to the weight of the grievance they feel.

WILLIAM BLACKSTONE, *COMMENTARIES ON THE LAWS OF ENGLAND*, BOOK 4, PARAGRAPH 13 (1769)

Blackstone's Commentaries *were the most influential synopsis of the English common law, and they were widely read by people in England and America, lawyers and lay persons alike. Here, Blackstone presents the common law definition of libel law, explaining it and defending its wisdom.*

[L]ibels . . . are malicious defamations of any person, and especially a magistrate, made public by either printing, writing, signs, or pictures, in order to provoke him to wrath, or expose him to public hatred, contempt, and ridicule. The direct tendency of these libels is the breach of the public peace, by stirring up the object of them to revenge, and perhaps to bloodshed.

The communication of a libel to any one person is a publication in the eye of the law: and therefore the sending of an abusive private letter to a man is as much a libel as if it were openly printed, for it equally tends to a breach of the peace. For the same reason it is immaterial with respect to the essence of a libel, whether the matter of it be true or false, since the provocation, and not the falsity, is the thing to be punished criminally: though, doubtless, the falsehood of it may aggravate its guilt, and enhance its punishment.

In a civil action . . . a libel must appear to be false, as well as scandalous; for, if the charge be true, the plaintiff has received no private injury, and has no ground to demand compensation for himself, whatever offence it may be against the public peace: and therefore, upon a civil action, the truth of the accusation may be pleaded in the bar of the suit. But, in a criminal prosecution, the tendency which all libels have to create animosities, and to disturb the public peace, is the sole consideration of the law.

In this . . . the liberty of the press, properly understood, is by no means infringed or violated. The liberty of the press is indeed essential to the nature of a free state: but this consists in laying no previous restraints upon publication, and not in the freedom from censure for criminal matter when published. Every freeman has an undoubted right to lay what sentiments he pleases before the public: to forbid this, is to destroy the freedom of the press: but if he publishes what is improper, mischievous, or illegal, he must take the consequences of his own temerity. To subject the press to the restrictive power of a licenser, as was formerly done, both before and since the revolution, is to subject all freedom of sentiment to the prejudices of one man, and make him the arbitrary and infallible judge of all controverted points in learning, religion, and government. But to punish (as the law does at present) any dangerous or offensive writings, which, when published, shall on a fair and impartial trail be adjudged of a pernicious tendency, is necessary for the preservation of peace and good order, of government and religion, the only solid foundations of civil liberty. Thus the will of individuals is still left free; the abuse only of that free will is the object of legal punishment. Neither is any restraint hereby laid upon freedom of thought or inquiry: liberty of private sentiment is still left; the disseminating, or making public, of bad sentiment, destructive of the ends of society, is the crime which society corrects. A man (says a fine writer on this subject) may be allowed to keep poisons in his closet, but not publicly vend them as cordials. . . . [T]o censure the licentiousness, is to maintain the liberty, of the press.

PUBLIUS [ALEXANDER HAMILTON],
FEDERALIST PAPER NO. 84 (1787)

In Federalist Paper *no. 84, written to persuade the citizens of New York to reject Anti-Federalist arguments and to vote to ratify the U.S. Consti-*

tution, Alexander Hamilton defended the omission of a Bill of Rights. In doing so, he advanced a now-neglected structural understanding of constitutional rights protection. Although the Constitution was ratified without the Bill of Rights, a promise was made to add one later, as was done in 1791.

The most considerable of the remaining objections is that the plan of the convention contains no bill of rights. Among other answers given to this, it has been upon different occasions remarked that the constitutions of several of the States are in a similar predicament. I add that New York is of the number. And yet the opposers of the new system, in this State, who profess an unlimited admiration for its constitution, are among the most intemperate partisans of a bill of rights. To justify their zeal in this matter, they allege two things: one is that, though the constitution of New York has no bill of rights prefixed to it, yet it contains, in the body of it, various provisions in favor of particular privileges and rights, which, in substance amount to the same thing; the other is, that the Constitution adopts, in their full extent, the common and statute law of Great Britain, by which many other rights, not expressed in it, are equally secured.

To the first I answer, that the Constitution proposed by the convention contains, as well as the constitution of this State, a number of such provisions.

Independent of those which relate to the structure of the government, we find the following: Article 1, section 3, clause 7 "Judgment in cases of impeachment shall not extend further than to removal from office, and disqualification to hold and enjoy any office of honor, trust, or profit under the United States; but the party convicted shall, nevertheless, be liable and subject to indictment, trial, judgment, and punishment according to law." Section 9, of the same article, clause 2 "The privilege of the writ of habeas corpus shall not be suspended, unless when in cases of rebellion or invasion the public safety may require it." Clause 3 "No bill of attainder or ex-post-facto law shall be passed." Clause 7 "No title of nobility shall be granted by the United States; and no person holding any office of profit or trust under them, shall, without the consent of the Congress, accept of any present, emolument, office, or title of any kind whatever, from any king, prince, or foreign state." Article 3, section 2, clause 3 "The trial of all crimes, except in cases of impeachment, shall be by jury; and such trial shall be held in the State where the said crimes shall have been committed; but when not committed within any State, the trial shall be at such place or places as the Congress may by law have directed." Section 3, of the same article "Treason against the United States shall consist only in levying war against them, or in adhering to their enemies, giving them aid and comfort. No person shall be convicted of treason, unless on the testimony of two witnesses to the same overt act, or on confession in open court." And clause 3, of the same section "The Congress shall have power to declare the punishment of treason; but no attainder of treason shall work corruption of blood, or forfeiture, except during the life of the person attainted." It may well be a question, whether these are not, upon the whole, of equal importance with any which are to be found in the constitution of this State. The establishment of the writ of habeas corpus, the prohibition of ex-post-facto laws, and of TITLES OF NOBILITY, *to which we have no corresponding provision in our constitution,* are perhaps greater securities to liberty and republicanism than any it contains. The creation of crimes after the commission of the fact, or, in other words, the subjecting of men to punishment for things which, when they were done, were breaches of no law, and the practice of arbitrary imprisonments, have been, in all ages, the favorite and most formidable instruments of tyranny. . . .

. . . [As] to the pretended establishment of the common and state law by the Constitution, I answer, that they are expressly made subject "to such alterations and provisions as the legislature shall from time to time make concerning the same." They are therefore at any moment liable to repeal by the ordinary legislative power, and of course have no constitutional sanction. The only use of the declaration was to recognize the ancient law and to remove doubts which might have been occasioned by the Revolution. This consequently can be considered as no part of a declaration of rights, which under our constitutions must be intended as limitations of the power of the government itself.

It has been several times truly remarked that bills of rights are, in their origin, stipulations between kings and their subjects, abridgements of prerogative in favor of privilege, reservations of rights not surrendered to the prince. Such was MAGNA CHARTA, obtained by the barons, sword in hand, from King John. Such were the subsequent confirmations of that charter by succeeding princes. Such was the *petition of right* assented to by Charles I, in the beginning of his reign. Such, also, was the Declaration of Right presented by the Lords and Commons to the Prince of Orange in 1688, and afterwards thrown into the form of an act of parliament called the Bill of Rights. It is evident, therefore, that, according to their primitive signification, they have no application to constitutions professedly founded upon the power of the people, and executed by their immediate representatives and servants. Here, in strictness, the people surrender nothing; and as they retain every thing they have no need of particular reservations. "WE, THE PEOPLE of the United States, to secure the blessings of liberty to ourselves and our posterity, do *ordain* and *establish* this Constitution for the United States of America." Here is a better recognition of popular rights, than volumes of those aphorisms which make the principal figure in several of our State bills of rights, and which would sound much better in a treatise of ethics than in a constitution of government.

But a minute detail of particular rights is certainly far less applicable to a Constitution like that under consideration, which is merely intended to regulate the general political interests of the nation, than to a constitution which has the regulation of every species of personal and private concerns. If, therefore, the loud clamors against the plan of the convention, on this score, are well founded, no epithets of reprobation will be too strong for the constitution of this State. But the truth is, that both of them contain all which, in relation to their objects, is reasonably to be desired.

I go further, and affirm that bills of rights, in the sense and to the extent in which they are contended for, are not only unnecessary in the proposed Constitution, but would even be dangerous. They would contain various exceptions to powers not granted; and, on this very account, would afford a colorable pretext to claim more than were granted. For why declare that things shall not be done which there is no power to do? Why, for instance, should it be said that the liberty of the press shall not be restrained, when no power is given by which restrictions may be imposed? I will not contend that such a provision would confer a regulating power; but it is evident that it would furnish, to men disposed to usurp, a plausible pretense for claiming that power. They might urge with a semblance of reason, that the Constitution ought not to be charged with the absurdity of providing against the abuse of an authority which was not given, and that the provision against restraining the liberty of the press afforded a clear implication, that a power to prescribe proper regulations concerning it was intended to be vested in the national government. This may serve as a specimen of the numerous handles which would be given to the doctrine of constructive powers, by the indulgence of an injudicious zeal for bills of rights.

On the subject of the liberty of the press, as much as has been said, I cannot forbear adding a remark or two: in the first place, I observe, that there is not a syllable concerning it in the constitution of this State; in the next, I contend, that whatever has been said about it in that of any other State, amounts to nothing. What signifies a declaration, that "the liberty of the press shall be inviolably preserved"? What is the liberty of the press? Who can give it any definition which would not leave the utmost latitude for evasion? I hold it to be impracticable; and from this I infer, that its security, whatever fine declarations may be inserted in any constitution respecting it, must altogether depend on public opinion, and on the general spirit of the people and of the government.* And here, after all, as is intimated upon another occasion, must we seek for the only solid basis of all our rights.

There remains but one other view of this matter to conclude the point. The truth is, after all the declamations we have heard, that the Constitution is itself, in every rational sense, and to every useful purpose, A BILL OF RIGHTS. The several bills of rights in Great Britain form its Constitution, and conversely the constitution of each State is its bill of rights. And the proposed Constitution, if adopted, will be the bill of rights of the Union. Is it one object of a bill of rights to declare and specify the political privileges of the citizens in the structure and administration of the government? This is done in the most ample and precise manner in the plan of the convention; comprehending various precautions for the public security, which are not to be found in any of the State constitutions. Is another object of a bill of rights to define certain immunities and modes of proceeding, which are relative to personal and private concerns? This we have seen has also been attended to, in a variety of cases, in the same plan. Adverting therefore to the substantial meaning of a bill of rights, it is absurd to allege that it is not to be found in the work of the convention. It may be said that it does not go far enough, though it will not be easy to make this appear; but it can with no propriety be contended that there is no such thing. It certainly must be immaterial what mode is observed as to the order of declaring the rights of the citizens, if they are to be found in any part of the instrument which establishes the government. And hence it must be apparent, that much of what has been said on this subject rests merely on verbal and nominal distinctions, entirely foreign from the substance of the thing.

Another objection which has been made, and which, from the frequency of its repetition, it is to be presumed is relied on, is of this nature: "It is improper say the objectors to confer such large powers, as are proposed, upon the national government, because the seat of that government must of necessity be too remote from many of the States to admit of a proper knowledge on the part of the constituent, of the conduct of the representative body." This argument, if it proves any thing, proves that there ought to be no general government whatever. For the powers which, it seems to be agreed on all hands, ought to be vested in the Union, cannot be safely intrusted to a body which is not under every requisite control. But there are satisfactory reasons to show that the objection is in reality not well founded. There is in most of the arguments which relate to distance a palpable illusion of the imagination. What are the sources of information by which the people in Montgomery County must regulate their judgment of the conduct of their representatives in the State legislature? Of personal observation they can have no benefit. This is confined to the citizens on the spot. They must therefore depend on the information of intelligent men, in whom they confide; and how must these men obtain their information? Evidently from the complexion of public measures, from the public prints, from correspondences with their representatives, and with other persons who reside at the place of their deliberations. This does not apply to Montgomery County only, but to all the counties at any considerable distance from the seat of government.

It is equally evident that the same sources of information would be open to the people in relation to the conduct of their representatives in the general government, and the impediments to a prompt communication which distance may be supposed to create, will be overbalanced by the effects of the vigilance of the State governments. The executive and legislative bodies of each State will be so many sentinels over the persons employed in every department of the national administration; and as it will be in their power to adopt and pursue a regular and effectual system of intelligence, they can never be at a loss to know the behavior of those who represent their constituents in the national councils, and can readily communicate the same knowledge to the people. Their disposition to apprise the community of whatever may prejudice its interests from another quarter, may be relied upon, if it were only from the rivalship of power. And we may conclude with the fullest assurance that the people, through that channel, will be better informed of the conduct of their national representatives, than they can be by any means they now possess of that of their State representatives.

It ought also to be remembered that the citizens who inhabit the country at and near the seat of government will, in all questions that affect the general liberty and prosperity, have the same interest with those who are at a distance, and that they will stand ready to sound the alarm when necessary, and to point out the actors in any pernicious project. The public papers will be expeditious messengers of intelligence to the most remote inhabitants of the Union. . . .

*To show that there is a power in the Constitution by which the liberty of the press may be affected, recourse has been had to the power of taxation. It is said that duties may be laid upon the publications so high as to amount to a prohibition. I know not by what logic it could be maintained, that the declarations in the State constitutions, in favor of the freedom of the press, would be a constitutional impediment to the imposition of duties upon publications by the State legislatures. It cannot certainly be pretended that any degree of duties, however low, would be an abridgment of the liberty of the press. We know that newspapers are taxed in Great Britain, and yet it is notorious that the press nowhere enjoys greater liberty than in that country. And if duties of any kind may be laid without a violation of that liberty, it is evident that the extent must depend on legislative discretion, respecting the liberty of the press, will give it no greater security than it will have without them. The same invasions of it may be effected under the State constitutions which contain those declarations through the means of taxation, as under the proposed Constitution, which has nothing of the kind. It would be quite as significant to declare that government ought to be free, that taxes ought not to be excessive, etc., as that the liberty of the press ought not to be restrained. [Note in original.]

U.S. Constitution (1787)

Article 1, Section 6 (Speech and Debate Clause)

The Senators and Representatives . . . shall in all Cases, except Treason, Felony and Breach of the Peace, be privileged from Arrest during their Attendance at the Session of their respective Houses, and in going to and returning from the same; and for any Speech or Debate in either House, they shall not be questioned in any other Place.

Article 3, Sections 1 and 2

The judicial Power of the United States shall be vested in one supreme Court, and in such inferior Courts as the Congress may from time to time ordain and establish. The Judges, both of the supreme and inferior Courts, shall hold their offices during good Behaviour, and shall, at stated Times, receive for their Services, a Compensation, which shall not be diminished during their Continuance in Office.

The judicial Power shall extend to all Cases, in Law and Equity, arising under this Constitution, the Laws of the United States, and Treaties made, or which shall be made, under their Authority. . . .

Article 3, Section 3

Treason against the United States, shall consist only in levying War against them, or in adhering to their Enemies, giving them Aid and Comfort. No Person shall be convicted of Treason unless on the Testimony of two Witnesses to the same overt Act, or on Confession in open Court.

Article 4, Section 4 (Guarantee Clause)

The United States shall guarantee to every State in this Union a Republican Form of Government, and shall protect each of them against Invasion; and on Application of the Legislature, or of the Executive (when the Legislature cannot be convened) against domestic Violence.

First Amendment (1791)

Congress shall make no law respecting an establishment of religion, or prohibiting the free exercise thereof; or abridging the freedom of speech, or of the press; or the right of the people peaceably to assemble, and to petition the Government for a redress of grievances.

Fifth Amendment (1791)

No person shall . . . be compelled in any criminal case to be a witness against himself. . . .

Tenth Amendment (1791)

The powers not delegated to the United States by the Constitution, nor prohibited by it to the States, are reserved to the States respectively, or to the people.

SEDITION ACT (1798)

Led by President John Adams, the Federalists passed the Sedition Act in an attempt to silence the incessant criticisms and attacks of their political opponents, whom they believed to be fomenting dangerous instability. The act and the politically motivated prosecutions under it proved highly controversial.

[I]f any person shall write, print, utter, or publish, or shall cause or procure to be written, printed, uttered, or published, or shall knowingly and willingly assist or aid in writing, printing, uttering, or publishing, any false, scandalous, and malicious writing or writings against the Government of the United States, or either House of the Congress of the United States, or the President of the United States, with an intent to defame the said Government or either House of the said Congress, or the President, or to bring them or either of them into contempt or disrepute; or to excite against them, or either or any of them, the hatred of the good people of the United States, or to stir up sedition within the United States, or to excite any unlawful combinations therein, for opposing or resisting any law of the United States, or any act of the President of the

United States, done in pursuance of any such law, or of the powers in him vested by the Constitution of the United States, or to resist, oppose, or defeat any such law or act; or to aid, encourage or abet any hostile designs of any foreign nation against the United States, their people or government, then such person, being thereof convicted before any court of the United States having jurisdiction thereof, shall be punished by a fine not exceeding two thousand dollars, and by imprisonment not exceeding two years.

And be it further enacted and declared, that if any person shall be prosecuted under this act, for the writing or publishing any libel aforesaid, it shall be lawful for the defendant, upon the trial of the cause, to give in evidence in his defence, the truth of the matter contained in the publication charged as a libel, and the jury who shall try the cause, shall have a right to determine the law and the fact, under the direction of the court, as in the other cases.

LETTER, JOHN MARSHALL TO
A FREEHOLDER (1798)

John Marshall (1755–1835), patriot, diplomat, congressman, secretary of state, and chief justice of the United States (1801–1835), was a staunch Federalist. He was appointed to the Supreme Court by President John Adams as Adams was leaving office after a defeat in large part due to intense opposition to the Sedition Act. Marshall offered a partial apology for, though not an outright defense of, that act.

I am not an advocate for the alien and sedition bills; had I been in Congress when they passed, I should . . . certainly have opposed them. Yet, I do not think them fraught with all those mischiefs which many gentlemen ascribe to them. I should have opposed them because I think them useless; and because they are calculated to create unnecessary discontents and jealousies at a time when our very existence, as a nation, may depend on our union.

I believe that these laws, had they been opposed [in Congress] on these principles by a man, not suspected of intending to destroy the government, or being hostile to it, would never have been enacted. With respect to their repeal, the effort will be made before I can become a member of Congress. If it succeeds, that will be the end of the business. . . .

[Otherwise, my hope is that] the laws will expire of themselves . . . [and] I shall indisputably oppose their revival. . . .

JAMES MADISON, REPORT ON THE
VIRGINIA RESOLUTION (1800)

In his report to the Virginia House of Delegates, James Madison success-fully persuaded that body to declare the Sedition Act unconstitutional. (He expected no relief from the Federalist-controlled courts). In doing so, Madison broke sharply from English law and formulated a distinctively American understanding of the freedom of speech.

[T]he Sedition Act, in its definitions of some of the crimes created, is an abridgement of the freedom of publication, recognized by principles of the common law in England. The freedom of the press under the common law is, in the defenses of the Sedition Act, made to consist in an exemption from all *previous* restraints on printed publications by persons authorized to inspect and prohibit them. It appears to the committee that this idea of the freedom of the press can never be admitted to be the American idea of it; since a law inflicting penalties on printed publications would have a similar effect with a law authorizing a previous restraint on them. It would be a mockery to say that no laws should be passed preventing publications being made, but that laws might be passed for punishing them in case they should be made.

The essential difference between the British Government and the American Constitutions will place this subject in the clearest light. . . . Parliament is unlimited in its power; or, in their own language, is omnipotent. Hence, too, all the ramparts for protecting the rights of the people—such as their Magna Charta, their Bill of Rights, etc.—are not reared against the Parliament, but against the royal prerogative. They are merely legislative precautions against executive usurpations. Under such a government as this, an exemption of the press from previous restraint, by licensers appointed by the King, is all the freedom that can be secured to it. In the United States the case is altogether different. The People, not the Government, possess the absolute sovereignty. The legislature, no less than the Executive, is under limitations of power. Encroachments are regarded as possible from the one as from the other. Hence, in the

United States the great and essential rights of the people are secured against legislative as well as against executive ambition. . . . The state of the press, therefore, under the common law, cannot, in this point of view, be the standard of its freedom in the United States.

The nature of governments elective, limited, and responsible in all their branches, may well be supposed to require a greater freedom of animadversion than might be tolerated by the genius of such a government as that of Great Britain. . . . In the United States the executive magistrates are not held to be infallible, nor the Legislatures to be omnipotent; and both being elective, are both responsible. Is it not natural and necessary, under such different circumstances, that a different degree of freedom in the use of the press should be contemplated?

The freedom of conscience and of religion are found in the same instruments which assert the freedom of the press. It will never be admitted that the meaning of the former, in the common law of England, is to limit their meaning in the United States.

Had "Sedition Acts," forbidding every publication that might bring the constituted agents into contempt or disrepute, or that might excite the hatred of the people against the authors of unjust or pernicious measures, been uniformly enforced against the press, might not the United States have been languishing at this day under the infirmities of a sickly Confederation? Might they not, possibly, be miserable colonies, groaning under a foreign yoke?

When the Constitution was under discussions which preceded its ratification, it is well known that great apprehensions were expressed by many, lest the omission of some positive exception, from the powers delegated, of certain rights, and of the freedom of the press particularly, might expose them to the danger of being drawn, by construction, within some of the powers vested in Congress, more especially of the power to make all laws necessary and proper for carrying their other powers into execution. In reply to this objection, it was invariably urged to be a fundamental and characteristic principle of the Constitution, that all powers not given by it were reserved; that no powers were given beyond those enumerated in the Constitution, and such as were fairly incident to them; that the power over the rights in question, and particularly over the press, was neither among the enumerated powers, nor incident to any of them; and consequently that an exercise of any such power would be manifest usurpation. It is painful to remark how much the arguments now employed in behalf of the Sedition Act are at variance with the reasoning which then justified the Constitution, and invited its ratification. . . . Without tracing farther the evidence on this subject, it would seem scarcely possible to doubt that no power whatever over the press was supposed to be delegated by the Constitution, as it originally stood, and that the amendment was intended as a positive and absolute reservation of it.

Is, then, the Federal Government, it will be asked, destitute of every authority for restraining the licentiousness of the press, and for shielding itself against the libellous attacks which may be made on those who administer it? . . . [T]he answer must be, that the Federal Government is destitute of all such authority.

[The] right of freely examining public characters and measure, and of free communication among the people thereon . . . has ever been justly deemed the only effectual guardian of every other right. . . . Should it happen, as the Constitution supposes it may happen, that either of [the] branches of the Government may not have duly discharged its trust; it is natural and proper, that, according to the cause and degree of their faults, they should be brought into contempt or disrepute, and incur the hatred of the people. Whether it has, in any case, happened that the proceedings of either or all of those branches evince such a violation of duty as to justify a contempt, a disrepute, or hatred among the people, can only be determined by a free examination thereof, and a free communication among the people thereon. Whenever it may have actually happened that proceedings of this sort are chargeable on all or either of the branches of the Government, it is the duty, as well as right, of intelligent and faithful citizens to discuss and promulge them freely. . . . [I]t is manifestly impossible to punish the intent to bring those who administer the Government into disrepute or contempt, without striking at the right of freely discussing public characters and measures. . . .

Let it be recollected, lastly, that the right of electing the members of the Government constitutes more particularly the essence of a free and responsible government. The value and efficacy of this right depends on the knowledge of the comparative merits and demerits of the candidates for public trust. . . . Should there happen, then, as is extremely probable in relation to some or other of the branches of the Government, to be competitions between those who are and those who are not members of the Government, what will be the situations of the competitors? Not equal; because the characters of the former will be covered by the Sedition Act from animadversions exposing them to disrepute among the people, whilst the latter may be exposed to the contempt and hatred of the people without a violation of the act. What will be the situation of the people? Not free; because they will be compelled to make their election between competitors whose pretensions they are not permitted by the act equally to examine, to discuss, and to ascertain. . . . It is with justice, therefore . . . [to affirm] that the right of freely examining public characters and measures, and of free communication thereon, is the only effectual guardian of every other right.

Thomas Jefferson, First Inaugural Address, Washington, D.C. (March 4, 1801)

Jefferson triumphed in the election of 1800 in large part due to anger over his predecessor John Adams's passage and enforcement of the Sedition Act. The election was bitterly contested, and Jefferson's inaugural address sought to calm and reconcile the country as it undertook a transfer of power.

During the contest of opinion through which we have passed the animation of discussions and of exertions has sometimes worn an aspect which might impose on strangers unused to think freely and to speak and to write what they think; but this being now decided by the voice of the nation, announced according to the rules of the Constitution, all will, of course, arrange themselves under the will of the law, and unite in common efforts for the common good. All, too, will bear in mind this sacred principle, that though the will of the majority is in all cases to prevail, that will to be rightful must be reasonable; that the minority possesses their equal rights, which equal law must protect, and to violate would be oppression. Let us, then, fellow-citizens, unite with one heart and one mind. Let us restore to social intercourse that harmony and affection without which liberty and even life itself are but dreary things.

And let us reflect that, having banished from our land that religious intolerance under which mankind so long bled and suffered, we have yet gained little if we countenance a political intolerance as despotic, as wicked, and capable of as bitter and bloody persecutions.... [E]very difference of opinion is not a difference of principle. We have called by different names brethren of the same principle. We are all Republicans, we are all Federalists. If there be any among us who would wish to dissolve this Union or to change its republican form, let them stand undisturbed as monuments of the safety with which error of opinion may be tolerated where reason is left free to combat it....

ST. GEORGE TUCKER, EDITOR, *BLACKSTONE'S COMMENTARIES: WITH NOTES OF REFERENCE TO THE CONSTITUTION AND LAWS OF THE FEDERAL GOVERNMENT OF THE UNITED STATES; AND OF THE COMMONWEALTH OF VIRGINIA* (1803)

St. George Tucker, a professor of law at the College of William and Mary, produced an edition of Blackstone's Commentaries, *with appended notes and comments, that was the most widely used version of that work among lawyers in the early-nineteenth-century United States.*

Whoever makes use of the press as the vehicle of his sentiments on any subject, ought to do it in such language as to show he has a deference for the sentiments of others; that while he asserts the right of expressing and vindicating his own judgment, he acknowledges the obligation to submit the judgment of those whose authority he cannot legally, or constitutionally dispute. In his statement of facts he is bound to adhere strictly to the truth; for every deviation from the truth is both an imposition upon the public, and an injury to the individual whom it may respect. In his restrictures on the conduct of men, in public stations, he is bound to do justice to their characters, and not to criminate them without substantial reason. The right of character is a sacred and invaluable right, and is not forfeited by accepting a public employment. Whoever knowingly departs from any of these maxims is guilty of a crime against the community, as well as against the person injured; and though both the letter and the spirit of our federal constitution wisely prohibit the Congress of the United States from making any law, by which the freedom of speech, or of the press, may be exposed to restraint or persecution under the authority of the federal government, yet for injuries done the reputation of any person, as an individual, the state-courts are always open, and may afford ample, and competent redress, as the records of the [state courts of Virginia] abundantly testify.

ALEXANDER HAMILTON'S SPEECH IN HARRY CROSWELL'S CASE (1804)

In his argument as an attorney in defending Harry Croswell, a Federalist newspaper editor accused of libeling President Thomas Jefferson, Alexander Hamilton set out the understanding of the free speech and press with which he is commonly associated (People v. Croswell, 3 Johns Cas. 337 [N.Y. 1804]).

The Liberty of the Press consists, in my idea, in publishing the truth, from good motives and for justifiable ends, though it reflect on government, on magistrates, or individuals. If it be not allowed, it excludes the privilege of canvassing men, and our rulers. It is vain to say, you may canvass measures. This is impossible without the right of looking to men. . . . I do not say that there ought to be an unbridled license. . . . I do not stand here to say that no shackles are to be laid on this license. I consider this spirit of abuse and calumny as the pest of society. . . . I contend for the liberty of publishing truth, with good motives and for justifiable ends, even though it reflect on government, magistrates, or private persons. I contend for it under the restraint of our tribunals.—When this is exceeded, let them interpose and punish.

No man can think more highly of our judges, and I may say personally so, of those who now preside, than myself. . . . [Y]et, if once they enter into the views of government, their power may be converted into the engine of oppression. . . . [T]he independence of our judges is not so well secured as in England. . . . It must be the Jury to decide on the intent,—they must in certain cases be permitted to judge of the law, and pronounce on the combined matter of law and fact. . . . [T]rial by jury [is] the palladium of public and private liberty.

JOSEPH STORY, *COMMENTARIES ON THE
CONSTITUTION OF THE UNITED STATES* (1833)

In expounding upon the meaning of the First Amendment, Story's Commentaries *insisted that a clear distinction must be drawn between liberty
and license.*

That [the First Amendment] was intended to secure to every citizen
an absolute right to speak, or write, or print, whatever he may please,
without any responsibility, public or private, . . . is a supposition too
wild to be indulged by any rational man. This would be to allow to every citizen a right to destroy, at his pleasure, the reputation, the peace,
the property, and even the personal safety of every other citizen. A man
might, out of mere malice and revenge, accuse another of the most infamous of crimes; might excite against him the indignation of all his fellow citizens by the most atrocious calumnies; might disturb, nay, over-
turn all his domestic peace, and embitter his parental affections; might
inflict the most distressing punishments upon the weak, the timid, and
the innocent; might prejudice all a man's civil, and political, and private
rights; and might stir up sedition, rebellion, and treason even against the
government itself, in the wantonness of his passions, or the corruption
of his heart. Civil society could not go on under such circumstances.
Men would be obliged to resort to private vengeance, to make up for
the deficiencies of the law; and assassinations, and savage cruelties,
would be perpetrated with all the frequency belonging to barbarous
and brutal communities. It is plain, then, that the language of this
amendment imports no more, than that every man shall have a right to
speak, write, and print his opinions upon any subject whatsoever, without any prior restraint, so always, that he does not injure any other person in his rights, person, property, or reputation; and so always, that he
does not thereby disturb the public peace, or attempt to subvert the
government. . . .

[The First Amendment is no more or less than an expansion of the
doctrine that] every man shall be at liberty to publish what is true, with
good motives and for justifiable ends. And with this reasonable limitation it is not only right in itself, but it is an inestimable privilege in a free
government. Without such a limitation, it might become the scourge of
the republic, first denouncing the principles of liberty, and then, by ren-

dering the most virtuous patriots odious through the terrors of the press, introducing despotism in its worst form.

There is a good deal of loose reasoning on the subject of the liberty of the press, as if its inviolability were constitutionally such, that, like the king of England, it could do no wrong, and was free from every inquiry, and afforded perfect sanctuary for every abuse; that, in short, it implied a despotic sovereignty to do every sort of wrong, without the slightest accountability to private or public justice. Such a notion is too extravagant to be held by any sound constitutional lawyer. . . . If it were admitted to be correct, it might be justly affirmed, that the liberty of the press was incompatible with the permanent existence of any free government. . . .

[F]ree, but not licentious, discussion must be encouraged. But the exercise of a right is essentially different from an abuse of it. The one is no legitimate inference from the other. Common sense here promulgates the broad doctrine, *sic utere tuo, ut non alienum laedas;* so exercise your own freedom, as not to infringe the rights of others, or the public peace and safety. The doctrine laid down by Mr. Justice Blackstone, respecting the liberty of the press, has not been repudiated (as far as is known) by any solemn decision of any of the state courts. . . . [I]t has farther been held, that the truth of the facts is not alone sufficient to justify the publication, unless it is done from good motives and for justifiable purposes, or, in other words, on an occasion, (as upon the canvass of candidates for public office,) when public duty, or private right requires it.

BARRON V. BALTIMORE, 32 U.S. 243 (1833)

The Barron *case involved a suit brought by a Baltimore wharf owner seeking financial compensation from the city for the deprival of his rights under the Fifth Amendment's takings clause ("nor shall private property be taken for public use, without just compensation"). The case arose when a municipal public works project filled his wharf with sand, rendering it useless. The Supreme Court dismissed Barron's claim on the grounds that the Bill of Rights limited the federal government, not states and their subdivisions.*

Chief Justice John Marshall, writing for the Court:

The question thus presented is, we think, of great importance, but not of much difficulty. The Constitution was ordained and established by the people of the United States for themselves, for their own government, and not for the government of the individual States. Each State established a constitution for itself, and in that constitution provided such limitations and restrictions on the powers of its particular government as its judgment dictated. The people of the United States framed such a government for the United States as they supposed best adapted to their situation, and best calculated to promote their interests. The powers they conferred on this government were to be exercised by itself; and the limitations on power, if expressed in general terms, are naturally, and, we think, necessarily applicable to the government created by that instrument. They are limitations of power granted in the instrument itself; not of distinct governments, framed by different persons and for different purposes. . . .

Had the framers of [the Bill of Rights] intended them to be limitations on the powers of the State governments they would have imitated the framers of the original Constitution, and expressed that intention. . . . [T]hey would have declared this purpose in plain and intelligible language. . . . These amendments demanded security against the apprehended encroachments of the general government—not against those of the local governments.

ALEXIS DE TOCQUEVILLE,
DEMOCRACY IN AMERICA (1833)

After observing Americans during an extended visit to the United States in the 1830s, Tocqueville concluded that their democratic and egalitarian mores were a serious hindrance to independent thought and speech. This extract is reproduced as translated by George Lawrence, edited by J. P. Mayer (1969).

Thought is an invisible power and one almost impossible to lay hands on, which makes sport of all tyrannies. In our day the most absolute sovereigns in Europe cannot prevent certain thoughts hostile to their power from silently circulating in their states and even in their own courts. It is not like that in America; while the majority is in doubt, one talks; but when it has irrevocably pronounced, everyone is silent, and friends and enemies alike seem to make for its bandwagon. The reason is simple: no monarch is so absolute that he can hold all the forces of society in his hands, and overcome all resistance, as a majority invested with the right to make the laws, and to execute them, can do. Moreover, a king's power is physical only, controlling actions but not influencing desires, whereas the majority is invested with both physical and moral authority, which acts as much upon the will as upon the behavior and at the same moment prevents both the act and the desire to do it. I know no country in which, speaking generally, there is less independence of mind and true freedom of discussion than in America.

In a democracy organized on the model of the United States there is only one authority, one source of strength and of success, and nothing outside of it. In America the majority has enclosed thought within a formidable fence. A writer is free inside that area, but woe to the man who goes beyond it. Not that he stands in fear of an auto-da-fé, but he must face all kinds of unpleasantness and everyday persecution.

We need seek no other reason for the absence of great writers in America so far; literary genius cannot exist without freedom of the spirit, and there is no freedom of the spirit in America. In Spain the Inquisition was never able to prevent the circulation of books contrary to the majority religion. The American majority's sway extends further and has rid itself even of the thought of publishing such books. One finds unbelievers in America, but unbelief has, so to say, no organ. One finds governments striving to protect mores by condemning authors of licentious books. No one in the United States is condemned for works of that sort, but no one is tempted to write them. Not that all the citizens are chaste in their mores, but those of the majority are regular.

"GAG RULE,"
U.S. HOUSE OF REPRESENTATIVES (1836)

The "gag rule" banning the receipt of antislavery petitions in the U.S. Congress, passed by a vote of 117–68, with both pro-slavery southerners and northerners seeking to diffuse tensions voting in its favor.

[A]ll petitions, memorials, resolutions, propositions, or papers relating in any way, or to any extent whatsoever, to the subject of slavery, or the abolition of slavery, shall, without being either printed or referred,

be laid upon the table, and no further action whatever shall be had
thereon.

JOHN STUART MILL, *ON LIBERTY* (1859)

*The English philosopher John Stuart Mill penned one of the most elegant
and influential defenses of the freedom of thought and speech. Mill's defense was based on considerations of the search for truth as well as claims
on behalf of individual autonomy and human flourishing. His argument
was a touchstone for Oliver Wendell Holmes, Jr., who launched the
Supreme Court's modern free speech jurisprudence, as well as the starting
point for much of Anglo-American liberal thought on the subject.*

The time, it is to be hoped, is gone by when any defense would be necessary of the "liberty of the press" as one of the securities against corrupt
or tyrannical government. No argument, we may suppose, can now be
needed, against permitting a legislature or an executive, not identified in
interest with the people, to prescribe opinions to them, and determine
what doctrines or what arguments they shall be allowed to hear. This aspect of the question, besides, has been so often and so triumphantly enforced by preceding writers, that it needs not be specially insisted on in
this place. . . . Were an opinion a personal possession of no value except
to the owner; if to be obstructed in the enjoyment of it were simply a private injury, it would make some difference whether the injury was in-
flicted only on a few persons or on many. But the peculiar evil of silencing the expression of an opinion is, that it is robbing the human race;
posterity as well as the existing generation; those who dissent from the
opinion, still more than those who hold it. If the opinion is right, they are
deprived of the opportunity of exchanging error for truth: if wrong, they
lose, what is almost as great a benefit, the clearer perception and livelier
impression of truth, produced by its collision with error. . . .

First: the opinion which it is attempted to suppress by authority may
possibly be true. Those who desire to suppress it, of course deny its
truth; but they are not infallible. They have no authority to decide the
question for all mankind, and exclude every other person from the
means of judging. To refuse a hearing to an opinion, because they are
sure that it is false, is to assume that their certainty is the same thing as

absolute certainty. All silencing of discussion is an assumption of infalli-bility. Its condemnation may be allowed to rest on this common argu-ment, not the worse for being common. . . .

. . . There is the greatest difference between presuming an opinion to be true, because, with every opportunity for contesting it, it has not been refuted, and assuming its truth for the purpose of not permitting its refutation. Complete liberty of contradicting and disproving our opin-ion, is the very condition which justifies us in assuming its truth for pur-poses of action; and on no other terms can a being with human faculties have any rational assurance of being right. . . .

It still remains to speak of one of the principal causes which make di-versity of opinion advantageous, and will continue to do so until mankind shall have entered a stage of intellectual advancement which at present seems at an incalculable distance. We have hitherto considered only two possibilities: that the received opinion may be false, and some other opinion, consequently, true; or that, the received opinion being true, a conflict with the opposite error is essential to a clear apprehen-sion and deep feeling of its truth. But there is a commoner case than ei-ther of these; when the conflicting doctrines, instead of being one true and the other false, share the truth between them; and the nonconform-ing opinion is needed to supply the remainder of the truth, of which the received doctrine embodies only a part. Popular opinions, on subjects not palpable to sense, are often true, but seldom or never the whole truth. They are a part of the truth; sometimes a greater, sometimes a smaller part, but exaggerated, distorted, and disjoined from the truths by which they ought to be accompanied and limited. Heretical opinions, on the other hand, are generally some of these suppressed and neglected truths, bursting the bonds which kept them down, and either seeking reconciliation with the truth contained in the common opinion, or fronting it as enemies, and setting themselves up, with similar exclusive-ness, as the whole truth. The latter case is hitherto the most frequent, as, in the human mind, one-sidedness has always been the rule, and many-sidedness the exception. Hence, even in revolutions of opinion, one part of the truth usually sets while another rises. Even progress, which ought to superadd, for the most part only substitutes one partial and incom-plete truth for another; improvement consisting chiefly in this, that the new fragment of truth is more wanted, more adapted to the needs of the time, than that which it displaces. Such being the partial character of prevailing opinions, even when resting on a true foundation; every opinion which embodies somewhat of the portion of truth which the common opinion omits, ought to be considered precious, with whatever amount of error and confusion that truth may be blended. No sober judge of human affairs will feel bound to be indignant because those who force on our notice truths which we should otherwise have overlooked, overlook some of those which we see. Rather, he will think that so long as popular truth is one-sided, it is more desirable than otherwise that unpopular truth should have one-sided asserters too; such being usually the most energetic, and the most likely to compel reluctant attention to the fragment of wisdom which they proclaim as if it were the whole. . . .

I do not pretend that the most unlimited use of the freedom of enunciating all possible opinions would put an end to the evils of religious or philosophical sectarianism. Every truth which men of narrow capacity are in earnest about, is sure to be asserted, inculcated, and in many ways even acted on, as if no other truth existed in the world, or at all events none that could limit or qualify the first. I acknowledge that the tendency of all opinions to become sectarian is not cured by the freest discussion, but is often heightened and exacerbated thereby; the truth which ought to have been, but was not, seen, being rejected all the more violently because proclaimed by persons regarded as opponents. But it is not on the impassioned partisan, it is on the calmer and more disinterested bystander, that this collision of opinions works its salutary effect. Not the violent conflict between parts of the truth, but the quiet suppression of half of it, is the formidable evil: there is always hope when people are forced to listen to both sides; it is when they attend only to one that errors harden into prejudices, and truth itself ceases to have the effect of truth, by being exaggerated into falsehood. And since there are few mental attributes more rare than that judicial faculty which can sit in intelligent judgment between two sides of a question, of which only one is represented by an advocate before it, truth has no chance but in proportion as every side of it, every opinion which embodies any fraction of the truth, not only finds advocates, but is so advocated as to be listened to.

We have now recognized the necessity to the mental well-being of mankind (on which all their other well-being depends) of freedom of opinion, and freedom of the expression of opinion, on four distinct grounds; which we will now briefly recapitulate. First, if any opinion is compelled to silence, that opinion may, for aught we can certainly know, be true. To deny this is to assume our own infallibility. Secondly, though the silenced opinion be an error, it may, and very commonly does, contain a portion of truth; and since the general or prevailing opinion on any object is rarely or never the whole truth, it is only by the collision of adverse opinions that the remainder of the truth has any chance of being supplied. Thirdly, even if the received opinion be not only true, but the whole truth; unless it is suffered to be, and actually is, vigorously and earnestly contested, it will, by most of those who receive it, be held in the manner of a prejudice, with little comprehension or feeling of its rational grounds. And not only this, but, fourthly, the meaning of the doctrine itself will be in danger of being lost, or enfeebled, and deprived of its vital effect on the character and conduct: the dogma becoming a mere formal profession, inefficacious for good, but cumbering the ground, and preventing the growth of any real and heartfelt conviction, from reason or personal experience.

Before quitting the subject of freedom of opinion, it is fit to take notice of those who say, that the free expression of all opinions should be permitted, on condition that the manner be temperate, and do not pass the bounds of fair discussion. Much might be said on the impossibility of fixing where these supposed bounds are to be placed; for if the test be offense to those whose opinion is attacked, I think experience testifies that this offense is given whenever the attack is telling and powerful, and that every opponent who pushes them hard, and whom they find it difficult to answer, appears to them, if he shows any strong feeling on the subject, an intemperate opponent. But this, though an important consideration in a practical point of view, merges in a more fundamental objection. Undoubtedly the manner of asserting an opinion, even though it be a true one, may be very objectionable, and may justly incur severe censure. But the principal offenses of the kind are such as it is mostly impossible, unless by accidental self-betrayal, to bring home to conviction. The gravest of them is, to argue sophistically, to suppress facts or arguments, to misstate the elements of the case, or misrepresent the opposite opinion. But all this, even to the most aggravated degree, is so continually done in perfect good faith, by persons who are not considered, and in many other respects may not deserve to be considered, ignorant or incompetent, that it is rarely possible on adequate grounds conscientiously to stamp the misrepresentation as morally culpable; and still less could law presume to interfere with this kind of controversial misconduct. With regard to what is commonly meant by intemperate discussion, namely, invective, sarcasm, personality, and the like, the denunciation of these weapons would deserve more sympathy if it were ever proposed to interdict them equally to both sides; but it is only desired to restrain the employment of them against the prevailing opinion: against the unprevailing they may not only be used without general disapproval, but will be likely to obtain for him who uses them the praise of honest zeal and righteous indignation. Yet whatever mischief arises from their use, is greatest when they are employed against the comparatively defenseless; and whatever unfair advantage can be derived by any opinion from this mode of asserting it, accrues almost exclusively to received opinions. The worst offense of this kind which can be committed by a polemic, is to stigmatize those who hold the contrary opinion as bad and immoral men. To calumny of this sort, those who hold any unpopular opinion are peculiarly exposed, because they are in general few and uninfluential, and nobody but themselves feels much interest in seeing justice done them; but this weapon is, from the nature of the case, denied to those who attack a prevailing opinion: they can neither use it with safety to themselves, nor if they could, would it do anything but recoil on their own cause. In general, opinions contrary to those commonly received can only obtain a hearing by studied moderation of language, and the most cautious avoidance of unnecessary offense, from which they hardly ever deviate even in a slight degree without losing ground: while unmeasured vituperation employed on the side of the prevailing opinion, really does deter people from professing contrary opinions, and from listening to those who profess them. For the interest, therefore, of truth and justice, it is far more important to restrain this employment of vituperative language than the other; and, for example, if it were necessary to choose, there would be much more need to discourage offensive attacks on infidelity, than on religion. It is, however, obvious that law and authority have no business with restraining either, while opinion ought, in every instance, to determine its verdict by the circumstances of the individual case;

condemning every one, on whichever side of the argument he places himself, in whose mode of advocacy either want of candor, or malignity, bigotry or intolerance of feeling manifest themselves, but not inferring these vices from the side which a person takes, though it be the contrary side of the question to our own; and giving merited honor to every one, whatever opinion he may hold, who has calmness to see and honesty to state what his opponents and their opinions really are, exaggerating nothing to their discredit, keeping nothing back which tells, or can be supposed to tell, in their favor. This is the real morality of public discussion; and if often violated, I am happy to think that there are many controversialists who to a great extent observe it, and a still greater number who conscientiously strive towards it. . . .

Let us next examine whether . . . men should be free to act upon their opinions—to carry these out in their lives, without hindrance, either physical or moral, from their fellow men, so long as it is at their own risk and peril. . . . The liberty of the individual must be thus far limited; he must not make himself a nuisance to other people. . . . It is desirable . . . that in things which do not primarily concern others, individuality should assert itself. Where, not the person's own character, but the traditions or customs of other people are the rule of conduct, there is wanting one of the principal ingredients of human happiness, and quite the chief ingredient of individual and social progress. . . . It is not by wearing down into uniformity all that is individual in themselves, but by cultivating it and calling it forth, within the limits imposed by the rights and interests of others, that human beings become a noble and beautiful object of contemplation. . . . Whatever crushes individuality is despotism. . . . Genius can only breath freely in an atmosphere of freedom. . . .

There are many who consider as an injury to themselves any conduct which they have a distaste for, and resent it as an outrage to their feelings; as a religious bigot, when charged with disregarding the religious feelings of others, has been known to retort that they disregard his feelings, by persisting in their abominable worship or creed. But there is no parity between the feeling of a person for his own opinion, and the feeling of another who is offended at his holding it; no more than between the desire of a thief to take a purse, and the desire of the right owner to keep it. And a person's taste is as much his own peculiar concern as his opinion or his purse. . . .

FOURTEENTH AMENDMENT, U.S. CONSTITUTION, SECTION 1 (1868)

All persons born or naturalized in the United States and subject to the jurisdiction thereof, are citizens of the United States and of the State wherein they reside. No State shall make or enforce any law which shall abridge the privileges or immunities of citizens of the United States; nor shall any State deprive any person of life, liberty, or property, without due process of law; nor deny to any person within its jurisdiction the equal protection of the laws.

THOMAS M. COOLEY, *A TREATISE ON THE CONSTITUTIONAL LIMITATIONS WHICH REST UPON THE LEGISLATIVE POWER OF THE STATES OF THE AMERICAN UNION* (1868)

Cooley's Treatise on Constitutional Limitations, *which evinced a strong commitment to the freedom of speech and press, was one of the most influential works of legal scholarship of the second half of the nineteenth century.*

[The provisions of the First Amendment] do not create new rights, but their purpose is to protect the citizen in the enjoyment of those already possessed. We are at once, therefore, turned back from these provisions to the common law, in order that we may ascertain what the rights are which are thus protected, and what is the extent of the privileges they assure. At the common law, however, it will be found that liberty of the press was neither well protected nor well defined. The art of printing, in the hands of private persons, has, until within a comparatively recent period, been regarded rather as an engine of mischief.... [L]iberty of the press, as now exercised, is of modern origin, and commentators seem to be agreed in the opinion that the term itself means only that liberty of publication without the previous permission of the government, which was obtained by the abolition of censorship.

The constitutional liberty of speech and of the press, as we understand it, implies a right to freely utter and publish whatever the citizen may please, and to be protected against any responsibility for the publication, except so far as such publications, from their blasphemy, obscenity, or scandalous character, may be a public offense, or as by their falsehood and malice they may injuriously affect the private character of individuals. Or, to state the same thing in somewhat different words, we understand liberty of speech and of the press to imply not only liberty to publish, but complete immunity for the publication, so long as it is not harmful in its character, when tested by such standards as the law affords. For these standards, we must look to the common law rules which were in force when the constitutional guarantees were established.

THEODORE SCHROEDER, *LIBERTY OF CONSCIENCE, SPEECH, AND PRESS* (1906)

Theodore Schroeder (1864–1953) was an influential early-twentieth-century free speech theorist and legal activist. A founder of the Free Speech League, an early civil liberties group, Schroeder frequently came to the defense of political and sexual radicals. In this pamphlet, Schroeder defended the general principle of free speech and called for greater tolerance of sex-related speech.

The desire to persecute, even for mere opinion's sake, seems to be an eternal inheritance of humans. We naturally and as a matter of course encourage others in doing and believing whatever for any reason, or without reason, we deem proper. Even though we have a mind fairly well disciplined in the duty of toleration, we quite naturally discourage others and feel a sense of outraged propriety, whenever they believe and act radically different from ourselves. Our resentment becomes vehement just in proportion as our reason is impotent and our nerves diseasedly sensitive. That is why it is said that "man is naturally, instinctively intolerant and a persecutor."

From this necessity of our undisciplined nature comes the stealthy but inevitable recurrence of legalized bigotry, and its rehabilitation of successive inquisitions. From the days of pagan antiquity to the present hour, there has never been a time or country wherein mankind could claim immunity from all persecution for intellectual differences. This cruel intolerance has always appealed to a "sacred and patriotic duty," and masked behind an ignorantly made and unwarranted pretense of morality.

"Persecution has not been the outgrowth of any one age, nationality or creed; it has been the ill-favored progeny of all." Thus, under the disguise of new names and new pretensions, again and again we punish unpopular, though wholly self-regarding, nonmoral conduct, imprison men for expressing honest intellectual differences, deny the duty of toleration, destroy a proper liberty of thought and conduct, and always under the same old false pretenses of "morality," "law and order."

Whenever our natural tendency toward intolerance is reinforced by abnormally intense feelings, such as diseased nerves produce, persecution follows quite unavoidably, because the intensity of associated emotions is transformed into a conviction of inerrancy. Such a victim of diseased emotions, even more than others, "knows because he feels, and is firmly convinced because strongly agitated." Unable to answer logically the contention of his neighbor, he ends by desiring to punish him as his enemy. . . .

The concurrence of many in like emotions, associated with and centered upon the same focus of irritation, makes the effective majority of the state view the toleration of their opponents as a crime, and their heresy, whether political, religious, ethical or sexual, is denounced a danger to civil order, and the heretic must be judicially silenced. Thus all bigots have reasoned in all past ages. Thus do those afflicted with our present sex superstition again defend their moral censorship of literature and art.

These are the processes by which we always become incapable of deriving profit from the lessons of history. That all the greatest minds of every age believed in something now known to be false, and in the utility of what is now deemed injurious or immoral, never suggests to petty intellects that the future generations will also pity us for having entertained our most cherished opinions.

The presence of these designated natural defects, which so very few have outgrown, makes it quite probable that the battle for intellectual freedom will never reach an end. The few, trained in the duty of toleration, owe it to humanity to restate, with great frequency, the arguments for mental hospitality. Only by this process can we contribute directly toward the mental discipline of the relatively unevolved masses, and prepare the way for those new and therefore unpopular truths by which the race will progress. The absolute liberty of thought, with opportunity, unlimited as between adults for its oral or printed expression is a condition precedent to the highest development of our progressive morality.

Men of strong passions and weak intellects seldom see the expediency of encouraging others to disagree. Thence came all of those terrible persecutions for heresy, witchcraft, sedition, etc., which have prolonged the midnight of superstition into "dark ages." The passionate zeal of a masterful few has always made them assume that they only could be trusted to have a personal judgment upon moral questions, while all others must be coerced, unquestioningly to accept them upon authority.

Such egomania always resulted in the persecution of those who furnished the common people with the materials upon which they might base a different opinion, or outgrow their slave virtues. . . .

So now we have many who . . . esteem it to be of immoral tendency for others than themselves to secure such information as may lead to a personal and different opinion about the physiology, psychology, hygiene, or ethics of sex, and by law, they make it a crime to distribute any specific and detailed information upon the subject, especially if it be unprudish in the manner of its presentation or is accompanied with unorthodox opinions about marriage or sexual ethics. This is repeating the old folly that the adult masses cannot be trusted to form an opinion of their own. The "free" people of the United States cannot be allowed to have the information which might lead to a change of their own statute laws upon sex. . . .

Formerly, when bigots were rampant and openly dominant, the old superstition punished the psychological crime of "immoral thinking," because it was irreligious, and it was called "sedition," "blasphemy," etc. Under the present verbal disguise, the same old superstition punishes the psychological crime of immoral thinking, because it may discredit the ethical claims of religious asceticism, and now we call it "obscenity" and "indecency." What is the difference between the old and the new superstition and persecution?

The argument against the expediency of truth is ever the last refuge of retreating error, the weakest subterfuge to conceal a dawning consciousness of ignorance. In all history, one cannot find a single instance in which an enlargement of opportunity for the propagation of unpopular allegations of truth has not resulted in increased good.

"If I were asked, 'What opinion, from the commencement of history to the present hour, had been productive of the most injury to mankind?' I should answer, without hesitation: 'The inexpediency of publishing sentiments of supposed bad tendency.'" It is this infamous opinion which has made the world a vale of tears, and drenched it with the blood of martyrs.

I am fully mindful of the fact that an unrestricted press means that some abuse of the freedom of the press will result. However, I also remember that no man can tell a priori what opinion is of immoral tendency. I am furthermore mindful that we cannot argue against the use of a thing, from the possibility of its abuse, since this objection can be urged against every good thing, and I am not willing to destroy all that makes life pleasant. Lord Littleton aptly said: "To argue against any breach of liberty from the ill use that may be made of it is to argue against liberty itself, since all is capable of being abused. . . ."

No argument for the suppression of "obscene" literature has ever been offered which will not justify by unavoidable implication, and which has not already justified, every other limitation that has ever been put upon mental freedom. No argument was ever made to justify intolerance, whether political, theological, or scientific, which has not been restated in support of our present sex superstitions and made to do duty toward the suppressing of information as to the physiology, psychology, or ethics of sex. All this class of arguments that have been made have always started with the false assumption that such qualities as morality or immorality could belong to opinions, or to a static fact. . . .

There may still be those, who, like Dr. Johnson, argue that the persecutors of Christians were right, because the persecution of an advocate is a necessary ordeal through which his truth always passes successfully; legal penalties, in the end, being powerless against the truth, though sometimes beneficially effective against mischievous error.

It may be a historical fact that all known truths, for a time, have been crushed by the bigot's heel, but this should not make us applaud his iniquity. It is an aphorism of unbalanced optimists, that truth crushed to earth will always rise. Even if this were true, it must always remain an unprovable proposition, because it postulates that at every particular moment we are ignorant of all those suppressed truths, not then resurrected, and since we do not know them, we cannot prove that they ever will be resurrected. It would be interesting to know how one could prove that an unknown truth of past suppression is going to be rediscovered, or that the conditions which alone once made it a cognizable fact will ever again come into being. And yet a knowledge of it might have a very important bearing on some present controversy of moment.

Surely, many dogmas have been wholly suppressed which were once just as earnestly believed to be as infallibly true as some that are now accepted as inspired writ. Just a little more strenuosity in persecution would have wiped out Christianity. How can we prove that all the suppressed, and now unknown, dogmas were false? If mere survival after persecution is deemed evidence of the inerrancy of an opinion, then which of the many conflicting opinions, each a survivor of persecution, are unquestionably true, and how is the choice to be made from the mass? Is it not clear that neither a rediscovery, nor a survival after persecution, can have any special relation to truth as such? If it is, then let us unite to denounce as an unprovable hallucination the statement that truth crushed to earth will rise again.

The abettors of persecution are more damaged than those whom they deter from expressing and defending unpopular opinions, since as between these, only the former are depriving themselves of the chief means of correcting their own errors. But the great mass of people belong neither to the intellectual innovators, nor to their persecutors. The great multitude might be quite willing to listen to or read unconventional thoughts if ever permitted, amid opportunity, to exercise an uncoerced choice. . . .

Observance of natural law is the unavoidable condition of all life, and a knowledge of those laws is a condition precedent to all effort for securing well-being, through conscious adjustment to them. It follows that an opportunity for an acquaintance with nature's processes, unlimited by human coercion, is the equal and inalienable right of every human being, because an essential to his life, liberty, and the pursuit of happiness. No exception can be made for the law of our sex nature.

It also follows that in formulating our conception of what is the law of nature, and in its adjustment or application by us to our infinitely varied personal constitutions, each sane adult human is the sovereign of his own destiny and never properly within the control of any other person, until some one, not an undeceived voluntary participant is directly affected thereby to his injury.

The laws for the suppression of "obscene" literature as administered, deny to adults the access to part of the alleged facts and arguments concerning our sex nature, and therefore are a violation of the above rules of right and conduct.

We all believe in intellectual and moral progress. Therefore, whatever may be the character or subject of a man's opinions, others have the right to express their judgments upon them; to censure them, if deemed censurable; or turn them to ridicule, if deemed ridiculous. If such right is not protected by law, we should have no security against the exposition or perpetuity of error, and therefore we should hamper progress. . . .

Since advancement in the refining of our ethical conceptions is conditioned upon experimentation and the dissemination of its observed results, it follows that the most immoral of present tendencies is that which arrests moral progress by limiting the freedom of speech and press. When viewed in long perspective it also follows that we must conclude that the most immoral persons of our time are those who are now successfully stifling discussion and restricting the spread of sexual intelligence, because they are most responsible for impeding moral progress, as to the relations of men and women.

Those who in these particulars deny a freedom of speech and press and the correlative right to hear, unlimited as to all sane adults, by their very act of denial, exercise a right which they would suppress in others. The true believer in equality of liberty allows others the right to speak against free speech, though he may not be so hospitable as to its actual suppression. No man is truly liberal who is unwilling to defend the right of others to disagree with him, even about free love, polygamy or stirpiculture [the scientific breeding of human beings in the interest of progress].

If our conceptions of sexual morality have a rational foundation, then they are capable of adequate rational defense, and there is no need for legislative suppression of discussion. If our sex ethics will not bear critical scrutiny and discussion, then to suppress such discussion is infamous, because it is a legalized support of error. In either case the freest possible discussion is a condition of the progressive elimination of error. . . .

EMMA GOLDMAN, "SYNDICALISM: ITS THEORY AND PRACTICE," *MOTHER EARTH* (JANUARY–FEBRUARY 1913)

In this essay, Emma Goldman, the nation's most outspoken and influential anarchist, outlines both the core of her revolutionary, anticapitalist views and the tactics she believed necessary to precipitate the revolution.

The fundamental difference between Syndicalism and old trade methods is this: while the old trade unions, without exception, move within the wage system and capitalism, recognizing the latter as inevitable, Syndicalism repudiates and condemns present industrial arrangements as unjust and criminal, and holds out no hope to the worker for lasting results from this system.

Of course Syndicalism, like the old trade unions, fights for immediate gains, but it is not stupid enough to pretend that labor can expect humane conditions from inhuman economic arrangements in society. Thus it merely wrests from the enemy what it can force him to yield; on the whole, however, Syndicalism aims at, and concentrates its energies upon, the complete overthrow of the wage system. Indeed, Syndicalism goes further: it aims to liberate labor from every institution that has not for its object the free development of production for the benefit of all humanity. In short, the ultimate purpose of Syndicalism is to reconstruct society from its present centralized, authoritative and brutal state to one based upon the free, federated grouping of the workers along lines of economic and social liberty.

With this object in view, Syndicalism works in two directions: first, by undermining the existing institutions; secondly, by developing and educating the workers and cultivating their spirit of solidarity, to prepare them for a full, free life, when capitalism shall have been abolished.

Syndicalism is, in essence, the economic expression of Anarchism. That circumstance accounts for the presence of so many Anarchists in the Syndicalist movement.

Like Anarchism, Syndicalism prepares the workers along direct economic lines, as conscious factors in the great struggles of to-day, as well as conscious factors in the task of reconstructing society along autonomous industrial lines, as against the paralyzing spirit of centralization with its bureaucratic machinery of corruption, inherent in all political parties.

Realizing that the diametrically opposed interests of capital and labor can never be reconciled, Syndicalism must needs repudiate the old, rusticated, worn-out methods of trade unionism, and declare for an open war against the capitalist régime, as well as against every institution which to-day supports and protects capitalism.

As a logical consequence Syndicalism, in its daily warfare against capitalism, rejects the contract system, because it does not consider labor and capital equals, hence cannot consent to an agreement which the one has the power to break, while the other must submit to without redress.

For similar reasons Syndicalism rejects negotiations in labor disputes, because such a procedure serves only to give the enemy time to prepare his end of the fight, thus defeating the very object the workers set out to accomplish. Also, Syndicalism stands for spontaneity, both as a preserver of the fighting strength of labor and also because it takes the enemy unawares, hence compels him to a speedy settlement or causes him great loss.

Syndicalism objects to a large union treasury, because money is as corrupting an element in the ranks of labor as it is in those of capitalism. We in America know this to be only too true. If the labor movement in this country were not backed by such large funds, it would not be as conservative as it is, nor would the leaders be so readily corrupted. However, the main reason for the opposition of Syndicalism to large treasuries consists in the fact that they create class distinctions and jealousies within the ranks of labor, so detrimental to the spirit of solidarity. The worker whose organization has a large purse considers himself superior to his poorer brother, just as he regards himself better than the man who earns fifty cents less per day.

The chief ethical value of Syndicalism consists in the stress it lays upon the necessity of labor's getting rid of the element of dissension, parasitism and corruption in its ranks. It seeks to cultivate devotion, solidarity and enthusiasm, which are far more essential and vital in the economic struggle than money. . . .

Syndicalism has grown out of the disappointment of the workers with politics and parliamentary methods. In the course of its development Syndicalism has learned to see in the State—with its mouthpiece, the representative system—one of the strongest supports of capitalism; just as it has learned that the army and the church are the chief pillars of the State. It is therefore that Syndicalism has turned its back upon parliamentarism and political machines, and has set its face toward the economic arena wherein alone gladiator Labor can meet his foe successfully. . . .

Now, as to the methods employed by Syndicalism—Direct Action, Sabotage, and the General Strike.

DIRECT ACTION: *Conscious individual or collective effort to protest against, or remedy, social conditions through the systematic assertion of the economic power of the workers.*

Sabotage has been decried as criminal, even by so-called revolutionary Socialists. Of course, if you believe that property, which excludes the producer from its use, is justifiable, then sabotage is indeed a crime. But unless a Socialist continues to be under influence of our bourgeois morality—a morality which enables the few to monopolize the earth at the expense of the many—he cannot consistently maintain that capitalist property is inviolate. Sabotage undermines this form of private possession. Can it therefore be considered criminal? On the contrary, it is ethical in the best sense, since it helps society to get rid of its worst foe, the most detrimental factor of social life.

Sabotage is mainly concerned with obstructing, by every possible method, the regular process of production, thereby demonstrating the determination of the workers to give according to what they receive, and no more. For instance, at the time of the French railroad strike of 1910, perishable goods were sent in slow trains, or in an opposite direction from the one intended. Who but the most ordinary philistine will call that a crime? If the railway men themselves go hungry, and the "innocent" public has not enough feeling of solidarity to insist that these men should get enough to live on, the public has forfeited the sympathy of the strikers and must take the consequences.

Another form of sabotage consisted, during this strike, in placing heavy boxes on goods marked "Handle with care," cut glass and china and precious wines. From the standpoint of the law this might have been a crime, but from the standpoint of common humanity it was a very sensible thing. The same is true of disarranging a loom in a weaving mill, or living up to the letter of the law with all its red tape, as the Italian railway men did, thereby causing confusion in the railway service. In other words, sabotage is merely a weapon of defense in the industrial warfare, which is the more effective, because it touches capitalism in its most vital spot, the pocket.

By the General Strike, Syndicalism means a stoppage of work, the cessation of labor. Nor need such a strike be postponed until all the workers of a particular place or country are ready for it. As has been pointed out ... the General Strike may be started by one industry and exert a tremendous force. It is as if one man suddenly raised the cry "Stop the thief!" Immediately others will take up the cry, till the air rings with it. The General Strike, initiated by one determined organization, by one industry or by a small, conscious minority among the workers, is the industrial cry of "Stop the thief," which is soon taken up by many other industries, spreading like wildfire in a very short time.

One of the objections of politicians to the General Strike is that the workers also would suffer for the necessaries of life. In the first place, the workers are past masters in going hungry; secondly, it is certain that a General Strike is surer of prompt settlement than an ordinary strike. . . . Besides, Syndicalism recognizes the right of the producers to the things which they have created; namely, the right of the workers to help themselves if the strike does not meet with speedy settlement. . . . I think that the General Strike will become a fact the moment labor understands its full value—its destructive as well as constructive value, as indeed many workers all over the world are beginning to realize.

These ideas and methods of Syndicalism some may consider entirely negative, though they are far from it in their effect upon society to-day. But Syndicalism has also a directly positive aspect. In fact, much more time and effort is being devoted to that phase than to the others. Various forms of Syndicalist activity are designed to prepare the workers, even within present social and industrial conditions, for the life of a new and better society. To that end the masses are trained in the spirit of mutual aid and brotherhood, their initiative and self-reliance developed, and an *esprit de corps* maintained whose very soul is solidarity of purpose and the community of interests of the international proletariat. . . .

[Syndicalists are committed to forming extensive systems of education that train] the worker in his daily struggle, but [serve] also to equip him for the battle royal and the future, when he is to assume his place in society as an intelligent, conscious being and useful producer, once capitalism is abolished. Nearly all leading Syndicalists agree with the Anarchists that a free society can exist only through voluntary association, and that its ultimate success will depend upon the intellectual and moral development of the workers who will supplant the wage system with a new social arrangement, based on solidarity and economic well-being for all. That is Syndicalism, in theory and practice.

ESPIONAGE ACT (OF 1917, AS AMENDED BY THE SEDITION ACT OF 1918)

At the behest of the Wilson administration and amid national concern that spying and sabotage would undermine the U.S. war effort during World War I, Congress passed the Espionage Act. The act was roundly criticized on free speech grounds by political radicals, critics of the war, and civil libertarians.

Whoever, when the United States is at war, shall willfully make or convey false reports or false statements with intent to interfere with the operation or success of the military or naval forces of the United States or to promote the success of its enemies and whoever, when the United States is at war, shall willfully cause or attempt to cause insubordination, disloyalty, mutiny, or refusal of duty, in the military or naval forces of the United States, or shall willfully obstruct the recruiting or enlistment service of the United States, shall be punished by a fine of not more than $10,000 or imprisonment for not more than twenty years, or both.

[The act also forbade, while the United States was at war] any disloyal . . . scurrilous or abusive language about the form of government of the United States, or the Constitution, or the flag, or the uniform of the Army or Navy . . . [and] any language intended to bring the form of government of the United States . . . into contempt, scorn, contumely, or disrepute.

MASSES PUBLISHING CO. V. PATTEN, 244 FED. 535 (S.D.N.Y. 1917)

Judge Learned Hand's opinion in the Masses *case involved the federal government's decision to deny mailing privileges to Max Eastman's so-*

cialist magazine The Masses *on the grounds that it encouraged violation of the Espionage Act. Hand's opinion advanced a highly speech-protective Incitement test for the freedom of speech.*

U.S. District Judge Learned Hand, writing for the Court:

It may be that the peril of war, which goes to the very existence of the state, justifies any measure of compulsion, any measure of suppression which Congress deems necessary to its safety, the liberties of each being in subjection to the liberties of all. . . .

[M]en who become satisfied that they are engaged in an enterprise dictated by the unconscionable selfishness of the rich, and effectuated by a tyrannous disregard for the will of those who must suffer and die, will be more prone to insubordination than those who have faith in the cause and acquiesce in the means. . . . Yet to interpret . . . [the language of the Espionage Act permitting the prosecution of those who "willfully cause . . . insubordination, disloyalty, mutiny, or refusal of duty" in the armed forces] broadly would . . . involve necessarily as a consequence the suppression of all hostile criticism, and of all opinion except what encouraged and supported the existing policies, or which fell within the range of temperate argument. It would contradict the normal assumption of democratic government that the suppression of hostile criticism does not turn upon the justice of its substance or the decency and propriety of its temper. Assuming that the power to repress such opinion may rest in Congress in the throes of a struggle for the very existence of the state, its exercise is so contrary to the use and wont of our people that only the clearest expression of such a power justifies the conclusion that it was intended. . . .

Yet [that said], there has always been a recognized limit to such expressions, incident indeed to the existence of any compulsive power of the state itself. One may not counsel or advise others to violate the law as it stands. Words are not only the keys of persuasion, but the triggers of action, and those which have no purport but to counsel the violation of law cannot by any latitude of interpretation be part of that public opinion which is the final source of government in a democratic state. The defendant asserts not only that the magazine indirectly through its propaganda leads to a disintegration of loyalty and a disobedience of law, but that in addition it counsels and advises resistance to existing law, especially the draft. . . . To counsel or advise a man to an act is to urge upon him either that it is in his interest or his duty to do it. While, of course, this may be accomplished as well by indirection as expressly, since words carry the meaning that they impart, the definition is exhaustive, I think, and I shall use it. Political agitation, by the passions it arouses or the convictions it engenders, may in fact stimulate men to the violation of the law. Detestation of existing policies is easily transformed into forcible resistance of the causal relation between the two. Yet to assimilate agitation, legitimate as such, with direct incitement to violent resistance, is to disregard the tolerance of all methods of political agitation which in normal times is a safeguard of free government. The distinction is not a scholastic subterfuge, but a hard-bought acquisition in the fight for freedom, and the purpose to disregard it must be evident when the power exists. If one stops short of urging upon others that it is their duty or their interest to resist the law, it seems to me one should not be held to have attempted to cause its violation. If that be not the test, I can see no escape from the conclusion that under [the Espionage Act] every political agitation which can be shown to be apt to create a seditious temper is illegal. I am confident that by such language Congress had no such revolutionary purpose in view.

Zechariah Chafee, Jr., from *The New Republic* (1918)

Chafee, a Harvard Law School professor and one of the founding fathers of modern civil libertarian understandings of the freedom of speech, began to formulate his free speech theories in response to the speech restrictions put in place during World War I.

The true meaning of freedom of speech seems to be this. One of the most important purposes of society and government is the discovery and spread of truth on subjects of general concern. This is possible only through absolutely unlimited discussion, for . . . once force is thrown into the argument, it becomes a matter of chance whether it is thrown on the false side or the true, and truth loses all its natural advantage in the contest. Nevertheless, there are other purposes of government, such as order, the training of the young, protection against external aggression. Unlimited discussion sometimes interferes with these purposes, which must then be balanced against freedom of speech, but freedom of speech ought to weigh heavily in the scale. The First Amendment gives binding force to this principle of political wisdom.

California Criminal Anarchy Statute (Cal. Pen. Code, sec 403a, 1919)

California's Criminal Anarchy Statute (1919) was typical of many state statutes passed during the Red Scare. It was later declared unconstitutional by the Supreme Court in Stromberg v. California, 283 U.S. 359 *(1931).*

Any person who displays a red flag, banner or badge or any flag, badge, banner, or device of any color or form whatever in any public place or in any meeting place or public assembly, or from or on any house, building or window as a sign, symbol or emblem of opposition to organized government or as an invitation or stimulus to anarchistic action or as an aid to propaganda that is of a seditious character is guilty of a felony.

Schenck v. United States, 249 U.S. 47 (1919)

This case involved the Wilson administration's prosecution of Charles Schenck, the leader of the Socialist Party, for printing and distributing antidraft leaflets during World War I in violation of the Espionage Act. While announcing a new Clear and Present Danger test, the Court sustained the government's claim that the leaflets caused insubordination in the military and frustrated the recruitment of soldiers during wartime.

Justice Oliver Wendell Holmes, Jr., writing for the Court:

It may well be that the prohibition of the laws abridging the freedom of speech is not confined to previous restraints, although to prevent them may have been the main purpose . . . [of the First Amendment]. We admit that in many places and in ordinary times the defendants in saying all that was said in the circular would have been within their constitutional rights. But the character of every act depends upon the circumstances in which it is done. The most stringent protection of free speech would not protect a man in falsely shouting fire in a theatre and causing a panic. It does not even protect a man from an injunction against uttering words that may have all the effect of force. The question in every case is whether the words used are used in such circumstances and are of such a nature as to create a clear and present danger that they will bring about the substantive evils that Congress has a right to prevent. It is a question of proximity and degree. When a nation is at war, many things that might be said in times of peace are such a hindrance to its effort that their utterance will not be endured so long as men fight and that no Court could regard them as protected by any constitutional right. . . .

ABRAMS V. UNITED STATES, 250 U.S. 616 (1919)

This case involved the prosecution under the Espionage Act of five Russian immigrants for printing and distributing leaflets stridently opposing U.S. involvement in World War I and sharply criticizing the Wilson administration's war policies. Although the Court upheld the convictions, Justice Holmes, in dissent, penned one of the most famous defenses of free speech in U.S. history.

Justice John Clarke, writing for the Court:

It will not do to say . . . that the only intent of these defendants was to prevent injury to the Russian cause [rather than to the war effort of the United States against Germany]. Men must be held to have intended, and to be accountable for, the effects which their acts were likely to produce. Even if their primary purpose and intent was to aid the cause of the Russian Revolution [which the United States was opposing], the plan of action which they adopted necessarily involved, before it could be realized, defeat of the war program of the United States. . . . [T]he plain purpose of their propaganda was to excite, at the supreme crisis of the war, disaffection, sedition, riots, and, as they hoped, revolution, in this country for the purpose of embarrassing and if possible defeating the military plans of the Government in Europe. . . . [T]he defendants . . . plainly urged and advocated a resort to a general strike of workers in ammunition factories for the purpose of curtailing the production of ordinance and munitions necessary and essential for the prosecution of the war. . . .

Justice Oliver Wendell Holmes, Jr., joined by Justice Louis D. Brandeis, dissenting:

I do not doubt for a moment that . . . the United States constitutionally may punish speech that produces or is intended to produce a clear
and imminent danger that it will bring about forthwith certain substantive evils that the United States constitutionally may seek to prevent.
The power undoubtedly is greater in time of war than in time of peace
because war opens dangers that do not exist in other times. . . . But . . . it
is only the present danger of immediate evil or intent to bring it about
that warrants Congress in setting a limit to the expression of opinion
where private rights are not concerned. Congress certainly cannot forbid
all effort to change the mind of the country. Now nobody can suppose
that the surreptitious publishing of a silly leaflet by an unknown man,
without more, would present any immediate danger that its opinions
would hinder the success of the government arms or have any apprecia-
ble tendency to do so. . . .

Persecution for the expression of opinions seems to me perfectly logical. If you have no doubt of your premises or your power and want a
certain result with all your heart you naturally express your wishes in
law and sweep away all opposition. To allow opposition by speech
seems to indicate that you think the speech impotent, as when a man
says that he has squared the circle, or that you do not care whole-heart-
edly for the result, or that you doubt either your power or your
premises. But when men have realized that time has upset many fighting
faiths, they may come to believe even more than they believe the very
foundations of their own conduct that the ultimate good desired is better reached by free trade in ideas—that the best test of truth is the power
of the thought to get itself accepted in the competition of the market,
and that truth is the only ground upon which their wishes safely can be
carried out. That at any rate is the theory of our Constitution. It is an experiment, as all life is an experiment. Every year if not every day we have
to wager our salvation upon some prophecy based upon imperfect
knowledge. While that experiment is part of our system I think that we
should be eternally vigilant against attempts to check the expression of
opinions that we loath and believe to be fraught with death, unless they
so imminently threaten immediate interference with the lawful and
pressing purposes of the law that an immediate check is required to save
the country. I wholly disagree with the argument of the Government
that the First Amendment left the common law of seditious libel in

force. . . . I had conceived that the United States through many years had shown its repentance for the Sedition Act of 1798. . . . I regret that I cannot put into more impressive words my belief that in their conviction upon this indictment the defendants were deprived of their rights under the Constitution of the United States.

A. MITCHELL PALMER, "THE CASE AGAINST THE REDS," *FORUM* 63 (1920): 173–185

In the aftermath of the Bolshevik Revolution and a wave of bombings at home, and fearful that the U.S. government was on the verge of being overthrown, Woodrow Wilson's attorney general, A. Mitchell Palmer, initiated a series of round-ups of anarchists, Communists, and other suspected political radicals. He justified his actions in this article.

In this brief review of the work which the Department of Justice has undertaken, to tear out the radical seeds that have entangled American ideas in their poisonous theories, I desire not merely to explain what the real menace of communism is, but also to tell how we have been compelled to clean up the country almost unaided by any virile legislation. Though I have not been embarrassed by political opposition, I have been materially delayed because the present sweeping processes of arrests and deportation of seditious aliens should have been vigorously pushed by Congress last spring. The failure of this is a matter of record in the Congressional files.

The anxiety of that period in our responsibility when Congress, ignoring the seriousness of these vast organizations that were plotting to overthrow the Government, failed to act, has passed. The time came when it was obviously hopeless to expect the hearty cooperation of Congress in the only way to stamp out these seditious societies in their open defiance of law by various forms of propaganda.

Like a prairie-fire, the blaze of revolution was sweeping over every American institution of law and order a year ago. It was eating its way into the homes of the American workmen, its sharp tongues of revolutionary heat were licking the altars of the churches, leaping into the belfry of the school bell, crawling into the sacred corners of American homes, seeking to replace marriage vows with libertine laws, burning up the foundations of society.

Robbery, not war, is the ideal of communism. This has been demonstrated in Russia, Germany, and in America. As a foe, the anarchist is fearless of his own life, for his creed is a fanaticism that admits no respect of any other creed. Obviously it is the creed of any criminal mind, which reasons always from motives impossible to clean thought. Crime is the degenerate factor in society.

Upon these two basic certainties, first that the "Reds" were criminal aliens and secondly that the American Government must prevent crime, it was decided that there could be no nice distinctions drawn between the theoretical ideals of the radicals and their actual violations of our national laws. An assassin may have brilliant intellectuality, he may be able to excuse his murder or robbery with fine oratory, but any theory which excuses crime is not wanted in America. This is no place for the criminal to flourish, nor will he do so so long as the rights of common citizenship can be exerted to prevent him. . . .

It has always been plain to me that when American citizens unite upon any national issue they are generally right, but it is sometimes difficult to make the issue clear to them. If the Department of Justice could succeed in attracting the attention of our optimistic citizens to the issue of internal revolution in this country, we felt sure there would be no revolution. The Government was in jeopardy; our private information of what was being done by the organization known as the Communist Party of America, with headquarters in Chicago, of what was being done by the Communist Internationale under their manifesto planned at Moscow last March by Trotzky, Lenin and others addressed "To the Proletariats of All Countries," of what strides the Communist Labor Party was making, removed all doubt. In this conclusion we did not ignore the definite standards of personal liberty, of free speech, which is the very temperament and heart of the people. The evidence was examined with the utmost care, with a personal leaning toward freedom of thought and word on all questions.

The whole mass of evidence, accumulated from all parts of the country, was scrupulously scanned, not merely for the written or spoken differences of viewpoint as to the Government of the United States, but, in spite of these things, to see if the hostile declarations might not be sincere in their announced motive to improve our social order. There was no hope of such a thing.

By stealing, murder and lies, Bolshevism has looted Russia not only of its material strength but of its moral force. A small clique of outcasts from the East Side of New York has attempted this, with what success we all know. Because a disreputable alien—Leon Bronstein, the man who now calls himself Trotzky—can inaugurate a reign of terror from his throne room in the Kremlin, because this lowest of all types known to New York can sleep in the Czar's bed, while hundreds of thousands in Russia are without food or shelter, should Americans be swayed by such doctrines?

Such a question, it would seem, should receive but one answer from America.

My information showed that communism in this country was an organization of thousands of aliens who were direct allies of Trotzky. Aliens of the same misshapen caste of mind and indecencies of character, and it showed that they were making the same glittering promises of lawlessness, of criminal autocracy to Americans, that they had made to the Russian peasants. How the Department of Justice discovered upwards of 60,000 of these organized agitators of the Trotzky doctrine in the United States is the confidential information upon which the Government is now sweeping the nation clean of such alien filth. . . .

Behind, and underneath, my own determination to drive from our midst the agents of Bolshevism with increasing vigor and with greater speed, until there are no more of them left among us, so long as I have the responsible duty of that task, I have discovered the hysterical methods of these revolutionary humans with increasing amazement and suspicion. In the confused information that sometimes reaches the people they are compelled to ask questions which involve the reasons for my acts against the "Reds." I have been asked, for instance, to what extent deportation will check radicalism in this country. Why not ask what will become of the United States Government if these alien radicals are permitted to carry out the principles of the Communist Party as embodied in its so-called laws, aims and regulations?

There wouldn't be any such thing left. In place of the United States Government we should have the horror and terrorism of bolsheviki tyranny such as is destroying Russia now. Every scrap of radical literature demands the overthrow of our existing government. All of it demands obedience to the instincts of criminal minds, that is, to the lower appetites, material and moral. The whole purpose of communism appears to be a mass formation of the criminals of the world to overthrow the decencies of private life, to usurp property that they have not earned, to disrupt the present order of life regardless of health, sex or religious rights. By a literature that promises the wildest dreams of such low aspirations, that can occur to only the criminal minds, communism distorts our social law. . . .

It has been inferred by the "Reds" that the United States Government, by arresting and deporting them, is returning to the autocracy of Czardom, adopting the system that created the severity of Siberian banishment. My reply to such charges is that in our determination to maintain our government we are treating our alien enemies with extreme consideration. To deny them the privilege of remaining in a country which they have openly deplored as an unenlightened community, unfit for those who prefer the privileges of Bolshevism, should be no hardship. It strikes me as an odd form of reasoning that these Russian Bolsheviks who extol the Bolshevik rule should be so unwilling to return to Russia. The nationality of most of the alien "Reds" is Russian and German. There is almost no other nationality represented among them.

It has been impossible in so short a space to review the entire menace of the internal revolution in this country as I know it, but this may serve to arouse the American citizen to its reality, its danger, and the great need of united effort to stamp it out, under our feet, if needs be. It is being done. The Department of Justice will pursue the attack of these "Reds" upon the Government of the United States with vigilance, and no alien, advocating the overthrow of existing law and order in this country, shall escape arrest and prompt deportation.

It is my belief that while they have stirred discontent in our midst, while they have caused irritating strikes, and while they have infected our social ideas with the disease of their own minds and their unclean morals we can get rid of them! and not until we have done so shall we have removed the menace of Bolshevism for good.

GITLOW V. NEW YORK, 268 U.S. 652 (1925)

This case involved the constitutionality of the prosecution of Benjamin Gitlow, a radical socialist, under New York State's criminal anarchy statute, which prohibited advocacy of the violent overthrow of the government. The "Left Wing Manifesto," which Gitlow had published, read in part, "The proletariat revolution and the Communist reconstruction of society—the struggle for these—is now indispensable. . . . The Communist International calls the proletariat of the world to the final struggle!" Gitlow's conviction was upheld, but the Court here took a significant step, announcing that the First Amendment free speech provision was "incorporated" as a constitutional limitation on state conduct. Gitlow himself later became a staunch anticommunist.

Justice Edward Sanford, writing for the Court:

The Manifesto, plainly, is neither the statement of abstract doctrine nor . . . mere prediction that industrial disturbances and revolutionary mass strikes will result spontaneously in an inevitable process of evolution in the economic system. It advocates and urges in fervent language mass action which shall progressively foment industrial disturbances and through political mass strikes and revolutionary mass action overthrow and destroy organized parliamentary government. . . . This is not the expression of philosophical abstraction, the mere prediction of future events; it is the language of direct incitement. . . .

That a State in the exercise of its police power may punish those who abuse [the constitutionally protected freedom of speech] by utterances inimical to the public welfare, tending to corrupt public morals, incite to crime, or disturb the public peace, is not open to question. . . . That utterances inciting to the overthrow of organized government by unlawful means, present a sufficient danger of substantive evil to bring their punishment within the range of legislative discretion, is clear. Such utterances, by their very nature, involve danger to the public peace and the security of the State. They threaten breaches of the peace and ultimate revolution. And the immediate danger is none the less real and substantial, because the effect of a given utterance cannot be accurately foreseen. The State cannot reasonably be required to measure the danger from every such utterance in the nice balance of a jeweler's scale. A single revolutionary spark may kindle a fire that, smouldering for a time, may burst into a sweeping and destructive conflagration. . . . We cannot hold that the present statute is an arbitrary or unreasonable exercise of the police power of the State. . . .

Justice Oliver Wendell Holmes, Jr., with whom Justice Louis D. Brandeis joins, dissenting:

[T]here was [here] no present danger of an attempt to overthrow the government by force on the part of the admittedly small minority who shared the defendant's views. It is said that this manifesto was more than a theory, that it was an incitement. Every idea is an incitement. It offers itself for belief and if believed it is acted on unless some other belief outweighs it or some failure of energy stifles the movement at its birth. The only difference between the expression of an opinion and an incitement in the narrower sense is the speaker's enthusiasm for the result. Eloquence may set fire to reason. . . . If in the long run the beliefs expressed in proletarian dictatorship are destined to be accepted by the dominant forces of the community, the only meaning of free speech is that they should be given their chance to have their way. . . .

WHITNEY V. CALIFORNIA, 274 U.S. 357 (1927)

This case involved the prosecution of Charlotte Whitney, an Oakland, California, Communist, for violating the state's Criminal Syndicalism Act, which forbade the use of violence, general strikes, sabotage, and other illicit methods in union or labor efforts to seize control of the means of production. Whitney was prosecuted because, as a member of a political party advocating violent revolution and the workers' seizure of the means of production, she was teaching, advocating, and abetting criminal syndicalism. The Court upheld Whitney's conviction.

Justice Louis D. Brandeis, with whom Justice Oliver Wendell Holmes, Jr., joins, concurring:

Those who won our independence believed that the final end of the State was to make men free to develop their faculties; and that in its government the deliberative forces should prevail over the arbitrary. They valued liberty both as an end and as a means. They believed liberty to be the secret of happiness and courage to be the secret of liberty. They believed that freedom to think as you will and to speak as you think are means indispensable to the discovery and spread of political truth; that without free speech and assembly discussion would be futile; that with them, discussion affords ordinarily adequate protection against the dissemination of noxious doctrine; that the greatest menace to freedom is an inert people; that public discussion is a political duty; and that this should be a fundamental principle of the American government. [The nation's founders] recognized the risks to which all human institutions are subject. But they knew that order cannot be secured merely through fear of punishment for its infraction; that it is hazardous to discourage thought, hope and imagination; that fear breeds repression; that repression breeds hate; that hate menaces stable government; that the path of safety lies in the opportunity to discuss freely supposed grievances and proposed remedies; and that the fitting remedy for evil counsels is good ones. Believing in the power of reason as applied through public discussion, they eschewed silence coerced by law—the argument of force in its worst form. Recognizing the occasional tyrannies of governing majorities, they amended the Constitution so that free speech and assembly should be guaranteed.

Fear of serious injury cannot alone justify suppression of free speech and assembly. Men feared witches and burnt women. It is the function of speech to free men from the bondage of irrational fears. To justify suppression of free speech there must be reasonable ground to fear that serious evil will result if free speech is practiced. There must be reasonable ground to believe that the danger apprehended is imminent. There must be reasonable ground to believe that the evil to be prevented is a serious one. Every denunciation of existing law tends in some measure to increase the probability that there will be violation of it. Condonation of a breach enhances the probability. Propagation of the criminal state of mind by teaching syndicalism increases it. Advocacy of law-breaking heightens it still further. But even advocacy of violation, however reprehensible morally, is not a justification for denying free speech where the advocacy falls short of incitement and there is nothing to indicate that the advocacy would be immediately acted on. The wide difference between advocacy and incitement, between preparation and attempt, between assembling and conspiracy, must be borne in mind. In order to support a finding of clear and present danger it must be shown either that immediate serious violence was to be expected or was advocated, or that the past conduct furnished reason to believe that such advocacy was then contemplated. . . .

MOTION PICTURE PRODUCERS AND DISTRIBUTORS ASSOCIATION OF AMERICA, MOTION PICTURE PRODUCTION CODE (HAYS CODE), STATEMENT OF GENERAL PRINCIPLES (JANUARY 1931)

Under political pressure from the Catholic church and its Legion of Decency, which threatened a massive boycott and anti-Hollywood campaign, the movie industry agreed to abide by a code ensuring that every film made and exhibited in the United States would uphold certain specified moral standards.

1. No picture shall be produced which will lower the moral standards of those who see it. Hence the sympathy of the audience shall never be thrown to the side of crime, wrong-doing, evil, or sin.

2. Correct standards of life, subject only to the requirements of drama and entertainment, shall be presented.

3. Law, natural or human, shall not be ridiculed, nor shall sympathy be created for its violation.

PALKO V. CONNECTICUT, 302 U.S. 319 (1937)

In this criminal procedure case holding the Fifth Amendment's double jeopardy provision applicable to the federal government and not to the states (i.e., holding that that provision was not "incorporated"), Justice Benjamin Cardozo included an important statement about those provisions of the Bill of Rights that the Court would regard differently.

Justice Benjamin Cardozo, writing for the Court:

The argument . . . is that whatever is forbidden by the Fifth Amendment is forbidden by the Fourteenth also. The Fifth Amendment, which is not directed to the states, but solely to the federal government, creates immunity from double jeopardy. . . . [But in fact, the] thesis is even broader. Whatever would be a violation of the original bill of rights (Amendments I to VIII) if done by the federal government is now equally unlawful by force of the Fourteenth Amendment if done by a state. There is no such general rule. . . .

On the other hand, the due process clause of the Fourteenth Amendment may make it unlawful for a state to abridge by its statutes the free-

dom of speech which the First Amendment safeguards against encroach-
ment by Congress . . . or the like freedom of the press . . . or the free exercise of religion . . . or the right of peaceable assembly, without which
speech would be unduly trammeled. . . . In these and other situations
immunities that are valid as against the federal government by force of
the specific pledges of particular amendments have been found to be implicit in the concept of ordered liberty, and thus, through the Fourteenth
Amendment, become valid as against the states.

The line of division may seem to be wavering and broken if there is a
hasty catalogue of the cases on the one side and the other. Reflection and
analysis will induce a different view. There emerges the perception of a
rationalizing principle which gives to discrete instances a proper order
and coherence. . . . [Rights not considered incorporated as protections
against the conduct of the states] are not of the very essence of a scheme
of ordered liberty. To abolish them is not to violate a "principle of justice so rooted in the traditions and conscience of our people as to be
ranked as fundamental. . . . Few would be so narrow or provincial as to
maintain that a fair and enlightened system of justice would be impossible without them. . . . If the Fourteenth Amendment has absorbed [cer-
tain provisions of the Bill of Rights], the process of absorption has had
its source in the belief that neither liberty nor justice would exist if they
were sacrificed. . . . This is true, for illustration, of freedom of thought,
and speech. Of that freedom one may say that it is the matrix, the indispensable condition, of nearly every other form of freedom. With rare
aberrations a pervasive recognition of that truth can be traced in our history, political and legal.

CAROLENE PRODUCTS CO. V. UNITED STATES, 304 U.S. 144 (1938)

*In this otherwise obscure New Deal era regulatory case concerning fed-
eral standards for the shipping of skim milk, the Court set out a post-New
Deal agenda in which the Court would apply higher levels of scrutiny to
laws infringing on specific constitutional provisions (including the Bill of
Rights), laws burdening the political process, and laws animated by prejudice against "discrete and insular minorities." The Court would, in con-*

trast, apply lower levels of scrutiny to laws affecting "mere" economic rights.

Justice Harlan Fiske Stone, writing for the Court:

[T]he existence of facts supporting the legislative judgment is to be presumed, for regulatory legislation affecting ordinary commercial transactions is not to be pronounced unconstitutional unless in light of the facts made known or generally assumed it is of such a character as to preclude the assumption that it rests upon some rational basis within the knowledge and experience of the legislators.[4]

[4][But] there may be narrower scope of the presumption of constitutionality when legislation appears on its face to be within a specific prohibition of the Constitution, such as those of the first ten amendments, which are deemed equally specific when held to be embraced within the Fourteenth. [Note in original.]

It is unnecessary to consider now whether legislation which restricts those political processes which can ordinarily be expected to bring about repeal of undesirable legislation is to be subjected to more exacting judicial scrutiny under the general prohibitions of the Fourteenth Amendment than are other types of legislation [citing cases involving restrictions on the right to vote, restrictions upon the dissemination of information (citing free press and free speech cases), interferences with political organizations (citing free speech cases), and limitations on peaceable assembly].

Nor need we inquire whether similar considerations enter into the review of statutes directed at particular religions ... or national ... or racial minorities ... ; whether prejudices against discrete and insular minorities may be a special condition, which tends seriously to curtail the operation of those political processes ordinarily thought to be relied upon to protect minorities, and which may call for a correspondingly more searching judicial inquiry. ...

LOVELL V. CITY OF GRIFFIN,
303 U.S. 444 (1938)

This case involved a Jehovah's Witness's challenge to a Griffin, Georgia, ordinance that required that she get written permission from the city manager before publicly distributing printed materials. The Witness, Alma Lovell, who distributed religious books and pamphlets in town, asserted that this requirement forced her to commit "an act of disobedience to His commandment." The Supreme Court sided with Lovell, declaring the city ordinance to be an unconstitutional prior restraint and violation of the freedom of the press.

Chief Justice Charles Evans Hughes, writing for the Court:

We think that the ordinance is invalid on its face. Whatever the motive which induced its adoption, its character is such that it strikes at the very foundation of the freedom of the press by subjecting it to license and censorship. The struggle for the freedom of the press was primarily directed against the power of the licensor. It was against that power that John Milton directed his assault by his "Appeal for the Liberty of Unlicensed Printing." And the liberty of the press became initially a right to publish "without a license what formerly could be published only with one." While this freedom from previous restraint upon publication cannot be regarded as exhausting the guaranty of liberty, the prevention of that restraint was a leading purpose in the adoption of the constitutional provision.... Legislation of the type of the ordinance in question would restore the system of license and censorship in its baldest form.

The liberty of the press is not confined to newspapers and periodicals. It necessarily embraces pamphlets and leaflets. These indeed have been historic weapons in the defense of liberty, as the pamphlets of Thomas Paine and others in our own history abundantly attest. The press in its connotation comprehends every sort of publication which affords a vehicle of information and opinion.... [Finally], [t]he ordinance cannot be saved because it relates to distribution and not publication....

THORNHILL V. ALABAMA, 310 U.S. 88 (1940)

Declaring it to be a coercive means of infringing upon private property rights, the state of Alabama had outlawed picketing. When Byron Thornhill, a union member, was arrested for picketing during a strike led by the American Federation of Labor at a wood-preserving plant in Tuscaloosa, he challenged the state's ban on the grounds that it violated his freedom of speech. In an opinion written by the former pro-labor governor of Michigan, Frank Murphy, the Court sided with Thornhill.

Justice Frank Murphy, writing for the Court:

The freedom of speech and of the press guaranteed by the Constitution embraces at the least the liberty to discuss publicly and truthfully all matters of public concern without previous restraint or fear of subsequent punishment. The exigencies of the colonial period and the efforts to secure freedom from oppressive administration developed a broadened conception of these liberties as adequate to supply the public need for information and education with respect to the significant issues of the times. . . . Freedom of discussion, if it would fulfill its historic function in this nation, must embrace all issues about which information is needed or appropriate to enable the members of society to cope with the exigencies of their period. . . . [T]he dissemination of information concerning the facts of a labor dispute must be regarded as within that area of free discussion that is guaranteed by the Constitution. . . .

The State urges that the purpose of the challenged statute is the protection of the community from the violence and breaches of the peace, which, it asserts, are the concomitants of picketing. The power and the duty of the State to take adequate steps to preserve the peace and to protect the privacy, the lives, and the property of its residents cannot be doubted. But no clear and present danger of destruction of life or property, or invasion of the right of privacy, or breach of the peace can be thought to be inherent in the activities of every person who approaches the premises of an employer and publicizes the facts of a labor dispute involving the latter. . . .

CANTWELL V. CONNECTICUT, 310 U.S. 296 (1940)

This case involved the prosecution of a Jehovah's Witness for failing to secure the proper permit before going door-to-door in a heavily Catholic neighborhood, asking residents if they would like to accept a pamphlet or hear a record, and then handing out or playing vehemently anti-Catholic messages. The Court held that on the facts of the case, the state's permit system exceeded the bounds of constitutionally appropriate time, place, and manner regulations.

Justice Owen Roberts, writing for the Court:

In the realm of religious faith, and in that of political belief, sharp differences arise. In both fields the tenets of one man may seem the rankest error to his neighbor. To persuade others to his own point of view, the pleader, as we know, at times, resorts to exaggeration, to vilification of men, who have been, or are, prominent in church or state, and even to false statement. But the people of this nation have ordained in the light of history, that, in spite of the probability of excesses and abuses, these liberties are, in the long view, essential to the enlightened opinion and right conduct on the part of the citizens of a democracy. . . .

THE ALIEN REGISTRATION ACT (1940) (SMITH ACT)

The Smith Act was passed shortly after the creation of the House Un-American Activities Committee and was aimed at fighting Communist subversion.

Whoever knowingly or willfully advocates, abets, advises, or teaches the duty, necessity, desirability, or propriety of overthrowing or destroying the government of the United States or the government of any State, Territory, District or Possession thereof, or the government of any political subdivision therein, by force or violence, or by the assassination of any officer of any such government; or Whoever, with intent to cause the overthrow or destruction of any such government, prints, publishes, edits, issues, circulates, sells, distributes, or publicly displays any written or printed matter advocating, advising, or teaching the duty, necessity, desirability, or propriety of overthrowing or destroying any government in the United States by force or violence, or attempts to do so; or Whoever organizes or helps or attempts to organize any society, group, or assembly of persons who teach, advocate, or encourage the overthrow or destruction of any such government by force or violence; or becomes or is a member of, or affiliates with, any such society, group, or assembly of persons, knowing the purposes thereof—

Shall be fined under this title or imprisoned not more than twenty years, or both, and shall be ineligible for employment by the United States or any department or agency thereof, for the five years next following his conviction.

If two or more persons conspire to commit any offense named in this section, each shall be fined under this title or imprisoned not more than twenty years, or both, and shall be ineligible for employment by the United States or any department or agency thereof, for the five years next following his conviction.

FRANKLIN DELANO ROOSEVELT, STATE OF THE UNION ADDRESS ("FOUR FREEDOMS" SPEECH) (JANUARY 6, 1941)

Roosevelt's "four freedoms" speech, delivered at a time when the United States was one of the last standing democracies and the world was descending into war, explained what the United States stood for and why it had to triumph.

I address you, the members of this new Congress, at a moment unprecedented in the history of the union. I use the word "unprecedented" because at no previous time has American security been as seriously threatened from without as it is today. . . . I suppose that every realist knows that the democratic way of life is at this moment being directly assailed in every part of the world—assailed either by arms or by secret spreading of poisonous propaganda by those who seek to destroy unity and promote discord in nations that are still at peace. During sixteen months this assault has blotted out the whole pattern of democratic life in an appalling number of independent nations, great and small. And the assailants are still on the march, threatening other nations, great and small. . . .

As men do not live by bread alone, they do not fight by armaments alone. Those who man our defenses and those behind them who build our defenses must have the stamina and the courage which come from an unshakable belief in the manner of life which they are defending. The mighty action that we are calling for cannot be based on a disregard of all the things worth fighting for. . . .

The basic things expected by our people of their political and economic systems are simple. They are: Equality of opportunity for youth and for others; jobs for those who can work; security for those who need it; the ending of special privilege for the few; the preservation of civil liberties for all; the enjoyment of the fruits of scientific progress in a wider and constantly rising standard of living. . . .

In the future days which we seek to make secure, we look forward to a world founded upon four essential human freedoms. The first is freedom of speech and expression—everywhere in the world. The second is freedom of every person to worship God in his own way—everywhere in the world. The third is freedom from want—which translated into world terms, means economic understandings which will secure to every nation a healthy peacetime life for its inhabitants—everywhere in the world. The fourth is freedom from fear, which translated into world terms, means a world-wide reduction of armaments to such a point and in such a thorough manner that no nation will be in a position to commit an act of physical aggression against any neighbor—anywhere in the world. . . .

This nation has placed its destiny in the hands, heads and hearts of its millions of free men and women, and its faith in freedom under the guidance of God. Freedom means the supremacy of human rights everywhere. Our support goes to those who struggle to gain those rights and keep them. Our strength is in our unity of purpose. To that high concept there can be no end save victory.

CHAPLINSKY V. NEW HAMPSHIRE, 315 U.S. 568 (1942)

This case involved the prosecution of a Jehovah's Witness for violating a New Hampshire law banning name-calling and derisive or offensive public speech. After attracting a hostile crowd and being told to move on by a city marshal, the Witness denounced the official as a "racketeer" and a "fascist." In upholding Walter Chaplinsky's conviction, the case launched the Supreme Court's two-tiered approach to free speech issues, which distinguishes high-value from low-value speech, and set out its "fighting words" doctrine.

Justice Frank Murphy, writing for the Court:

There are certain well-defined and narrowly limited classes of speech, the prevention and punishment of which have never been thought to raise any Constitutional problem. These include the lewd and obscene, the profane, the libelous, and the insulting or "fighting" words—those which by their very utterance inflict injury or tend to incite an immediate breach of the peace. It has been well observed that such utterances are no essential part of any exposition of ideas, and are of such slight social value as a step to truth that any benefit that may be derived from them is clearly outweighed by the social interest in order and morality. . . .

WEST VIRGINIA STATE BOARD OF EDUCATION V. BARNETTE, 319 U.S. 624 (1943)

Walter Barnette, a Jehovah's Witness, challenged the constitutionality of a West Virginia statute that required schoolchildren (including his own) to salute the flag. Saluting the flag, Barnette asserted, ran counter to his religion's prohibition on the worship of graven images. In a decision reversing the Court's much-criticized decision in a previous Witness flag salute case of just three years earlier (Minersville School District v. Gobitis, 310 U.S. 586 [1940]), the Court voided the West Virginia law.

Justice Robert Jackson, writing for the Court:

Here . . . we are dealing with a compulsion of students to declare a belief. . . . [T]he flag salute is a form of utterance. . . .To sustain the compulsory flag salute we are required to say that a Bill of Rights which guards the individual's right to speak his own mind, left it open to public authorities to compel him to utter what is not in his mind. Whether the First Amendment to the Constitution will permit officials to order observance of rituals of this nature does not depend upon whether as a voluntary exercise we would think it to be good, bad, or merely innocuous. . . .Nor does the issue as we see it turn on one's possession of particular religious views or the sincerity with which they are held. While religion supplies [the student's] motive for enduring the discomforts of making the issue in this case, many citizens who do not share these religious views hold such a compulsory rite to infringe constitutional liberty of the individual. . . .

The very purpose of a Bill of Rights was to withdraw certain subjects from the vicissitudes of political controversy, to place them beyond the reach of majorities and officials and to establish them as legal principles to be applied by the courts. . . .

If there is any fixed star in our constitutional constellation, it is that no official, high or petty, can prescribe what shall be orthodox in politics, nationalism, religion, or other matters of opinion or force citizens to confess by word or act their faith therein. . . . We think the action of the local authorities in compelling the flag salute and pledge transcends constitutional limitations on their power and invades the sphere of intellect and spirit which it is the purpose of the First Amendment to our Constitution to reserve from all official control. . . .

Justice Felix Frankfurter, dissenting:

One who belongs to the most vilified and persecuted minority in history is not likely to be insensible to the freedoms guaranteed by our Constitution. Were my purely personal attitude relevant I should wholeheartedly associate myself with the general libertarian views in the Court's opinion. . . . But as judges we are neither Jew nor Gentile, neither Catholic nor agnostic. We owe equal attachment to the Constitution. . . . "For the removal of unwise laws from the statute books appeal lies, not to the courts, but to the ballot and to the processes of democratic government." . . . [T]his Court's only and very narrow function is to determine whether within the broad grant of authority vested in legislatures they have exercised a judgment for which reasonable justification can be offered. . . . [I]t is not for this Court to make psychological judgments as to the effectiveness of a particular symbol in inculcating indispensable feelings, particularly if the state happens to see fit to utilize the symbol that represents our heritage and our hopes. . . .

We have not before us any attempt by the State to punish disobedient children or visit penal consequences on their parents. All that is in question is the right of the state to compel participation in this exercise by those who choose to attend public schools. . . . All channels of affirmative free expression are open to both children and parents. . . .

UNIVERSAL DECLARATION OF HUMAN RIGHTS
(DECEMBER 10, 1948)

Shortly after the United Nations was founded, its General Assembly adopted the Universal Declaration of Human Rights. The declaration had been drafted by a small international committee of scholars and diplomats chaired by Eleanor Roosevelt.

Article 18

Everyone has the right to freedom of thought, conscience and religion; this right includes freedom to change his religion or belief, and freedom, either alone or in community with others and in public or private, to manifest his religion or belief in teaching, practice, worship and observance.

Article 19

Everyone has the right to freedom of opinion and expression; this right includes freedom to hold opinions without interference and to seek, receive and impart information and ideas through any media regardless of frontiers.

KOVACS V. COOPER, 336 U.S. 77 (1949)

Responding to a challenge mounted by proselytizing Jehovah's Witnesses, the Court in Kovacs *declared unconstitutional a Trenton, New Jersey, ordinance barring from its streets sound systems producing "loud and raucous" noises. The case led to debate on the Court concerning the propriety of its emerging "preferred freedoms" doctrine.*

Justice Stanley Reed, joined by Chief Justice Fred Vinson and Justice Harold Burton, writing for the Court:

City streets are recognized as a normal place for the exchange of ideas by speech or paper. But this does not mean the freedom is beyond all control. We think it is a permissible exercise of legislative discretion to bar sound trucks with broadcasts of public interest, amplified to loud and raucous volume, from the public ways of municipalities. . . .

The right of free speech is guaranteed every citizen that he may reach the minds of willing listeners, and to do so there must be opportunity to win their attention. This is the phase of freedom of speech that is involved here. We do not think the Trenton ordinance abridges that freedom. . . . Surely such an ordinance does not violate our people's "concept of ordered liberty" so as to require federal intervention to protect a citizen from the action of his own local government. . . . Opportunity to gain the public's ears by objectionably amplified sound on the streets is not more assured by the right of free speech than is the unlimited opportunity to address gatherings on the streets. The preferred position of freedom of speech in a society that cherishes liberty for all does not require legislators to be insensible to claims by citizens to comfort and convenience. To enforce freedom of speech in disregard of the rights of others would be harsh and arbitrary in itself. . . .

Justice Felix Frankfurter, concurring:

My brother Reed speaks of "The preferred position of freedom of speech," though, to be sure, he finds that the Trenton ordinance does not disregard it. This is a phrase that has uncritically crept into some recent opinions of this Court. I deem it a mischievous phrase, if it carries the thought, which it may subtly imply, that any law touching communication is infected with presumptive invalidity. . . . So long as a legislature does not prescribe what ideas may be noisily expressed and what may not be, nor discriminate among those who would make inroads upon the public peace, it is not for us to supervise the limits the legislature may impose in safeguarding the steadily narrowing opportunities for serenity and reflection. Without such opportunities freedom of thought becomes a mocking phrase, and without freedom of thought there can be no free society. . . .

Justice Hugo Black, joined by Justices William O. Douglas and Wiley Rutledge, dissenting:

The basic premise of the First Amendment is that all present instruments of communication, as well as others that inventive genius may bring into being, shall be free from governmental censorship or prohibition. Laws which hamper the free use of some instruments of communication thereby favor competing channels. Thus unless constitutionally prohibited, laws like this Trenton ordinance can give an overpowering influence to views of owners of legally favored instruments of communication. This favoritism, it seems to me, is the inevitable result of today's decision. . . .

There are many people who have ideas that they wish to disseminate but who do not have enough money to own or control publishing plants, newspapers, radios, moving picture studios, or chains of show places. Yet everybody knows the vast reaches of these powerful channels of communication which from the very nature of our economic system must be under the control and guidance of comparatively few people. On the other hand, public speaking is done by many men of divergent minds with no centralized control over the ideas they entertain so as to limit the causes they espouse. . . . [I]t is an obvious fact that public speaking today without sound amplifiers is a wholly inadequate way to reach the people on a large scale. Consequently, to tip the scales against transmission of ideas through public speaking as the Court does today, is to deprive the people of a large part of the basic advantages of the receipt of ideas that the First Amendment was designed to protect. . . .

SPEECH BY SENATOR JOSEPH McCARTHY, WHEELING, WEST VIRGINIA (FEBRUARY 9, 1950)

Senator Joseph McCarthy's speech in Wheeling, West Virginia, alleging extensive Communist infiltration of the State Department, marked the beginning of what is known as "the McCarthy era" (1950–1954).

Six years ago, at the time of the first conference to map out the peace—Dumbarton Oaks—there was within the Soviet orbit 180,000,000 people. Lined up on the antitotalitarian side there were in the world at that time roughly 1,625,000,000 people. Today, only six years later, there are 800,000,000 people under the absolute domination of Soviet Russia—an increase of over 400 percent. On our side, the figure has shrunk to around 500,000,000. In other words, in less than six years the odds have changed from nine to one in our favor to eight to five against us. This indicates the swiftness of the tempo of Communist victories and American defeats in the cold war. As one of our outstanding historical figures once said, "When a great democracy is destroyed, it will not be because of enemies from without, but rather because of enemies from within." . . .

At war's end we were physically the strongest nation on earth and, at least potentially, the most powerful intellectually and morally. Ours could have been the honor of being a beacon in the desert of destruction, a shining living proof that civilization was not yet ready to destroy itself. Unfortunately, we have failed miserably and tragically to arise to the opportunity.

The reason why we find ourselves in a position of impotency is not because our only powerful potential enemy has sent men to invade our shores, but rather because of the traitorous actions of those who have been treated so well by this Nation. It has not been the less fortunate or members of minority groups who have been selling this Nation out, but rather those who have had all the benefits that the wealthiest nation on earth has had to offer—the finest homes, the finest college education, and the finest jobs in Government we can give. This is glaringly true in the State Department. There the bright young men who are born with silver spoons in their mouths are the ones who have been the worst. . . .

In my opinion the State Department, which is one of the most important government departments, is thoroughly infested with Communists. I have in my hand fifty-seven cases of individuals who would appear to be either card-carrying members or certainly loyal to the Communist Party, but who nevertheless are still helping to shape our foreign policy.

One thing to remember in discussing Communists in our Government is that we are not dealing with spies who get thirty pieces of silver to steal the blueprints of a new weapon. We are dealing with a far more sinister type of activity because it permits the enemy to guide and shape our policy. . . . This brings us down to the case of one Alger Hiss who is important not as an individual agent any more, but rather because he is so representative of a group in the State Department. . . .

[L]ate in 1948 . . . when the Un-American Activities Committee called Alger Hiss to give an accounting, President Truman at once issued a Presidential directive ordering all Government agencies to refuse to turn over any information whatsoever in regard to the Communist activities of any Government employees to a congressional committee. . . .

If time permitted, it might be well to go into detail about the fact that Hiss was Roosevelt's chief advisor at Yalta when Roosevelt was in admittedly ill health and tired physically and mentally . . . and when, according to the Secretary of State, Hiss and Grombyko drafted the report of the conference. As you hear this story of high treason, I know that you are saying to yourself, "Well, why doesn't Congress do something about it?" Actually, ladies and gentlemen, one of the most important reasons for the graft, the corruptions—one of the most important reasons why this continues is the lack of moral uprising on the part of 140,000,000 American people. . . .

[T]his pompous diplomat in striped pants, with a phony British accent . . . has lighted the spark which is resulting in a moral uprising and will end only when the whole sorry mess of twisted, warped thinkers are swept from the national scene so that we may have a new birth of national honesty and decency in Government.

DENNIS V. UNITED STATES,
341 U.S. 494 (1951)

The Dennis *decision, which conventional wisdom has long condemned as a classic example of McCarthyite hysteria, involved the Smith Act prosecution of Eugene Dennis and the other leaders of the American Communist Party for conspiring to teach and advocating the violent overthrow the U.S. government. The Court upheld the constitutionality of the convictions.*

Chief Justice Fred Vinson, with whom Justices Stanley Reed, Harold Burton, and Sherman Minton join, writing for the Court:

The obvious purpose of the statute is to protect existing Government, not from change by peaceable, lawful, and constitutional means, but from change by violence, revolution, and terrorism.... We reject any principle of governmental helplessness in the face of preparation for revolution.... The very language of the Smith Act ... is directed at advocacy, not discussion.... Congress did not intend to eradicate the discussion of political theories.... [T]he inflammable nature of world conditions, similar uprisings in other countries, and the touch-and-go nature of our relations with countries with whom petitioners were in the very least ideologically attuned, convince us that their convictions were justified on this score....

Justice Felix Frankfurter, concurring:

The soil in which the Bill of Rights grew was not a soil of arid pedantry. The historic antecedents of the First Amendment preclude the notion that its purpose was to give unqualified immunity to every expression that touched on matters within the range of political interests.... The demands of free speech in a democratic society as well as the interest in national security are better served by candid and informed weighing of the competing interests, within the confines of the judicial process, than by announcing dogmas too inflexible for the non-Euclidian problems to be solved.... [W]ho is to balance the relevant factors? ... Full responsibility for the choice cannot be given to the courts. Courts are not representative bodies. They are not designed to be a good reflex of a democratic society.... Primary responsibility for adjusting the interests which compete in the situation before us of necessity belongs to the Congress.... Free speech cases are not an exception to the principle that we are not legislators, that direct policy-making is not our province. How best to reconcile competing interests is the business of legislatures....

Justice Robert Jackson, concurring:

The "clear and present danger" test was an innovation by Justice Holmes in the *Schenck* case, reiterated and refined by him and Justice Brandeis in later cases, all arising before the era of World War II revealed the subtlety and efficacy of modernized revolutionary techniques used by totalitarian parties.... When the issue is criminality of a hot-headed speech on a street corner, or circulation of a few incendiary pamphlets, or parading by some zealots behind a red flag, or refusal of a handful of school children to salute our flag, it is not beyond the capacity of the judicial process to gather, comprehend, and weigh the necessary materials for decision whether it is a clear and present danger of substantive evil or a harmless letting off of steam.... [Now, however, we face] a well-organized, nation-wide conspiracy.... The authors of the clear and present danger test never applied it to a case like this, nor would I.... The Constitution does not make conspiracy a civil right....

Justice Hugo Black, dissenting:

These petitioners were not charged with an attempt to overthrow the Government. They were not charged with overt acts of any kind designed to overthrow the Government. They were not even charged with saying anything or writing anything designed to overthrow the Government. The charge was that they agreed to assemble and to talk and publish certain ideas at a later date: The indictment is that they conspired to organize the Communist Party and to use speech or newspaper and other publications in the future to teach and advocate the forcible overthrow of the Government.... [T]his is a virulent form of ... prior restraint.... [T]he First Amendment command[s] that "Congress shall make no law ... abridging the freedom of speech." ... I have always believed that the First Amendment is the keystone of our Government ... [and hope that] this or some later Court will restore the First Amendment liberties to the high preferred place where they belong in a free society.

BEAUHARNAIS V. ILLINOIS,
343 U.S. 250 (1952)

This case involved the prosecution of Joseph Beauharnais, president of the White Circle League of Chicago, under a group libel law forbidding defamation of a race or class of people. Beauharnais had publicly distributed leaflets calling attention to "the aggressions . . . rapes, robberies, knives, guns, and marijuana of the negro" and demanding that blacks be excluded from the city's white neighborhoods. The Supreme Court, in part citing its Chaplinsky *decision, narrowly upheld the constitutionality of the law.*

Justice Felix Frankfurter, writing for the Court:

No one will gainsay that it is libelous falsely to charge another with being a rapist, robber, carrier of knives and guns, and user of marijuana. The precise question before us, then, is whether the protection of "liberty" in the Due Process Clause of the Fourteenth Amendment prevents a State from punishing such libels—as criminal libel has been defined, limited, and constitutionally recognized time out of mind—directed at designated collectivities and flagrantly disseminated. . . . It is certainly clear that some American jurisdictions have sanctioned their punishment under ordinary criminal libel statutes. We cannot say, however, that the question is concluded by history and practice. But if an utterance directed at an individual may be the object of criminal sanctions, we cannot deny to a State power to punish the same utterance directed at a defined group, unless we can say that this is a willful and purposeless restriction unrelated to the peace and well-being of the State.

Illinois did not have to look beyond her own borders or await the tragic experience of the last three decades to conclude that willful purveyors of falsehood concerning racial and religious groups promote strife and tend powerfully to obstruct the manifold adjustments required for free, ordered life in a metropolitan, polyglot community. . . . In the face of this history and its frequent obligato of extreme racial and religious propaganda, we would deny experience to say that the Illinois legislature was without reason in seeking ways to curb false or malicious defamation of racial and religious groups, made in public places and by means calculated to have a powerful emotional impact on those to whom it was presented. . . .

It may be argued, and weightily, that this legislation will not help matters; that tension and on occasion violence between racial and religious groups must be traced to causes more deeply embedded in our society than the rantings of modern Know-Nothings. Only those lacking responsible humility will have a confident solution for problems as intractable as the frictions attributable to differences or race, color, or religion. This being so, it would be out of bounds for the judiciary to deny the legislature a choice of policy, provided it is not unrelated to the problem and not forbidden by some explicit limitation on the State's power. That the legislative remedy might not in practice mitigate the evil, or might itself raise new problems, would only manifest once more the paradox of reform. It is the price to be paid for the trial-and-error inherent in legislative efforts to deal with obstinate social issues. . . .

We are warned that the choice open to the Illinois legislature may be abused, that the law may be discriminatorily enforced; prohibiting libel of a creed or of a racial group, we are told, is but a step from prohibiting libel of a political party. Every power may be abused, but the possibility of abuse is a poor reason for denying Illinois the power to adopt measures against criminal libels sanctioned by centuries of Anglo-American law. . . . Libelous utterances not being within the area of constitutionally protected speech, it is unnecessary, either for us or for the State courts, to consider the issues behind the phrase "clear and present danger." Certainly no one would contend that obscene speech, for example, may be punished only upon a showing of such circumstances. Libel, as we have seen, is in the same class. We find no warrant in the Constitution for denying Illinois the power to pass the law here under attack. . . .

Justice Hugo Black, dissenting:

The Court's holding here and the constitutional doctrine behind it leave the rights of assembly, petition, speech, and press almost completely at the mercy of state legislative, executive, and judicial agencies. I say "almost" because state curtailment of these freedoms may still be invalidated if a majority of this Court conclude that a particular infringement is "without reason," or is a "willful and purposeless restriction un-related to the peace and well-being of the State." But lest this encouragement should give too much hope as to how and when this Court might protect these basic freedoms from state invasion, we are cautioned that state legislatures must be left free to "experiment" and to make "legislative" judgments. . . . Consolation can be sought and must be found in the philosophical reflection that state legislative error in stifling speech and press "is the price to be paid for the trial-and-error inherent in legislative efforts to deal with obstinate social issues." My own belief is that no legislature is charged with the duty or vested with the power to decide what public issues Americans can discuss. In a free country that is the individual's choice, not the state's. . . .

This Act sets up a system of state censorship which is at war with the kind of free government envisioned by those who forced adoption of our Bill of Rights. The motives behind the state law may have been to do good. But the same can be said about most laws making opinions punishable as crimes. History indicates that urges to do good have led to the burning of books and even to the burning of witches. . . . If there be minority groups who hail this holding as their victory, they might consider the possible relevancy of this ancient remark: "Another such victory and I am undone." . . .

Justice William O. Douglas, dissenting:

My view is that if in any case other public interests are to override the plain command of the First Amendment, the peril of speech must be clear and present, leaving no room for argument, raising no doubts as to the necessity of curbing speech in order to prevent disaster. The First Amendment is couched in absolute terms—freedom of speech shall not be abridged. Speech has therefore a preferred position as contrasted to some other civil rights. . . .

Today a white man stands convicted for protesting in unseemly language against our decisions invalidating restrictive covenants. Tomorrow a Negro will be haled before a court for denouncing lynch law in heated terms. Farm laborers in the West who compete with field hands drifting up from Mexico; whites who feel the pressure of orientals; a minority which finds employment going to members of the dominant religious group—all of these are caught in the mesh of today's decision. Debate and argument even in the courtroom are not always calm and dispassionate. Emotions sway speakers and audiences alike. Intemperate speech is a distinctive characteristic of man. Hotheads blow off and release destructive energy in the process. They shout and rave, exaggerating weaknesses, magnifying error, viewing with alarm. So it has been from the beginning; so it will be throughout time. . . .

Justice Robert Jackson, dissenting:

In this case, neither the court nor jury found or were required to find any injury to any person, or group, or to the public peace, nor to find any probability, let alone any clear and present danger, of injury to any of these. Even though no individuals were named or described as targets of this pamphlet, if it resulted in a riot or caused injury to any individual Negro, such as being refused living quarters in a particular section, house, or apartment, or being refused employment, certainly there would be no constitutional obstacle to imposing civil or criminal liability for actual results. But in this case no actual violence and no specific injury was charged or proved. . . .

Punishment of printed words, based on their tendency either to cause breach of the peace or injury to persons or groups, in my opinion, is justifiable only if the prosecution survives the "clear and present danger" test. It is the most just and workable standard yet evolved for determining criminality of words whose injurious or inciting tendencies are not demonstrated by the event but are ascribed to them on the basis of probabilities. . . .

No group interest in any particular prosecution should forget that the shoe may be on the other foot in some prosecution tomorrow. In these, as in other matters, our guiding spirit should be that each freedom is balanced with a responsibility, and every power of the State must be checked with safeguards. Such is the spirit of our American law of criminal libel, which concedes the power of the State, but only as a power restrained by recognition of individual rights. I cannot escape the conclusion that as the Act has been applied in this case it lost sight of the rights.

YATES V. UNITED STATES, 354 U.S. 298 (1957)

Like Dennis v. United States *(341 U.S. 494 [1951]),* Yates *involved the prosecution of leaders of the American Communist Party under the Smith Act. Here, in an altered political context, the Court reversed the convictions, although it did sanction retrials for the defendants on some of the charges.*

Justice John Marshall Harlan, writing for the Court:

We are thus faced with the question whether the Smith Act prohibits advocacy and teaching of forcible overthrow as an abstract principle, divorced from any effort to instigate action to that end, so long as such advocacy or teaching is engaged with evil intent. We hold that it does not. The distinction between advocacy of abstract doctrine and advocacy directed at promoting unlawful action is one that has been consistently recognized in the opinions of this Court. . . . The legislative history of the Smith Act and related bills shows beyond all question that Congress was aware of the distinction between the advocacy or teaching of abstract doctrine and the advocacy or teaching of action, and that it did not intend to disregard it. The statute was aimed at the advocacy and teaching of concrete action for the forcible overthrow of the Government, and not of principles divorced from action. . . .

Justices Hugo Black and William O. Douglas, concurring in part and dissenting in part:

In [our] judgment the statutory provisions on which these prosecutions are based abridge freedom of speech, press and assembly in violation of the First Amendment to the United States Constitution. . . .

ROTH V. UNITED STATES,
354 U.S. 476 (1957)

This case involved the prosecution of Samuel Roth, the publisher of American Aphrodite, a magazine of literary erotica and nude photographs, for violating a federal statute criminalizing sending "obscene, lewd, lascivious, or filthy" materials through the U.S. mails. The Court upheld Roth's conviction.

Justice William Brennan, writing for the Court:

All ideas having even the slightest redeeming social importance—unorthodox ideas, controversial ideas, even ideas hateful to the prevailing climate of opinion—have the full protection of the guaranties, unless excludable because they encroach upon the limited area of more important interests. But implicit in the history of the First Amendment is the rejection of obscenity as utterly without redeeming social importance.

NAACP v. ALABAMA, 357 U.S. 449 (1958)

As part of the intense battles between the State of Alabama and the civil rights movement, the state moved to halt the operations of the National Association for the Advancement of Colored People (NAACP) by forcing it to comply with a rule requiring out-of-state corporations doing business in Alabama to comply with state reporting requirements. These included a requirement that the state be provided with the names and addresses of all organization members living in the state (which would have been potentially life threatening, given the violent defense of segregation taking place at the time in the Deep South). The NAACP refused, citing its constitutional rights to free association. The Court sided unanimously with the group. Free association issues arose repeatedly in the context of Communist organizations, as well as with regard to the disclosure requirements of campaign finance laws.

Justice John Marshall Harlan, writing for the Court:

Effective advocacy of both public and private points of view, particularly controversial ones, is undeniably enhanced by group association, as this Court has more than once recognized by remarking upon the close nexus between the freedoms of speech and assembly. It is beyond debate that freedom to engage in association for the advancement of beliefs and ideas is an inseparable aspect of the "liberty" assured by the Due Process Clause of the Fourteenth Amendment.... Of course it is immaterial whether the beliefs sought to be advanced by association pertain to political, economic, religious or cultural matters, and state action which may have the effect of curtailing the freedom to associate is subject to the closest scrutiny....

Compelled disclosure of membership in an organization engaged in advocacy of particular beliefs is of the same order. Inviolability of privacy in group association may in many circumstances be indispensable to the preservation of freedom of association, particularly where a group espouses dissident beliefs....

NEW YORK TIMES V. SULLIVAN, 376 U.S. 254 (1964)

This landmark civil-rights-era free press case involved a libel action filed by L. B. Sullivan, a Montgomery, Alabama, city commissioner supervis-

ing the city's police force, against the New York Times, *which had run an ad containing false statements concerning civil rights demonstrations in that city. The* Times *defended itself by appealing to the First Amendment. The Supreme Court sided unanimously with the paper.*

Justice William J. Brennan, writing for the Court:

If neither factual error nor defamatory content suffices to remove the constitutional shield from criticism of official conduct, the combination of the two elements is no less inadequate. This is the lesson to be drawn from the great controversy over the Sedition Act of 1798 . . . which first crystallized a national awareness of the central meaning of the First Amendment. . . . [T]he restraint [that the Sedition Act] imposed upon criticism of government and public officials, was inconsistent with the First Amendment. . . .

[W]e consider this case against the backdrop of a profound national commitment to the principle that debate on public issues should be un-inhibited, robust, and wide-open, and that it may well include vehement, caustic, and sometimes unpleasantly sharp attacks on government and public officials. . . .

INTERNATIONAL COVENANT ON CIVIL AND POLITICAL RIGHTS (DECEMBER 16, 1966)

The International Covenant on Civil and Political Rights was adopted by the U.N. General Assembly in 1966.

Article 19

1. Everyone shall have the right to hold opinions without interference.

2. Everyone shall have the right to freedom of expression; this right shall include freedom to seek, receive and impart information and ideas of all kinds, regardless of frontiers, either orally, in writing or in print, in the form of art, or through any media of his choice.

3. The exercise of the rights provided for in paragraph 2 of this article carries with it special duties and responsibilities. It may therefore be subject to certain restrictions, but these shall only be such as are pro-

vided by law and are necessary: (a) For respect of the rights and reputations of others; (b) For the protection of national security or of public order . . . or of public health and morals.

Article 20

1. Any propaganda for war shall be prohibited by law.
2. Any advocacy of national, racial or religious hatred that constitutes incitement to discrimination, hostility, or violence shall be prohibited by law.

GINZBURG V. UNITED STATES, 383 U.S. 463 (1966)

Over the dissent of four justices, the Court in Ginzburg *upheld the conviction of the proprietors of an erotic magazine,* Eros, *for violating a federal statute forbidding the sending of obscene materials through the U.S. mails.*

Justice William O. Douglas, dissenting:

Some of the tracts for which these publishers go to prison concern normal sex, some homosexuality, some the masochistic yearning that is probably present in everyone and dominant in some. Masochism is a desire to be punished or subdued. In the broad frame of reference the desire may be expressed in the longing to be whipped and lashed, bound and gagged, and cruelly treated. Why is it unlawful to cater to the needs of this group? They are, to be sure, somewhat offbeat, nonconformist, and odd. But we are not in the realm of criminal conduct, only ideas and tastes. Some like Chopin, others like "rock and roll." Some are "normal," some are masochistic, some deviant in other respects, such as the homosexual. Another group also represented here translates mundane articles into sexual symbols. This group, like those embracing masochism, are anathema to the so-called stable majority. But why is freedom of the press and expression denied them? Are they to be barred from communicating in symbolisms important to them? When the Court today speaks of "social value," does it mean a "value" to the majority? Why is not a minority "value" cognizable? The masochistic group is one; the deviant group is another. Is it not important that members of those groups communicate with each other? Why is communication by the "written word" forbidden? If we were wise enough, we might know that communication may have greater therapeutical value than any sermon that those of the "normal" community can ever offer. But if the communication is of value to the masochistic community or to others of the deviant community, how can it be said to be "utterly without redeeming social importance"? "Redeeming" to whom? "Importance" to whom? . . .

[P]eople are mature enough to pick and chose, to recognize trash when they see it, to be attracted to the literature that satisfies their deepest need, and, hopefully to move from plateau to plateau and finally to reach the world of enduring ideas. . . .

HERBERT MARCUSE, "REPRESSIVE TOLERANCE" (AND POSTSCRIPT) (1969)

Marcuse, a Marxist émigré political philosopher who taught for many years at Brandeis University, was an intellectual hero of the New Left and of the student movement of the 1960s. In "Repressive Tolerance," he argues that free speech is a sham and that socially retrograde views should be suppressed. Marcuse's views had a profound influence on key strains of contemporary feminism, and they served as a major inspiration for the political correctness now common among university professors and administrators, transnational human rights activists, and the bureaucratic elites of the European Union and United Nations.

. . . Tolerance is extended to policies, conditions, and modes of behavior which should not be tolerated because they are impeding, if not destroying, the chances of creating an existence without fear and misery. . . . [T]he passive toleration of entrenched and established attitudes and ideas even if their damaging effect on man and nature is evident . . . protects the already established machinery of discrimination. . . .

Under the conditions prevailing in this country, tolerance does not, and cannot, fulfill the civilizing function attributed to it by the liberal protagonists of democracy, namely, protection of dissent. The progressive historical force of tolerance lies in its extension to those modes and forms of dissent which are not committed to the status quo of society, and not confined to the institutional framework of the established society. Consequently, the idea of tolerance implies the necessity, for the dissenting group or individuals, to become illegitimate if and when the established legitimacy prevents and counteracts the development of dissent. This would be the case not only in a totalitarian society, under a dictatorship, in one-party states, but also in a democracy (representative, parliamentary, or "direct") where the majority does not result from the development of independent thought and opinion but rather from the monopolistic or oligopolistic administration of public opinion, without terror and (normally) without censorship. In such cases, the majority is self-perpetuating while perpetuating the vested interests which *made* it a majority. In its very structure this majority is "closed," petrified; it repels "a priori" any change other than changes within the system. But this means that the majority is no longer justified in claiming the democratic title of the best guardian of the common interest. And such a majority is all but the opposite of Rousseau's "general will": it is composed, not of individuals who, in their political function, have made effective "abstraction" from their private interests, but, on the contrary, of individuals who have effectively identified their private interests with their political functions. And the representatives of this majority, in ascertaining and executing its will, ascertain and execute the will of the vested interests which have formed the majority. The ideology of democracy hides its lack of substance.

In the United States, this tendency goes hand in hand with the monopolistic or oligopolistic concentration of capital in the formation of public opinion, i.e., of the majority. The chance of influencing, in any effective way, this majority is at a price, in dollars, totally out of reach of the radical opposition. Here too, free competition and exchange of ideas have become a farce. The Left has no equal voice, no equal access to the mass media and their public facilities—not because a conspiracy excludes it, but because, in good old capitalist fashion, it does not have the required purchasing power. And the Left does not have the purchasing power because it is the Left. These conditions impose upon the radical minorities a strategy which is in essence a refusal to allow the continuous functioning of allegedly indiscriminate but in fact discriminate tolerance, for example, a strategy of protesting against the alternate matching of a spokesman for the Right (or Center) with one for the Left. Not "equal" but *more* representation of the Left would be equalization of the prevailing inequality.

Within the solid framework of preestablished inequality and power, tolerance is practiced indeed. Even outrageous opinions are expressed, outrageous incidents are televised; and the critics of established politics are interrupted by the same number of commercials as the conservative advocates. Are these interludes supposed to counteract the sheer weight, magnitude, and continuity of system-publicity, indoctrination which operates playfully through the endless commercials as well as through the entertainment?

Given this situation, I suggested . . . the practice of discriminating tolerance in an inverse direction, as a means of shifting the balance between Right and Left, by restraining the liberty of the Right, thus counteracting the pervasive inequality of freedom (unequal opportunity of access to the means of democratic persuasion) and strengthening the oppressed against the oppressors. Tolerance would be restricted with respect to movements of a demonstrably aggressive or destructive character (destructive of the prospects for peace, justice, and freedom for all). Such discrimination would also be applied to movements opposing the extension of social legislation to the poor, weak, disabled. As against the virulent denunciations that such a policy would do away with the sacred liberalistic principle of equality for "the other side," I maintain that there are issues where either there is no "other side" in any more than a formalistic sense, or where "the other side" is demonstrably "regressive" and impedes possible improvement of the human condition. To tolerate propaganda for inhumanity vitiates the goals not only of liberalism but of every progressive political philosophy. . . .

Part of this struggle is the fight against an ideology of tolerance which, in reality, favors and fortifies the conservation of the status quo of inequality and discrimination. For this struggle, I [propose] the practice of discriminating tolerance. To be sure, this practice already presupposes the radical goal which it seeks to achieve. I committed this *petitio principii* in order to combat the pernicious ideology that tolerance is already institutionalized in society. The tolerance which is the life element, the token of a free society, will never be the gift of the powers that be; it can, under the prevailing conditions of tyranny by the majority, only be won in the sustained effort of radical minorities, willing to break this tyranny and to work for the emergence of a free and sovereign majority—minorities intolerant, militantly intolerant and disobedient to the rules of behavior which tolerate destruction and suppression.

TINKER V. DES MOINES, 393 U.S. 503 (1969)

After hearing about the plans of a group of students and adults in Des Moines, Iowa, to publicly demonstrate their opposition to the Vietnam War by wearing black armbands, the principals of the city's schools instituted a ban on such armbands in the public schools. Shortly thereafter, two students, John and Mary Beth Tinker, were suspended for defying the ban. They sued, alleging a violation of their First Amendment rights. The Supreme Court declared the ban unconstitutional.

Justice Abe Fortas, writing for the Court:

[T]he wearing of an armband for the purpose of expressing certain views is the type of symbolic act that is within the Free Speech Clause of the First Amendment. . . . It [is] closely akin to "pure speech" which, we have repeatedly held, is entitled to comprehensive protection under the First Amendment.

First Amendment rights, applied in light of the special characteristics of the school environment, are available to teachers and students. It can hardly be argued that either students or teachers shed their constitutional rights to freedom of speech or expression at the schoolhouse gate. . . .

The school officials banned and sought to punish petitioners for a silent, passive expression of opinion, unaccompanied by any disorder or disturbance on the part of petitioners. There is here no evidence whatever of petitioners' interference, actual or nascent, with the school's work or of collision with the rights of other students to be secure and to be let alone. Accordingly, this case does not concern speech or action that intrudes upon the work of the schools or the rights of other students. . . .

[T]he school authorities did not purport to prohibit the wearing of all symbols of political or controversial significance. . . . Instead, a particular symbol—black armbands worn to exhibit opposition to this Nation's involvement in Vietnam—was singled out for prohibition. Clearly, the prohibition of expression of one particular opinion, at least without evidence that it is necessary to avoid material and substantial interference with schoolwork or discipline, is not constitutionally permissible. . . .

Justice Hugo Black, dissenting:

Even a casual reading of the record shows that this armband did divert students' minds from the regular lessons. . . . I think the record overwhelmingly shows that the armbands did exactly what the elected school officials and principals foresaw they would, that is, took the students' minds off their classwork and diverted them to thoughts about the highly emotional subject of the Vietnam war. . . .

The schools of this Nation have undoubtedly contributed to giving us tranquillity and to making us more law-abiding people. Uncontrolled and uncontrollable liberty is an enemy to domestic peace. We cannot close our eyes to the fact that some of the country's greatest problems are crimes committed by the youth, too many of school age. School discipline, like parental discipline, is an integral and important part of training our children to be good citizens—to be better citizens. Here a very small number of students have crisply and summarily refused to obey a school order designed to give pupils who want to learn the opportunity to do so. One does not need to be a prophet or the son of a prophet to know that after the Court's holding today some students in Iowa schools and indeed in all schools will be ready, able, and willing to defy their teachers on practically all orders. This is the more unfortunate for the schools since groups of students all over the land are already running loose, conducting break-ins, sit-ins, lie-ins, and smash-ins. Many of these student groups, as is all too familiar to all who read the newspapers and watch the television news programs, have already engaged in rioting, property seizures, and destruction. . . . Students engaged in such activities are apparently confident that they know far more about how to operate public school systems than do their parents, teachers, and elected school officials. . . . Turned loose with lawsuits for damages and injunctions against their teachers as they are here, it is nothing but wishful thinking to imagine that young, immature students will not soon believe it is their right to control the schools rather than the right of the States that collect the taxes to hire the teachers for the benefit of the pupils. . . .

I wish, therefore, wholly to disclaim any purpose on my part to hold that the Federal Constitution compels the teachers, parents, and elected school officials to surrender control of the American public school system to public school students.

BRANDENBURG V. OHIO,
395 U.S. 444 (1969)

This case involved the prosecution of Charles Brandenburg, a Ku Klux Klan leader, under an Ohio criminal syndicalism statute for a speech he made to armed Klansman at a cross-burning on private property in rural Ohio. The speech was later broadcast on local and national television. The Court held the Ohio statute unconstitutional and reversed Brandenburg's conviction.

Per Curium:

[This Court's] decisions have fashioned the principle that the constitutional guarantees of free speech and free press do not permit a State to forbid or proscribe advocacy of the use of force or of law violation except where such advocacy is directed to inciting or producing imminent lawless action and is likely to incite or produce such action. As we said [in a previous decision], "the mere abstract teaching ... of the moral propriety or even moral necessity for a resort to force and violence, is not the same as preparing a group for violent action and steeling it to such action." A statute which fails to draw this distinction impermissibly intrudes upon the freedoms guaranteed by the First and Fourteenth Amendments. It sweeps within its condemnation speech which our Constitution has immunized from government control.

Measured by this test, Ohio's Criminal Syndicalism Act cannot be sustained. The Act punishes persons who "advocate or teach the duty, necessity, or propriety" of violence "as a means of accomplishing industrial or political reform"; or who publish or circulate or display any book or paper containing such advocacy; or who "justify" the commission of violent acts "with intent to exemplify, spread or advocate the propriety of the doctrines of criminal syndicalism"; or who "voluntarily assemble" with a group formed "to teach or advocate the doctrines of criminal syndicalism." Neither the indictment nor the trial judge's instructions to the jury in any way refined the statute's bald definition of the crime in terms of mere advocacy not distinguished from incitement to imminent lawless action.

Accordingly, we are here confronted with a statute which, by its own words and as applied, purports to punish mere advocacy and to forbid, on pain of criminal punishment, assembly with others merely to advocate the described type of action. Such a statute falls within the condemnation of the First and Fourteenth Amendments. The contrary teaching of *Whitney v. California,* cannot be supported, and that decision is therefore overruled.

Justice Hugo Black, concurring:

I agree with the views expressed by Mr. Justice Douglas in his concurring opinion in this case that the "clear and present danger" doctrine should have no place in the interpretation of the First Amendment. I join the Court's opinion, which, as I understand it, simply cites *Dennis v. United States* (1951), but does not indicate any agreement on the Court's part with the "clear and present danger" doctrine on which *Dennis* purported to rely.

Justice William O. Douglas, concurring:

While I join the opinion of the Court, I desire to enter a caveat. . . .

The "clear and present danger" test was adumbrated by Mr. Justice Holmes in a case arising during World War I—a war "declared" by the Congress, not by the Chief Executive. The case was *Schenck v. United States,* where the defendant was charged with attempts to cause insubordination in the military and obstruction of enlistment. The pamphlets that were distributed urged resistance to the draft, denounced conscription, and impugned the motives of those backing the war effort. The First Amendment was tendered as a defense. Mr. Justice Holmes in rejecting that defense said: "The question in every case is whether the words used are used in such circumstances and are of such a nature as to create a clear and present danger that they will bring about the substantive evils that Congress has a right to prevent. It is a question of proximity and degree."

In the 1919 Term, the Court applied the *Schenck* doctrine to affirm the convictions of other dissidents in World War I. The dissents in [the World War I decisions] show how easily "clear and present danger" is manipulated to crush what Brandeis called "the fundamental right of free men to strive for better conditions through new legislation and new institutions" by arguments and discourse even in time of war. Though I doubt if the "clear and present danger" test is congenial to the First

Amendment in time of a declared war, I am certain it is not reconcilable with the First Amendment in days of peace.

The Court quite properly overrules *Whitney v. California* (1927) which involved advocacy of ideas which the majority of the Court deemed unsound and dangerous. . . .

Out of the "clear and present danger" test came other offspring. Advocacy and teaching of forcible overthrow of government as an abstract principle is immune from prosecution. But an "active" member, who has a guilty knowledge and intent of the aim to overthrow the Government by violence, may be prosecuted. And the power to investigate, backed by the powerful sanction of contempt, includes the power to determine which of the two categories fits the particular witness. And so the investigator roams at will through all of the beliefs of the witness, ransacking his conscience and his innermost thoughts.

When one reads the opinions closely and sees when and how the "clear and present danger" test has been applied, great misgivings are aroused. First, the threats were often loud but always puny and made serious only by judges so wedded to the status quo that critical analysis made them nervous. Second, the test was so twisted and perverted in *Dennis* as to make the trial of those teachers of Marxism an all-out political trial which was part and parcel of the cold war that has eroded substantial parts of the First Amendment. . . .

Action is often a method of expression and within the protection of the First Amendment. Suppose one tears up his own copy of the Constitution in eloquent protest to a decision of this Court. May he be indicted? Suppose one rips his own Bible to shreds to celebrate his departure from one "faith" and his embrace of atheism. May he be indicted?

The line between what is permissible and not subject to control and what may be made impermissible and subject to regulation is the line between ideas and overt acts. The example usually given by those who would punish speech is the case of one who falsely shouts fire in a crowded theatre.

This is, however, a classic case where speech is brigaded with action. They are indeed inseparable and a prosecution can be launched for the overt acts actually caused. Apart from rare instances of that kind, speech is, I think, immune from prosecution. . . .

COHEN V. CALIFORNIA, 403 U.S. 15 (1971)

Paul Robert Cohen was prosecuted for walking through the halls of the Los Angeles County Courthouse wearing a jacket emblazoned with the words "Fuck the Draft" under a state law prohibiting "maliciously and willfully disturb[ing] the peace or quiet of any neighborhood or person ... by ... offensive conduct." Citing First Amendment protections, the Supreme Court reversed his conviction.

Justice John Marshall Harlan, writing for the Court:

The constitutional right of free expression is powerful medicine in a society as diverse and populous as ours. It is designed and intended to remove governmental restraints from the arena of public discussion, putting the decision as to what views shall be voiced largely into the hands of each of us, in the hope that use of such freedom will ultimately produce a more capable citizenry and more perfect polity and in the belief that no other approach would comport with the premise of individual dignity and choice upon which our political system rests. . . .

To many, the immediate consequence of this freedom may often appear to be verbal tumult, discord, and even offensive utterance. These are, however, within established limits, in truth necessary side effects of the broader enduring values which the process of open debate permits us to achieve. That the air may at times seem filled with verbal cacophony is, in this sense, not a sign of weakness but of strength. We cannot lose sight of the fact that, in what otherwise might seem a trifling and annoying instance of individual distasteful abuse of a privilege, these fundamental societal values are truly implicated. . . .

Against this perception of the constitutional policies involved, we discern certain more particularized considerations that peculiarly call for reversal of this conviction. First, the principle contended for by the State seems inherently boundless. How is one to distinguish this from any other offensive word? Surely the State has no right to cleanse the public debate to the point where it is grammatically palatable to the most squeamish among us. Yet no readily ascertainable general principle exists for stopping short of that result were we to affirm the judgment below. For, while the particular four-letter word being litigated here is perhaps more distasteful than most others of its genre, it is nevertheless often true that one man's vulgarity is another's lyric. Indeed, we think it is largely because governmental officials cannot make principled distinctions in this area that the Constitution leaves matters of taste and style so largely to the individual.

Justices Harry Blackmun, Chief Justic Warren Burger, Justice Hugo Black, and Justice Byron White (in part), dissented.

MILLER V. CALIFORNIA, 413 U.S. 15 (1973)

This case involved the prosecution under state obscenity laws of Marvin Miller for sending unsolicited advertising for adult books and movies through the mails. In Miller, *the Court attempts to promulgate clear standards concerning the power of government to regulate obscenity.*

Chief Justice Warren Burger, writing for the Court:

This case involves the application of a State's criminal obscenity statute to a situation in which sexually explicit materials have been thrust by aggressive sales action upon unwilling recipients who had in no way indicated any desire to receive such materials. . . . Obscene material is unprotected by the First Amendment. . . . We acknowledge, however, the inherent dangers of undertaking to regulate any form of expression. State statutes designed to regulate obscene materials must be carefully limited. As a result, we now confine the permissible scope of such regulation to works which depict or describe sexual conduct. That conduct must be specifically defined by the applicable state law, as written or authoritatively construed. A state offense must also be limited to works which, taken as whole, appeal to the prurient interest in sex, which portray sexual conduct in a patently offensive way, and which, taken as a whole, do not have serious literary, artistic, political, or scientific value.

The basic guidelines for the trier of fact must be: (a) whether "the average person, applying contemporary community standards" would find that the work, taken as a whole, appeals to the prurient interest; (b) whether the work depicts or describes, in a patently offensive way, sexual conduct specifically defined by the applicable state law; and (c) whether the work, taken as a whole, lacks serious literary, artistic, political, or scientific value.

Justice William O. Douglas, dissenting:

[T]here was no recognized exception to the free press at the time the Bill of Rights was adopted which treated "obscene" publications differently from other types of papers, magazines, and books. So there are no constitutional guidelines for deciding what is and what is not "obscene." The Court is at large because we deal with tastes and standards of literature. What shocks me may be sustenance for my neighbor. What causes one person to boil up in rage over one pamphlet or movie may reflect only his neurosis, not shared by others. We deal here with a regime of censorship which, if adopted, should be done by constitutional amendment after full debate by the people. . . .

BUCKLEY V. VALEO, 424 U.S. 1 (1976)

In this complicated decision, the Supreme Court ruled on the constitutionality of various provisions of the Federal Election and Campaign Finance Act, a statute that had been recently overhauled in the wake of the Watergate scandal (1974). The Court struck down a number of the law's expenditure limits on First Amendment grounds, but it upheld the law's contribution limits as reasonable regulations aimed at the legitimate goal of preventing corruption and the appearance of corruption in federal elections.

Per Curium:

The Act's contribution and expenditure limitations operate in an area of the most fundamental First Amendment activities. Discussion of public issues and debate on the qualifications of candidates are integral to the operation of the system of government established by our Constitution. The First Amendment affords the broadest protection to such political expression in order "to assure [the] unfettered interchange of ideas for the bringing about of political and social changes desired by the people. . . ."

Appellees contend that what the Act regulates is conduct, and that its effect on speech and association is incidental at most. Appellants respond that contributions and expenditures are at the very core of political speech, and that the Act's limitations thus constitute restraints on First Amendment liberty that are both gross and direct.

A restriction on the amount of money a person or group can spend on political communication during a campaign necessarily reduces the quantity of expression by restricting the number of issues discussed, the depth of their exploration, and the size of the audience reached. This is because virtually every means of communicating ideas in today's mass society requires the expenditure of money.... The expenditure limitations contained in the Act represent substantial rather than merely theoretical restraints on the quantity and diversity of political speech.... By contrast with a limitation upon expenditures for political expression, a limitation upon the amount that any one person or group may contribute to a candidate or political committee entails only a marginal restriction upon the contributor's ability to engage in free communication. A contribution serves as a general expression of support for the candidate and his views, but does not communicate the underlying basis for the support. The quantity of communication by the contributor does not increase perceptibly with the size of his contribution, since the expression rests solely on the undifferentiated, symbolic act of contributing. At most, the size of the contribution provides a very rough index of the intensity of the contributor's support for the candidate. A limitation on the amount of money a person may give to candidate or campaign organization thus involves little direct restraint on his political communication, for it permits the symbolic expression of support evidenced by a contribution but does not in any way infringe the contributor's freedom to discuss candidates and issues. While contributions may result in political expression if spent by a candidate or an association to present views to the voters, the transformation of contributions into political debate involves speech by someone other than the contributor.... The overall effect of the Act's contribution ceilings is merely to require candidates and political committees to raise funds from a greater number of persons and to compel people who would otherwise contribute amounts greater than the statutory limits to expend such funds on direct political expression, rather than to reduce the total amount of money potentially available to promote political expression....

Chief Justice Warren Burger, concurring in part, and dissenting in part:

I agree fully with that part of the Court's opinion that holds unconstitutional the limitations the Act puts on campaign expenditures which "place substantial and direct restrictions on the ability of candidates, citizens, and associations to engage in protected political expression, restrictions that the First Amendment cannot tolerate." Yet when it approves similarly stringent limitations on contributions, the Court ignores the reasons it finds so persuasive in the context of expenditures. For me contributions and expenditures are two sides of the same First Amendment coin. By limiting campaign contributions, the Act restricts the amount of money that will be spent on political activity—and does so directly. . . .

The Court's attempt to distinguish the communication inherent in political contributions from the speech aspects of political expenditures simply "will not wash." We do little but engage in word games unless we recognize that people—candidates and contributors—spend money on political activity because they wish to communicate ideas, and their constitutional interest in doing so is precisely the same whether they or someone else utters the words. . . . At any rate, the contribution limits are a far more severe restriction on First Amendment activity than the sort of "chilling" legislation for which the Court has shown such extraordinary concern in the past. See, e.g., *Cohen v. California* (1971). . . .

Justice Byron White, concurring in part, dissenting in part:

I dissent . . . from the Court's view that the expenditure limitations . . . violate the First Amendment. . . . Congress was plainly of the view that these expenditures . . . have corruptive potential; but the Court strikes down the provision, strangely enough claiming more insight as to what may improperly influence candidates than is possessed by the majority of Congress that passed this bill and the President who signed it. Those supporting the bill undeniably included many seasoned professionals who have been deeply involved in elective processes and who have viewed them at close range for many years. . . . It would make little sense to me, and apparently made none to Congress, to limit the amounts an individual may give to a candidate or spend with his approval but fail to limit the amounts that could be spent on his behalf. Yet the Court permits the former while striking down the latter limitation. . . .

FCC v. PACIFICA FOUNDATION, 438 U.S. 726 (1978)

This case arose when a father who was listening to the radio while driving with his young son complained to the Federal Communications Com-

mission (FCC) after happening upon Pacifica Radio's afternoon broadcast of George Carlin's comic monologue entitled "Filthy Words." The FCC had chastised the station for the inappropriateness of the broadcast, placed a letter concerning the broadcast in its file, and warned it that sanctions (potentially including the revocation of its license) would be imposed if a similar program was broadcast in the future. In the process, the FCC claimed full authority to regulate indecent programming on the public airwaves. The Court upheld the authority of the FCC to place limits on (but not to ban) indecent broadcasts.

Justice John Paul Stevens, with whom Chief Justice Warren Burger and Justice William Rehnquist join in part, writing for the Court:

This case requires that we decide whether the Federal Communications Commission has any power to regulate a radio broadcast that is indecent but not obscene. . . .

The question in this case is whether a broadcast of patently offensive words dealing with sex and excretion may be regulated because of its content. Obscene materials have been denied the protection of the First Amendment because their content is so offensive to contemporary moral standards. . . . But the fact that society may find speech offensive is not a sufficient reason for suppressing it. Indeed, if it is the speaker's opinion that gives offense, that consequence is a reason for according it constitutional protection. For it is a central tenet of the First Amendment that the government must remain neutral in the marketplace of ideas. If there were any reason to believe that the Commission's characterization of the Carlin monologue as offensive could be traced to its political content—or even to the fact that it satirized contemporary attitudes about four letter words—First Amendment protection might be required. But that is simply not the case. These words offend for the same reason that obscenity offends. . . . "Such utterances are no essential part of any exposition of ideas, and are of such slight social value as a step to truth that any benefit that may be derived from them is clearly outweighed by the social interest in order and morality. . . ."

Although these words ordinarily lack literary, political, or scientific value, they are not entirely outside the protection of the First Amendment. . . . In this case it is undisputed that the content of Pacifica's broadcast was "vulgar," "offensive," and "shocking." Because content of that character is not entitled to absolute constitutional protection under all circumstances, we must consider its context in order to determine whether the Commission's action was constitutionally permissible. . . .

We have long recognized that each medium of expression presents special First Amendment problems. And of all forms of communication, it is broadcasting that has received the most limited First Amendment protection. . . . The reasons for these distinctions are complex, but two have relevance to the present case. First, the broadcast media have established a uniquely pervasive presence in the lives of all Americans. . . . Second, broadcasting is uniquely accessible to children, even those too young to read. . . .

It is appropriate, in conclusion, to emphasize the narrowness of our holding. . . . The Commission's decision rested entirely on a nuisance rationale under which context is all-important. The concept requires consideration of a host of variables. The time of day was emphasized by the Commission. The content of the program in which the language is used will also affect the composition of the audience, and differences between radio, television, and perhaps closed-circuit transmissions, may also be relevant. . . . We simply hold that when the Commission finds that a pig has entered the parlor, the exercise of its regulatory power does not depend on proof that the pig is obscene. . . .

Justice William Brennan, with whom Justice Thurgood Marshall joins, dissenting:

Without question, the privacy interests of an individual in his home are substantial and deserving of significant protection. In finding these interests sufficient to justify the content regulation of protected speech, however, the Court commits two errors. First, it misconceives the nature of the privacy interests involved where an individual voluntarily chooses to admit radio communications into his home. Second, it ignores the constitutionally protected interests of both those who wish to transmit and those who desire to receive broadcasts that many—including the FCC and this Court—might find offensive. . . .

The Court's balance . . . fails to accord proper weight to the interests of listeners who wish to hear broadcasts the FCC deems offensive. It permits majoritarian tastes completely to preclude a protected message from entering the homes of a receptive, unoffended minority. . . .

Because the Carlin monologue is obviously not an erotic appeal to the prurient interests of children, the Court, for the first time, allows the government to prevent minors from gaining access to materials that are not obscene, and are therefore protected, as to them. . . . Taken to their logical extreme [the Court's] rationales would support the cleansing of public radio of any "four letter words" whatsoever, regardless of their context. The rationales could justify the banning from radio of a myriad of literary works, novels, poems, and plays by the likes of Shakespeare, Joyce, Hemingway, Ben Jonson, Henry Fielding, Robert Burns, and Chaucer; they could support the suppression of a good deal of political speech, such as the Nixon tapes; and they could even provide the basis for imposing sanctions for the broadcast of certain portions of the Bible. . . .

CONVENTION ON THE ELIMINATION OF ALL FORMS OF DISCRIMINATION AGAINST WOMEN (DECEMBER 18, 1979)

The Convention on the Elimination of All Forms of Discrimination against Women was approved by the U.N. General Assembly in 1979.

Article 5

States Parties shall take all appropriate measures: (a) to modify the social and cultural patterns of men and women, with a view to achieving the elimination of prejudices and customary and all other practices which are based on the idea of the inferiority or the superiority of either of the sexes or on stereotyped roles for men and women. . . .

Article 10

States Parties shall take all appropriate measures to eliminate discrimination against women in order to ensure to them equal rights with men in the field of education . . . [including] [t]he elimination of any stereotyped concept of the roles of men and women at all levels and in all forms of education by . . . the revision of textbooks and the adaptation of teaching methods. . . .

TEXAS V. JOHNSON, 491 U.S. 397 (1989)

Gregory Lee Johnson was convicted under a Texas flag-desecration law when he publicly burned a flag at the 1984 Republican National Convention in Dallas while protesting the policies of U.S. corporations and the Reagan administration. The Supreme Court declared his conviction unconstitutional.

Justice William J. Brennan, writing for the Court:

We must first determine whether Johnson's burning of the flag constituted expressive conduct permitting him to invoke the First Amendment in challenging his conviction. If his conduct was expressive, we next decide whether the State's regulation is related to the suppression of free expression. . . . That we have had little difficulty identifying an expressive element in conduct relating to flags should not be surprising. . . . Johnson burned an American flag as part—indeed, as the culmination—of a political demonstration that coincided with the convening of the Republican Party and its renomination of Ronald Reagan for President. The expressive, overtly political nature of this conduct was both intentional and overwhelmingly apparent. . . .

The State offers two separate interests to justify [its conviction of Johnson]: preventing breaches of the peace, and preserving the flag as a symbol of nationhood and national unity. We hold that the first interest is not implicated on this record and that the second is related to the suppression of expression. . . . [T]his restriction on Johnson's expression is content-based. . . .

If there is a bedrock principle underlying the First Amendment, it is that the Government may not prohibit the expression of an idea simply because society finds the idea itself offensive or disagreeable. . . . The First Amendment does not guarantee that . . . concepts virtually sacred to our Nation as a whole—such as the principle that discrimination on the basis of race is odious and destructive—will go unquestioned in the marketplace of ideas. . . . We decline, therefore, to create for the flag an exception to the joust of principles protected by the First Amendment.

Chief Justice William Rehnquist, with whom Justices Byron White and Sandra Day O'Connor join, dissenting:

The American flag . . . throughout more than 200 years of our history, has come to be the visible symbol embodying our Nation. It does not represent the views of any particular political party, and it does not represent any particular political philosophy. The flag is not simply another "idea" or "point of view" competing for recognition in the marketplace of ideas. Millions of Americans regard it with an almost mystical reverence regardless of what sort of social, political, or philosophical beliefs they may have. . . .

[T]he public burning of the American flag by Johnson was no essential part of any exposition of ideas, and at the same time it had a tendency to incite a breach of the peace. Johnson was free to make any verbal denunciation of the flag he wished; indeed, he was free to burn the flag in private. . . . He did lead a march through the streets of Dallas, and conducted a rally in front of the Dallas City Hall. He engaged in a "die-in" to protest nuclear weapons. He shouted out various slogans during the march, including: "Reagan, Mondale which will it be? Either one means World War III"; "Ronald Reagan, killer of the hour, Perfect example of U.S. power"; and "red, white and blue, we spit on you, you stand for plunder, you will go under." For none of these acts was he arrested or prosecuted; it was only when he proceeded to burn publicly an American flag stolen from its rightful owner that he violated the Texas statute. . . . Far from being a case of "one picture being worth a thousand words," flag burning is the equivalent of an inarticulate grunt or roar that, it seems fair to say, is most likely to be indulged in not to express any particular idea, but to antagonize others. . . .

Justice John Paul Stevens, dissenting:

The Court is . . . quite wrong in blandly asserting that respondent "was prosecuted for his expression of dissatisfaction with the policies of this country, expression situated at the core of our First Amendment values." Respondent was prosecuted because of the method he chose to express his dissatisfaction with those policies. . . .

RUST V. SULLIVAN, 500 U.S. 173 (1991)

In Rust, *the Supreme Court narrowly upheld the constitutionality of regulations imposed by the Reagan administration conditioning federal grants to family planning clinics on the willingness of those clinics to follow strict rules concerning abortion-related speech.*

Chief Justice William Rehnquist, writing for the Court:

The broad language of Title X plainly allows the Secretary's construction of the statute. . . . Based on the broad directives provided by Congress in Title X in general and Section 1008 in particular, we are unable to say that the Secretary's construction of the prohibition in Section 1008 to require a ban on counseling, referral, and advocacy within the Title X project, is impermissible. . . .

To hold that the Government unconstitutionally discriminates on the basis of viewpoint when it chooses to fund a program dedicated to advance certain permissible goals, because the program in advancing those goals necessarily discourages alternate goals, would render numerous government programs constitutionally suspect. When Congress established a National Endowment for Democracy to encourage other countries to adopt democratic principles, it was not constitutionally required to fund such a program to encourage competing lines of political philosophy such as Communism and Fascism. . . . By requiring that the Title X grantee engage in abortion-related activity separately from activity receiving federal funding, Congress has . . . not denied it the right to engage in abortion-related activities. Congress has merely refused to fund such activities out of the public fisc. . . . The same principles apply to [the] claim that the regulations abridge the free speech rights of the grantee's staff. Individuals who are voluntarily employed for a Title X project must perform their duties in accordance with the regulation's restrictions on abortion counseling and referral. . . .

Justice Harry Blackmun, dissenting:

Until today, the Court has never upheld viewpoint-based suppression of speech simply because that suppression was a condition upon the acceptance of public funds. Whatever may be the Government's power to condition the receipt of its largess upon the relinquishment of constitutional rights, it surely does not extend to a condition that suppresses the recipient's cherished freedom of speech based solely upon the content or viewpoint of that speech. . . . The regulations are . . . clearly viewpoint-based. While suppressing speech favorable to abortion with one hand, the Secretary compels antiabortion speech with the other. . . . One can imagine no legitimate governmental interest that might be served by suppressing such information. . . .

Roe v. Wade [confers upon a woman] a fundamental right to self-determination. . . . ."[L]iberty," if it means anything, must entail freedom from governmental domination in making the most intimate and personal of decisions. By suppressing medically pertinent information and injecting a restrictive ideological message unrelated to considerations of maternal health, the government places formidable obstacles in the path of Title X clients' freedom of choice and thereby violates their Fifth Amendment rights [to reproductive freedom]. . . .

R.A.V. v. St. Paul, 505 U.S. 377 (1992)

A teenager who burned a cross on a black family's lawn was charged under a St. Paul, Minnesota, Bias-Motivated Crime Ordinance, which banned the display of symbols one knows or has reason to know "arouses anger, alarm or resentment in others" on the basis of race, color, creed, religion, or gender. The Supreme Court held the St. Paul ordinance unconstitutional.

Justice Antonin Scalia, writing for the Court:

[T]he ordinance is facially unconstitutional. Although the phrase in the ordinance, "arouses anger, alarm or resentment in others," has been limited by the Minnesota Supreme Court's construction to reach only those symbols or displays that amount to "fighting words," the remaining, unmodified terms make clear that the ordinance applies only to "fighting words" that insult, or provoke violence, "on the basis of race, color, creed, religion, or gender. . . ." Those who wish to use "fighting words" in connection with other ideas—to express hostility, for example, on the basis of political affiliation, union membership, or homosexuality—are not covered. The First Amendment does not permit St. Paul to impose special prohibitions on those speakers who express views on disfavored subjects. In its practical operation, moreover, the ordinance goes even beyond mere content discrimination, to actual viewpoint discrimination. Displays containing some words—odious racial epithets, for example—would be prohibited to proponents of all views. But "fighting words" that do not themselves invoke race, color, creed, religion, or gender—aspersions upon a person's mother, for example—would seemingly be usable ad libitum in the placards of those arguing in favor of race, color, etc. tolerance and equality, but could not be used by that speaker's opponents. One could hold up a sign saying, for example, that all "anti-Catholic bigots" are misbegotten; but not that all "papists" are, for that would insult and provoke violence "on the basis of religion." St. Paul has no such authority to license one side of a debate to fight freestyle, while requiring the other to follow Marquis of Queensbury Rules. . . . Selectivity of this sort creates the possibility that the city is seeking to handicap the expression of particular ideas. . . .

Let there be no mistake about our belief that burning a cross in someone's front yard is reprehensible. But St. Paul has sufficient means at its disposal to prevent such behavior without adding the First Amendment to its fire. . . .

Justice Byron White, with whom Justices Harry Blackmun, Sandra Day O'Connor, and John Paul Stevens (in part) join, concurring:

I agree with the majority that the judgment of the Minnesota Supreme Court should be reversed. However, our agreement ends there. . . . [T]he Court's reasoning in reaching its result is transparently wrong. . . .

Should the government want to criminalize certain fighting words, the Court now requires it to criminalize all fighting words. . . . Fighting words are not a means of exchanging views, rallying supporters, or registering a protest; they are directed against individuals to provoke violence or to inflict injury. Therefore, a ban on all fighting words or on a subset of the fighting words category would restrict only the social evil of hate speech, without creating the danger of driving viewpoints from the market. Therefore, the Court's insistence on inventing its brand of First Amendment underinclusiveness puzzles me. The overbreadth doctrine has the redeeming virtue of attempting to avoid the chilling of protected expression, but the Court's new "underbreadth" creation serves no desirable function. . . . Indeed, by characterizing "fighting words as a form of debate," the majority legitimates hate speech as a form of public discussion. . . .

ROSENBERGER V. UNIVERSITY OF VIRGINIA, 515 U.S. 819 (1995)

In Rosenberger, *the Supreme Court struck down a University of Virginia policy that barred the funding through student activities fees of a student-run paper,* Wide Awake, *whose stated mission was "to challenge*

Christians to live, in word and deed, according to the faith they proclaim and to encourage students to consider what a personal relationship with Jesus Christ means." In contrast, the school freely permitted the use of such fees for the campus's secular papers.

Justice Anthony Kennedy, writing for the Court:

Once it has opened a limited forum . . . the State must respect the lawful boundaries it has itself set. The State may not exclude speech where its distinction is not "reasonable in light of the purpose served by the forum," nor may it discriminate against speech on the basis of its viewpoint. Thus, in determining whether the State is acting to preserve the limits of the forum it has created so that the exclusion of a class of speech is legitimate, we have observed a distinction between, on the one hand, content discrimination, which may be permissible if it preserves the purposes of that limited forum, and, on the other hand, viewpoint discrimination, which is presumed impermissible when directed against speech otherwise within the forum's limitations. . . . By the very terms of the SAF [Student Activities Fund] prohibition, the University does not exclude religion as a subject matter but selects for disfavored treatment those student journalistic efforts with religious editorial viewpoints. . . .

The prohibition on funding on behalf of publications that "primarily promote or manifest a particular belief in or about a deity or an ultimate reality," in its ordinary and commonsense meaning, has a vast potential reach. The term "promotes" as used here would comprehend any writing advocating a philosophic position that rests upon a belief in a deity or ultimate reality. . . . Were the prohibition applied with much vigor at all, it would bar funding of essays by hypothetical student contributors named Plato, Spinoza, and Descartes. And if the regulation covers, as the University says it does, those student journalistic efforts which primarily manifest or promote a belief that there is no deity and no ultimate reality, then undergraduates named Karl Marx, Bertrand Russell, and Jean-Paul Sartre would likewise have some of their major essays excluded from student publications. If any manifestation of beliefs in first principles disqualifies the writing, as seems to be the case, it is indeed difficult to name renowned thinkers whose writings would be accepted, save perhaps for articles disclaiming all connection to their ultimate philosophy. Plato could contrive perhaps to submit an acceptable essay on making pasta or peanut butter cookies. . . .

The governmental program here is neutral toward religion. . . . The category of support here is for "student news, information, opinion, entertainment, or academic communications media groups. . . ." It does not violate the Establishment Clause for a public university to grant access to its facilities on a religion-neutral basis to a wide spectrum of student groups, including groups which use meeting rooms for sectarian activities, accompanied by some devotional exercises. . . .

The viewpoint discrimination inherent in the University's regulation required public officials to scan and interpret student publications to discern their underlying philosophic assumptions respecting religious theory and belief. That course of action was a denial of the right of free speech and would risk fostering a pervasive bias or hostility to religion, which could undermine the very neutrality the Establishment Clause requires. . . .

Justice David Souter, with whom Justices John Paul Stevens, Ruth Bader Ginsburg, and Stephen Breyer, join, dissenting:

This writing is . . . [a] straightforward exhortation to enter into a relationship with God as revealed in Jesus Christ, and to satisfy a series of moral obligations derived from the teachings of Jesus Christ. . . . The subject is not the discourse of the scholar's study or the seminar room, but of the evangelist's mission station and the pulpit. . . . Using public funds for the direct subsidization of preaching the word is categorically forbidden under the Establishment Clause, and if the Clause was meant to accomplish nothing else, it was meant to bar this use of public money. . . .

Give the dispositive effect of the Establishment Clause's bar to funding the magazine, there should be no need to decide whether in the absence of this bar the University would violate the Free Speech Clause by limiting funding as it has done. . . . There is no viewpoint discrimination . . . it applies to Muslim and Jewish and Buddhist advocacy as well as to Christian. . . . [I]t applies to agnostics and atheists as well as it does to deists and theists. . . .

44 *LIQUORMART V. RHODE ISLAND,*
517 U.S. 484 (1996)

This case involved a challenge to a Rhode Island statute that prohibited advertising the price of alcoholic beverages "in any manner whatsoever" (aside from the actual price tag). 44 Liquormart placed a newspaper advertisement that, although mentioning no specific prices, placed the word "WOW" next to photos of vodka and rum bottles and called attention to the store's low prices. After being fined by the state, the liquor store sued on free speech grounds. The Court unanimously held the statute unconstitutional.

Justice John Paul Stevens, writing for the Court:

[W]hen a State regulates commercial messages to protect consumers from misleading, deceptive, or aggressive sales practices, or requires the disclosure of beneficial consumer information, the purpose of its regulation is consistent with the reasons for according constitutional protection to commercial speech and therefore justifies less than strict review. However, when a state entirely prohibits the dissemination of truthful, non-misleading commercial messages for reasons unrelated to the preservation of a fair bargaining process, there is far less reason to depart from the rigorous review that the First Amendment generally demands. Sound reasons justify reviewing the latter type of commercial speech regulation more carefully. Most obviously, complete speech bans, unlike content-neutral restrictions on the time, place, or manner of expression, are particularly dangerous because they all but foreclose alternative means of disseminating certain information. . . .

Precisely because bans against truthful, non-misleading commercial speech rarely seek to protect consumers from either deception or overreaching, they usually rest solely on the offensive assumption that the public will respond "irrationally" to the truth. The First Amendment directs us to be especially skeptical of regulations that seek to keep people in the dark for what the government perceives to be their own good. . . .

The State argues that the price advertising prohibition should nevertheless be upheld because it directly advances the State's substantial interest in promoting temperance. . . . Although the record suggests that the price advertising ban may have some impact on the purchasing patterns of temperate drinkers of modest means, the State has presented no evidence to suggest that its speech prohibition will significantly reduce market-wide consumption. . . . [Moreover,] higher prices [could] be maintained either by direct regulation or by increased taxation. . . . As a result, even under the less than strict standard that generally applies to commercial speech cases, the State has failed to establish a "reasonable

fit" between its abridgment of speech and its temperance goal. It necessarily follows that the price advertising ban cannot survive the more
stringent constitutional review. . . .

Justice Clarence Thomas, concurring:

In cases such as this, in which the government's asserted interest is to
keep legal users of a product or service ignorant in order to manipulate
their choices in the marketplace . . . [the asserted state interest] is per se
illegitimate and can no more justify regulation of "commercial" speech
than it can justify regulation of "noncommercial" speech. . . .

I do not see a philosophical or historical basis for asserting that "commercial" speech is of "lower value" than "noncommercial" speech. . . .
[I]nformed adults are the best judges of their own interests. . . .

Justice Sandra Day O'Connor, with whom Chief Justice William
Rehnquist, Justice David Souter, and Justice Stephen Breyer join, concurring:

Rhode Island says that the ban is intended to keep alcohol prices high
as a way to keep consumption low. . . . The fit between Rhode Island's
method and this particular goal is not reasonable. If the target is simply
higher prices generally to discourage consumption, the regulation imposes too great, and unnecessary, a prohibition on speech in order to
achieve it. The State has other methods at its disposal—methods that
would more directly accomplish this stated goal without intruding on
sellers' ability to provide truthful, nonmisleading information to cus-
tomers. . . . [The State is required] to show that the speech restriction directly advances its interest and is narrowly tailored. . . . [Under this standard,] Rhode Island's price-advertising ban clearly fails to pass
muster. . . .

RENO v. ACLU, 521 U.S. 844 (1997)

*The American Civil Liberties Union and others challenged the constitu-
tionality of the Communications Decency Act (CDA) of 1996, which was
aimed at protecting minors from sexually explicit material on the Internet. The Court declared the act unconstitutional.*

Justice John Paul Stevens, writing for the Court:

At issue is the constitutionality of two statutory provisions enacted to protect minors from "indecent" and "patently offensive" communications on the Internet. Notwithstanding the legitimacy and importance of the congressional goal of protecting children from harmful materials, [we conclude that] the statute abridges "the freedom of speech" protected by the First Amendment. . . .

Unlike communications received by radio or television, "the receipt of information on the Internet requires a series of affirmative steps more deliberate and directed than merely turning a dial. A child requires some sophistication and some ability to read to retrieve material and thereby to use the Internet unattended." Systems have been developed to help parents control the material that may be available on a home computer with Internet access. . . .

The Government offered no evidence that there was a reliable way to screen recipients and participants in such fora for age. . . . Credit card verification is only feasible . . . either in connection with a commercial transaction in which the card is used, or by payment to a verification agency. Using credit card possession as a surrogate for proof of age would impose costs on non-commercial Web sites that would require many of them to shut down. . . . Moreover, the imposition of such a requirement "would completely bar adults who do not have a credit card and lack the resources to obtain one from accessing any blocked material. . . ."

The CDA's broad categorical prohibitions are not limited to particular times and are not dependent on any evaluation by an agency familiar with the unique characteristics of the Internet. . . .

Neither before nor after the enactment of the CDA have the vast democratic fora of the Internet been subject to the type of government supervision and regulation that has attended the broadcast industry. Moreover, the Internet is not as "invasive" as radio or television. . . .

[The CDA's] many ambiguities concerning the scope of its coverage render it problematic for purposes of the First Amendment. For instance, each of the two parts of the CDA uses a different linguistic form. The first uses the word "indecent," while the second speaks of material that "in context, depicts or describes, in terms patently offensive as measured by contemporary community standards, sexual or excretory activities or organs." Given the absence of a definition of either term, this difference in language will provoke uncertainty among speakers about how the two standards relate to each other and just what they mean. Could a speaker confidently assume that a serious discussion about birth control practices, homosexuality . . . or the consequences of prison rape would not violate the CDA? This certainly undermines the likelihood that the CDA has been carefully tailored to the congressional goal of protecting minors from potentially harmful materials. . . .

[W]e have made it perfectly clear that "sexual expression which is indecent but not obscene is protected by the First Amendment." . . .

NATIONAL ENDOWMENT FOR THE ARTS V. FINLEY, 524 U.S. 569 (1998)

Performance artist Karen Finley sued the National Endowment for the Arts (NEA) after her application for grant funding was denied following the enactment of a law that required the endowment to "[take] into consideration general standards of decency and respect for the diverse beliefs and values of the American public" in awarding its grants. The Court upheld the constitutionality of the law.

Justice Sandra Day O'Connor, writing for the Court:

Respondents argue that the provision is a paradigmatic example of viewpoint discrimination because it rejects any artistic speech that either fails to respect mainstream values or offends standards of decency . . . [but the Act] imposes no categorical requirement. The advisory language stands in sharp contrast to congressional efforts to prohibit the funding of certain classes of speech. . . . [The Act] admonishes the NEA merely to take "decency and respect" into consideration. . . .

[A]lthough the First Amendment certainly has application in the subsidy context, we note that the Government may allocate competitive funding according to criteria that would be impermissible were direct regulation of speech or a criminal penalty at stake. So long as legislation does not infringe on other constitutionally protected rights, Congress has wide latitude to set spending priorities. . . .

Justice Antonin Scalia, with whom Justice Clarence Thomas joins, concurring:

"The operation was a success, but the patient died." What such a procedure is to medicine, the Court's opinion in this case is to law. It sustains the constitutionality of [the Act] by gutting it. . . . By its terms, [the Act] establishes content and viewpoint-based criteria upon which grant applications are to be evaluated. And that is perfectly constitutional. . . . I am at a loss to understand what the Court has in mind . . . when it speculates that the statute is merely "advisory." [The statute requires that general standards of decency and respect for Americans' beliefs and values] must always be considered. . . . This unquestionably constitutes viewpoint discrimination. That conclusion is not altered by the fact that the statute does not "compel" the denial of funding, any more than a provision imposing a five-point handicap on all black applicants for civil service jobs is saved from being race discrimination by the fact that it does not compel the rejection of black applicants. . . .

[The Act] is no more discriminatory, and no less constitutional, than virtually every other piece of funding legislation enacted by Congress. . . . As we noted in *Rust*, when Congress chose to establish the National Endowment for Democracy it was not constitutionally required to fund programs encouraging competing philosophies of government—an example of funding discrimination that cuts much closer than this one to the core of political speech which is the primary concern of the First Amendment. It takes a particularly high degree of chutzpah for the NEA to contradict this proposition, since the agency itself discriminates—and is required by law to discriminate—in favor of artistic (as opposed to scientific, or political, or theological) expression. . . . Surely the NEA itself is nothing less than an institutionalized discrimination against that point of view. Nonetheless it is constitutional, as is the congressional determination to favor decency and respect for beliefs and values over the opposite. [S]uch favoritism does not "abridge" anyone's freedom of speech. . . .

It is the very business of government to favor and disfavor points of view on (in modern times, at least) innumerable subjects—which is the main reason we have decided to elect those who run the government, rather than save money by making their posts hereditary. . . . None of this has anything to do with abridging anyone's speech. . . . I regard the distinction between "abridging" speech and funding it as a fundamental divide. . . .

Justice David Souter, dissenting:

One need do nothing more than read the text of the statute to conclude that Congress's purpose in imposing the decency and respect criteria was to prevent the funding of art that conveys an offensive message; the decency and respect provision on its face is quintessentially viewpoint based. . . . Boiled down to its practical essence, the limitation obviously means that art that disregards the ideology, opinions, or convictions of a significant segment of the American public is to be disfavored, whereas art that reinforces those values is not. After all, the whole point of the proviso was to make sure that works like Serrano's ostensibly blasphemous portrayal of Jesus would not be funded, while a reverent treatment, conventionally respectful of Christian sensibilities, would not run afoul of the law. . . .

A [key] strand in the Court's treatment of today's question, and the heart of Justice Scalia's, in effect assumes that whether or not the statute mandates viewpoint discrimination, there is no constitutional issue here because government art subsidies fall within a zone of activity free from First Amendment restraints. . . . The Government calls attention to the roles of government-as-speaker and government-as-buyer, in which the government is of course entitled to engage in viewpoint discrimination. . . . The Government freely admits, however, that it neither speaks through the expression subsidized by the NEA, nor buys anything for itself with its NEA grants. . . . [T]his patronage falls embarassingly on the wrong side of the line between government-as-buyer and government-as-regulator-of-private speech. . . . [G]overnment may not act on viewpoint when it "does not itself speak or subsidize transmittal of a message it favors but instead expends funds to encourage a diversity of views from private speakers. . . ." *Rosenberger* controls here. . . .

CHRONOLOGY

1275   English Parliament enacts statute criminalizing slander of the realm's most prominent men.

1523   Thomas More, speaker of the English House of Commons, advises King Henry VIII on the advantages of allowing disinterested "advice and counsel."

1534   King Henry VIII of England breaks with the Church of Rome.

1576   Puritan Parliamentarian Peter Wentworth delivers his speech "On the Liberties of the Commons."

1606   English Court of Star Chamber established.

1606   *De libellis famosis* decision by Court of Star Chamber declares criminal punishments for the publication of scurrilous libels appropriate.

1620   King James I of England issues a royal proclamation defending the freedom of speech that is conducive to sound, effective government.

1644   John Milton publishes *Areopagitica*.

1688   Glorious Revolution takes place in England.

1689   English Bill of Rights adopted.

1701   Act of Settlement passed, providing the judges will serve on good behavior rather than at the pleasure of the King, thus advancing the cause of judicial independence.

1720–1723	English writers John Trenchard and Thomas Gordon publish *Cato's Letters* in London.
1731	Benjamin Franklin publishes "Apology for Printers" in the Philadelphia *Gazette*.
1735	Seditious libel trial of newspaper publisher John Peter Zenger takes place in New York City.
1748	Montesquieu's *Spirit of the Laws* published.
1763	English M.P. John Wilkes publishes a provocative criticism of the King and his government, the *North Briton no. 45*.
1765–1769	William Blackstone publishes his *Commentaries on the Laws of England.*
1776	U.S. declares its independence from Great Britain.
1776	George Mason's draft of a "Declaration of Rights" becomes part of the Virginia Constitution.
1781	Cornwallis's surrender at Yorktown seals American victory in Revolution.
1781	Articles of Confederation ratified.
1786	Shay's Rebellion breaks out in Massachusetts.
1787	U.S. Constitution drafted in Philadelphia.
1787–1788	James Madison, Alexander Hamilton, and John Jay publish the newspaper editorials, known as *The Federalist Papers,* explaining and advocating the adoption of the U.S. Constitution.
1789	U.S. Constitution takes effect.
1789	In Paris, Bastille falls, Declaration of the Rights of Man and Citizen issued, and French Revolution begins.
1791	U.S. Bill of Rights ratified.
1792	Fox Libel Act passed in England.
1793	French King Louis XVI executed by guillotine in Paris's Place de la Concorde. Reign of Terror begins.
1794	Whiskey Rebellion takes place in western Pennsylvania.

1798	Alien and Sedition Acts passed.
1798	Virginia and Kentucky Resolutions passed in resistance to the Sedition Act.
1800	Democratic-Republican Thomas Jefferson defeats Federalist rival John Adams in race for Presidency. Political power passes from one party to another for the first time in U.S. history.
1801	Federalist John Marshall becomes Chief Justice of the United States.
1803	Louisiana Purchase.
1803	Chief Justice John Marshall articulates a bold defense of judicial review in *Marbury v. Madison.*
1804	Aaron Burr kills political rival Alexander Hamilton in duel at Weehawken, New Jersey.
1812	War of 1812 begins.
1814	Violent slave uprising takes place in Haiti.
1822	Denmark Vesey slave uprising takes place in South Carolina.
1826–1830	James Kent's *Commentaries on American Law* published.
1831	William Lloyd Garrison launches abolitionist newspaper, the *Liberator.*
1831	Nat Turner slave revolt takes place in Virginia.
1833	Great Britain abolishes slavery in its West Indian colonies.
1833	In *Barron v. Baltimore,* U.S. Supreme Court affirms that the Bill of Rights imposes limits on the powers of the national government and not on the states.
1833	Joseph Story's *Commentaries on the Constitution of the United States* published.
1833	Alexis de Tocqueville's *Democracy in America* published.
1835	Northern abolitionists undertake a mass mailing of abolitionist literature to the South.

1836	U.S. House of Representatives passes "gag rule" barring the reading of antislavery petitions in Congress.
1837	Abolitionist newspaper publisher Elijah Lovejoy murdered in Alton, Illinois.
1838	Pennsylvania Hall in Philadelphia, erected by abolitionists, is burned to the ground by proslavery mob.
1846–1848	Mexican War.
1848	As a wave of revolutions sweeps across Europe, Karl Marx and Friedrich Engels publish *The Communist Manifesto.*
1854	Kansas-Nebraska Act passed, instituting rule of "popular sovereignty" on slavery in the territories.
1854	Republican Party formed.
1856	Abolitionist U.S. Senator Charles Sumner of Massachusetts severely beaten on the floor of the Senate.
1857	In *Dred Scott v. Sanford,* U.S. Supreme Court declares the right to own slaves a fundamental national right.
1858	Lincoln-Douglas debates take place in Illinois.
1859	As prelude to what he hoped would be a massive slave uprising, radical abolitionist John Brown stages unsuccessful raid on the U.S. arsenal at Harper's Ferry, Virginia. Brown is captured, tried, and hanged.
1859	Charles Darwin publishes *On the Origin of Species.*
1859	John Stuart Mill publishes *On Liberty.*
1860	South Carolina secedes from the Union. U.S. Civil War begins.
1863	Abraham Lincoln issues the Emancipation Proclamation.
1863	Abraham Lincoln delivers the Gettysburg Address.

1865	Confederate General Robert E. Lee surrenders at Appomattox, Virginia, ending the U.S. Civil War.
1865	Black Codes enacted in southern states.
1865	Ku Klux Klan founded.
1868	Fourteenth Amendment ratified.
1868	Thomas Cooley publishes *A Treatise on the Constitutional Limitations which Rest upon the Legislative Power of the States of the American Union.*
1873	Comstock Postal Act passed.
1877	Reconstruction ends. U.S. troops withdraw from the South.
1877	In the midst of an economic depression, a massive railroad strike seizes the attention of the nation.
1881	Russian Czar Alexander II assassinated by nihilist radicals.
1886	Chicago's Haymarket Square bombed by anarchist radicals.
1890	Samuel Warren and Louis D. Brandeis publish their famous *Harvard Law Review* article, "The Right to Privacy."
1894	Great Pullman Railway strike paralyzes the nation's transportation system, training national attention on "the labor problem."
1897	In *Chicago, Burlington, and Quincy Railroad v. Chicago,* the Supreme Court for the first time incorporates a provision of the Bill of Rights as a restriction upon the powers of a state.
1898	Spanish-American War.
1901	U.S. President William McKinley assassinated by anarchist radical in Buffalo, New York.
1902	Oliver Wendell Holmes, Jr. appointed to the U.S. Supreme Court by President Theodore Roosevelt.
1902	Free Speech League organized in New York City.

1905	Radical labor union the Industrial Workers of the World ("IWW" or "Wobblies") founded.
1908	U.S. strips radical anarchist Emma Goldman of her citizenship.
1909–1913	IWW free speech fights garner national attention.
1911	Pioneering civil libertarian Theodore Schroeder publishes *Obscene Literature and Constitutional Law*.
1912	Liberal Club founded in Greenwich Village, New York City.
1913	Shocking modernist art showcased in exhibit at New York City Armory.
1914	World War I begins in Europe.
1914	American Union Against Militarism, the progenitor of the American Civil Liberties Union, founded.
1916	Louis D. Brandeis appointed to U.S. Supreme Court by President Woodrow Wilson.
1917	Bolshevik Revolution launched in Russia.
1917	Espionage Act and Trading with the Enemy Acts passed.
1917	U.S. enters First World War.
1917	Following a split in the American Union Against Militarism over support for the First World War, the National Civil Liberties Bureau, a precursor to the ACLU, is founded.
1917	U.S. District Judge Learned Hand issues decision in *Masses Publishing v. Patten*.
1918	Sedition Act passed.
1919	Wave of postwar strikes hits U.S.
1919–1920	Anticommunist and antiradical sentiment reaches a peak in "The Red Scare."
1919	Landmark "Red Scare" cases, *Schenck v. United States* and *Abrams v. United States* decided by U.S. Supreme Court, inaugurating the modern Supreme Court's active engagement with free speech issues.

1920	Roger Baldwin reorganizes the National Civil Liberties Bureau under a new name, the American Civil Liberties Union.
1920	Harvard Law School Professor Zechariah Chafee, Jr., publishes *Freedom of Speech*.
1924	"America must be kept American," declares President Calvin Coolidge, signing into law a measure sharply restricting European immigration.
1925	In *Gitlow v. United States,* the U.S. Supreme Court announces that the First Amendment is "incorporated" via the Fourteenth Amendment as a restriction upon the powers of the states.
1929	Stock market crashes. Great Depression begins.
1930	Legion of Decency, a prominent Catholic group, sends Hollywood producers a petition signed by eleven million Catholics, condemning indecent and immoral films and threatening a massive boycott if Hollywood does not change the content of its films.
1931	Motion Picture Production Code, familiarly known as the "Hays Code," promulgated by the Motion Picture Producers and Distributors of America.
1933	Adolph Hitler seizes power in Germany.
1935	After meeting in a basement room of the U.S. capitol for most of its history, the U.S. Supreme Court moves for the first time into its own home in the current court building.
1935	National Labor Relations Act (familiarly known as the "Wagner Act") passed, giving broad collective bargaining rights to organized labor.
1937–1938	Soviet Communist dictator Joseph Stalin launches Moscow Trials, followed by the Great Purge and Terror. Millions die.
1937	Sit-Down strike paralyzes General Motors Assembly plant in Flint, Michigan.

1938	House Un-American Activities Committee created by U.S. Congress.
1938	In Anschluss, Adolph Hitler invades Austria, uniting the two German nations.
1938	U.S. Supreme Court announces in Footnote Four of its *Carolene Products* decision that in the future it may be especially skeptical of the constitutionality of laws infringing upon specific provisions of the Constitution, including the Bill of Rights.
1939	Hitler invades Poland. World War II begins.
1940	Alien Registration Act (popularly known as the "Smith Act") passed.
1941	President Franklin Delano Roosevelt delivers "Four Freedoms" speech.
1941	On December 7, the United States Pacific fleet is attacked by the Japanese at Pearl Harbor, Hawaii. The United States enters World War II.
1943	U.S. Supreme Court issues its famous flag salute decision in *West Virginia State Board of Education v. Barnette,* reversing its decision in *Minersville School District v. Gobitis* (1940).
1945	World War II ends. Cold War between U.S. and U.S.S.R. begins.
1947	In *Everson v. Board of Education,* the U.S. Supreme Court creates the constitutional doctrine announcing the separation of Church and state.
1948	Universal Declaration of Human Rights adopted by U.N. General Assembly.
1948	McCarren-Walter Immigration Act passed, permitting exclusion from country of those holding dangerous political views.
1949	Federal Communications Commission promulgates the Fairness Doctrine requiring balanced coverage of public issues on the public airwaves.

1949	Chinese Communists, led by Mao Tse-tung, win control of China. Era of communist dictatorship begins.
1949	Soviet Union explodes its first atomic bomb.
1950	Communist North Korea invades South Korea, igniting Korean War, which lasts until 1953.
1950	Wisconsin Senator Joseph McCarthy delivers speech in Wheeling, West Virginia launching aggressive campaign to root communists out of the U.S. government. McCarthy era, which lasts until 1954, begins.
1950	Soviet spy and former Franklin Roosevelt advisor Alger Hiss convicted of perjury.
1951	U.S. Supreme Court upholds the constitutionality of the Smith Act in *Dennis v. United States.*
1953	Soviet spy Julius Rosenberg, and his wife, Ethel, executed in New York State's Sing-Sing prison.
1953	Earl Warren appointed Chief Justice of the United States. The era of the liberal "Warren Court," which lasts until 1969, begins.
1953	Soviet dictator and mass murderer Joseph Stalin dies.
1954	U.S. Supreme Court declares racial segregation in public schools unconstitutional in *Brown v. Board of Education.*
1954	Communist Control Act passed, outlawing the Communist Party USA.
1955	Civil rights leader the Reverend Martin Luther King, Jr., launches the Montgomery, Alabama, bus boycott.
1956	Soviet Premier Nikita Khrushchev acknowledges and denounces Stalin's crimes.
1956	Anti-Soviet uprising in Hungary put down by Soviet troops.

1956	Justice William J. Brennan, Jr. appointed to the Supreme Court by President Dwight D. Eisenhower.
1957	On June 17, "Red Monday," the Supreme Court issues a series of decisions evincing skepticism about the constitutionality of a number of domestic security initiatives targeting communists.
1960	Conservative group Young Americans for Freedom founded. Group issues "The Sharon Statement," affirming a commitment to the defeat of communism and the preservation of American sovereignty, institutions, and ideals.
1960	Birth control pill introduced.
1962	Students for a Democratic Society ("SDS") issues the Port Huron statement, inaugurating the student movement and the "New Left."
1963	Landmark feminist book *The Feminist Mystique* published by Betty Friedan.
1963	Rev. Martin Luther King, Jr. delivers "I Have a Dream Speech" at Lincoln Memorial in Washington, D.C.
1963	U.S. President John F. Kennedy assassinated in Dallas, Texas.
1964	Freedom Summer civil rights protests take place in Mississippi.
1964	Free Speech Movement launched by students at the University of California at Berkeley.
1964	American law of libel and free speech transformed by U.S. Supreme Court's decision in *New York Times Co. v. Sullivan.*
1964	Civil Rights Act, guaranteeing blacks equal rights in employment, housing, education, public accommodations, and other areas passed by U.S. Congress.
1965	Selma to Montgomery march for voting rights for African-Americans attacked by police on Selma, Alabama's Edmund Pettus Bridge.

1965	Voting Rights Act passed by U.S. Congress.
1965	Race riots break out in Watts section of Los Angeles.
1965	Marxist Professor Herbert Marcuse publishes *Repressive Tolerance.*
1965	U.S. begins bombing North Vietnam.
1965–1968	Ascendancy of antiwar (Vietnam) movement on university campuses.
1966	International Covenant on Civil and Political Rights adopted by U.N. General Assembly.
1966	National Organization for Women founded.
1967	Hippie "Summer of Love" celebrated in San Francisco. Beatles release landmark Sgt. Pepper's Lonely Hearts Club Band album.
1967	Urban riots break out in New York City, Newark, Cleveland, Chicago, Detroit, Washington, D.C., and Atlanta.
1968	Civil Rights leader Martin Luther King, Jr., assassinated in Memphis, Tennessee. Urban riots again sweep the nation.
1968	U.S. Senator and contender for the Democratic Party's nomination for the Presidency, Robert F. Kennedy, assassinated in Los Angeles.
1968	Riots by students and other activists take place at the Democratic Convention in Chicago.
1969	Manson murders take place in Los Angeles.
1969	U.S. Supreme Court announces the Incitement test for free speech in *Brandenburg v. Ohio.*
1969	Woodstock rock festival takes place in upstate New York.
1973	In *Roe v. Wade,* U.S. Supreme Court declares abortion to be a fundamental constitutional right.
1973	U.S. Supreme Court announces its "Miller Test" for obscenity in *Miller v. California.*
1974	Engulfed in Watergate scandal, U.S. President Richard M. Nixon resigns.

1976   U.S. Supreme Court issues its seminal campaign fi-
           nance decision in *Buckley v. Valeo.*
1979   Convention on the Elimination of All Forms of Dis-
           crimination against Women adopted by U.N. Gen-
           eral Assembly.
1980   Staunch anticommunist Ronald Reagan elected
           President of the United States.
1989   Berlin wall torn down. Eastern European revolu-
           tions triumph over communism. Cold War ends.
1992   Urban riot breaks out in Los Angeles following ac-
           quittal of police officers in beating of black motorist
           Rodney King.
2001   On September 11, radical Islamic terrorists attack
           the World Trade Center in New York City and the
           Pentagon in Washington, D.C., killing over 3,000
           people, the most deadly foreign attack on U.S. soil
           in American history. "War on Terror" begins.
2001   U.S.A. Patriot Act passed.
2002   McCain-Feingold Campaign Finance Reform Law
           passed by U.S. Congress.

TABLE OF CASES

STATUTES

BIBLIOGRAPHY

The freedom of speech is studied by a wide range of scholars in an array of disciplines. These scholars ask very different questions and have distinctive intellectual agendas. Historians, law professors, political scientists, philosophers, journalists, and judges, among others, have all contributed to our understanding of the freedom of speech. And someone new to the subject who stumbles inadvertently upon a single line of inquiry is likely to end up at the mercy of the much-cited problem of the blind man laying hands on an elephant: His conception of the whole will be distorted by the assumption that the whole resembles the part that he fortuitously rubs up against first.

Law students typically start by reading court opinions and the musings on the subject by professional legal theorists. The fullest perspective, however, and the best initial overview, is provided in histories. These have been written not only by historians but also by historically oriented law professors and political scientists. Perhaps the best comprehensive overview of free speech in America in the seventeenth and eighteenth centuries as well as in much of the nineteenth century is Norman Rosenberg's *Protecting the Best Men: An Interpretive History of the Law of Libel* (1986) Rosenberg's book, which gives sustained attention to local ordinances, statutes, and courts as well as to both formal and informal aspects of private and political disputes, is the best account of how the freedom of speech was actually lived in early America. Also strong on speech in the colonial and early national period are Leonard Levy's landmark books *Freedom of Speech and Press in Early America: Legacy of Suppression* (1960), *Jefferson and Civil Liberties: The Darker Side* (1963), and *Emergence of a Free Press* (1985) (the last book revises some of the claims Levy made in the earlier works and is thus is the most authoritative). Michael Kent Curtis's masterpiece *Free Speech, "The People's Darling Privilege": Struggles for Freedom of Expression in American History* (2000) is probably the best single overview of the history of the freedom of speech in America, paying simultaneous attention to both legal and political struggles over the freedom. Curtis, whose previous work focused on the Civil War era, is the indispensable source on free speech controversies in the nineteenth century, especially those involving slavery. Rochelle Gurstein's *The Repeal of Reticence: A History of America's Cultural and Legal Struggles over Free Speech, Obscenity, Sexual Liberation, and Modern Art* (1996) looks at the late nineteenth and early twentieth centuries and conveys in fascinating detail the birth of modern "anything goes" understandings of speech, considered in its broadest sense. Gurstein's book, which focuses on sex-related speech, is essential reading for those who want to understand how broader cultural and intellectual currents come to influence the shape of free speech law. Mark Graber's *Transforming Free Speech: The Ambiguous Legacy of Civil Libertarianism* (1991) and David Rabban's *Free Speech in Its Forgotten Years* (1997) focus on free speech law before the U.S. Supreme Court got into the act in a sustained way in 1919. Both chart the precursors of modern free speech law in the intellectual, political, and legal landscape of the late nineteenth and early twentieth centuries. Christine Stansell's *American Moderns: Bohemian New York and the Creation of a New Century* (2000) gives sustained attention to the influence of the Greenwich Village avant-garde of about the same time in shaping modern understandings of the freedom of speech. And Paul Murphy's *World War I and the Origin of Civil Liberties in the United States* (1979) focuses on the overlapping story of the impact of the war and opposition to it in setting the trajectory of modern civil liberties law. Chief Justice William Rehnquist's *All the Laws but One: Civil Liberties in Wartime* (1998) is an informative and engaging account of that subject, written for a general audience, with a significant amount of material on the fate of free speech in times of national emergency.

It is useful for those interested in the modern law of the freedom of speech to read accounts that put the Court's modern civil liberties jurisprudence in context and situate free speech within the work the Court was undertaking concerning such subjects as freedom of religion, criminal procedure, and equal protection. Traditional approaches present the emergence of the Court's modern civil liberties jurisprudence as the Court's belated willingness to finally do what is right and to realize the full promise of the Founding Fathers' vision. In recent years, though, scholars have developed much more sophisticated analyses that emphasize matters of institutional change, intellectual history, and politics. Excellent representatives of the latest thinking on the emergence of contemporary civil liberties are Akhil Amar's *The Bill of Rights: Creation and Reconstruction* (1998), Michael

Klarman's "Rethinking the Civil Rights and Civil Liberties Revolutions" (1996), G. Edward White's "The First Amendment Comes of Age" (1996), Howard Gillman's "Preferred Freedoms: The Progressive Expansion of State Powers and the Rise of Modern Civil Liberties Jurisprudence" (1994), and Lucas Powe's *The Warren Court and American Politics* (2000).

Although context is essential to genuine understanding, the truth is that much of the contemporary thinking concerning the freedom of speech takes place within relatively narrow confines. And this is especially true of the thinking on the subject done by lawyers and judges, including the justices of the Supreme Court. These legal professionals occupy themselves with an elaborate web of doctrinal categories, subcategories, distinctions, tensions, tests, and exceptions. For reasons of space (and inclination), I have merely outlined the elemental points of these complexities in this book. Law students are charged with mastering the intricacies of this web (often in near-total isolation from the history that prompted and surrounded it). Law professors take it as their duty to describe it, to elaborate upon it, and more often than not, to reform it. And not coincidentally—though perhaps less forthrightly—so too do judges, who were, after all, once law students themselves. As cases come before them one by one, judges, with the assistance of newly minted law school graduates (known as "law clerks") who read law reviews written by law professors, both apply First Amendment doctrine and, usually incrementally but occasionally boldly, alter it. As far as free speech is concerned these days, in short, legal doctrine is of primary importance in shaping the path of the law.

Those who want to learn the complexities of this web of doctrines, categories, and tests—to see the world of free speech as law students, lawyers, and judges see it—must have recourse to law school and law school–style casebooks. These books are organized around the categories of analysis, and they present case excerpts interspersed with commentary, questions, and abundant citations to law review articles on every possible First Amendment issue and subissue. One of the most comprehensive is Kathleen M. Sullivan and Gerald Gunther's *First Amendment Law* (1999). Those interested in more accessible variants of the doctrinal approach that place somewhat more emphasis on historical, political, and philosophical contexts and issues may wish to consult constitutional law casebooks oriented toward undergraduates. Two useful casebooks on the broader field of constitutional law are Louis Fisher's *American Constitutional Law* (1999), which emphasizes the ongoing dialogue among the legislative, executive, and judicial branches, and David O'Brien's *Constitutional Law and Politics: Civil Rights and Civil Liberties* (2000). These two books have well-assembled subparts on the freedom of speech. Terry Eastland's *Freedom of Expression in the Supreme Court: The Defining Cases* (2000) intersperses a judicious selection of excerpts from landmark cases with history, philosophical reflection, and, uniquely, contemporaneous excerpts from newspapers and magazines, hinting at popular reaction to the decisions at the time they were handed down. Eastland's book, like Sullivan and Gunther's more densely doctrinal work, would serve well as a stand-alone casebook for courses focused on the contemporary law of the freedom of speech.

A major vein of free speech scholarship, and the vein that predominates in the law schools, involves the promulgation of global theories of free speech, which seek to outline the "purpose" of the principle. Many of these works argue that the First Amendment has one overriding central purpose. Not surprisingly, law professors disagree over just what that purpose is. Zechariah Chafee, Jr.'s *Free Speech in the United States* (1941) (as well as Chafee's other, mostly earlier, writings) are highly readable and were very influential, though both David Rabban and Mark Graber have since shown that that influence depended in part on mythmaking in service of an explicitly political program. Alexander Meikeljohn's *Free Speech and Its Relation to Self-Government* (1948) was also a highly readable work in the grand style. It took up where Chafee left off. Performing the same function during and in the wake of the liberationism of the 1960s was Thomas Emerson's *Toward a General Theory of the First Amendment* (1967) and *The System of Freedom of Expression* (1970), though a sharp counterpoint was posed by Walter Berns in *The First Amendment and the Future of American Democracy* (1976). In more-recent years, free speech theory has become a full-time profession, and an elaborate literature has developed in the area. Among the more discussed works in this field are C. Edwin Baker's *Human Liberty and the Freedom of Speech* (1989), Vincent Blasi's "The Checking Value of the First Amendment" (1977), Robert Bork's "Neutral Principles and Some First Amendment Problems" (1971), Owen Fiss's *Irony of Free Speech* (1996) and *Liberalism Divided: Freedom of Speech and the Many Uses of State Power* (1996), Lee Bollinger's *The Tolerant Society: Freedom of Speech and Extremist Speech in America* (1986), Rodney Smolla's *Free Speech in an Open Society* (1992), Stephen Shiffrin's *The First Amendment, Democracy, and Romance* (1990), Martin Redish's *Freedom of Expression: A Critical Analysis* (1984), Frederick Schauer's *Free Speech: A Philosophical Inquiry* (1982), and Cass Sunstein's *Democracy and the Problem of Free Speech* (1993). In the 1980s and 1990s, a flurry of work by feminist and critical race scholars challenged mainstream doctrine and practice concerning the freedom of speech. Among the most provocative and influential of these works were Andrea Dworkin's *Pornography: Men Possessing Women* (1981), Andrea Dworkin and Catherine MacKinnon's *Pornography and Civil Rights: A New Day for Women's Equality* (1988), Catherine MacKinnon's *Only Words* (1993), and Mari Matsuda, Charles R. Lawrence III, Richard Delgado, and Kimberlè Williams Crenshaw's *Words That Wound: Critical Race Theory, Assaultive Speech, and the First Amendment* (1993).

The arguments for stricter regulations of speech by Dworkin, MacKinnon, Matsuda, and others during the 1990s prompted a number of spirited rejoinders from across the political spectrum. These include the feminist head of the American Civil Liberties Union (ACLU), Nadine Strossen's *Defending Pornography: Free Speech, Sex, and the Fight for Women's Rights* (1995), Nat Hentoff's broad-ranging *Free Speech for Me—but Not for Thee* (1992), Jonathan Rauch's *Kindly Inquisitors* (1993), and Alan Kors and Harvey Silverglate's exposé on campus political correctness, *The Shadow University: The Betrayal of Liberty on America's Campuses* (1998). David Horowitz's *Uncivil Wars: The Controversy over Reparations for Slavery* (2002) takes up one of the most current campus free speech controversies.

In recent years, in the wake of many years of argument over what the central purpose of the First Amendment is, some scholars have asserted that in fact it has no central purpose at all. Stanley Fish, in *There's No Such Thing as Free Speech, and It's a Good Thing, Too* (1994), argues, with characteristic verve, that free speech has always been about ideology and political power (and free speech theory about ideological efforts to obscure the play of political power), and not about transcendent principle. For the more ambitious, Fish places his argument concerning free speech within the context of his broader understanding of the place of principles in political life in *The Trouble with Principle* (1999). Other free speech pluralists, like Robert Post, have argued that free speech does not have any one purpose; rather, it actually has several purposes that relate to one another in different ways.

Of course, a major source of learning on the subject of free speech is the decisions in the cases of the Supreme Court itself. These are available on the subscription Websites Lexis-Nexis and Westlaw, where many lawyers find them. But they are also available on a number of free Websites, including Cornell Law School's Legal Information Institute (http://www.law.cornell.edu), Northwestern University's Oyez Website (http://www.oyez.nwu.edu), FindLaw (http://www.findlaw.com), and the U.S. Supreme Court's own Website (http://www.supremecourtus.gov). The Oyez Website also provides live recordings of the oral arguments made in many landmark

Supreme Court cases, including free speech cases. The Website of the federal courts (http://www.supremecourtus.gov) is also useful.

One can learn a great deal about free speech issues from advocacy groups as well. And many such groups maintain sites available to the public on the World Wide Web. The ACLU (http://www.aclu.org) maintains a site, as does the First Amendment Lawyers Association (http://www.fala.org), the Freedom Forum (http://www.freedomforum.org), and the Center for Individual Rights (http://www.cir-usa.org). The Foundation for Individual Rights in Education (http://www.thefire.org) focuses on free speech issues raised on college campuses. The Supreme Court practice group of the law firm of Mayer, Brown, Rowe, and Maw maintains a superb Website, with abundant links to just about every participant in the process of Supreme Court litigation http://www.appellate.net). The University of Pittsburgh's Jurist Website is the home of lively commentary on legal issues by the nation's law professors (http://www.jurist.law.pitt.edu).

For those new to the study of both the freedom of speech and U.S. constitutionalism more generally, several excellent reference books are available in which one can either look up information on specific topics or browse freely. These are Kermit Hall, James W. Ely, Jr., Joel Grossman, and William Wiecek, eds., *The Oxford Companion to the Supreme Court of the United States* (1992); Kermit Hall, ed., *The Oxford Guide to Supreme Court Decisions* (1999) and *The Oxford Companion to American Law* (2002); and Jethro K. Lieberman, *A Practical Companion to the Constitution* (1999).

Index

About the Author

Ken I. Kersch is assistant professor of politics at Princeton University.